Revelation and Mystery

in Ancient Judaism and Pauline Christianity

Markus N. A. Bockmuehl

WILLIAM B. EERDMANS PUBLISHING COMPANY

GRAND RAPIDS, MICHIGAN / CAMBRIDGE, U.K.

Originally published in 1990 as volume 36 in the series
Wissenschaftlich Untersuchungen zum Neuen Testament —
2. Reihe by J. C. B. Mohr (Paul Siebeck),
P.O. Box 2040, D-7400 Tübingen.
This edition published in 1997 in the United States of America
through special arrangement with J. C. B. Mohr (Paul Siebeck) by
Wm. B. Eerdmans Publishing Co.
255 Jefferson Ave. S.E., Grand Rapids, Michigan 49503 /
P.O. Box 163, Cambridge CB3 9PU U.K.

Printed in the United States of America

01 00 99 98 97   5 4 3 2 1

Library of Congress Cataloging-in-Publication Data

Bockmuehl, Markus N. A.
Revelation and mystery in ancient Judaism and
Pauline Christianity / by Markus N. A. Bockmuehl.
p.   cm.
Originally published: Tübingen : J.C.B. Mohr. c1990. (Wissenschaftliche
Untersuchungen zum Neuen Testament. 2. Reihe ; 36) Based on
the author's thesis (Ph.D.) — University of
Cambridge, 1987.
Includes bibliographical references and indexes.
ISBN 0-8028-4277-1 (pbk. : alk. paper)
1. Revelation (Jewish theology) — History of doctrines.   2. Judaism —
History — Post-exilic period, 586 B.C.–210 A.D.   3. Revelation —
History of doctrines — Early church, ca. 30-600.   4. Mystery —
History of doctrines.   5. Bible. N.T. Epistles
of Paul — Criticism, interpretation, etc.   I. Title.
[BM645.R5B63   1997]
231.7'4'09015 — dc21   96-6813
CIP

For my mother Elisabeth

and in memory of my father Klaus

(May 6, 1931 – June 10, 1989)

אַשְׁרֵי אָדָם עוֹז־לוֹ בָךְ   מְסִלּוֹת בִּלְבָבָם
עֹבְרֵי בְּעֵמֶק הַבָּכָא   מַעְיָן יְשִׁיתֻהוּ
גַּם־בְּרָכוֹת יַעְטֶה מוֹרֶה   יֵלְכוּ מֵחַיִל אֶל־חָיִל
יֵרָאֶה אֶל־אֱלֹהִים בְּצִיּוֹן:

Psalm 84:6–8 (5–7)

Preface

It was during an undergraduate course in classical studies and philosophy that I first developed an interest in the theory of knowledge, and in religious epistemology in particular. When I moved into the area of biblical studies during my subsequent work in theology, I became increasingly intrigued by the meaning and significance of the Bible's talk of divine disclosures and revelations. In particular, I wanted to discover how revelation "works" in the texts of Ancient Judaism and the New Testament, i. e., at a time when a significant body of sacred writings (whether formally "closed" or not) had already come to be generally accepted as authoritative Scripture. In order to channel this interest into a manageable critical investigation, I further decided to focus especially on the recurring motif of a revelation of divine secrets or "mysteries".

This research, then, first took shape in something like the present form as a 1987 Ph.D. dissertation at the University of Cambridge. Since then it has undergone a number of changes, chiefly consisting in the addition of Chapter 11 and the evaluation of such additional secondary literature as became available to me until the spring of 1989.

A comprehensive bibliography is almost by definition impossible in a work like this. Nevertheless, I feel compelled to mention two or three works which I should very much like to have seen before submitting the work to the publisher. Volume 2 of Peter Schäfer's *Konkordanz zur Hekhalot-Literatur* (TSAJ 13, Tübingen: J.C.B. Mohr [Paul Siebeck], 1988) as well as volume 1 of his *Übersetzung der Hekhalot-Literatur* (vol. 2 appeared in 1987 as TSAJ 17) have not been accessible to me. The former especially would have been a significant help in trading the use of pertinent words such as סוד, סתר, רז etc. in the Jewish mystical writings.

Two apparently important new works have only just come to my attention within the last few weeks; here I can do no more than to mention them. Peter Kuhn's *Offenbarungsstimmen im Antiken Judentum: Untersuchungen zur "bat qol" und verwandten Phänomenen,* TSAJ 20 (Tübingen: J.C.B. Mohr [Paul Siebeck], 1989), promises to offer much additional insight especially into some of the material discussed in Chapter 7 below. For the further theological integration which the results of this research call for, I should have liked to evaluate E. J.

Lott, *Vision, Tradition, Interpretation,* Religion and Reason 35 (Berlin / New York: de Gruyter, 1988).

For the production of this book I am indebted to the help of many — even though its remaining flaws and shortcomings are of course solely my own responsibility. My special thanks, however, are due to several people without whose counsel and support the project could not have seen the light of day.

First of all I am deeply grateful to my Cambridge *Doktorvater,* Dr. W. Horbury, for his tireless generosity and friendship in guiding, challenging and correcting my course of research throughout. Cheerful and unassuming in his depth and comprehensiveness of learning, always committed to a balanced and sympathetic reading of the ancient sources, he has been to me a model of the scholar of Scripture who "makes glad both God and mankind" (m. Abot 6:1, ed. Herford). I also wish to thank Professor M. D. Hooker, whose perceptive supervision during my first term in Cambridge helped to set my research on course.

The Association of Commonwealth Universities provided generous financial support of my postgraduate research through a Commonwealth Scholarship. My thanks must go also to the Tyndale House Council for library privileges, and to the Tyndale House librarian, Mr. D. Deboys, for his frequent generous assistance.

I wish to thank Prof. M. Hengel for accepting this work for publication in the WUNT series. Mr. Ulrich Gaebler and his team at J.C.B. Mohr (Paul Siebeck) have provided friendly and competent assistance in the production of the book. Mr. Paul Spilsbury kindly helped in checking the proofs, while Mr. Barry Nielsen compiled the Index of Passages and the Index of Modern Authors.

Finally, my deepest thanks go to my parents, who first taught me about revelation and the mystery of God in Christ. I have always been assured of their faithful and unwavering support, even when at times the relevance of my research may not have seemed apparent. And although it pleased God in His mercy and wisdom to call my father home before these words could appear in print, it would be sufficient tribute if these pages occasionally showed that his son *sequiturque patrem non passibus aequis.*

Vancouver, B. C.
June 15, 1989.

Table of Contents

Part Two: Pauline Christianity

List of Abbreviations

1. The system of abbreviations of Biblical books as well as of periodicals, reference works, and serial publications follows that of the *Journal of Biblical Literature,* with the following exceptions and additions (for fuller information see the Bibliography):

ADPB	*The Authorised Daily Prayer Book of the United Hebrew Congregations of the British Commonwealth of Nations*
BHM	Jellinek, *Bet ha-Midrasch*
BibSac	*Bibliotheca Sacra*
CPJ	*Corpus Papyrorum Judaicarum*
EWNT	*Exegetisches Wörterbuch zum Neuen Testament.* Edited by H. Balz und G. Schneider. 3 Vols. Stuttgart: Kohlhammer, 1980-1983.
FJB	*Frankfurter Judaistische Beiträge*
Jastrow	Jastrow, *Dictionary*
JETS	*Journal of the Evangelical Theological Society*
KlP	*Der kleine Pauly: Lexikon der Antike.* Edited by K. Ziegler and W. Sontheimer. 5 Vols. Munich: Deutscher Taschenbuchverlag, © 1979.
M–L	Montefiore/Loewe, *A Rabbinic Anthology*
MHG	M. H. Segal, *A Grammar of Mishnaic Hebrew* (Oxford: Clarendon, 1972).
NHL	*The Nag Hammadi Library in English.* Edited by J. M. Robinson. Leiden: Brill, 1977.
NIGTC	The New International Greek Testament Commentary
NJB	The New Jerusalem Bible
SHR	Studies in the History of Religion
SHVL	Skrifter Utgivna av. Kungl. Humanistiska Vetenskapsamfundet i Lund
TEV	Today's English Version (Good News Bible)
TSAJ	Texte und Studien zum Antiken Judentum
WBC	Word Biblical Commentary
α'	Aquila
σ'	Symmachus
ϑ'	Theodotion

2. Abbreviations of the Dead See Scrolls (DSS) are according to J. A. Fitzmyer, *The Dead Sea Scrolls: Major Publications and Tools for Study,* SBLSBS 8 (Missoula: Scholars Press, © 1977).

3. Abbreviations of Apocrypha, Pseudepigrapha, Rabbinic and Patristic literature are according to J. H. Charlesworth (ed.), *The Old Testament Pseudepigrapha* [=*OTP*], 2 Vols. (Garden City: Doubleday, 1985), with the following exceptions and additions:

Abot	Pirqe Abot	Mek	Mekhilta de–Rabbi
Apol 1–2	Justin, *Apology* 1–2		Ishmael
AscIsa	Ascension of Isaiah	*MidrPsa*	Midrash Tehillim
BM	Baba Mesia	*MM*	*Memar Marqah*
BQ	Baba Qamma	MQ	Mo'ed Qatan
Cant R	Shir ha-Shirim Rabbah	ParJer	*Paraleipomenta Jere-*
Dial	Justin, *Dialoque with*		*miou*
	Trypho	Taan	Ta'anit
Diogn	*Epistle to Diognetus*	Tg	Targum
EpApost	*Epistula Apostolorum*	TJ	Targum Jonathan to
EpBarn	Epistle of Barnabas		the Prophets
.FT	Fragment–Targums to	TJac	Testament of Jacob
	the Pentateuch	TN	Targum Neofiti I to
Git	Gittin		the Pentateuch
HermVis/	Shepherd of Hermas:	TNgl	Marginal Glosses to
	Visions/		Targum Neofiti I
HermSim	Similitudes	TO	Targum Onkelos to
IgnEph/	Ignatius: Ephesians/		the Pentateuch
IgnMagn/	Magnesians/	TPsJ	Targum Pseudo-Jona-
IgnPhld/	Philadelphians/		than (Yerushalmi) to
IgnPol/	Polycarp/		the Pentateuch
IgnRom/	Romans/	TR	Teacher of Right-
IgnSmyr/	Smyrnaeans/		eousness
IgnTrall	Trallians	VitAd	Life of Adam and Eve
MartPol	Martyrdom of Polycarp	VitProph	Lives of the Prophets

4. Works of Josephus are referred to as follows:

Ant	*Biblical Antiquities*	*BJ*	*The Jewish War*
Ap	*Against Apion*	*Vita*	*Life of Josephus*

5. Abbreviations for Philo's treaties follow the Loeb Classical Library edition (e.g. vol. 10, p. xxxv), omitting all punctuation and with the following exceptions:

Cont	*De Vita Contemplativa*	*Prob*	*Quod Omnis Probus*
Her	*Quis Rerum Divinarum*		*Liber sit*
	Heres Sit	*QE* 1–4	*Quaestiones et Solu-*
Immut	*Quod Deus Immutabilis*		*tiones in Exodum* 1-4
	sit	*QG* 1–2	*Quaestiones et Solu-*
LA 1–3	*Legum Allegoriae* 1–3		*tiones in Genesin* 1-2
LG	*De Legatione ad Gaium*	*Spec* 1–4	*De Specialibus Legi-*
Opif	*De Opificio Mundi*		*bus* 1-4

6. Other abbreviations follow established usage.

Citation Procedure for Secondary Literature

All secondary sources are cited by the author's name and a convenient short (or in some cases abbreviated) title. In ambiguous cases this short title will be identified under the author's name in the bibliography.

Foreign language works are cited according to the original where this has been easily accessible; otherwise available translations have been used.

The dating procedure for ancient Rabbis is explained in n. 1 of Chapter 7. The sigla used are e. g. T3 = third generation Tanna, A2 = second generation Amora, etc.

In Chapter 9—11 the pertinent commentaries are cited by author and page number only (e. g. Cranfield 1:137).

Introduction

Problem Definition and Method

גל — עיני ואביטה נפלאות מתורתך.

Psalm 119:18.

Mysteria sunt doctrinae coelestes, quae citra
DEI revelationem ignorantur ab hominibus.

J. A. Bengel, *Gnomon*, 618 (*ad* 1 Cor 4:1).

1. Thesis Statement

Faced with the theological problems of delayed deliverance and historical theodicy, Jewish religious thought in the Hellenistic period necessarily became engaged in a close reassessment of the received tradition and of the channels of revelation. Drawing on this re-reading of their Biblical heritage, and somewhat stimulated by the increasing secrecy of the surrounding popular pagan religions, many Jews found in the notion of revealed divine mysteries the key to a renewed understanding of God's sovereignty in history and the cosmos, being offered as it were an "insider's look" at God's dealings in heaven. It is significant in this respect that the theme of revealed heavenly mysteries is continued in early Christianity with its unique affirmation of God's decisive historical intervention in Jesus of Nazareth as the Messiah: the later correspondence e.g. of the apostle Paul repeatedly develops the theme of Christ as the mystery "hidden for ages and generations, but now made manifest" (cf. Col 1:26).

This book, then, offers a theological study of ancient Jewish and Pauline views of the revelation of heavenly mysteries. Exegetical surveys of the respective notions of revelation will be complemented by a broadly based literary documentation of the "mystery" motif in the Old Testament and early Jewish writings, without thereby losing sight of the influence of the Hellenistic religious milieu.[1]

The particular and, it is hoped, original contribution of this study will be to locate the Jewish and Pauline understanding of such divine secrets firmly within the wider framework of corresponding views of *revelation* both "old" and "new".

2. Definition of Terms

"A mystery", wrote E. M. Forster, "is only a high-sounding term for a muddle."[2] Modern society seems to use the word "mystery" for any sublime and nebulous truth which is marvelled at but not fully understood. Similarly, the word "revelation" today is often commandeered to describe any experience of cognitive realization ("the penny has dropped").[3]

However, in responsible scholarship such looseness of terminology is quite unhelpful. Before proceeding any further, therefore, I would like to offer the following as my *working definitions* for the purposes of this inquiry.

> 1. "Revelation" designates a) any divine disclosure communicated by visionary or prophetic means, or b) the manifestation of heavenly realities in a historical context.
> 2. By "Mystery" is meant any reality of divine or heavenly origin specifically characterized as hidden, secret, or otherwise inaccessible to human knowledge.

Lest I incur the charge of contrived results, I hasten to add that those who sailed in quest of a golden fleece must have had from the outset some notion of what they were after: but as in that expedition, the working definitions here may justly be expected to receive considerable clarification in the course of interaction with the sources.[4]

---

[1] Since the chosen field of inquiry is limited to "Ancient Judaism and Pauline Christianity", unfortunately no separate study of the mystery religions can here be offered. However, the most significant points of contact are noted where apposite; see especially Chapter Four below.

[2] *A Passage to India*, Ch. 7.

[3] Cf. Tillich, "Offenbarung", 406.

[4] In any theme study a working definition is unavoidable; this applies particularly to the subject of revelation (cf. Guillet, "Révélation", 601). The *broadly* outlined definition here suggested seems more suitable than pre- understandings of revelation as "proposition", as "history", as "experience", "dialectical Word", etc. (Cf. in detail Dulles, *Models,* 19–128.)

The quest for God's *self*-revelation, once fashionable (esp. in German theology), would be another inappropriate limitation on the study of revelation. For a vigorous criticism of the idea see Downing, "Revelation", esp. 185. However, Downing's thesis (*Has Christianity a Revelation?*) that Biblical faith is altogether without revelation does violence to a body of texts which do appeal for their statements about God to past divine

3. Problem Definition in Relation to Previous Research

There have been a number of relevant studies on the New Testament under-standing of revelation. Representative of these are the works of E. F. Scott, R. Bultmann, A. Oepke, H. Schulte, U. Wilckens, and D. Lührmann. Similarly, among the various surveys of ancient Jewish views of revelation mention may be made of O. Betz, J. Blenkinsopp, A. Chester, J. J. Petuchowski, and G. Scholem. Studies on the term "mystery" in the New Testament and its envi-ronment have been offered by many, from the excursus in J. A. Robinson's commentary on Ephesians and G. Bornkamm's seminal article in *TWNT* to the writings of K. Prümm, R. E. Brown, C. C. Caragounis, R. Penna, and A. E. Harvey.[5] These works and others have been taken into account in the ap-propriate chapters below; my agreements and differences with several of the most important will be outlined in the Conclusion.

But although the intimate link between divine "revelation" and divine "mys-teries" has sometimes been noted, rarely if ever have these two concepts been analysed *together*, in light of each other, and in their larger theological context. It is here that I would like to see my contribution: viz., in a study of the Jewish notion of heavenly mysteries as an aspect of the view of revelation.

4. Method

In approaching this project I have attempted to include significant informa-tion from a wide range of Jewish literature, the delimitation of which will be explained below. But since the primary interest of this work is in the examina-tion of an idea (rather than a precise word study of the terms "revelation" or "mystery"), my approach to the texts has had at times to be fairly inductive. I have taken into account various Greek, Hebrew, and Aramaic words denoting "disclosure" and "hiddenness", while trying at the same time to keep an eye open for passages where the theme in question may be expressed in different terms, or where in fact it occurs only implicitly. In order to limit the scope of the investigation, the subjects of miracles, of epiphanies, and of "natural" re-velation have for the most part been excluded (cf. the definition of "revelation" above). Further, my interest has not been in heavenly secrets *as such* but in "re-vealed secrets", i. e. *mysteria revelata* or *revelanda*. The theme of a disclosure of *human* secrets, which occurs in our texts with perhaps surprising regularity, will be addressed only incidentally.

---

actions and disclosures as well as to future fulfilments of promises. For the Biblical wri-ters, God can be loved and obeyed only because He has made His love and His will known. Cf. Dulles, *Models*, 11—13.

[5] Full references given in the bibliography.

In the interest of methodological integrity, it is appropriate at this point to issue a caveat. This study intends to treat the ancient Jewish and Pauline literature
independently, each on its own terms. There is no conscious concern to present
Paul as the sum and culminating "fulfilment" of Judaism, or on the other hand
to treat each in complete isolation. However, it is true that as a theologian and
a historian of ideas I am trying to understand something of the religious context
out of which Paul speaks; and hence it is perhaps inevitable that my investigation will be guided in part by "Pauline" questions and ideas. Nevertheless, I
have endeavoured to bear this in mind, and to regard my task as one of critical
perception and description rather than of systemic harmonization. My aim
throughout has been to proceed from a broad textual base in the primary sources, and to note similarities as well as differences.

5. Order of Presentation

After a general introduction to the "Ancient Judaism" here in view, the structure of the argument in Part One will be to offer first a *précis* of what constitutes
divine revelation in a given body of literature. This will address, where helpful,
the respective view of the identity and theological place of the "original" revelation (*Uroffenbarung*: i. e. the giving of Torah, though this is sometimes ex-
panded to include oral tradition).

The presentation will then proceed in a second step to highlight the problems
and possiblities of on-going *contemporary* revelation as understood in the respective group of writings. Finally, this general overview will in each case serve
as the backdrop for a more specific investigation of the nature and function of
revealed heavenly mysteries for these same writers. Part One concludes with a
brief attempt at a synthetic presentation of previous conclusions.

Part Two on the letters of Paul will be organized in analogous fashion. A separate introduction will be followed by a survey of the constituent elements of
Paul's view of revelation. Chapters Nine and Ten will then address the "revealed mysteries" theme in the letters to the Corinthians, Romans and Colossians, while the final Chapter surveys the remaining letters of the Pauline corpus and briefly assesses the continuing influence of the motif in the Apostolic
Fathers.

Part One

Ancient Judaism

Introduction

1. Outline of an Old Testament Topology of Revelation

1.1. Religious Background

At the risk of over-simplification, the Ancient Near Eastern view of divine revelation could perhaps be summarized under three headings: the interlacing of the visible and the invisible, the world of man and the world of god; secondly, the sovereign, overruling involvement of the deity in the events, indeed *all* events, of nature and of history;[1] and finally, the disclosure of the divine character and intentions — through the threefold channels of nature, mantic technique, and the corpus of mythology and religious historiography. Mesopotamian gods frequently reveal things to man — not simply through their regular manifestations in the realm of nature, but also and more specifically by disclosing in *words* the truths about themselves and about human fate which they wish to communicate.[2]

Nevertheless, actual religious practice apparently never fully developed this doctrine for application in the realm of daily life. Thus, it seems that the lack of regular effectual revelation may have been compensated by means of mantic procedures.[3] Notwithstanding the silence of the gods in daily life, they could still be induced to make known the answers to man's questions in other ways, such as signs and omens.[4]

---

[1] Cf. esp. Albrektson, *History and the Gods*.

[2] N. B. mythic heroes such as Gilgamesh are forever receiving special dispensations of "divine secrets": e.g. *Epic of Gilgamesh* 1:5; 11:9f., 186f., 266f. Similarly in *Poem of Adapa* 57f.; the *Etana Myth* 2:143ff.; and often. Compare Hesiod on Prometheus: *Works* 45f., 49–51. Cf. Labat, *Religions*, 39 n. 3: "La révélation des secrets des dieux est un ressort habituel du déroulement des mythes babyloniens." These mysteries tend to be concerned with secret divine knowledge about the past or about nature. Secrets of haruspicy are particularly common: Borger, "Geheimwissen", 191. On religious secrecy in Egypt see Assmann, *Re,* 23f., 195–199 and passim; Altenmüller, "Geheimnis", 510 (esp. mysteries of Hades).

[3] Lutzmann, "דבר", 98, 100.

[4] See esp. Gadd, "Methods", 25.

1.2. External Media of Revelation

Recognizable traces of such religious thought survive in the Old Testament.

1.2.1. Dreams. Basic Ancient Near Eastern dream types in the OT include (i) divine revelations; (ii) expressions of the dreamer's physical, spiritual, or mental state of health; and (iii) mantic (predictive) dreams.[5] However, dreams as media of revelation seem relatively rare in the OT.[6]

1.2.2. Lots. Perhaps the only remaining *mechanical* medium of revelation (divination) was the sacred lot, "Urim and Thummim", which was cast "before Yahweh".[7] Although the decision so obtained was regarded as Yahweh's final word on the matter,[8] a conclusive answer was apparently not always available (e.g. 1 Sam 28:6; cf. 14:37). In later texts, the term גורל is often used metaphorically of an allotment or appointment, whether of land[9] or of one's "lot" in life.[10] Overall, the rare use of the lot represents a survival of "older and widespread ideas and practices which Israel shared with many other peoples."[11]

1.2.3. Portents. Portentous events in nature or history demonstrate God's majesty, goodness, displeasure, etc.; as such they, too, are not peculiar to Israelite religion.[12]

1.2.4. Miscellaneous Signs and Symbols. Prophetic revelation could also be triggered by ordinary (but timely, hence ominous) "chance" experiences or encounters;[13] examples include Amos's plumbline (Amos 7:7 ff.) and basket of

---

[5] Thus Oppenheim, *Interpretation,* 184. Cf. Ehrlich, *Traum,* 135 on revelation dreams e.g. in Gen 20:3 ff., 31:24, 31:11 ff. See also, more recently, Gnuse, *Dream Theophany.*

[6] According to Fohrer, *Grundstrukturen,* 39, dreams are limited to "E" (Genesis), early cultic prophecy, late prophecy and apocalyptic.

[7] E.g. Num 27:21; cf. Lev 16:8−10. Note also the divinatory bronze altar of 2 Kgs 16:15 (Gray, *Kings,* 578 assumes haruspicy). Lindblom, *Gesichte,* 16 recognizes hydromancy in Gen 44:5.

[8] Dommershausen, "גורל", 994; cf. e.g. Prov 16:33.

[9] Cf. Josh, 1 Chr; and in the NT period see e.g. Luke 1:9; Acts 1:26; Josephus *BJ* 4:153 ff.

[10] E.g. Isa 57:6; Dan 12:13; the meaning of גורל in such passages approaches that of חלק or נחלה. Even in this sense it can apply to the land of Israel (e.g. Psa 125:3). Cf. Sir 11:22 [Heb]; and e.g. 1 QS 11:7; 1 QSa 1:9, 20; 1 QM 1:5, 15:1, 17:7, etc. (see further below on Qumran).

[11] Rowley, *Faith,* 30 f. Lindblom, "Vorstellung", 279, suggests omens of divination in 2 Sam 5:22 ff. or Num 23:3 ff. (cf. 24:1); but the evidence is inconclusive.

[12] E.g. Exod 19:16 ff.; Psa 18:9 ff. (thunderstorm); 1 Kgs 19:12 ("gentle whisper" of the wind); 2 Sam 5:24 (sound of balsam trees); cf. possibly the pillar of cloud/fire (primarily a symbol of epiphany). On portentous signs in Egypt see e.g. Hornung, *Der Eine,* 122 ff. Cf. also Rowley, *Faith,* 25 f.

[13] Fishbane (*Biblical Interpretation,* 449 ff.) sees this as an example of "mantological" interpretation, similar in kind to the reinterpretation of prophetic oracles e.g. in Daniel (and later the *pesher* at Qumran).

fruit (8:1 ff.), and Jeremiah's almond branch and boiling pot (Jer 1:11–14; cf. also 24:1 ff.), as well as his visit at the potter's workshop (18:1 ff.).[14] On a somewhat different level, cultic objects such as the ark, tabernacle, sacrifice, temple, etc. serve not as media of revelation in themselves, but as pledges of Yahweh's presence; they may constitute *loci* of divine revelation.[15]

1.3. Prophecy and the Social and Cultic Locus of Revelation

Revelation in the Old Testament is not normally given to an individual for his private benefit. This of course is most obvious for the constitutive revelation of Torah. But elsewhere, too, individuals are chosen to *receive* revelation in order then to mediate it to the whole community: even revelations for patriarchs or kings (e.g. 2 Sam 7; 2 Kgs 20) pertain to God's intentions for His people and thus to the greater dimension of salvation history.[16]

The organized cult was a special focus of revelation. Prophets commonly received their visions in a cultic setting,[17] and priests were the primary dispensers of תורה, instruction.[18] In this sense the bearer of revelation, whether priest or prophet (or both), is almost never properly independent of the cult.[19]

However, it is fitting to re-emphasize the importance of the *word*: even where revelation in the OT involves visions as part of the cultic experience, it expres-

---

[14] N. B. such "stimuli" should not be reduced to "the ordinary 'mechanics' of how the divine message came to the prophets" (thus Rogerson, *Supernatural*, 15). The prophets did distinguish between the triggering *stimulus* and the acting *source* of revelation: note e.g. Jer 18; also König, *Offenbarungsbegriff*, 2:299. Cf. the sequence of "seeing" and "hearing", vision and interpretation, in apocalyptic literature.

[15] Cf. e.g. Eichrodt, "Offenbarung", 1599; Sauer, "עד", 745; Levine, "Presence", 82.

[16] Cf. Haag, "Révélation", 599.

[17] Isa 6 is only the most obvious example; cf. cultic theophanies in Psa 18:7–15; 97:1–5; 114; Hab 3:34 ff.; Nah 1:3 ff. See further Kuntz, *Self- Revelation*, 215–231 and passim; Westermann (*Lob*, 75 f.) and Jeremias (*Theophanie*, 154) relate the cultic epiphany and theophany motifs respectively to the Red Sea and Sinai traditions. The frequency of cultic visions (not only in pre-exilic texts) would seem to militate against a sharp polarization between a visionary and a priestly party in Israel, posited by P. D. Hanson as the origin of apocalyptic (*Dawn*, 209 ff., 280 ff.; cf. Plöger, *Theocracy*, 45 ff.). Contrast e.g. Eaton, Vision, passim; Meyers, "*Tôrâ*", 70–74.

[18] Cf. Deut [17:8–11; 19:16–19]; 31:9; 33:8, 10; Judg 18:5 f.; 1 Sam 23:9–12; 30:7 f.; Jer 2:8; 18:18; Ezek 44:23; Hos 4:6; Mic 3:11; Mal 2:7; 2 Chr 15:3. See Thomson, *Revelation*, 42 f. Also e.g. Josephus *Ap* 1:29.

[19] Gyllenberg, "Kultus", 77. Note Clements, *Prophecy*, on Torah, priesthood and prophecy (71 ff.); and conversely, on the prophetic censure of cultic abuse and corruption (93 ff.).

ses and brings to bear a *message* from God.[20] Rendtorff's 1961 call to arms of "revelation [sc. exclusively] through history" fails to recognize that revelation in the Bible is impossible without the word: "Il n'y a révélation qu'à partir du moment où il y a parole."[21]

1.4. Revelation and the Hiddenness of God

The origins of the theme of a revelation of divine secrets can, I submit, be traced with fair probability to the Old Testament theology of God's hiddenness.

1.4.1. The Problem of Divine Hiddenness

Prophetic revelation and the cult granted the believer the possibility of knowing God and His intentions. But this was not an unequivocal confession: "O Lord, by your favour you made my mountain to stand strong; but when you hid your face, I was dismayed" (Psa 30:8). The Old Testament also displays an acute familiarity with God's silence and hiddenness.

This hiddenness is not an abnormality, an unfortunate occasional blemish in an otherwise predictable system of theology.[22] New revelation from God may not in fact be forthcoming for long periods of time: "In those days it was rare for Yahweh to speak; visions were uncommon" (1 Sam 3:1 NJB). Characters like Job, David, Hezekiah, Jeremiah, all have to cope at one time or another with the torment and agony of God's silence. True, God's silence and absence are never His last word, and therefore the hiddenness of Yahweh is not ultimately a cornerstone of an OT theology of revelation. Nevertheless, God is not simply "available" to man, whether in daily experience or in the cult.[23]

---

[20] See Psa 50:3; cf. Kraus, *Psalmen*, 1:80 (*pace* Mowinckel, Weiser et al.): "Die Theophanie ist ein Lautwerden der קול־יהוה (Ps 29,3 ff.). Jahwe 'redet' (דבר) und 'ruft' (קרא): Ps 50,1." He also identifies this as the distinction between theophany and the "Theoria" of Greek religion: *Theologie*, 45.

[21] De Pury, "Sagesse", 26. See Rendtorff, "Offenbarungsvorstellungen", 40 and passim; he has since modified his view in "Offenbarung und Geschichte" (1981), e.g. 48. For the "revelation through history" debate see titles by Rendtorff, Zimmerli, Barr, Muschalek/Gamper, et al. in the bibliography.

[22] Cf. Balentine's statistical observations (*Hidden God*, 7 f. (cf. 85)): on 26 occasions God is said to hide His face (סתר); seven times He hides Himself (עלם, סתר); and ten times the things of God are said to be hidden (כחד, צפן, סתר).

[23] Cf. Weiser, "Beziehungen", 522: even in the cult, God's familiarity was never allowed to overshadow His mysterious awesomeness (see e.g. Psalm 68:36); this tension engendered much fruitful theological reflection in the Psalms and elsewhere. Cf. Kraus, *Psalmen*, 80 (on Psa 80:4, 94:1); Eaton, "Self-Revelation", 331; Perlitt, "Verborgenheit", 373.

God's self-concealment is not arbitrary or capricious, but often relates to reckless disobedience and guilt on the part of His people and their leaders (e.g. Mic 3:1—4; Isa 59:1 ff.; Ezek 39:24, etc.).[24] The problem of God's felt absence is thus laid at the people's doorstep, so that "what had been the people's complaint against God became God's complaint against his people."[25] Nevertheless, not all occurrences e.g. of the expression סתר + פנים are due to human sinfulness and the wrath of God, as Balentine points out.[26] God may be hidden for a number of different reasons, of which the sin of the people is only one. His sovereignty in this matter is never questioned.

1.4.2. The Response of Faith

But how does the Old Testament cope existentially and theologically with the problem of God's hiddenness?

Modern scholarship has variously suggested that one way of coming to terms with God's silence was in fact to take it as a sign of His saving intention. Isa 45:15 reads, "You are indeed a God who hides Himself (אתה אל מסתתר), O God of Israel, Saviour!" God's use of the Gentile Cyrus amounts to a new message of salvation amidst His continuing hiddenness.[27]

Another approach is more typical: where prayers of distress are uttered before God, there is often a subtle appeal to His promises or His character as He has revealed it in the past. Thus e.g. in Exod 5:22f. Moses bitterly complains about God's failure to act — all the while appealing to past revelation: "Why did you ever send me?"[28]

The attitude taken here and in many of the lament psalms is dialectical: God's silence now is indeed painfully real — but that does not make His past promise *un*real. Both horns of this dilemma are fully relevant to the believer's situation. Often the Psalmist draws comfort from the one side when facing the other: he remembers the days of old and longs for God (Psa 143:5); he recalls that God saved him in battle (140:8); and a passionate historical appeal can be heard to resound in his prayer to "God my stronghold" or "the God of Israel" (Psa 59:6, 10, etc.). Such reasoning would of course be actively encouraged by the liturg-

---

[24] Perlitt, "Verborgenheit", 375.

[25] Balentine, *Hidden God*, 161.

[26] Balentine, *Hidden God*, e.g. 76—79.

[27] But we should not go on with Westermann, *Jesaja,* 138, to postulate in this obscure passage a decisive turning point of OT thought, after which God's actions are *on principle* no longer perceptible in history. The glory and majesty of God are still intended to be recognizable even to the Gentiles: Psa 98:2; Isa 40:5, 52:10, etc.; cf. Zobel, "גלה", 1030f. (Some have questioned the integrity of the text, suggesting an emendation אתך for אתה: e.g. BHS; Whybray, *Isaiah 40—66,* 110; McKenzie, *Second Isaiah,* 80, 82f.)

[28] Cf. e.g. Num 11:10ff.; Jer 20:7ff.

ical use of credal and confessional formulae relating precisely to God's past saving activity.

Many more examples could be named.[29] But the pattern is clear: in the face of Yahweh's hiddenness both individual and nation could recall "His grace and favour to our fathers in distress." Here as in later Judaism, the insistence on God's unaltered character serves to buttress a passionate hope that absence and hiddenness will give way to epiphany and revelation.[30]

1.4.3. The Eclipse of Prophetic Revelation

In the post-exilic period, the *deus absconditus* problem became subject to particular complications. Considering the great accomplishments of the eighth-century prophets, an editor[31] confidently affirmed that "the Lord God does nothing unless He reveals (גלה) His secret counsel (סודו) to His servants the prophets" (Amos 3:7). But at the same time, individual claims to contemporary prophetic revelation were becoming increasingly suspect, perhaps not least in the aftermath of Ezra's reforms.

Prophets like Jeremiah, Ezekiel, and Zechariah frequently encounter the problem of *false* prophecy; חזון ("vision"), the standard term for prophetic revelation, is now often used negatively, as the mark of the *false* prophet.[32] Jeremiah in particular utters some sharply critical words about the role of dreams in revelation.[33] Clearly there was need for a test criterion to distinguish canonical ("true") prophecy from the pronouncements of a host of contemporary charlatans whose banner was the appeal to dreams and ecstatic visions. The post-exilic religious and political environment faced the believing community with the increasingly intractable problem of how to interpret one's times.[34]

---

[29] Cf. e.g. Zimmerli, "Offenbarung", 31, on Psa 44, 77.

[30] Cf. e.g. Rochais, "Apocalyptique", 284−286; also Chapter 8 below on the three-dimensional nature of revelation in Paul.

[31] Most commentators regard Amos 3:7 as the work of a Deuteronomic redactor. See also Blenkinsopp, *History*, 89.

[32] E.g. Jer 14:14; 23:16; Ezek 12:24; 13:6−9, 16, 23; 21:34; Zech 10:2; 13:4. Cf. also Isa 28:7; 29:9f.; 30:10.

[33] Jer 23:25−32, 27:9f., 29:8f.; cf. Zech 10:2; Eccl 5:6. Deut 13:1−5 and 18:14−22, being incorporated into the Deuteronomic code, would have become particularly influential guidelines in this respect: see e.g. Jer 28:9.

[34] In practice the main test criterion appears to have been moral and spiritual, i.e. exposing sin and affirming Yahweh's sovereignty: e.g. Isa 55:8, Mic 3:5−12; Jer 23:25−29; Lam 2:14; Ezek 23:26; also Deut 13:1−5; 18:18−22. Oepke, "καλύπτω", 578 lists four criteria: (i) the prophet's personality and motive, (ii) the manner in which the revelation is received, (iii) the fulfilment of relevant predictions, and (iv) unrelenting loyalty to the will of God rather than to the popular trends of the day. On the general problem cf. further Crenswhaw, *Conflict*, passim.

Alongside the dispute over false prophecy, prophetic activity was becoming anonymous (e.g. Mal; Zech 9—14; Isa 40—66). Moreover, there arose the belief that contemporary prophecy was really not to be compared with the prophets of old. For the first time we encounter here the suggestion that prophecy may altogether be coming to an end: the Psalmist writes (74:9), "We do not see our signs; there is no longer any prophet אֵין עוֹד נָבִיא, nor is there any among us who knows how long." This late OT sentiment (cf. e.g. Zech 13:3; Lam 2:9; also Ezek 7:26; Amos 8:11) foreshadows a common trend in postcanonical Jewish literature, as we will see.

Despite these emerging reservations about the possibility and legitimacy of contemporary prophecy, there can be little doubt that prophetic activity in one form or another continued until well after the exile. At the same time, two important *theologoumena* from this period gradually evolved into virtual substitutes for prophetic revelation: exegesis and apocalyptic.

1.4.4. Revelation, Torah, and Exegesis

In the postexilic writings of Scripture there is an undeniable trend towards accepting the *received, written* word as a significant means of revelation. Early indications of this have been seen e.g. in Ezekiel's eating of the scroll (3:1 f.)[35] or in recurring Deuteronomic phrases like "the words of this law", which stress the givenness of the revealed word.[36] Torah piety begins to manifest itself clearly in Ezra/Nehemiah and in several of the Psalms (esp. 1, 19, 119). Alongside the emerging influence of the Pentateuch as canon there arose the belief in Torah as embodiment of wisdom[37] — a conviction also commonly found in later Judaism, and one which amounts in effect to a nationalization of wisdom.

Thus Psalm 19 argues, *a minore ad maius*,[38] that just as creation declares the glory of Elohim, so even more Yahweh's Torah is perfect, restoring the soul and making wise the simple. Instruction was now to be sought in the book of Torah and from those who study it.[39] At the same time, although God's sovereignty in creation and history is still affirmed (see above), adverse historical circumstances increasingly drive the believer to search God's word written. This, above all, has become the place where Israel is to know the Lord's will: "Where there is no revelation [חָזוֹן] the people are unrestrained; but happy is he who keeps Torah" (Prov 29:18).[40]

---

[35] Latourelle, *Theology*, 26.
[36] Deut 17:19; 27:3, 8, 26; 28:58; 29:28; 31:12, 24; 32:46; Josh 1:7 f.; 8:34, etc. Latourelle, *Theology*, 25.
[37] E.g. Ezra 7:25; Psa 111:10; cf. Job 28. See Chapter 3 below.
[38] Haag, "Révélation", 597 f.
[39] E.g. Psa 1, 19, 119 passim; Neh 8; 2 Chr 35:6, 12 f.
[40] Cf. Bartlett, "Revelation", 23; Zobel, "גלה", 1031. Note also the exhortation to

But of course no mere human exegesis can replace divine revelation. Wisdom is hidden with God, inaccessible to human search and understanding (esp. Job 28; Psa 51:8); he alone can dispense it (Prov 1:7; 2:6; 20:27; Job 11:5 f.; 12:22, etc.). Although this theme is only fully elaborated in the postcanonical writings, Psalm 119:18 already hints at an important implication: "Open my eyes, that I may behold wonderful things [נפלאות] from your law." The suggestion here is that God may disclose the wonders of Torah through the process of exegesis (cf. vv. 27, 129 f.).[41] Just as one searches and mines for treasures of silver, so for hidden secrets of wisdom and of Torah — and God meets this search in revelation (Job 28:1 ff.; cf. 11:6; 12:22; also Prov 2:4—6). This view lies near the beginning of a long tradition of Jewish thought which held that the Scriptures contain some things which are obvious and straightforward, and others which are "wondrous" and hidden but whose meaning can be revealed to the sage. It was this belief which ensured that in many circles the acceptance of a canon led not to religious stagnation[42] but to a dynamic process of creative and yet theologically mature and responsible interpretation.[43]

1.4.5. The Secrets of Heaven

"The hidden things belong to the Lord our God, but the things revealed belong to us and to our children forever, that we may follow all the words of this law" (Deut 29:28). Despite such apparent commitment to the adequacy and clarity of received revelation (cf. Deut 30:11—14), we find in post-exilic thought the conviction that Scripture alone was not sufficient to explain God's sovereignty in creation and redemption. Indeed, perhaps it was precisely the "hidden things" which held the clue to God's intentions for salvation history.[44] Here for the first time in the Bible, God's plans for future judgement and redemption are understood to be firmly determined and laid up in heavenly treasure stores, in order to be manifested in history at the proper time.[45]

Alongside the seeming decline of "classical" prophecy, then, there developed a new form of special revelation in the prophetic tradition. Those who thus un-

---

"remember the law of Moses my servant" (Mal 3:22 [Heb]) at the conclusion of the book of Prophets.

[41] Cf. Levenson, "Sources", 564: "in Psalm 119 God himself is the teacher" of Torah (broadly understood: 565 ff.). See further Fishbane, *Biblical Interpretation*, 540; idem, "Revelation", 350; and compare Psa 119:18 with references in the Dead Sea Scrolls to "wondrous mysteries" רזי פלא, etc. (esp. 1 QH 1:21; 1 QM 14:14).

[42] *Pace* Williams, *Form and Vitality*, 84, 87 and passim.

[43] Fishbane, "Exegesis", 35 speaks of the "strategic subordination of the human exegetical voice to divine revelation". Cf. idem, "Revelation", passim.

[44] Even the enigmatic Deut 29:28 appears to pertain to salvation history; see vv. 21 ff.

[45] Deut 32:34 f. Cf. Jer 50:25; Mal 3:10.

derstood and communicated God's "secrets" no longer posed as traditional prophets; yet at the same time they quite specifically absorbed and reapplied the concerns of the prophets to the vexing questions of a new day.[46] We obviously stand here on the brink of apocalyptic; Chapter One will further treat of this subject and its origin in prophecy and mantic wisdom.

Excursus: סוד/רז

Of particular significance for their use in postcanonical literature (e.g. in the Dead Sea Scrolls) are the Hebrew terms סוד and (only Daniel) רז. We will repeatedly have occasion to return to these words, but this may be a suitable moment to give an initial overview of their use in the Old Testament.

The word סוד appears to be related to the root יסד II "to associate, conspire together" (Psa 2:2; 31:14).[47] It is found 21 times in the Old Testament, always in the singular. It never appears in apocalyptic material, and only once in the Pentateuch.

The meaning is perhaps best summarized as a "fellowship of intimate friends taking counsel [for action]." All of the occurrences in the Old Testament can be accounted for by this description. Nevertheless, we can distinguish between two semantic categories, each in turn supporting two related shades of meaning: (i) a confidential human fellowship[48] or counsel/plan;[49] and (ii) the divine council/fellowship[50] or secret plan.[51] Most significant appears to be the element of intimate fellowship and consultation, and the resulting plan;[52] both are intended to be kept from inappropriate disclosure. Reference to a *divine* counsel or plan may be further qualified in the context as pertaining to God's sovereign action in history through judgement or redemption.[53]

The word רז occurs nine times and is found only in the Aramaic section of Daniel.[54] While its meaning shares certain similarities with that of סוד, never-

---

[46] Dan 9:2 ff., 22 ff. (cf. Jer 25:11) and Zech 6:12 f. (cf. Jer 23:5 f.) are but two obvious examples of the reappropriation of earlier prophecy. See more fully Fishbane, *Biblical Interpretation,* esp. 458–499. For the idea of a prophecy as "hidden" or "encoded" until the latter days cf. already Isa 8:16; 29:11 f.; Hab 2:2 f.; and see below.

[47] Cf. Koehler/Baumgartner, *Lexikon* 4 (3rd ed. 1983): 709.

[48] Gen 49:6; Jer 6:11; 15:17; Ezek 13:9; Psa 55:15; 64:3; 111:1; Job 19:19.

[49] Psa 83:4; Prov 11:13; 15:22; 20:19; 25:9.

[50] Jer 23:18, 22; Psa 89:8 [there explicitly the heavenly council]; Job 15:8; [29:4]; Prov 3:32.

[51] Amos 3:7; Psa 25:14.

[52] Cf. Sæbø, "סוד", 146; Fabry, "סוד", 104; Fohrer, "Aspects", 103; Wewers, *Geheimnis,* 191 f.

[53] E.g. Jer 23:16–22; Amos 3:3–8; and cf. Psa 25:13 f.

[54] Dan 2:18, 19, 27, 28, 29, 30, 47 (2x); 4:6. Its use in Dan closely resembles that at Qumran: Finkel, "Pesher".

theless a clear semantic distinction is possible. *Prima facie* the term designates the solution of an inscrutable problem of divination, especially the exposition of dreams and visions. This solution can be the object of inquiry (2:18, 27; [4:6]) and of revelation (2:19, 28–30, 47), and it pertains to events of the near or distant future (cf. 2:21, 28 f.; and passim). As such, it is clearly removed from the sociological dimension suggested by סוד: רז implies neither a confidential consultation nor a plan thereby conceived.[55] It is, however, at the same time the exclusive property of God and can only be revealed by Him as an act of grace to a man of His favour (2:22, 28; 4:5 f., 15).

We will discuss the Greek versions in due course, but it is significant to mention for the time being that in the LXX μυστήριον never renders Hebrew סוד, and that outside Daniel (where it consistently translates רז) the word occurs only in the apocryphal books (see Chapter Six below).

2. "Ancient Judaism": Definition

It now remains for us to indicate the chronological, literary, and religious scope of the "Judaism" whose beliefs[57] are here under examination.

2.1. General Identification

We will trace our theological theme in the Jewish literature of the period bounded very approximately by the Maccabean uprising and the collapse of the revolt under Hadrian. The validity of my results will of necessity be limited by my reconstruction of Judaism from *literary* sources, inasmuch as these are still the main quarry of evidence. Greater emphasis will be given to the Palestinian sources, although important diaspora writers have also been included.[58]

---

[55] Willi-Plein, "Geheimnis", 70 f. keenly observes the difference between the two terms; רז in this sense is "ein statischer Begriff".

[56] This foreshadows the fact that, despite a degree of interchangeable usage in Rabbinic literature, רז is for our purposes the more important word. N. B. Fiddes, "Hiddenness", 225–228 asserts, *pace* many authors (cf. recently Couturier, "Visions"), that סוד and the idea of the divine council "cannot be maintained to be the explanation for the basic idea of divine mysteries" (227).

[57] It must be noted that beliefs are, of course, only one aspect of a religion in which beliefs and practices form a complex whole.

[58] I have not included one ambiguous body of literature, the magical texts (cf. P. S. Alexander in Schürer/Vermes, *HJPAJC* 3.1:342–379). However, if even "mainstream" Jewish writers exhibit both positive and negative attitudes to various forms of magic (e.g. Philo *Spec* 3:100–102; Josephus *Ant* 8:45–49; cf. Cohen, *Talmud,* 274 ff. and Ur-

The headings chosen for the discussion are apocalyptic literature, Qumran, wisdom literature, Philo, Josephus, the Targums and Greek versions, and rabbinic literature. This selection reflects to some extent the approach of my research; but it is also intended as a basic structuring device to help present the data in meaningful and somewhat representative units. Clearly some of the categories are vague, and some documents in turn of a character which matches more than one description (e.g. Jub, 3 En). The following paragraph, therefore, will attempt to assess the degree to which such a collection of evidence may in fact be considered representative of the Judaism here examined.

2.2. Belief and "Orthodoxy" in Early Judaism

Since the classic treatments of the early 20th century,[59] there has been increasing discussion of whether any "mainstream" of belief can be detected, especially in pre-Rabbinic Judaism. A full discussion would obviously require detailed interaction with a vast and growing body of literature. Two observations may here suffice: one, regarding the *type* of writing most likely to embody religious *homologoumena*; and the other, pertaining to the question of "distinguishing" beliefs and practices which would mark off a confessing Jew from an apostate.

2.2.1. Types of Functionally Representative Religious Writing

Clearly some religious documents are more ephemeral and partisan expressions of faith than others. But it is usually safe to regard a public credal statement as more broadly representative of a community's belief than an occasional polemical treatise on a matter of current concern. Similarly, liturgical texts by their very nature and use are likely to express ideas of wider currency than an individual writer's work — witness four centuries of the Book of Common

---

bach, *Sages,* 1:101 f. on the Rabbis), it would seem that the importance of "mysteries" in the magical texts further accentuates the broad influence of Jewish thought on mysteries, illustrating the varying significance of the concept in Graeco-Roman as well as in specifically Jewish settings.

Thus, "mystery" (רזא) can denote on the one hand the magical ritual or formula (a δρώμενον): e.g. Isbell, *Corpus,* Nos. 3:13; 8:1; 11:11; 25:8; 36:4, 5; 38:4; 58:1, 10; Montgomery, *Incantation* Texts, Nos. 38:6; 39:7; Naveh/Shaked, *Amulets,* Amulet 3:3; Bowl 1:7 (cf. Montgomery 37:8); 6:1; Genizah 6.2.1, 9. Cf. the theurgic mysteries of *Hekhalot* texts; and note e.g. 1 En 9:6 (the illegitimate mysteries of the Watchers, which are also "performed"); cf. VitProph 2:5. On the other hand there seem to be cosmological "mysteries of heaven" (e.g. Naveh/Shaked Bowl 1:3 (cf. Montgomery 37:4); 5:2; 13:21; *Sefer Ha-Razim* 2:1 ff.; 3:1 ff.; 4:1 ff.; 8:13 f.) resembling those more fully discussed below.

[59] See the works of Weber, Bousset, Moore, Montefiore, Schürer, Billerbeck, et al.

Prayer.[60] Congregational prayers must clearly formulate a piety held in common. What is more, such "public" texts, along with older documents which are either explicitly or implicitly (e.g. by frequent citation) accorded a status of some authority, may in time become part of the way in which a community defines and understands itself over against its environment.

Finally, another literary category likely to contain widely held views includes writings whose purpose is partly or entirely apologetic. A writer who accounts for his religious beliefs and practices before a hostile or skeptical audience will probably portray his faith in a favourable light and to the best of his knowledge; he is in any case unlikely to defend "extreme" views held only by minority fringe groups.

Given these criteria, the documents here under examination are "representative" to quite different degrees. The apocalyptic writings, though sometimes idiosyncratic in detail, share the claim to be speaking for the (or a) believing community. They also agree in the shaping of certain influential motifs such as throne visions, interpreting angels, the heavenly architecture, coordination of celestial and earthly forces, and the nature of mysteries. Philo distinctly betrays the perspective of an Alexandrian philosopher, Josephus that of a Roman historian; yet because of their frequently apologetic purpose both would appear to support *inter alia* a basic stock of views which appertain to a "mainstream" Judaism.[61] A number (though by no means all) of the Dead Sea Scrolls are more clearly sectarian in content, but they have nevertheless revolutionized our understanding of early Palestinian hermeneutics. From frequent citations, the book of Ben Sira is known to have been widely influential among the Rabbis; moreover, its translation and inclusion in the LXX suggests that it was a significant bridge between Palestinian and diaspora Judaism.[62] Early Rabbinic discussion contains some highly academic subject matter (e.g. technical halakhic debate or exegesis), but also material which will have been more commonly known in the synagogues (prayers, homiletical midrashim, popular teachings of the famous sages). Ancient liturgical texts such as Targums and prayers offer recurring indications of being influenced by notions developed e.g. in apocalyptic and even mystical circles.[63]

---

[60] Thus see e.g. Psalms; PssSol; 18 Benedictions; Piyyutim; Targumim; also 1 QH, Lukan Canticles, OdSol.

[61] Josephus in particular turns out to be a helpful source of contemporary Palestinian views on prophecy. See below, Chapter 5.

[62] Josephus's works are a similar bridge; cf. further Esther 10:3*l* LXX.

[63] Cf. Baeck, "Mysticism", 103; Petuchowski, "Liturgy", 39.

2.2.2. Distinguishing Doctrines: "Judaism" and "Apostasy"

If the debate of recent years[64] has taught us anything about the nature of doctrine in Second Temple Judaism, it is the impossibility of establishing the existence of an "orthodoxy" which could be precisely delineated by means of credal or doctrinal statements. But are there criteria which might distinguish those who were clearly Jews from those who were clearly not?

Latet dolus in generalibus; but at the risk of caricature, the pillars of "mainstream" Jewish belief might be summarized as a) exclusive monotheism, b) "revelation"[65] and orthopraxis, and c) election and redemption. Heretics and apostates appear to have been identified chiefly on the grounds not of specific doctrinal dissent but of the denial of and practical non-conformity with this religious basis of Judaism;[66] criteria for such an identification were obtained from the laws pertaining to (i) ritual fitness for membership in the congregation, and (ii) faithfulness to the covenant.[67]

A good example of "apostasy" by this definition is Elisha b. Abuya (T2), who a) allowed for the heresy of "two powers (רשויות) in heaven" (e.g. b.Hag 15a); b) consciously rebelled against Torah and the "power" of God although he knew better;[68] and c) denied the eschatological reward for the righteous and the resurrection from the dead.[69] Several other pertinent examples could be cited.[70] Whether or not such people were explicitly excommunicated, clearly they were regarded as falling outside the framework of "acceptable" Judaism.

---

[64] See e.g. the articles of Aune, McEleney, Grabbe, Dexinger, Horbury.

[65] I.e. Torah, tradition and interpretation. Cf. Schiffman, "Crossroads", 125: conversion requires the acceptance of both written and oral Torah. See also t.Dem 2:5 (R. Jose b. Judah T4); b.Shab 31a (Hillel/Shammai).

[66] But see Dexinger, "Limits", 111 f.: "One should never forget ... that behind ... orthopraxy there is always a significant amount of orthodoxy." Cf. e.g. SifDeut 329 (on 32:39; ed. Finkelstein, 379) regarding those who say "there is no power/there are two powers in heaven", and those who claim "He has no ability either to kill or to make alive, to do evil or to do good". M.Sanh 10:1 excludes "the one who denies that the Torah is from heaven" from the world to come. See more generally Philo Spec 1:324–345.

[67] Horbury, "Extirpation", 16 f.; cf. also Schiffman, "Crossroads", 145 (= idem, *Jew*, 48).

[68] E.g. RuthR 6:4/EcclR 7.8.1; b.Hag 15a–b; y.Hag 2, 77b; N.B. see also Heb 6:4–6.

[69] RuthR 6:4/EcclR 7.8.1 (in view of R. Judah the baker's martyrdom). But although a *bat qôl* denied him the possibility of repentance (b. Hag 15a; RuthR 6:4/EcclR 7.8.1 [on Jer 3:22; Mal 3:7]), there was apparently no absolute consensus about Aher's final salvation or perdition. Cf. b. Hag 15b; esp. RuthR 6:4/Eccl 7.8.1 (R. Meir T3, Aher's student); see further Segal, *Two Powers,* 60 ff. and passim.

[70] (i) Dositheus the son of Drimylus left Judaism (μεταβαλὼν τὰ νόμιμα καὶ τῶν πατρίων δογμάτων ἀπηλλοτριωμένος: 3 Macc 1:3) and became a priest of Alexander and the deified Ptolemies Adelphoi and Euergetai (*CPJ* 3:235 f., No. 127d–e; cf. p. 230 f.). Note the exclusion of initiates in the Mysteries as πολέμιοι τοῦ ἔθνους (3 Macc 2:32 f.);

But conversely, on these same premises the so-called Qumran community with its range of sectarian beliefs and practices[71] should probably *not* be seen to fall outside the perimeter of the mainstream of the Jewish religion: for despite their criticism of the temple these people did not abandon circumcision, engage in idolatry, or the like.[72] Moreover, if the identification of these sectarians with the Essenes be correct, we have all the more reason not to suspect them of apostasy: Philo and Josephus, while allowing for their distinctiveness,[73] regard the Essenes as an integral and important part of Palestinian Judaism.[74]

2.3. Judaism and the Pagan Religions

This is not the place for a discussion of the impact of "Hellenism" on Judaism in general. Nor indeed can the ultimately religious Hellenistic origin of the term μυστήριον here be examined.[75] The purpose of these remarks is, rather, to indicate in brief the view I have taken of the Hellenistic mystery religions as regards my thesis in particular: viz., that their popularity serves as an apt illustration of an Eastern Mediterranean milieu increasingly fascinated with secret knowledge and esoteric religious truth. The interest in privileged access to the supernatural was "in the air", so to speak — manifested in the accelerated proliferation of personal dream revelations, oracles and their interpretation, magic and astrology, and numerous exclusive groups offering initiates higher knowledge for their personal weal and salvation.[76]

But while the amount of cross-fertilization between Judaism and the general Hellenistic culture was clearly very substantial, theological parallels in the sub-

---

cf. further Horbury, "Extirpation", 23. (ii) The Hasmoneans revolted against the enforced apostasy (ἀποστασίαν, 1 Macc 2:15) of idolatry and other offences against the covenant (cf. 2:27 and passim). (iii) Tiberius Julius Alexander (Philo's nephew): see Josephus *Ant* 20:100; *BJ* 5:45 and passim. (iv) Miriam daughter of Bilgah: t.Suk 4:28.

[71] Peculiar exegesis and halakhhah as well as conscious separation from the temple and from the life of the nation at large clearly mark Qumran as sectarian. Furthermore, criteria for apostasy appear here to have been rather more strictly defined: cf. Sanders, *PPJ*, 255–257.

[72] With regard to the Qumran community's reserved attitude about the Jerusalem temple, note the surprisingly limited criticism of Leontopolis (בית חניו) in m. Men 13:10.

[73] Josephus *BJ* 2:128 describes their piety as ἰδίως.

[74] Josephus *BJ* 2:126–161; Philo *Prob* 75–91; *Hyp* 11:1–18. Contrast Josephus's treatment of the Samaritans: Shechem was inhabited ὑπὸ τῶν ἀποστάτων τοῦ Ἰουδαίων ἔθνους, *Ant* 11:340 (cf. 9:291; 11:19(ff.), 84(ff.), 114f., 174f., 341, 346; 12:257).

[75] The most comprehensive discussion of the Hellenistic religious use of "mysteries" is still Prümm, "Mystères", 1–225; on the religious origin of the μυστήριον terminology also Caragounis, *Mysterion*, 3–19; Harvey, "Mystery Language", esp. 321–324; and most recently Wedderburn, *Baptism*, 148 ff.

[76] See further Hengel, *Judentum*, 381–394; Festugière, *Révélation*, 1:309–354.

ject matter here under consideration would appear for the most part to lie in the realm of religious commonplace, i.e. of the phenomenology and psychology of religion.[77] Outsiders began, rightly or wrongly, to regard the Jewish preoccupation with a mysterious lawbook and with enigmatic rules of cleanliness as an obvious parallel to more familiar patterns of religion.[78] At the same time the more cosmopolitan Jewish writers seized upon this comparison as an apologetic device to demonstrate how Judaism matched and surpassed even the finest of Greek spirituality and morality (e.g. Wisd, EpArist, Artapanus); and thereby, as Cerfaux says, they "faisaient vibrer une corde très sensible de l'âme religieuse de leur temps."[79] And although these Jews maintained all the while a deep-seated antipathy to the substance of the pagan religions, the spread of Greek language, culture, and commerce (even in Palestine) created a milieu in which "Hellenistic" reflection about Yahweh's secret counsels was further encouraged. After initial resistance (see below on the LXX), some of the new religious and philosophical terminology was used positively to express existing and developing ideas of Jewish thought.

2.4. Jewish Mysteries?

In modern scholarship the name of E. R. Goodenough has become associated with the idea that Diaspora Judaism itself became for all practical considerations a mystery religion.[80] Inscriptional evidence from the Diaspora clearly confirms that in many places Jewish religion was significantly influenced by pagan symbolism and pagan religious ideas;[81] indeed the existence of even thoroughly syncretistic Jews in the Diaspora cannot be denied.[82] Goodenough's main assertion is not all-out syncretism, but the use of pagan symbols with Jewish meanings in order to frame Jewish religious practice in conscious analogy to the religious symbolism of the pagan mysteries.[83]

It is of course true that ancient Judaism exercised a considerable attraction on many pagan contemporaries. And although outright proselytes may have been

---

[77] The major literary exception may be Alexandrian Judaism.

[78] See esp. Juvenal *Sat* 14:102–104: "Tradidit arcano quodcumque volumine Moyses, Non monstrare vias eadem sacras nisi sacra colenti, Quaesitum ad fontem solos deducere verpos." Cf. the Gentile Christian perspective voiced in SibOr 8:307f.

[79] Cerfaux, "Influence", 63.

[80] See the classic statement in Goodenough, *Light,* 5 and passim, and its painstaking elaboration in the massive *Jewish Symbols* (13 vols.).

[81] E.g. *Jewish Symbols,* Vols. 2, 9.

[82] Cf. Gnostic and magical texts, also e.g. 1 Macc 1:11–15, 43– 53; 2 Macc 4:10–17; 3 Macc 2:28–31; Acts 13:6; regarding nonobservant Jews in the Diaspora.

[83] E.g. *Jewish Symbols* 9:6–8.

limited in number, our information about Jews in the Roman empire is quite compatible with widespread religious and cultural interaction. Especially (but not only) the uneducated on both sides of the "fence" must be considered a likely source of much indiscriminate folk religion, as indeed we find it in many of the charms, amulets, epitaphs, images, etc. which Goodenough adduces.[84]

On the other hand, Goodenough has come in for a good deal of criticism. The Jewishness of some of his evidence has been challenged.[85] More significantly, few scholars have accepted his underlying claim that religious symbols carry an inherent emotional "value" which is unchanging and independent of an interpretive framework.[86] In particular (and most damaging for his overall argument), his notion of a universal pagan sacramental mysticism has not been accepted.[87]

Moreover, it remains doubtful to what extent one can fairly reconstruct the nature of Judaism on the basis largely of a Philonic reading of non-literary evidence.[88] No clear reference, either critical or supportive, is made to Jewish mystery rites by the literary spokesmen of Judaism (or for that matter of Christianity).[89] The statements of *pagan* writers, whether comparing Judaism to other foreign cults[90] or abhorring its distinctives as alien to piety and decorum (*profana illic omnia quae apud nos sacra*[91]), tend to reflect ignorance rather than considered judgements of comparative religion.

Nevertheless, the case mounted by Goodenough should alert us to the possibility that Jewish use of Hellenistic mystery language may at times have been *more* than a mere "bluff"[92] to affirm the superiority of Judaism. We must allow that various symbols, terms and patterns of Hellenistic religion would in some

---

[84]   E.g. *Jewish Symbols* 2:121−295.

[85]   Cf. Smith, *"Symbols"*, 67 f. (Additional Note 2).

[86]   *Jewish Symbols* 12:70; cf. e.g. Smith, *"Symbols"*, 55 f.

[87]   Cf. Smith, *"Symbols"*, 58 f.

[88]   (Even his interpretation of Philo is open to question.) F. Millar's recent assessment of diaspora archaeological evidence comes to rather different conclusions (Schürer/Vermes, *HJPAJC* 3.1:1−176, esp. 138−149).

[89]   Goodenough himself admits (*Jewish Symbols,* 9:8), "We know no Jewish literature that shows any need of pagan symbols to express itself." The supposed "sacramental" references of JosAsen have been thought to point to some kind of Jewish initiatory rite or meal, but against this see Burchard, "Importance", 112 ff.; Wedderburn, *Baptism*, 157 f.; also Sänger, *Judentum*, passim (though N. B. Kee, "Setting", 399 ff. envisions substantial influence from the Isis cult.)

[90]   E.g. Juvenal *Sat* 6:542−547 (in context); Tacitus, *Hist* 5:5; Valerius Maximus, *Facta et Dicta Memorabilia* 1.3.3 (cult of Jupiter Sabazius); Plutarch, *Quaestiones Convivales* 4.6.1 f.

[91]   Thus Tacitus *Hist* 5:4. Cf. Dio Cassius *Hist* 37:17.2; Philostratus, *Vita Apollonii* 5:33. But N.B. Juvenal *Sat* 15:1 ff. speaks with similar derision about Egyptian religion.

[92]   Thus Lagrange, "Mystères", 152.

settings have been employed as ways of expressing Jewish religious truth.[93] This might occur for internal or for propaganda purposes (a clear example of the former is the use of מסטירין in rabbinic literature; the latter is present e.g. in Philo's description of the *Therapeutae*). What is more, in a pagan environment such adiaphorous religious idiom (much like the pattern of synagogal architecture) could be expected to develop quite naturally.[94]

The extent to which pagan thought has ultimately "influenced" the Jewish and/or Pauline idea of revealed mysteries cannot here be discussed; indeed in the realm of religious commonplace (e.g. secrecy, mysticism, divine disclosure) a call for absolute distinction is quite futile. The discussion below is limited to a more or less representative range of relevant *Jewish* religion; and it will lend further support to the now widely held view of a fundamentally Palestinian Jewish origin of Paul's idea of divine mysteries.[95] Nevertheless it will attempt to remain vigilant regarding any obvious *double entendre*, intentional or unintentional, of metaphors from the pagan cults.[96]

The following chapters examine the Jewish material on revealed mysteries in its own right; Part Two will then discuss Paul's thought both in its novel ideas about revelation and in its fundamental continuity with Jewish views of revealed mysteries.

---

[93] Cf. also Petuchowski, "Mystery", 141 f., 152.

[94] Wedderburn, offering a much fuller discussion, argues a similar point (indirect conceptual familiarity; separate development) with regard to Paul: *Baptism*, passim, esp. 158–161, 393 f.

[95] Championed most confidently (perhaps too confidently) in the word study of Brown (*Mystery*, esp. 69).

[96] Note the critical (perhaps too critical) words of A. E. Harvey ("Mystery Language", esp. 331), calling for greater awareness of a possible residual "echo" of the Greek mystery-metaphor in the New Testament texts.

Chapter One

Apocalyptic Literature

1. Introduction

"Si nous hésitons à parler d'Apocalyptique, c'est parce que nous voudrions savoir si elle est un genre littraire ou bien un pudding théologique."[1] This somewhat comical confession of J. Carmignac captures well the quandary besetting any treatment of "apocalyptic". To forestall a long discussion (and without losing track of the distinction), the term shall here be used in both customary senses: viz., of the literary genre of apocalypse[2] and of a more broadly defined theological perspective.[3] If for this reason my deliberations may at times incur Carmignac's charge of spooning out a "theological pudding", I would call on the reader's patience and considered judgement: the subject matter is undeniably complex and may at any rate better suit the Dickensian description of a "highly geological home-made cake."[4]

The following remarks offer some general observations regarding the *locus* of apocalyptic thought within Second Temple Judaism.

---

[1] Carmignac, "Description", 163.

[2] N.B. the most common genre in "apocalyptic literature" may well be that of *testament* rather than apocalypse: von Rad, *Theologie,* 2:330 n. 28; cf. K. Müller, "Propheten", 180.

[3] Aune, *Prophecy,* 107 (following Hanson, "Apocalypticism", 28–34), discerns *three* distinct phenomena: the literary genre, the system of religious beliefs, and "a religiously motivated social movement called 'apocalypticism'." My own remarks are primarily concerned with literary and theological considerations.

[4] *Martin Chuzzlewit,* Ch. 5. At the same time Davies (*PRJ,* 9) gives pause for thought with his remark that apocalyptic literature is on the whole remarkably free of significant sectarian tendencies and thus may well represent a type of piety close to the mainstream of Jewish life.

2. Introductory Observations

2.1. On the Nature of Apocalyptic

There is undoubtedly foreign influence on apocalyptic thought;[5] but motifs such as Yahweh's revelation and hiddenness, His election and deliverance of Israel, and His coming day of judgement are all inherited from a prophetic tradition reaching from Ezekiel and Deutero-Isaiah to Joel, Zechariah, and Daniel. Other antecedents of apocalyptic thinking are to be found in passages like Gen 15, 28; Exod 24 and Isa 6 (arguably the determining exemplars of all later throne visions); and the visions of Num 24; 2 Kgs 2; Isa 24–27; Job 4, 28, 38 ff.[6]

But the apocalyptic visionaries are not simply heirs of the prophetic tradition. Significantly, these writers do not on the whole adopt prophetic pseudonyms or claim to dispense prophecy;[7] and nowhere do they appear particularly perturbed by the canonical prophets' vexing problem of false prophecy.[8] The apocalyptic writings notably constitute a *scribal* phenomenon, thus inviting comparison with the Israelite sapiential tradition.[9]

G. von Rad's statement[10] that wisdom is the origin of apocalyptic has become one of the classic *antilegomena* of contemporary scholarship;[11] the preferred option has been to describe apocalyptic as being most closely indebted to the prophetic tradition. But H.-P. Müller, while joining the critics of von Rad in questioning the derivation of apocalyptic from OT didactic wisdom, has advanced a shrewd case for a significant influence from *mantic* wisdom;[12] joined

---

[5] E.g. Persian dualism, Babylonian and Hellenistic astronomy.

[6] Otzen ("Heavenly Visions", 200–204) argues for an origin of the apocalypses in OT cultic theophany and prophetic call visions (and even for a priestly *Sitz im Leben,* 204–212). Cf. also Hamerton-Kelly, "Temple", passim; Lebram, "Apokalyptik", 523 f.

[7] Prophetic pseudonyms are generally later and occur only after a crystallization of the canon (e.g. AscIsa; ParJer; AssMos; ApZeph; cf. 4 Ezra [1:1]; 12:42. Cf. also Willi-Plein, "Geheimnis", 65; Aune, *Prophecy,* 109 and n. 54. Note 2 Bar 85:3 ("the prophets have gone to sleep"), etc.; but contrast the explicit claim to prophecy in Rev 1:3; cf. 19:10.

[8] Russell, *Method,* 163 n. 1. An important exception is AscIsa (2:12, 15; 3:1, 7; 5:2, etc.); cf. Rev 2:2, 14 f., 20.

[9] Cf. e.g. Aune, *Prophecy,* 113; also J. Z. Smith, "Wisdom", 135–140, 154. Jeremias, *Jerusalem,* 271 in fact believes that the apocalyptic writings contain the secret doctrines of the scribes, being as it were esoteric midrashim (272 n. 1). Cf. n. 53 below.

[10] *Theologie,* esp. 2:319–21.

[11] But see e.g. Grelot, "Eschatologie", 177; Lührmann, *Offenbarungsverständnis,* 101 n. 3; H. W. Kuhn, *Enderwartung,* esp. 149–153; Küchler, *Weisheitstraditionen,* 67 ff.

[12] "Mantische Weisheit", passim: esp. on the OT image of Joseph and Daniel (271 ff.). Cf. also e.g. Jacob's dream (Gen 31:10 ff.) and the view of Balaam as a mantic prophet

with prophetic eschatology, this helps to explain the unique apocalyptic blend of interpretation, determinism, and universal history.[13] The interaction of mantic wisdom and classical prophecy provides a plausible origin for the apocalyptic interest in secret symbolic visions and their divinely revealed interpretation.[14]

2.2. On History and Eschatology

R. H. Charles rightly stressed that apocalyptic thought must not be defined just in terms of eschatology. The literature in question contains no homogeneous eschatology; indeed often an equal or greater interest in other subjects (e.g. heavenly cosmology) prevails.[15]

However, while apocalyptic fascination with the secrets of heaven betrays a significant alienation between present and ultimate reality,[16] it need not diminish the writers' deep commitment to the outworking of God's plan of deliverance within history.

> There was an air of eager, even desperate, expectancy that soon, very soon, God's rule would suddenly and devastatingly break in and God himself, either in person or through his Messiah, would right all wrongs and reward the patience and longsuffering of the righteous.[17]

---

and dream interpreter (e.g. *LAB* 18:2, 12; Josephus *Ant* 4:104, 125; but cf. already Num 23 f. and the Balaam inscription of Deir 'Alla).

[13] Müller, "Mantische Weisheit", 281−283. His proposal is taken up by VanderKam, "Origins", 167 f.; cf. further Hengel, *Judentum*, 345 f. Nickelsburg, "Apocalyptic Message", 327 f. sees in Ben Sira and Baruch a possible *locus* for such a combination of wisdom and prophetic elements.

[14] A return to dreams and visions after the passionate resistance e.g. of Isa 28:7; Jer 23:25 ff.; Ezek 13:6 ff.; Zech 10:2; even Sir 34:1−8, etc. may be possible *inter alia* because of the emerging "canon": thus the authority of the book of Jeremiah is never in doubt in Dan 9. In relation to the Scriptures, apocalyptic visions are only "metar-evelations" which do not threaten canonical works (even in 4 Ezra 14; cf. below on Torah and Sinai). After Dan itself came to be accepted as canonical (see e.g. Josephus and the Synoptic gospels), 4 Ezra 12:11 based further revelation on Dan 9; HermVis 2.3.4, on "the book of El-dad and Modad"; also cf. TLevi 14:1, 16:1; TJud 18:1; TNaph 4:1, etc. regarding the "Book of Enoch". Charles, *Development*, 26, also points to Ezek 38:17.

[15] Charles, *Development*, 17; idem, History, 178. Cf. more recently Rowland, *Open Heaven*, esp. 23 ff.; idem, *Origins*, 56−58.

[16] Cf. Suter, "Apocalyptic Patterns", 10.

[17] Russell, *Method*, 263. Cf. similarly Rowland, *Open Heaven*, 38; Noth, "Geschichts-verständnis", 264. *Pace* the ahistorical eschatology supposed e.g. by Murdock, "History", 187; Lombard, "Character", 25 f.; Betz, "Concept", 199 ff. Some deny any notion of *Heilsgeschichte* in postbiblical Judaism: Noack, *Spätjudentum*, 84; Murdock, "History", 180; von Rad, *Theologie*, 2:316. Against such a view stands the sequentialization of eschatology; the fervent activity of apocalyptic visionaries e.g. in Jerusalem during the

Combined with this expectation was a universalistic and firmly deterministic view of history.[18] Despite an abundance of possible indications to the contrary, the God of Israel was still in sovereign control of the history of all the nations.[19] And the corollary of this conviction was not a historical defeatism[20] or escapism,[21] but the dialectical[22] conviction that external circumstances notwithstanding, the complete plan of Israel's salvation was already waiting to be implemented.[23] The apocalyptic view of history thrives on the paradoxical assurance that divine deliverance is guaranteed to take place in defiance of the present historical phenomena.[24]

3. The Visions: Scripture, Revelation, Interpretation

Having established a few general coordinates for the discussion, we must now consider the apocalyptic writers' estimation of their own teaching in relation to the Scriptures. Two perspectives suggest themselves: first, revelation as expressed at Sinai, in Torah, and in tradition; and secondly, the apocalyptic "revelations" as interpretation.

Jewish revolt (Josephus, *BJ* 6); or Rabbi Aqiba's identification of Simon Bar Koseba (nicknamed בר כוכבא, cf. Num 24:17) as the promised King Messiah (y.Taan 4:8, 68d48–50).

[18] Cf. already Hab 2:2f.; Dan 8:17, 19, 26; Gen 41:32; etc. On determinism see also Rowland, *Open Heaven*, 90f., and passim.

[19] Cf. Rowland, *Open Heaven*, 144 ("there is no suggestion that the present age is in any sense abandoned by God").

[20] *Pace* Lombard, "Character", 25; von Rad, *Theologie*, 2:318.

[21] With Russell, *Method*, 102. *Pace* Rowland, *Open Heaven*, 22 ("flight from reality"), 445 (contact with the realm above "undermines the concern for the historical fulfilment of the divine promises"). Contrast his p. 144, cited above; see the more circumspect statement in *Origins*, 101–104.

[22] Cf. e.g. Russell, *Method*, 223f., quoting H. W. Robinson. Aune, *Prophecy*, 121, appropriately describes the apocalyptic literary effort as both "quiescent" and "revolutionary".

[23] Koch aptly speaks of apocalypse as "the revelation of the divine revelation" (*Rediscovery*, 33), i.e. the anticipatory glimpse of the impending eschatological manifestation.

[24] Cf. Bertholet, *Theologie*, 2:369. Nevertheless, the apocalyptists are not unfamiliar with the problem of "delayed parousia": e.g. Dan 9:16–19; 4 Ezra 3:1 ff.; 2 Bar 3:3 ff., etc.

3.1. Sinai, Torah, and Tradition

3.1.1. The Status of Torah

Several modern authors have argued that the Law exercises at best an incidental function for apocalyptic theology.[25] While some documents may indeed show a certain skepticism about the *sufficiency* of the written books of the OT (e.g. 4 Ezra 14),[26] it is nevertheless reductionistic to conclude that the apparent lack of explicitly exegetical passages and the quest for additional revelation imply *eo ipso* a reduced relevance of the Law.[27]

For in point of fact apocalyptic literature abounds with both implicit and explicit allusions to the Torah. Thus 1 En pronounces woe to those who distort "the eternal law" (99:2), and to the law-transgressing Watchers (106:13f.).[28] TLevi 14:4 speaks of the "light of the law" given for the enlightenment of every man, and 2 Bar describes the law as an eternal lamp (17:4–18:2; 59:2; 77:13, 15f.)[29] and fountain (77:13, 15f.) for the nation of Israel. The Torah is dialectically opposed to the works of Belial as light is to darkness (TLevi 19:1; cf. TNaph 2:6). On several occasions the newly revealed "secret knowledge" turns out to be identified with insight into the Law, a proposition not without parallels at Qumran.[30] At the heart of concern in 2 Bar is the substitution of Torah for Temple after the calamity of A. D. 70.[31] D. S. Russell rightly concludes that "to the apocalyptists every bit as much as to the Pharisees the written Torah was the revelation of God to his people."[32]

---

[25] E.g. Rössler, *Gesetz*, 49; cf. Wilckens, "Bekehrung", 288; de Villiers, "Revealing", 64 (on 1 Enoch). The notion of apocalyptic disinterest in Torah in general and in commandments in particular is rightly criticized by Nissen, "Torah", 260ff.; cf. Blenkinsopp, *Wisdom*, 152; Rowland, *Open Heaven*, 30; the most serious weakness of this view is its negligence of books like Jubilees.

[26] Thus e.g. Lebram, "Piety", 207.

[27] *Pace* e.g. Myers, *I and II Esdras*, 326, who believes that the apocalyptic books "were obviously valued more highly than the canonical books"; cf. similarly Rowland, "Literature", 183.

[28] Cf. Black, *Enoch*, 321.

[29] For Torah as light see e.g. in the OT Psa 19:9; 119:105, 130; Prov 6:23; Isa 51:4. Also cf. *LAB* 9:8; 11:1; 12:2; 15:6; 19:6; 23:10; 33:3; Sir 24:27; Wisd 18:4; 4 Ezra 10:22; 14:20f.; Bar 4:2; 2 Bar 17:4; 59:2; TLevi 14:4; 19:1; TBenj 11:2; TJ Isa 2:5; 21:12; 24:16; 42:7; 45:17. See further Lührmann, *Offenbarungsverständnis*, 49; Hollander/de Jonge, *Testaments*, 170.

[30] E.g. 1 En 99:10; 4 Ezra 8:12, 13:54f.; 2 Bar 38:1–4, 44:14, 46:4f., 48:24, 77:13–16. Cf. Kuhn, *Enderwartung*, 149.

[31] See 2 Bar 31:4–32:1; 44:5–7; 77:13–16; 85:3, 14. Cf. also Bogaert, *Apocalypse*, 1:391; Nickelsburg, *Jewish Literature*, 286f.; Murphy, *Structure*, esp. 113–116. That this is perhaps only a *temporary* substitution until the eschaton (*pace* Murphy, 113) is borne out e.g. by 2 Bar 7:9; 32:4f.; 68:5.

[32] Russell, *Method*, 26.

3.1.2. The Visions and Mt. Sinai

This close commitment to the Scriptures on the one hand is matched by a high estimation of the apocalyptic visions on the other. Thus the new revelations themselves are described in terms of the image of a "spring" or "fountain", used elsewhere of the Torah.[33]

The apocalyptic teachings were believed to be handed down by God at Mount Sinai along with the written Torah.[34] This notion becomes understandable on the basis of an increasing canonical sedimentation: in light of the prior authority and givenness of a written Bible (esp. the Torah), any contemporary claim of additional divine disclosures must of necessity have recourse to Mount Sinai as the unquestioned touchstone and reference point. In a sense, all new revelation (even genuine revelation, which some at least of the apocalypses undoubtedly claim to be) now will always be "meta-revelation".[35]

3.2. Revelation and Interpretation

Apocalyptic literature shares the post-biblical reluctance to recognize present-day prophetic revelation, although explicit manifestations of this are comparatively rare.[36] The agency of the Holy Spirit tends to be invoked only on behalf of the ancient worthy in whose name an author is writing.[37] At a time when prophecy has ceased and history is still awaiting a decisive act of God, the word of the Lord for the present generation must be expressed in other ways.[38]

---

[33] E.g. 4 Ezra 14:47; 1 En 48:1; 49:1; OdSol 6:8 ff.; cf. Chapters 2, 3 below. Manson ("Reflections", 142 n. 2) cites approvingly the interesting statement of Sabatier that "l'apocalypse est à la prophétie ce que la Mischna est à la Thora."

[34] Jub Prologue; 1:1−5; (cf. 6:30); 4 Ezra 14:3−6 (cf. 2:33); AssMos 1:1 ff.; 10:11, 11:1; *LAB* 19:10. Cf. e.g. Manson, "Reflections", 145; Nickelsburg, *Jewish Literature,* 73; Russell, *Method,* 86. Stone also cites 1 En 93:11−14 ("Lists", 425). The reference to mediating angels need not be incompatible with this: see Acts 7:53; Gal 3:19; Heb 2:2; cf. Deut 33:2 LXX; Jub 1:29 f.; Philo *Somn* 1:141−143; Josephus *Ant* 15:136. Cf. further n. 86 below and Chapter 7 on "oral Torah".

[35] I.e. revelation which in some way takes previous revelation as its object or starting point. Cf. also Willi-Plein, "Geheimnis", 66 (apocalyptic revelation as indirect and "immer schon vermitteltes Wort"); Rowland, "Literature", 180.

[36] Cf. e.g. 2 Bar 85:3; Dan 3:38 LXX. See also on the withdrawal of wisdom, 4 Ezra 5:9 f.; 1 En 42:1−3; contrast 1 En 48:1, etc.; and cf. Küchler, *Weisheitstraditionen,* 70.

[37] (N.B. all the while leaving the reader in doubt about the writer's self-estimation!) E.g. 1 En 70:2, 91:1; 4 Ezra 5:22, 14:22; AscIsa 1:7, 5:14; TAbr (A) 4:7; 2 Bar 6:3, 7:2(?). On the apparent absence of the Spirit cf. Kuhn, *Enderwartung,* 119 f.; Russell, *Method,* 160 and n. 1.

[38] But one need not therefore speak of mere "pseudo-revelation" (e.g. Fishbane, *Interpretation,* 517). For while the literary features are often stylized and stereotyped, we find

Closely related to the role of Torah in apocalyptic literature is the question of interpretation. In Dan 9 and 4 Ezra 12, mentioned earlier, a mediating angel gives further insight as to the apocalyptic significance of a previous prophetic revelation. But in most other cases, too, the new revelation involves interpretation, whether of visions, dreams, or Scripture;[39] Collins aptly calls this process "prophecy by interpretation".[40]

It might be objected that there are only relatively few occasions when this interpretation explicitly takes as its object a written text of Scripture: e.g. in Daniel the hermeneutical disclosure is based on a Biblical passage only once, but pertains in most cases to a dream or vision. Apocalypses are on the whole not properly commentaries on Scripture.[41]

Having said that, however, there is a wide range of hermeneutical activity left to explore. Thus in 2 Bar 38:1−4 Baruch requests an interpretation of the vision he has received: "Your law (*nmws*) is life and your wisdom the true guide. Explain to me, therefore, what this vision means" (38:2 f.). The angel's subsequent interpretation concerns the four kingdoms and the time when the Messiah will be revealed. The passionate appeal to "your law" in 2 Bar 38, followed by the Danielic idea of the four kingdoms, demonstrates a specific dependence on Scripture without needing to be an explicit "commentary". Numerous texts e.g. in 1 En or Rev show similar characteristics;[42] indeed in-

---

the authors at times going out of their way e.g. to describe the means by which such visions were induced: prayer, fasting, special food or drink, etc. − see e.g. Ezek 3:1−3(?); Dan 9:3; 4 Ezra 9:23 f.; 14:39; 2 Bar 21:1; 47:2; ApAbr 9:7; AscIsa 2:11 (hallucinogens?); PastHerm Vis. 2.1.1, 3.1.1; and as early as 1 Sam 28:20. Cf. Russell, *Method*, 158 ff. passim; Rowland, *Open Heaven*, 234 ff.; further Francis, "Humility", 167−171. See also Baeck, "Mysticism", 102 f. on merkabah visions; esp. on t.Meg 4(3):28 ("many expounded the merkabah but never beheld it") and his quotation of Hai Gaon (c. A. D. 1000): "he should fast on certain days, put his head between his knees, and whisper into the earth many songs and hymns exactly as they are written. Thereupon he beholds . . . the porticos. . . ."

[39] (An exception is e.g. Jub 32:21 ff.) Cf. Vanderkam, *Enoch*, 190; Willi-Plein, "Geheimnis", 63, 66. Hellenistic parallels include e.g. the Egyptian Demotic Chronicle: cf. Collins, "Jewish Apocalyptic", 32 f.; Fishbane, "Pesher", 101; also Hengel, *Judentum*, 390 f. regarding Thessalos of Alexandria.

[40] Thus Collins, "Jewish Apocalyptic", 32. Willi-Plein, "Geheimnis", 66 regards the angel as almost a hypostasis of interpretation; cf. 3 Bar 11:7 "interpreter of revelations".

[41] Cf. Aune, *Prophecy*, 113; O. Betz, "Vision", 114; Rowland, "Literature", 170.

[42] E.g. 1 En 2−5, 6:1 ff.; Rev 1:11 ff., 4:1 ff., etc. Suter, *Tradition*, finds in 1 En midrashim on the following texts: Gen 6:1−4 (p. 37); Exod 14−15 (pp. 113 ff.); Isa 24:17−23 (pp. 39 ff.); Dan 7:9−14 (p. 14 and passim). Cf. also EzekTrag 68−81 with Dan 7. Aune, *Prophecy*, 108 (cf. 112) sees "the tendency to make frequent allusion to, but not quote, the OT" as one of the major characteristics of apocalyptic literature. Rowland (e.g. *Origins*, 62) points to clear elements of *bereshit/merkabah* meditations (i.e. on Gen 1/ Ezek 1): see his references, and cf. ApMos 2 f.; 22:3; VitAd 25:3; TIsaac 11:4; JosAsen 17:6.

stances of such "impromptu midrashim" occur already in prophetic texts of the OT.[43]

The main paradigm of apocalyptic revelation, therefore, seems to be that of inspired interpretation — i.e. an indirect, "hermeneutical" revelation.[44] Although this involves *prima* facie the interpretation not only of Biblical passages but of a range of symbolic phenomena in dreams and visions, the substance of apocalyptic discourse does depend most typically on Biblical precedents and source materials.[45] Christopher Rowland speaks of Scripture as "being in the imaginations of the apocalyptic visionaries a door of perception in which the text could become a living reality as its details merged with parallel passages to form the distinctive visions...."[46] One may cautiously accept the hypothesis that both visions and interpretations were frequently received while the author was meditating on a Scripture passage or passages relating e.g. to unfulfilled prophecy or the secrets of heaven.[47]

4. The Revelation of Mysteries

"To speak of apocalyptic, therefore, is to concentrate on the theme of the direct communication of the heavenly mysteries in all their diversity."[48] While this statement may be something of a caricature,[49] it renders due account of the extraordinary apocalyptic interest in divine "mysteries" and their revelation.

For these writers, "mysteries" subsist in heaven at present but a glimpse of their reality and relevance can be disclosed to select visionaries who pass on this

---

[43] See Fishbane, *Interpretation,* esp. 292 ff.; Buchanan, "Word", 192.

[44] Cf. von Rad, *Theologie,* 2:321: "Überhaupt wird man die geistige Leistung der Apokalyptiker ziemlich erschöpfend mit dem Begriff 'Interpretation' umschreiben können."

[45] Cf. Rowland, "Literature", 180: "lack of midrashic precision should not blind us to the clear scriptural archetype which undergirds the apocalyptic framework of the revelations."

[46] Rowland, "Literature", 173. Cf. also Hartman, *Prophecy,* 102−141 passim.

[47] Paradigmatic examples include Dan 9 and 4 Ezra 12 f. Cf. Frey, "Apocalyptique", 339 f.; Charles, *History,* 184−187; Russell, *Method,* 183 ff.; Willi-Plein, "Geheimnis", 76 f.; Rowland, *Origins,* 60−62; Gruenwald, *Apocalyptic,* 219 ff. (also with reference to Qumran).

[48] Rowland, *Open Heaven,* 14; cf. idem, *Origins,* 64; similarly Bornkamm, "μυστήριον", 821.

[49] We should not ignore e.g. the literary and theological significance of the almost invariably present *narrative* framework of the revelations, be it ever so skeletal (Rowland himself now allows for the significance of this framework: "Literature", 174). Then, too, not *all* parts of the revealed message are designated as "mysteries".

information to the faithful few (the "wise", i.e. the righteous[50]) to encourage
them in waiting for the impending deliverance (1 En 1:1–9, 37:1–5, etc.). At
present the divine wisdom is known only through such revealed mysteries,
since her abode is in heaven (1 En 42:1–3; 48:1, 49:1 f.). Old Testament antecedents notwithstanding, this notion of heavenly mysteries appears to have become popular only in the wake of early apocalyptic documents like Daniel and
1 Enoch.[51]

The term "mystery" applies to a wide variety of subjects. Nevertheless, most
of the pertinent material can here be divided under the two general headings of
cosmological and eschatological mysteries.[52] In addition, there is a third and separate category of evil or illegitimate mysteries. (The specifically exegetical
mysteries of the DSS and other writings are here rather less obviously repres-
ented.)[53]

In the following remarks a short excursus on the use of ἀποκαλύπτω and
ἀποκάλυψις will precede a discussion of the "cosmological" and "eschatological" mysteries and their revelation as encountered in the literature at hand. This
section concludes with a brief discussion of illegitimate mysteries as well as of
the occasional Hellenistic use of "mysteries".

Excursus: ἀποκαλύπτω / ἀποκάλυψις in the Apocalyptic Literature

Time and space do not permit a full word study, desirable though this might
be.[54]

In the Septuagint the noun ἀποκάλυψις is never, and the verb ἀποκαλύπτω
only rarely, used to denote theological revelation. Instead, the two words carry

---

[50] E.g. 1 En 82:3 f.; 4 Ezra 14:6, 26, 45 f.; also 2 Bar 54:5; AscIsa 4:20 (public vs. private
prophecies). The suggestion that the motif of secrecy in apocalyptic lore may be a mere
literary device (cf. Stemberger, "Esoterik", 368) or natural corollary of the subject matter (cf. Collins, *Athens*, 202 f.) should probably be rejected. Cf. below on the Dead Sea
Scrolls and on 1 Cor 2:6.

[51] Cf. Black, *Enoch*, 131. See above on Dan; relevant uses in 1 En (outside 37–71) include 9:6; 10:7; 16:3; 104:10; 106:19. But N.B. the frequency of the term may itself imply
a previously established usage: cf. Dexinger, *Zehnwochenapokalypse*, 87.

[52] Similarly e.g. Collins, "Morphology", 9; Rowland, *Open Heaven*, 10; Kuhn, *Enderwartung*, 152; Sjöberg, *Menschensohn*, 109; Willi-Plein, "Geheimnis", 79.

[53] But see perhaps JosAsen 16:1–8; 17:2 f., 6. Note also that some of the major visionary pseudonyms are of *scribes* (and thus exegetes?): Baruch, Ezra; but also Enoch. From
Ben Sira through Qumran and to the Rabbis it is consistently the scribal office which is
most closely linked with the mysteries revealed through exegesis. Cf. n. 9 above.

[54] See Oepke, "καλύπτω" and recently Smith, "History"; cf. also Section 3.2 in
Chapter 6 below.

a wide range of secular connotations, many of which broadly relate to the notion of "uncovering".[55] Outside the LXX the noun is never and the verb rarely found before the first century B. C.[56] No comparable religious usage occurs until much later.[57]

In light of the scant surviving literary evidence from Hellenistic sources, we may with M. Smith register surprise at finding in the apocalyptic writings and the NT[58] such a widespread idiomatic usage of a term whose suitability for the description of theological revelation is by no means obvious: "Apocalyptic revelations are not customarily effected by removing a cover; the heavens are not stripped away, nor the lid of the earth taken off...."[59] While the secular usage has not completely disappeared in apocalyptic literature,[60] its significance is overshadowed by the specifically theological application to (mostly visionary) divine disclosures.[61]

4.1. "Cosmological" Mysteries

The apocalyptic writings (esp. 1 and 2 En, 3 Bar) speak in considerable detail of the secrets of creation, astronomy, and the heavenly worlds. One example is 1 En 41:1−7:[62]

> And after this I saw all the secrets of heaven, and how the kingdom is divided, and how the deeds of men are weighed in the balance. There I saw the dwelling of the chosen and the resting-places of the holy; and ... all the sinners who deny the name of the Lord of Spirits being driven from there .... And there my eyes saw the secrets of the flashes of lightning and of the thunder, and the secrets of the winds ... and ... of the clouds and of the dew. ... And there I saw closed storehouses from which the winds are distributed, and the storehouses of the hail, and the storehouses of the mist, and the storehouses of the clouds. ... And I saw the chambers of the sun and the moon, whence they go out and whither they return. ...

---

[55] Terms such as sexual "uncovering", "uncovering the ear", etc. agree with the OT use of גלה.

[56] Smith, "History", 12 cites as a reference point Philodemus (110−40 B.C.), who uses both verb and noun.

[57] Cf. Oepke, "καλύπτω", 572.

[58] Especially Pauline and Deutero-Pauline writings: cf. Smith, "History", 14.

[59] Smith, "History", 12.

[60] E.g. ParJer 5:26 (uncovering a fig-basket); TJud 16:4.

[61] E.g. TLev 1:2, 18:2; TJos 6:6; TBenj 10:5; JosAsen 16:7; 3 Bar Prologue 1 f., 4:13 f., 11:7, 17:4. Also cf. 1 En 9:6 (Greek).

[62] My ignorance of Ethiopic necessitates, and our purposes would seem to permit, that the terms *xabu*ˣ ("hidden, secret") and *meštir* ("mystery", μυστήριον) will be treated on an equal footing. Cf. Dillmann, *Lexicon*, 181, 600; and Sjöberg, *Menschensohn*, 105, both with references.

This passage is quite representative of the kinds of subjects generally featured in lists of the "cosmological" class of secrets: the topography of heaven and hell, as well as the intricacies of creation, meteorology and astronomy.[63]

Certainly a concern for God's sovereignty in the unfolding of history is here not at first apparent. It is, rather, the common apocalyptic interest in understanding the nature and significance of the given, *ontic* structures of the universe, which Biblical scholars have often tended to discount or overlook.[64] Such "lists of secrets" are in many ways anticipated in wisdom texts like Job 9:2−12; 26:5−14; or 38:1 ff.[65]

The revelation of "cosmological" secrets fulfills both an evident literary and a more or less subtle theological function. With regard to the former, M. E. Stone observes that lists of secrets tend to occur "at the high point of a revelation, where a brief statement of its contents is desired, or else as a summary."[66] The literary effect of such lists is to convey an impression of the comprehensiveness of the revelation and hence of the message which accompanies it.[67]

More important, however, is the theological purpose of these esoterica about heaven and the universe.[68] Having lamented before God the fate of Israel, Baruch receives this answer: "Argue with God no more, and I will show you mysteries, greater than these. ... Come and I will show you the mysteries of God" (3 Bar 1:6, 8). In other words, the disclosure of the orderly operation of the heavenly spheres is intended to reassure the audience of God's sovereign lordship over all of reality.[69]

But in the same vein these mysteries also bear upon the authors' *soteriological* expectations. For the revelation of cosmological secrets demonstrates, as Frey observes, "comment le gouvernement divin s'étend aux moindres détails de la

---

[63] E.g. 1 En 22:1 ff.; 43:2; 60:11 ff.; 71:4 ff.; 2 En 3 ff., 24 ff.; 2 Bar 48:2−6; 59:4−12 (in context); 3 Bar 1:6−17:1; TLevi 3:2; *LAB* 19:10, 28:6−10. Cf. Hollander/de Jonge, *Testaments*, 137. A particular interest in hell occurs e.g. in ApPet; *Paradise and Gehenna* (*BHM* 5:50.30−51.13); etc.

[64] Similarly Rowland, "Visions", 138.

[65] Cf. also Stone, "Lists", 435; Brown, *Mystery*, 18. OT references to heavenly "storehouses" include Deut 28:12 (rain); Jer 10:13 (wind); Psa 33:7 (waters of the deep); Job 38:22 (snow/hail). VanderKam (*Enoch*, 140) considers the cosmological interest to reflect an "early", "scientific" stage of apocalyptic thought, whereas surveys of history first entered the Enoch tradition in the "Epistle of Enoch", the "Apocalypse of Weeks", the "Book of Dreams", and the "Animal Apocalypse". But N.B. historical surveys are in some ways already implicit e.g. in Gen 49; Deut 33.

[66] Stone, "Lists", 418. But longer passages occur in 1 En 60:11 ff., 3 Bar 1:6 ff.

[67] A desire for comprehensiveness is indicated by the recurring phrase "*all* the secrets": Bornkamm, "μυστήριον", 822.

[68] *Pace* e.g. Charles, Enoch, 147 ("the author has no other interest save a scientific one"). Cf. Brown, *Mystery*, 20.

[69] Sjöberg (*Menschensohn*, 110) stresses the fundamental link of cosmological secrets with the glory of God; Brown (*Mystery*, 14 f.), the connection with divine providence.

machine du monde et dispose toutes choses pour le plus grand bien des justes."[70] The secrets of lightning and thunder at God's direction "flash to bring blessing and satisfaction" (1 En 59:2 f.), as indeed the secrets of raindrops, wind, and snow demonstrate the creator's sovereignty.[71] There is an intimate link, then, between the cosmological mysteries of heaven and the questions of theodicy addressed by the visionaries.[72]

These mysteries, moreover, are associated with those of mercy and righteousness (1 En 71:3 ff.), and the secrets of the depth of the earth relate to the resurrection (1 En 61:5).[73] Cosmological and eschatological secrets repeatedly occur in tandem;[74] some instances deal specifically with the heavenly *localities* where the righteous are rewarded and the wicked are punished.[75] There is, as Stone suggests, ultimately "no real distinction between the meteorological and other eschatological or religious spheres" — that is, at least in regard to their relevance for the believer.[76] While the revelation of cosmological mysteries gives assurance of salvation through God's *a priori* sovereignty over creation and the heavens, eschatological secrets constitute God's pre-existent heavenly plan of redemptive action in the imminent climax of history.

4.2. Eschatological Mysteries

There my eyes saw the secrets of heaven, everything that will occur on earth. . . . And I asked the angel who went with me, saying, What are these things which I have seen in secret? And he said to me, All these things which you have seen serve the authority of his Messiah, that he may be strong and powerful on the earth.

---

[70] Frey, "Apocalyptique", 330. Cf. Hanson, *Dawn*, 381.

[71] Cf. Stone, "Lists", 434. Cosmic secrets are linked with God's enthronement in 2 En 24:3−25:4. For the relevance of the contents of heaven for the believer's present life in early Christian apocalyptic see Rev; also e. g. *Passio Perpetuae:* Perpetua's vision of the rewards of heaven serves at least *inter alia* to strengthen her for martyrdom (*pace* Rowland, *Open Heaven,* 399).

[72] Thus also Hengel, "Anonymität", 266 f.; cf. Barton, *Oracles,* 256; Rowland, "Literature", 185. Cf. already Isa 40:12−31, a passage to which Paul appeals in 1 Cor 2:16; also Job 38−40 (though this deals with personal theodicy rather than national redemption). Hanson, *Dawn,* 380 argues similarly for Zech 14:6−9.

[73] Cf. Stone, "Lists", 433.

[74] See also 1 En 2:1−5:3, 41:1−7, 43:4; poss. 52:1−9; 2 Bar 48:2− 8; 51:10; TNaph 3:2; 4 Ezra 7:97, 125; AssMos 10:9; cf. Sir 16:28; 4 Macc 17:5; TJ Isa 14:13. And see Stone, "Lists", 430 f.

[75] E. g. 1 En 41:1 f.; 2 Bar 59:5−11; cf. above on "topography".

[76] Stone, "Lists", 433. Hengel, *Judentum,* 377 firmly links cosmological mysteries and *Heilsgeschichte* in 1 Enoch. But Hanson (*Dawn,* 381) discusses 1 En 60:11−24 as a list which in his opinion merely serves to "stress the immutability of the natural order". Even if this is not entirely adequate (cf. 60:24 Garden of Righteousness, v. 24 f. judgement and punishment), it does provide a proper balance to Hengel's suggestion. Contrast also the "de-historicized" eschatology e. g. of 3 Bar.

This quotation from 1 En 52:2—4 is but one example of a large number of texts which speak of "mysteries" bearing a clearly discernible historical-eschatological relevance: "everything that will occur on earth". It seems that while much of the Enoch literature and parts of 3 Bar show greater interest in the "cosmological" mysteries, the secrets of an eschatological/ historical kind stand closer to the centre of attention in Daniel,[77] 4 Ezra,[78] 2 Bar,[79] as well as in the Similitudes (37—71) and "Epistle" (91—108) of 1 En,[80] and other books.[81] Of course here too the constitutive quality of these "mysteries" is not in the first instance their hiddenness, but their belonging to the heavenly world.[82]

4.2.1. Content

What are the subjects of these soteriological mysteries? Quite commonly we find references to "everything that will occur on earth", "for how long the generations will endure", the "advent of the hours", etc.[83] — i.e. in other words, the time and course of events of the divinely appointed eschaton. These "mysteries" are best understood as the individual components of God's salvific design.

Among the mysteries to be realized at the eschaton is the heavenly city of Jerusalem with its temple;[84] also the eschatological judgement and its aftermath, decribed as the secrets of righteousness (1 En 49:2, 58:5; cf. 38:3; 49:2; 4 Ezra 7:70).[85] Similarly we hear of the judgement of hidden things (1 En 49:4, 61:9, 68:5), and of a mystery, sometimes read on heavenly tablets,[86] consisting of the

---

[77] The term רז in Dan always relates in some way to a disclosure of the future. *Pace* Brown, *Mystery*, 8 this is not likely synonymous with סוד as in Amos 3:7; moreover the author of Dan arguably does *not* present himself as a "prophet".

[78] E.g. 4 Ezra 8:54, 10:38, 12:36, 14:4 f. (cf. *LAB* 19:10). 4 Ezra seems to feature only this eschatological type of mystery (cf. Brown, *Mystery*, 21 f.); indeed a reaction against the concern with cosmological esoterica may be present in 7:39—42.

[79] E.g. 2 Bar 48:3 (*gl'* + *r'z*), 81:4; cf. 83:2 f.

[80] E.g. 1 En 52:2, 68:1 f., 103:2 ff., 104:10—13, 106:19.

[81] E.g. TLevi 2:10; ParJer 9:22, 28 (in context with 9:13—18); ApAbr 9:6; also Vit-Proph 2:10, 19 (cf. 1:7).

[82] Cf. rightly Sjöberg, *Menschensohn*, 106 f.

[83] 1 En 52:22; 2 Bar 48:3, 81:4; cf. also 1 En 18:16 ("year of mystery"), etc.

[84] 4 Ezra 7:26, 8:52; 10:27, 44, 50—55; 13:36; 2 Bar 4:3—6; 1 En 90:29; Rev 21:10—27 (but note v. 22!); also cf. 5 Q15; and e.g. *Sefer Eliahu BHM* 3:65.12 ff.; *Mysteries of R. Shim'on b. Yohai BHM* 3:80.26 ff. Hamerton-Kelly, "Temple", 1—15 (cf. Otzen, "Heavenly Visions", 199—204) suggests a priestly origin for the idea of a heavenly sanctuary, also present e.g. in Exod 25:40, 1 Chr 28:19; Ezek 40:2; cf. Heb 8:5. See further Himmelfarb, "Ascent", 210—217.

[85] Probably the enigmatic phrase "the secrets of all the sin of the earth" of 1 En 83:7 refers to the eschatological judgement (see 83:4, 7 ff.). Cf. Black, *Enoch*, 255.

[86] E.g. 1 En 81:1; 103:2; 106:19, etc. Heavenly tablets containing future events occur

reward of the righteous and punishment of the wicked.[87] Related eschatological revelations are the community of the righteous (1 En 38:1, 53:6), the attacking nations (2 Bar 70:7; cf. TLevi 3:3), the joy and rest of heaven (2 Bar 73:1), Behemoth and Leviathan (2 Bar 29:4; cf. 4 Ezra 6:49 ff.; 1 En 60:7−10; also Rev 13:1 ff., 11 ff.), and of course hell and paradise (e.g. 4 Ezra 7:36; 8:52; 2 Bar 4:6).[88]

Excursus: Messiah / Son of Man

On a number of occasions especially in 1 Enoch the eschatological mystery is substantively linked with the Messiah and/or the Son of Man.[89] Since this constellation of motifs (i.e. mystery / Messiah) becomes significant in our examination of Paul's letters, it seems appropriate to devote a brief excursus to it.

We already encountered above a link between the eschatological mysteries and a "pre-incarnate" Messiah (1 En 52:2−4; cf. 46:2, 49:2−4, 62:7 f.; 63:3, 11). Indeed 1 En frequently features the conviction that the Messiah/Son of Man is already present and hidden with God since the beginning of the world, in order to be revealed in the eschaton (1 En 38:2, 48:2−7, 62:6 f., 69:26−29).[90] Simi-

---

already in Babylonian mythology; cf. further Jub 5:13 and passim; TAsh 7:5; PrJos frg. B, C (Charlesworth, *OTP* 2:714); 4 Q180 1:3; also Eth. ApPet 3 (on Christ's right palm the image of that which shall be fulfilled at the last day). Secret books, tablets etc. constituted a favourite channel of revelation in the ancient Hellenistic world: cf. e.g. Hengel, *Judentum*, 383 ff. For a recent treatment see García Martínez, "Tablas" (N.B. bibliography p. 333 n. 1). He distinguishes five categories of heavenly tablets in Jub (dependent on 1 En): tablets containing the Torah; a record of good and evil works; destiny; calendars and feasts; new *halakhot* (the last two should probably be merged). Most significant is his conclusion that in more than half the cases in Jub the heavenly tablets are the functional equivalent of Oral Torah (p. 348 f.).

[87] 2 Bar 21:12; 59:2; 4 Ezra 7:35, 83 f., 93; 3 Bar 2:7−4:9; 10:1 ff. Cf. further 1 En 11:2, 25:7, 103:3; 2 Bar 52:7, 81:4, 84:6; 4 Ezra 7:14, 13:18; also 2 Macc 12:45; Rev 2:10, 17; 22:12; 1 Pet 5:4; Jas 1:12; 2 Tim 4:8; AscIsa 8:26.

[88] For Rabbinic parallels see e.g. b.Pes 54a (the name of the Messiah, Torah, repentance, Garden of Eden, Gehenna, throne of glory, Temple are pre-existent); b.Ḥag 12a (the light of the first day of creation is stored up for the future world); GenR 1:1 (the new heavens).

[89] W. Horbury has recently (in the face of oppposition e.g. from Lindars, *Jesus*, 3 ff.; Vermes, *World*, 95−98) made a new case for the existence of an established messianic understanding of the term "Son of Man" by the time of Christ at the latest ("Associations", esp. 38 ff.); cf. also Bittner, "Gott", 343−72. Kim, *Son*, 20−22 cites Fitzmyer's restoration of 4 QPsDan A^a (= 4 Q243) in support of a pre-Christian, messianic link of the Danielic Son of Man with a "Son of God".

[90] The date of 1 En 37−71 continues to be disputed. Nickelsburg (*Jewish Literature*, 222 f.) rightly discounts Christian influence; no Christian would identify the Son of Man with Enoch (59:10, 71:14). The Messianic Son of Man here as in 4 Ezra could plausibly derive from Dan 7:13. Cf. also Suter, *Tradition*, 12 f., 23 ff. (he sees an influence of the Si-

larly, 4 Ezra knows of the future revelation of the Messiah hidden in heaven (7:28; 12:32; 13:25 f.; 13:26; 13:32). At least in 1 En and 4 Ezra it would seem to be reasonable to suggest that even in the absence of an explicit identification of Messiah and "mystery", the complex and substantive[91] connection between the Messiah and the hidden heavenly realities encourages a view of the "pre-exist-ent" Messiah himself as one of the mysteries.[92] Although 2 Bar is less specific, here too one reads of a "revelation" (Ethpe'el *gl'*) of the Messiah (2 Bar 29:3) and of his kingdom (39:7)[93] — making it reasonable to assume his previous hid-denness.[94] A large number of other relevant texts make at least implicit refe-rence to the hidden Messiah being revealed.[95] In 1 En this Son of Man/Messiah who is the mystery to be revealed becomes in turn a source of revelation of the secrets of wisdom (cf. on Col 2:3 below, Chapter Ten).[96]

In sum: the Messiah and/or Son of Man figures prominently in relation to the eschatological mysteries which, though presently concealed, are already exist-ent in heaven and await their imminent manifestation.

4.2.2. Revelation

Having established some of the objects of the revelation of eschatological mysteries, we must now inquire into the *mode* of their disclosure. The apoca-lyptic description of soteriological mysteries (i.e. the components and modali-

---

militudes on the Gospel of Matthew). Milik's argument (in Enoch, 4, 78, 89 ff.) for a late date in view of the absence of 1 En 37—71 from the DSS, is too one-sidedly *e silentio*. A date between 50 B. C. and A. D. 50 seems not impossible. For a recent summary of the debate see Charlesworth, *OT Pseudepigrapha and NT*, 89 f.; also pp. 103—106, 108—110 regarding the views of Milik and Black.

[91] Similarly Kamlah, "Untersuchungen", 110.

[92] Cf. Russell's (somewhat unguarded) statement, "The greatest secret is the Son of Man himself" (*Method*, 329).

[93] For a revelation of the kingdom cf. SibOr 3:47 f.; AssMos 10:1; 3 En 44:7; Luke 19:11; and see below, Chapter 6. The kingdom's "appearance" does not *a priori* imply its pre-existence (cf. *LAB* 62:2 "tunc apparebit David regnum") — but the common apoca-lyptic idea of eschatological *soteriologoumena* hidden in heaven nevertheless requires such an understanding.

[94] Bogaert, *Apocalypse*, 418; *pace* Rowland, *Open Heaven*, 177.

[95] E.g. 1 En 48:2 (the name of the Messiah: cf. 69:26, b.Pes 54a); PssSol 18:5; TLevi 2:10; John 1:31 (?); Justin *Dial* 8, 109 f.; also ProtJames 12:2 (Gabriel's annunciation to Mary as disclosure of mysteries); b.Sukk 52a; b.Sanh 98a (the Messiah comes from Rome); PesR 36:2 R. Isaac [T4?]; and cf. Chapter 6 below. See Volz, *Eschatologie*, 208 f.; Vermes, *Jesus the Jew*, 137—139; Hartman, *Prophecy*, 37; most fully Schimanowski, *Weis-heit*, passim.

[96] See 1 En 46:3, 51:3; cf. TLevi 18:2; *Sefer Eliyahu* (HebApEl: Ibn Shmuel Text, trans. in Buchanan, *Revelation*, 436). The origin of this idea may well lie in passages like Deut 18:15; Isa 42:4.

ties of the future salvation) commonly presents them as already objectively *existent* in heaven, only to be manifested in the eschaton at God's behest.[97]

4.2.2.1. Revelation as Historical Dialectic. This dual conviction of present transcendental concealment and impending historical actualization gives rise to a strong salvation-historical dialectic. Thus 2 Bar 55:5−8 contrasts the mere announcement of judgement and of the coming day of the Lord, which Baruch has only seen in his vision, with the actual arrival of the same as "happening before your eyes", "when the event reveals marvels". And yet the eschatological "mysteries" of God are revealed not simply as designs, but as actually existent in heaven.[98]

It is clear how such an idea could be a powerful device to assure believers of the certainty of the coming salvation. Pre-existence and eschatological revelation are then not mutually exclusive,[99] but together constitute the apocalyptic argument: the mystery is already there, and it is about to be materially concretized.[100]

4.2.2.2. Apocalyptic Preview for the Saints. Mediating between the two poles of present hiddenness and future manifestation is the belief that select individual saints of the past have, as it were, been granted a glimpse of the mysteries of God;[101] their visions − duly recorded in the apocalyptic books! − now give a share in this knowledge to the believing remnant. Of course the visionary is well aware that his anticipatory "glimpse" cannot itself be equated with the eschatological revelation of the mysteries, but merely constitutes a selective disclosure of their content.[102] Thus Ezra is granted a fleeting glance at the heavenly city and sanctuary awaiting the final implementation on earth (4 Ezra 7:26, 10:27, 10:50−5, 13:36). Other recipients of this celestial "tourist's view" of the mysteries are Adam, Enoch, Jacob, Moses, Abraham, Baruch, and Jeremiah.[103] From their privileged visions of the salvific realities in heaven, belie-

---

[97] For further documentation of the following discussion cf. also Volz, *Eschatologie,* 114 f.

[98] See also Volz, *Eschatologie,* 116.

[99] *Pace* de Villiers, "Revealing", 56, who seems to envision an exclusive relationship between "eschatological events" and "the present existence of the heavenly secrets".

[100] Cf. Murdock, "History", 186; Bornkamm, "μυστήριον", 822.

[101] Note 4 Ezra 13:52 ("only to you this has been revealed").

[102] *Pace* Rössler, *Gesetz,* 61: the disclosure of the divine mysteries is not *eo ipso* one of the *Heilsgüter.* Unlike gnosticism, Jewish apocalyptic does not equate the disclosure of hidden information with salvation − a point well put e.g. by Chernus, *Mysticism,* 15; cf. Rowland, "Literature", 182. But neither are the mysteries disclosed exhaustively and without remainder (*pace* Lacocque, *Daniel,* 147 f.).

[103] Cf. e.g. Jub 1:4, 26; 4:19, 21; 32:21; 1 En 52:2−9; 2 Bar 4:3−5, 59:4−12; 4 Ezra 3:14; Life of Adam and Eve 29:4−5; ApAbr 9:6−10; also cf. ParJer 9:13−28; *LAB* 19:10; Rev 21:2 ff.; and EzekTrag 68−81 (cosmological mysteries). Cf. also b.BB 16b−17a on Abraham, Isaac, and Jacob.

vers derive comfort and hope regarding the events to come: for "as it is on high, so also is it on earth: what happens in the vault of heaven happens similarly here on earth" (AscIsa 7:10).[104]

4.3. Illicitly Revealed Mysteries

The idea of evil and/or illegitimately revealed mysteries is occasionally found in apocalyptic literature and elsewhere (see below, Chapter Two, on Qumran; 2 Thes 2:7). Here it is particularly prevalent in the Book of Watchers (1 En 1−17), where in fact *only* illicit mysteries are referred to.[105] Under the leadership of Semyaza and Azazel (or Asael), the fallen angels ("Watchers") take human wives and disclose "eternal secrets which were made in heaven" (1 En 9:6, cf. 10:7). These secrets should not have been revealed, since on earth they lead to great sin and destruction (8:2, 9:8): among them are weapons of war and women's cosmetics (8:1), as well as magic, divination, and astrology (8:3). However, Enoch is told to advise the Watchers on behalf of God that the secrets they disclosed to the women are not in fact the mysteries of God but are worthless (1 En 16:3):

> You were in heaven, but its secrets had not yet been revealed to you and a worthless mystery you knew. This you made known to the women in the hardness of your hearts, and through this mystery the women and the men cause evil to increase on the earth.

These "mysteries" fall outside the cosmological or eschatological mysteries of God assuring the salvation of His people, constituting instead a kind of true but inferior[106] celestial knowhow which is inappropriate and harmful for human society, disclosed only as a result of an angelic revolt against God's authority.[107] Such secrets are evil and "worthless" inasmuch as they do not advance the lordship of God in creation, history, and salvation.[108]

---

[104] Cf. e.g. Barrett, "Eschatology", 138 f.; Rowland, *Open Heaven*, 169; Barth, *Diesseits*, 98; Thoma, "Apokalyptik", 143. This belief is common to OT and Ancient Near Eastern religion: see e.g. Ringgren, *Religions*, 95; Knierim, "Offenbarung", 212 ff.

[105] With Brown, *Mystery*, 13 n. 50.

[106] *Pace* Bietenhard, *Himmlische Welt*, 268 (who cites 1 En 8:3 − but unfortunately not 16:3 − in claiming that the Watchers do reveal "wirkliche und echte Geheimnisse"); similarly Sjöberg, *Menschensohn*, 112 f.

[107] Cf. VanderKam, *Enoch*, 125. For other cases of illicitly disclosed divine secrets cf. *LAB* 25 ff., esp. 26:6; 27:10; 34:2 f.; also b. Yoma 67b; EpArist 315. Frequently encountered is the notion of an illegitimate human inquiry into hidden things: see Deut 29:28; Sir 3:21 f.; *LAB* 25:13, 26:6; cf. subsequent chapters.

[108] Illegitimate disclosure of divine secrets can also occur through drunkenness: e.g. TJud 16:4; cf. NumR 10:8. Closely related (but outside the purview of this study) are fre-

"In den Apokalypsen ist der tote Schutt der Phantastik oder Reflexion so hoch über die pneumatischen Erlebnisse ... gehäuft, daß das eigentlich Lebendige ... längst ertötet ist."[109] Such assessments, still all too common, must be judged to be quite inadequate appraisals of the apocalyptic experience of divine revelation. Instead, a fervent belief in the universal sovereignty of God came to spiritual and literary fruition in revelations of the eschatological and cosmological secrets of heaven. Often arising out of a deep interaction with Scripture, such "meta-revelation" opens up the divine perspective on the world, and from this vantage point addresses pressing issues of cosmic and historical theodicy.[110]

---

quent passages about a betrayal of human secrets: e.g. TJud 12:6; 16:4 TZeb 1:6; TGad 6:5. In Jub 27:1 Esau's secret intention is *divinely* disclosed in a dream to Rebecca; similarly (with a dream angelophany) TReub 3:15 and TJos 6:6. In 2 Bar 60:1 the mysteries [*dr'zyhwn*] of the Amorites (i.e. idolatrous Gentiles: Jub 29:11; m. Shab 6:10; m. Hull 4:7; cf. Cohen *Talmud*, 291 f.) are pagan cultic and magical rites perhaps a conscious allusion to the mystery religions. Cf. possibly SibOr 12:64.

[109] Büchsel, *Geist*, 62 f.

[110] Cf. Rowland, "Literature", 185 f.: "By its appeal to revelation and its stress on the need to pierce behind appearances to the realities which explain the incoherent jumble of history, apocalyptic supports continued attachment to Scripture and tradition."

Chapter Two

Qumran

1. Introduction

The major Qumran manuscripts published to date give the impression of a community marked by a particularly rigid compliance with the Torah and the Prophets.[1] In contrast e.g. to the Rabbinic writings, we find here no allowance for debate in matters of exegesis, much less any concession of different possibilities of interpretation. Instead, generous abuse is heaped upon the promoters of explanations which deviate from what to the Qumran writers seems the only authorized and acceptable exegesis.

One looks in vain for prophecy, or dreams and their interpretation[2] (or indeed affirmations of divine action in contemporary history). What factors, then, fuelled this community's faith and its understanding of revelation? With this question as a springboard for our inquiry, the following remarks evaluate the material from several different angles, starting once again with the relationship of Scripture and revelation.

2. "Secret Things and Things Revealed": Exegesis at Qumran

2.1. נגלות and נסתרות in the Torah

1 QS 5:11 f. nicely illustrates the distinction commonly drawn at Qumran between two categories of legal material in the Torah. Here the outsiders and opponents of the sect (אנשי העול) are excluded from God's covenant because a)

---

[1] The identification of the Qumran community with the Essenes (on which see Josephus, *BJ* 2:119–161 and Ant 12:171 f., 18:18–22; Philo, *Prob* 75–91; Pliny, *Hist.Nat.* 5:37) is here taken as likely but not established beyond doubt. See e.g. Ringgren, *Faith,* 235–242; Vermes, *Scrolls,* esp. 125–130; Yadin, *Message,* esp. 173–186.

[2] Except in writings whose provenance is not distinctively Essene, such as 1 QapGen 19:14 ff., 4 QEnGiants^b 2:3 ff., etc.

they have not searched the commandments to discover the hidden things (הנסתרות) regarding which they went astray, and b) they have done the revealed things (הנגלות) wantonly. Without at once taking for granted the identity of these "revealed" and "hidden things", it is clear that the writer assumes the latter to be accessible through intensive searching (בקש/דרש) of the Torah (similarly 1 QS 8:11 f., 15 f.). The "revealed things", on the other hand, appear to be known to the offenders already, since they have "done" (i.e., presumably, "transgressed against") them wantonly.[3] Thus it seems reasonable to take the נגלות as referring to matters in the Torah which are clear to everyone (cf. CD 15:13?), whereas נסתרות are commandments not immediately obvious, and ascertainable only to careful scrutiny of the Torah — the particular kind of scrutiny, that is, which is carried out only by the Qumran sectarians (1 QS 8:1, 11 f., 15 f.; also CD 3:14).[4]

Proceeding from here to inquire into the identity of the נסתרות, we come upon an interesting discovery in CD 3:12—16, one of the earliest sectarian documents.

> But with the remnant which held fast to the commandments of God, He made His Covenant with Israel for ever, revealing to them the hidden things in which all Israel had gone astray (לגלות להם נסתרות אשר תעו בם כל ישראל). He unfolded before them His holy Sabbaths and His glorious feasts, the testimonies of His righteousness and the ways of His truth, and the desires of His will which a man must do in order to live.

Here the "hidden things" are by apposition identified as "God's holy sabbaths and glorious feasts" (שבתות קדשו ומועדי כבודו). These Sabbaths and feasts[5] have been disclosed by revelation[6] to the righteous remnant, i.e. the community itself. נסתרות, then, are matters in the Torah whose interpretation is not self-evident to all, and to which the sect claims privileged access.[7]

---

[3] ביד רמה: cf. Exod 14:8; Num 15:30, 33:3; CD 8:8, 10:3.

[4] Cf. Schiffman, *Halakhah*, 22 ff.; Leaney, *Rule*, 172. The idea of ignorant sin occurs already in Psa 19:12; 90:8; Job 34:32; but cf. Kosmala, *Hebräer*, 256: the fact that Israel sinned against the "hidden things" is not expressed in terms of unwitting sin but of going astray, תעה — cf. 1 QS 5:11; CD 3:14. Note that even David did not keep the "sealed book of the law", CD 5:1—5 (i.e. 11 QTemple and its stipulation of monogamy, 57:17 f.? Cf. CD 4:21).

[5] The specific reference here would appear to be to Qumran's solar calendar, closely patterned on that of Jub. Cf. 1 QS 10:1.

[6] Aside from this theological usage, גלה is also used transitively with the human ear (1 QH 1:21; 6:4, 18:4 f.; CD 2:2; 11 QtgJob 27:3 f.), heart (1 QH 12:34, 18:24), and eyes (1 QH 18:19, CD 2:14) as its object — cf. already 1 Sam 9:15; 2 Sam 7:27/1 Chr 17:25; Job 33:16, 36:10, 15. גלה "to go into exile" occurs only in CD 7:14 f. (quoting Amos 5:27); sexual "uncovering" (frequent in the OT) is found e.g. in 11 QTemple 66:12 f.

[7] Cf. Gabrion, "L'interprétation," 820 f.; also Nötscher, *Terminologie*, 71; and Wieder, *Scrolls*, 54, who notes a similar distinction in Karaite exegesis (57—62). Cf. also Phi-

The נגלות, in turn, are neither simply Scripture[8] nor merely its revealed interpretation;[9] rather, as O. Betz keenly observes, they include both the self-evident subjects in the Torah (as above) and interpretations previously revealed to the sect (as e.g. 1 QS 1:9; 5:9; 9:13, 19).[10] All of the Torah must be kept, including both the "revealed" and the "hidden" things — and the non-sectarians have failed on both counts.[11]

2.2. "Revelation" and Exegesis of the Torah

Revelation from the Torah occurred עת בעת ("from time to time": 1 QS 8:15, 9:13), and thus was probably "progressive" in character.[12] In 1 QS 9:13 the Instructor (משכיל)[13] is to "do the will of God according to all that has been revealed from time to time. He shall measure out all knowledge discovered according to the times, together with the statute of the time. . . ."[14]

What, then, is the manner in which this revelation was received? The primary (possibly the only) means of present-day revelation appears to have been the intensive searching of the Torah, as was tentatively suggested above (cf. e.g. 1 QS 8:15; CD 6:7, 7:18). It is clear from 1 QS 5:9, 11 f. that the Torah is opened up and revealed to the priests, the searchers of the will of God (דורשי רצונו). "Revelation" takes place, then, where the diligent search of the

---

lo's reference to the Essenic exegesis of the "things not understood" (ὅσα μὴ γνώριμα): *Prob* 82.

[8] *Pace* Schiffman, *Halakhah*, 32; Wacholder, *Dawn*, 89 and 254 n. 350 (N.B. on p. 89 Wacholder considers "Scripture" at Qumran to include Jub, a view which unfortunately he does not sufficiently substantiate).

[9] Westermann/Albertz, "גלה," 426; cf. Zobel, "גלה", 1031.

[10] Betz, *Offenbarung*, 7 ("den schon früher klargelegten oder selbstverständlichen Weisungen").

[11] Cf. Deut 29:28, apparently (intentionally?) never quoted: "The secret things (הנסתרת) belong to the Lord our God, but the things revealed (והנגלת) belong to us and to our children forever, that we may observe all the words of this Torah." Cf. 4 Q508 [= PrFêtes] 2:4 (ואתה ידעתה הנסתרות והנגלות) and passim.

[12] Thus e.g. Gabrion, "L'interprétation," 820; Nötscher, *Terminologie*, 68 f.; Schiffman, *Halakhah*, 22 ff.

[13] Vermes, *DSSE* (2nd ed.), 22–25 argues from DSS and post-exilic Biblical texts (Dan 11:33; 12:3; Ezra 8:18; 2 Chr 30:32, etc.) that the *maskîlîm* must be the levitical instructors of post-exilic Israel; and further, that at Qumran one such *maskîl* was singled out, as a "Guardian" (מבקר). Cf. Leaney, *Rule*, 72 f., 229 f.; he also (118) follows Carmignac, "Conjecture", 85–87 in reading 1 QS 1:1 as למשכיל לאנ[שים ל]א[חיון] ספר סר[ך היחד, i.e. dealing in the first instance with this eminent Instructor.

[14] Cf. Vermes, *DSSE*, 74, who translates the word עת as "age". This implies successive dispensations of redemptive history, at least one of which for Qumran falls into the present.

priestly exegete-teacher is met by God's gift.[15] In addition to the rule that community members were to spend one third of every night in the study of "the book" (1 QS 6:7), one man in ten (or, possibly, in a *minyan* of ten)[16] was required to "search in the Torah by day and by night" (1 QS 6:6). Significant discoveries illuminating the "hidden things" in the Torah had to be disclosed to the responsible council of twelve men and three priests (1 QS 8:11 f.; cf. p. 49 below), and thus presumably became an integral part of the halakhic code of "revealed things".[17]

2.3. Torah and Halakhah

The Scrolls appear to be unfamiliar with the Rabbinic distinction between the "written Torah" of Scripture (תורה שבכתב) and the "oral Torah" of tradition (תורה שבעל פה).[18] Biblical and sectarian law are found side by side on equal terms, and the Qumran interpretations breathe an air of finality which permits of no further discussion.[19] Conversely, the high authority vested in the "new", exegetically derived halakhic[20] revelation of hidden things goes hand in hand with a strict adherence to the letter of the law.[21] Some have concluded that therefore no qualitative distinctions between the Torah and Qumran's Halakhah can remain.[22]

---

[15] "Human exertion and divine illumination are interdependent elements of the process of uncovering the hidden portions of the Torah" (Wieder, *Scrolls*, 81 f.). Cf. Psa 119, discussed in the Introduction above. See also Gabrion, "L'interprétation", 827; more generally Hengel, *Judentum*, 416 on the trend of "intellectualizing" of religion and piety. An appeal to 1 Macc 3:48 (Betz, *Offenbarung*, 48), albeit intriguing, is perhaps not entirely fair.

[16] See 1 QS 6:3 and cf. Leaney, *Rule*, 181, 184.

[17] Cf. Schiffman, *Sectarian Law*, 29. N.B. Patte, *Hermeneutic*, 221 rightly cautions that not *every* Biblical precept was subject to such exegesis, but apparently only difficult ones.

[18] Cf. e.g. Gabrion, "L'interprétation," 822.

[19] Cf. Baumgarten, "Unwritten Law", 15 ff. on 1 QSa 1:1 ff.; 11 QTemple; 4 Q159 (Ord); also Jub, etc.

[20] The נסתרות all appear to be in the realm of halakhah. Patte, *Hermeneutic*, 227 offers a helpful two-phase distinction between these "hidden things" and "mysteries" (רזים, cf. §§ 2.4; 4 below): the latter pertain to a first stage of reflection, which interprets "contemporary salient history" in light of Scripture, thus arriving at statements constitutive for the community's self-estimation as the end-time elect. The discovery of halakhic נסתרות is, in turn, epiphenomenal upon this self-appraisal, being concerned with interpreting the life of the newly constituted eschatological community.

[21] Driver, *Scrolls*, 579, compares Matt 5:17 ff. But the difference, he concedes, lies in Qumran's extreme legalism.

[22] E.g. Baumgarten, "Unwritten Law", 17.

But is this conclusion sound? I would submit that such a reading fails to give due appreciation to the implicit *structural* priority of the Torah in the sectarian hermeneutic. Any and all so-called "revelation", authoritative and idiosyncratic though it may appear, is in fact an epiphenomenon to the primary writings of Scripture.

Qumran's halakhah always derives from exegesis — as poorly or well executed as that may be. In a very real sense, therefore, it carries no *independent* authority of its own.[23] This is not of course to deny that *a posteriori* the sectarian pronouncements share in the Biblical authority: indeed they can even assume a kind of "topical" epistemological priority (inasmuch as the understanding of certain parts of the Torah depends on them).[24] However, that is merely a consequence of the community's fervent devotion to the Torah and its unceasing search for the true interpretation.[25] Thus, in the extensive garden parable of 1 QH 8:1 ff. (where the covenant community is compared to a plantation which sends forth roots to the water channels[26]), the interpretive work of the author serves as the crucial instrument for the provision of water; yet this work is obviously in turn dependent on the prior God-givenness of the spring. Given the presuppositional framework of Qumran's principles of exegesis, then, the Torah does retain at least a *hermeneutical* priority over the authoritative halakhic "revelation" which derives from it.[27]

2.4. Prophets and *Pesher*

A famous passage in 1 QpHab reads,

> And God told Habakkuk to write down that which would happen to the final generation, but He did not make known to him when time would come to an end (ואת גמר הקץ לוא הודעו). . . . This concerns the Teacher of Righteousness, to whom God made known all the mysteries of the words of His servants the Prophets

---

[23] Cf. Gabrion, "L'interprétation", 822 n. 204, 823.

[24] Cf. Gabrion, "L'interprétation", 823, n. 210.

[25] See also Josephus on Essene devotion to the Scriptures, *BJ* 2:159. And cf. Philo *Prob* 82.

[26] Cf. CD 3:16; 6:3 ff.; cf. 19:33 f.: exegesis as the digging of a well. Cf. Psa 1; Sir 24:30 f. Wieder, *Scrolls*, 62–67 lists Karaite parallels.

[27] Cf. Gabrion, "L'interprétation," 822 n. 204. He continues (823 n. 210), "L'autorité de la halakha essénienne ne vient pas tant du fait qu'elle est issue d'une révélation que du fait qu'elle repose uniquement sur la seule autorité scripturaire, sur l'autorité de la Loi de Moïse vénérée par la Communauté de Qumrân". N.B. only the Torah itself is quoted (e.g. "He has said" or "it is written", cf. esp. CD 9:2 ff.); but see below on 11 QTemple.

(אשר הודיעו אל את כול רזי דברי עבדיו הנבאים).... The final age shall be prolonged, and shall exceed all that the Prophets have said; for the mysteries of God are astounding.[28]

Irenaeus's comment on Ebionite exegesis seems strangely apposite to this fascinating passage: "Quae autem sunt prophetica curiosius exponere nituntur" (*Contra Haereses* 1.26.2). It would seem that the prophets (including David[29] and thus presumably the Writings[30]) are here treated differently from the Torah: while sectarian exegesis of the latter seeks to uncover the "hidden" (but nevertheless *given*) intentions of the Mosaic Law, the prophetic word is in fact limited and *incomplete* in itself. Although it is assumed to be "revealed" (e.g. 1 QS 8:15 f.;[31] CD 5:21 f.; 11 QPs^a 27:11) and can even be mentioned together with Moses (e.g. 1 QS 1:3), it had to be augmented by Qumran's Teacher of Righteousness, the interpreter *par excellence* who received the complement and culmination of the prophetic word directly "from the mouth of God" (מפי אל, 1 QpHab 2:2 f.). The prophets received revelation about eschatological mysteries, but only the Teacher of Righteousness was given to understand the גמר הקץ ("the consummation of the time"[32]), i.e. knowledge of the time of the eschaton.[33] The Teacher may not have experienced special visions,[34] but his interpretation nevertheless is divinely authorized.[35]

---

[28] 1 QpHab 7:1–8 (Vermes, *DSSE*, 286). For the mysteries of "His servants the prophets" cf. esp. Rev 10:7.

[29] See 11 QPsa 27:11 (on which see Worrell, "Wisdom", 359–364); note the existence of a *pesher* on Psa 37. Cf. Acts 2:30; AscIsa 11:2; Josephus *Ant* 6:166; Philo *Agr* 50; *Her* 290; Justin *Dial* 85, 110; b.Suk 52a; and esp. Tg Psa 45:1; 46:1, 49:16; 51:13; 103:1 and passim. The idea itself may derive from passages like 1 Sam 16:13; 2 Sam 23:1 (נאם), 2; etc.

[30] Cf. possibly the "three books" 4 QMess ar; also Philo *Cont* 25.

[31] Betz, *Offenbarung*, 7 and n. 1 takes 1 QS 8:15 f. to indicate that the prophets, too, are merely revealing the Torah, just as this is done "from time to time" in the sect's interpretation. However, this reading is not as obvious from the text as Betz would have it.

[32] For this and similar phrases see also 2 Bar 30:3; 59:4, 69:4; AssMos 1:18; TReub 6:8; TLevi 10:2; TZeb 9:9; Tob 14:5; VitProph 2:10, 19; 4:13; also e.g. 1 Cor 10:11; Gal 4:4; Eph 1:10; etc. Wieder, "קץ", 22 f. observes that קץ means "period" or "time"; cf. Mertens, *Daniel*, 146–148; *pace* Silberman, "Unriddling", 345 f. (קץ = חזון). See further p. 138 f. below.

[33] See 1 QpHab 2:6–9, 7:2, etc. (cf. Dan 9:24–27; also e.g. 4 Ezra 12:11 f., for a similar procedure; and note Josephus' comment about Essene predictions of the future on the basis of the prophetic writings, *BJ* 2:159). Cf. Betz, *Offenbarung*, 82; Horgan, *Pesharim*, 237; Elliger, *Studien*, 154; Brownlee, *Midrash*, 110; *pace* Wieder, *Scrolls*, 86 f. A late example of striking similarity is Naḥmanides's *Book of Redemption* 4:3 (in Buchanan, *Revelation*, 166): Daniel understood the Secret but not the time of the end.

[34] Patte, *Hermeneutic*, 218 explicitly contrasts apocalyptic literature. But cf. Section 3.4 below.

[35] Rigaux, "Révélation", 247.

As has variously been observed, the pattern of this so called *midrash pesher* exegesis — also found outside the DSS[36] — is in some ways closely akin to the interpretation of dreams.[37] Particularly interesting parallels occur in Daniel[38]: the mystery (רז) given in an obscure nocturnal disclosure must be "decoded" (פשר) by an interpreter who may (e.g. Dan 2) or may not (e.g. Dan 4) have been given a separate revelation for this purpose.

The two basic ingredients of the *pesher* type of "revelation", then, are the רז (often plural) and its corresponding פשר:[39] the former is supplied by the prophets, the latter by the Teacher of Righteousness (or his subsequent agents). "Revealed" interpretation thus attained thrives on allegory and clever semantics (cf. also Philo, *Prob* 82), and does not shy away from changing the letters or words of the primary text where necessary to suit a particular expository purpose.

Finally it is interesting to note briefly the ethical intention of *pesher* revelation: 1 QS 9:19 makes it clear that the aim of such interpretation is to enable the sectarian to live his life in accordance with the revealed will of God (i.e. להלך תמים איש את רעהו בכול הנגלה להם) and thus to be one of the תמימים, i.e. the mature (1 QS 4:22).[40]

---

[36] Fishbane, *Interpretation,* 454 f. discusses the development of *pesher* in Talmud, Midrash, 4 Ezra, Targumim, etc. For the identification of the genre cf. further Brooke, "Pesher", 483—503. Silberman, "Unriddling", 324—330 compares esp. the Rabbinic Petirah Midrash.

[37] See esp. Fishbane, *Interpretation,* 455: *pašaru* "to solve, interpret" is used in Akkadian magical, divinatory, and dream contexts. In the OT cf. further Gen 40:12, 18; see Fishbane, "Pesher", 105—110. The connection between Scriptural prophets and dream interpretation may derive from the idea that the books of the prophets contain their visions and dreams: see Silberman, "Unriddling", 327—31 (followed by Patte, *Hermeneutic,* 301 f.), with reference to SifNum 12:6.

[38] See esp. Bruce, "Exposition", 77 f.; Horgan, *Pesharim,* 252 ff. Wacholder, *Dawn,* 90 f., even suggests the influence might have gone in either direction (assuming an early date for 1 QpHab). Another significant parallel is 1 En 106:19 = 4 QEn^c 5.ii.26 f. (ed. Milik, 209 f.): "I know the mysteries of God which the Holy Ones have told me and shown to me and which I read in the heavenly tablets." Note also אפשר דבראז אלהא in Tg Job 15:8.

[39] Vermes ("Interpretation", 91) lists four basic logical principles of the *pesher*: (i) the mysteriousness of the prophetic writings and their need of new revelation; (ii) the eschatological character of this new revelation; (iii) the imminence of the end of the world and hence the application of prophecy to the present generation; and (iv) the Teacher of Righteousness himself is the recipient of this revelation. Cf. also Horgan, *Pesharim,* 244 f.

[40] Cf. Rigaux, "Révélation," 248: "Le parfait était celui qui acceptant cette doctrine la vivait intégralement." See ibid., 237—241; Betz, *Offenbarung,* 74 f.; Nötscher, *Terminologie,* 74. On the ethical import of "revelation" cf. further Philo, *Prob* 82 f.; and see below, e.g. section 1.2 in Chapter Nine.

2.5. The Teacher of Righteousness as Mediator of Revelation

The author of the Qumran Hymns (1 QH) makes some remarkable claims of having received and passed on divine revelation (e.g. 1 QH 1:21; 4:23 ff.; 8:16 ff.; 12:12 f., 33 f., etc.).[41] Although not expressly stated, all indications are that the intended speaker is the Teacher of Righteousness himself. Besides this Teacher and of course certain Old Testament figures,[42] only the priests ("sons of Zadok") are specifically mentioned as recipients of revelation (see above; cf. CD 5:5 [Hilkiah]).[43] The primary function of the priests is to carry on the heritage of the Teacher of Righteousness, whose access to revelation is considered to be unmatched (see also CD 1:11).[44] He is the primary mediator of the sectarian revelation; the priests are its primary stewards; the whole community (N. B. only they),[45] its ultimate addressees.

While the Teacher of Righteousness resembles Moses in some ways and the prophets in others, he is different from both: being neither lawgiver nor prophet but a teacher,[46] his revelation is based on the interpretation of Scripture. His person and his work are constitutive for the self-understanding and theology of the community at Qumran.

---

[41] Cf. Holm-Nielsen, *Hodayot*, 285; also Casciaro Ramirez, "Himnos", 34, who sees here a precedent for Paul's self-understanding as a mediator of revelation and steward of mysteries.

[42] E.g. Moses (e.g. 1 QS 1:3; 1 Q22 [= DM]), Amram (4 Q'Amram), Samuel (4 Q160 [= VisSam]), and the prophets (e.g. 1 QpHab 7).

[43] Rigaux ("Révélation", 243−245) includes the council of twelve elders and three priests (1 QS 8:1) and the Instructor (משכיל − e.g. 1 QS 3:13); but it remains unclear in the texts whether these figures do anything more than to preserve and handle received revelation. Betz, *Offenbarung*, 11 f. (followed e.g. by Schnabel, *Law*, 174) includes Ezra, but his prooftext CD 1:6−12 seems less than convincing. A different situation may prevail in 1 QM 10:10−12, where Israel (the "true Israel"? cf. n. 45) is granted the revelation of celestial secrets.

[44] Schreiner, "Geistbegabung", 180 n. 75; Foerster, "Geist", 125.

[45] Holm-Nielsen, *Hodayot*, 284: the new revelation is not addressed to all Israel but only to those who accept it, i.e. the members of the new covenant. See 4 Ezra 14:26, 46; cf. also Rom 9:6 ff. Leaney, *Rule*, 72 observes that the community's image of itself as the people of the new covenant, receiving new revelation, is reflected in its organization as a "miniature Israel", with fully formulated functions for priests, Levites, etc.

[46] Rigaux, "Révélation," 246 f.; Betz, *Offenbarung*, 62 f., 67 f., 92, 98. Kosmala, *Hebräer*, 263 insists that the absence of prophetic nomenclature need not imply that the Teacher's office had no prophetic overtones.

2.6. Revelation and the Spirit

An important passage for the doctrine of spirit at Qumran is 1 QS 3:17−4:26.
Two spirits have been assigned to the world by God: the spirit of truth and the
spirit of falsehood (they also carry a number of other names),[47] who continually
wage war with each other.[48] However, most relevant for this inquiry is the
view of the Holy Spirit or spirit of God (probably not to be equated with the
"spirit of truth", which moreover does not seem to bear on revelation).[49]

The main function of the Holy Spirit as God's gift to the community seems
to be the purification and sanctification of the believer (1 QH 3:21, 4:20−22,
14:25−27, 16:10−12, etc.).[50] In a number of cases it is instrumental in dispensing revelation (e.g. 1 QH 13:18 f.; cf. 1 QS 4:2−6), including the revelation of
mysteries (1 QH 12:11 f.).[51] Indeed the Spirit grants a knowledge of mysteries
both to the prophets and to the Qumran community;[52] the latter benefits from
the special charisma of the Spirit which the Teacher of Righteousness has received in his exegesis.[53] Betz aptly summarizes the relationship between Scripture, the Spirit, and the giving of revelation: "Die Offenbarung ist für die Sekte
an die Schrift gebunden und Werk des Heiligen Geistes, der den Menschen rei-
nigt, erleuchtet, stärkt und mit Gott verbindet."[54]

2.7. An Exception? The Temple Scroll

On numerous occasions the Temple Scroll renders divine discourse in the
first person singular, when its OT source text refers to God's speech in the third
person, or not at all. Examples of the latter include the passages about marriage

---

[47] Significant for our concern is the fact that the spirit of falsehood, who governs the
"men of perdition", is later also called "spirit of secrecy" (ברוח הסתר, 1 QS 9:22).

[48] Cf. Schreiner, "Geistbegabung", 180; Schäfer, "Geist", 173 f. See also TJud 20:1 ff.;
TAsh 1:3−9.

[49] Betz, *Offenbarung*, 147 ff.: as minister of truth, the good spirit (angel of light, etc.)
only intervenes in the eschaton.

[50] See also Betz, *Offenbarung*, 140; Foerster, "Geist", 129 f.; Schreiner, "Geistbegabung", 175 ff.; Schäfer, "Geist", 173 f.

[51] Betz, *Offenbarung*, 18 (cf. (Hengel, *Judentum*, 403; Schnabel, *Law*, 173) notes a
stronger emphasis on Spirit-given revelation in 1 QH and on revelation through *Schriftforschung* e.g. in 1 QS. The different emphasis seems due primarily to the prayerful and
poetic language of 1 QH; here too revelation is mediated by virtue of God given knowledge of Torah: 1 QH 4:10; 5:11 f. See further Schäfer, "Geist", 173.

[52] Bruce, "Spirit", 51; cf. Coppens, "Mystère", 146; Schäfer, "Geist", 174.

[53] E.g. 1 QpHab 7:1 ff.; 1 QH. Cf. Schreiner, "Geistbegabung", 179; *pace* Kuhn, *Enderwartung*, 147, who denies a special charisma.

[54] Betz, *Offenbarung*, 149 (cf. 141).

with a niece (66:15—17; cf. CD 5:7), death penalty for betrayal (esp. 64:9—11), and a new, detailed charter for the king (56:12 ff.).[55]

Obviously the nature and intention of 11 QTemple is of fundamental importance. If it is for Qumran, as Wacholder suggests, the authoritative and surpassing Second Torah,[56] then (at least in large part[57]) it cannot constitute "revelation" merely in the sense of authoritative Torah interpretation. The fact that God here speaks a new word in the first person singular would have to mean that 11 QTemple contains indeed a major body of new and underived revelation.

Obviously a great deal rests on our assessment of the origin, nature and use of 11 QTemple. Without being able to enter fully into this on-going discussion, I would venture to suggest that in form, if not perhaps in intention, this document does in fact diverge from the pattern of exegesis described above. Among the other documents discovered at Qumran, only 4 Q159 [Ord] and 1Q 22 [DM] somewhat resemble it. Schiffman for one contrasts the halakhah of 11 QTemple (part of the original revelation to Moses) with that of the other Scrolls (the result of ongoing exegesis).[58]

What is more, in a number of ways the Temple Scroll may be functionally similar to the Mishnah. Despite undeniable formal differences between 11 QTemple and Rabbinic literature (esp. the feature of direct divine speech, though N. B. e.g. m. Abot 2:2), many topics are addressed in both bodies of literature — even those not found in Scripture. It may be that 11 QTemple represents a pre-Mishnaic restatement of Torah (*mishneh torah*) in which minority opinions are not included and the first-person address is intended to emphasize the divine origin of the rules.[59]

---

[55] Cf. the tabular arrangement in Wilson/Wills, "Sources", 278 ff.; and see Yadin, *Temple Scroll*, 1:46 f.

[56] *Dawn*, passim; his argument is based *inter alia* on the identification of 11 QTemple with the Book of *Hagu* (הגו/הגי — 1 QSa 1:6—8; CD 10:4—6, 13:2—3), the "sealed Book of the Law" (CD 5:1—5), and the "Book of the Second Law" (4 QpPs37 4:6—8, 4 QCatena[a] 1—4:13 f.). Cf. Yadin, *Temple Scroll*, 1:392—397; also Vermes in Schürer/Vermes, *HJPAJC* 3:411 f., Wacholder considers 11 QTemple to be the work of the Teacher of Righteousness (= "Zadok").

[57] An exception might be the rule (11 QTemple 66:17) about marriage with a niece, which in CD 5:7 *is* in fact defended on exegetical grounds.

[58] Schiffman, Review, 124. What is more, he considers the terminological, morphological, and orthographical affinities with the Mishnah to be significant enough to question "the assumption that the *Temple Scroll* was authored by the same group that authored the sectarian scrolls."

[59] See Falk, "*Temple Scroll*", 33—44; Schiffman, Review, 124; *pace* Wacholder, *Dawn*, passim; Yadin, *Temple Scroll*, 1:392 (but contrast 1:87); Maier, *Temple Scroll*, 6 ("Urdeuteronomy"). Apart from the book of Deuteronomy itself, precedents of such a phenomenon are admittedly rare.

Whether the Temple Scroll can actually offer us further *substantive* information about the idea of revelation at Qumran will have to await further research.

3. Other Means of Revelation?

3.1. No properly prophetic revelation appears to have been experienced at
Qumran. The prophets were a phenomenon of the past (e.g. 1 QS 8:16), and
the eschatological prophet promised in Deuteronomy 18:15 was still to come in
the future (see 1 QS 9:10 f.).[60]

3.2. There are frequent references to the "lot" (גורל); this can either designate a person's portion in life (e.g. 1 QS 11:7; 1 QSa 1:9, 20; 1 QM 1:5; 15:1;
17:7; etc.), or be linked with communal decision making (1 QS 5:3, 6:16 ff., 9:7,
CD 13:4). However, the texts imply that the reference is not to an actual "casting of lots" but periphrastically to a decision taken by the council of the community.[61]

3.3. Neither is divine revelation in the proper sense intended in 4 Q186 and
4 QMess ar, both of which could be classified as horoscopes.[62] While there is an
attempt to predict what otherwise would be hidden to man, there is no appeal
to God for this information. Perhaps such horoscopes were purely literary devices.[63]

3.4. Instances of explicit visionary language are rare and non-specific in the
major sectarian documents; they can best be explained as poetic descriptions of
the exegetical insights of the community and their soteriological impact (e.g.
1 QS 11:3, 6, 19).[64] A possible exception is 1 QM 10:10−12, which speaks
about visions of angels (N. B. cf. Josephus *BJ* 2:142) and of heavenly secrets;
perhaps 1 QH 4:18 (חזון דעת) should also be mentioned.

Beyond this, the only clearly identifiable non-Biblical accounts of visionary
experiences are to be found in 1 QapGen (2:10 f., 19:14 ff., 20:22, 21:8 ff.,
22:27 ff.);[65] 4 Q'Amram[b] (1:10 ff.); and 5 Q15 [= JN ar; cf. 1 Q32; 2 Q24].[66] But

---

[60] E.g. Burrows, "Prophecy", 225 f.

[61] See e.g. 1 QS 6:16, 18, 22; contrast poss. 4 Q176 [= Tanḥ] 16:2. See further Betz,
Offenbarung, 49; Beardslee, "Lots", 245 ff.; Dommershausen, "גורל", 998. Cf. also p. 85
n. 22 below regarding Urim and Thummim.

[62] Vermes, *DSSE*, 305 f. On 4 QMess ar contrast Fitzmyer, "Elect of God", esp.
370 ff.

[63] Vermes, *DSSE*, 305.

[64] Cf. Kuhn, *Enderwartung*, 173; Betz, *Offenbarung*, 141 f.; Foerster, "Geist," 131.
However, such passages do indicate a strong belief in the proleptic participation of the
community in the glory of heaven and the angels; cf. e.g. Rowland, *Open Heaven*, 116 ff.

[65] Dehandschutter ("Rêve", 54) suggests that the dreams in 1 QapGen follow a standard "schéma de révélation visionnaire" of apocalyptic literature.

[66] Despite its title, 4 Q160 [= 4 QVisSam] does not really describe a vision; moreover

these documents are written in Aramaic, not in Hebrew, and nothing in the content of 1 QapGen and quite arguably also 4 Q'Amram and 5 Q15 betrays doctrinal biases peculiar to Qumran. Possibly, therefore, these writings were merely "imported" in much the same way as several other known apocrypha. Although several documents manifest apocalyptic perspectives,[67] the genre of apocalypse seems to be absent from the sectarian Scrolls.[68] Despite their detailed descriptions of celestial worship, even the recently published *Songs of the Sabbath Sacrifice* do not supply an explicit revelatory framework.[69]

4. Revelation of Mysteries

The Qumran texts speak frequently about "mysteries" which are known to God but inaccessible to man except by revelation. Through the Teacher of Righteousness and its exegetes, the community has been granted a disclosure of such mysteries, as we saw, but it must guard them from outsiders unable or unworthy to understand.[70] The most important word for our purposes is רז, which occurs approximately 65 times in the texts I have been able to see.[71] Other significant terms include סוד, סתר (esp. nifal ptc.), חבה/חבא, etc.

The frequent occurrence of רז and סוד in similar contexts (e.g. 1 QH 4:28) might seem to imply their synonymity.[72] However, a semantic differentiation becomes desirable when it is realized e.g. that רז invariably denotes a mystery

---

its subject matter closely parallels 1 Sam 3:15 ff. Visionary material is arguably contained in the Angelic Liturgy and merkabah fragments (4 QŠirŠabb), but an explicit narrative framework is there lacking. 11 QMelch is a midrash; on its relation to apocalyptic thought cf. e.g. Kobelski, *Melchizedek*, esp. 49—83.

[67] Cf. Philonenko, "L'Apocalyptique", 217.

[68] Rowland, *Open Heaven*, 39—42; Russell, *Method*, 24.

[69] Cf. Newsom, "Merkabah Exegesis", 29: "Unlike many of the uses of Ezekiel's vision in contemporary apocalyptic literature, the Sabbath songs do not associate the merkabah with a scene of revelatory disclosure."

[70] 1 QS 4:6, 17, 22; 5:11; 1 QH 13:13 f.; and cf. Josephus *BJ* 2:142. Patte, *Hermeneutic*, 219 suggests this secrecy may be a secondary development arising from external opposition.

[71] 1 QpHab 7:5, 8, 14; 1 QS 3:23; 4:6, 18; 9:18; 11:3, 5, 19; 1 QM 3:9, 15; 14:9, 14; 16:11, 16; 17:9; 1 QH 1:11, 13, 21, 29; 2:13; 4:27; 5:25, 36; 7:27; 8:6, 11 (2x); 9:23; 11:10; 12:13, 20; 13:2, 13; 1 QH frg 3:7; 6:5; 17:3; 25:1; 50:5; 1 Q26 1:1, 4; 1 Q27 [= Myst] I 1:2, 3, 4, 7; 13:3; 1 Q30 4:1; 1 Q36 9:2; 16:2; 1 Q40 1:2; 4 QMᵃ 12; CD 3:18; 1 QapGen 1:2, 3; 1 Q23 9/14/15:2; 4 QMess ar 1:8 (2x); 4 Q176 [= Tanḥ] 16:2; 4 Q401 14.ii:24, 17:6; 4 Q403 1.ii:27 (2x); 4 Q405 3.ii:9; Q511 [= Shirᵇ] 2 II 6; 44—47 I 6; 48—51 II 7. A few of these readings are based on admittedly conjectural reconstructions. Kuhn's listing (in his *Konkordanz*) of 1 QH 13:13 is almost certainly incorrect.

[72] Thus Couturier, "Vision", 40 f.

or secret purpose, while סוד often does not.[73] Wewers suggests the useful distinction between the chiefly *sociological* import of סוד (as the private, hence "secret" communication of the "in-group" in its privileged access to God), and the more narrowly *theological* meaning of רז (as primarily an "apocalyptic" designation of the divine plan and order of salvation).[74]

R. E. Brown has identified four different categories of mysteries at Qumran, which form a useful starting point for the present discussion: (4.1) mysteries of divine providence (including eschatology); (4.2) mysteries of the sect's interpretation of the law (on which see § 2.1 above); (4.3) cosmic mysteries (above all the phenomena of nature); and (4.4) mysteries of evil.[75] This structure may not be comprehensive,[76] but it covers the vast majority of pertinent examples.

4.1. The first category of soteriological mysteries may be said to include the mysteries of knowledge (e.g. 1 QS 4:6) and understanding (1 QS 4:18), of marvellous truth (1 QS 9:18), and a host of similar terms — in so much as they appear to refer quite generally to the counsels and decrees of God's plan and will. These divine purposes, pertaining in particular to eschatology,[77] are divinely revealed only to the Teacher of Righteousness and thus to his community.[78] As for the *hiddenness* of these mysteries, it too proves to be eschatological in orientation: the final phase of history has been inaugurated, but its consummation still appears to tarry[79] and must thus remain a "mystery of God", to be realized shortly. It is interesting in this respect that the Messianic dimension of the mys-

---

[73] E.g. 1 QS 6:19; 11:7 ff.; 1 QH 4:25; 14:18, etc. Cf. Casciaro Ramirez, "Regla", 487 and n. 3.

[74] Wewers, *Geheimnis*, 192 ff. Cf. Fabry, "סוד", 100; see also p. 15 f. above. The use of רז specifically of *halakhic* secrets is comparatively rare (but cf. e.g. 1 QS 9:18 f.).

[75] Brown, *Mystery*, 22—29. Compare Coppens, "Mystère", 145 f.; Vogt, "Mysteria", 256 f.

[76] What, for example, is the category of "mysteries of the casting of the lot" (4 Q176 [=Tanḥ] 16:2)?

[77] E.g. 1 Q27 1:1, 3—6 (רזי נהיה with גלה) and passim. For the form רז נהיה cf. 1 Q27 1:1, 4; 1 QS 11:3. That this was indeed understood as a future participle is clear from Sir 42:19; 48:25 Heb. (= LXX τὰ ἐσόμενα); cf. also Nötscher, *Terminologie*, 74 f.; Betz, *Offenbarung*, 84; Mertens, *Daniel*, 125 f.

[78] Vogt, "Mysteria", 257; cf. Coppens, "Mystère", 144; also Nötscher, *Terminologie*, 74; Bruce, *Exegesis*, 19.

[79] Cf. 1 QpHab 7:5—13; 4 QpPs37 2:7 f.; CD 20:14; also Jub 50:2—4. Lincoln, *Paradise*, 143 believes 1 QS 11:5—8 to be proof that some mysteries are already *presently* realized. Such realized eschatology (joint worship with the angels, etc.) is undoubtedly a motif found in the Scrolls (cf. e.g. Aune, *Cultic Setting*, 31 ff.; and see Chapter 9 below), but 1 QS 11:6 suggests that there nevertheless remains a future component. (Present realization may also occur in 1 QH 8:11—13, where the fruit of the symbolic plantation (the psalmist's community) is protected "by the mystery of mighty heroes and of spirits of holiness and of the whirling flame of fire.")

tery motif, so prominent in apocalyptic literature (notably 1 En), is virtually absent in the Scrolls.[80]

Passing over (4.2) the secrets of halakhah (discussed above), we come to (4.3) mysteries of a cosmological dimension. Perhaps one of the most comprehensive texts is 1 QH 13:1–13; but other examples are the contents of heaven in 1 QM 14:14, celestial dimensions and beings in 1 QM 10:11 f., and astronomical and meteorological wonders in 1 QH 1:11 f. Further interest concerns the ocean and the deep and its inhabitants (1 QH 1:14; 1 Q27 [= Myst] frg. 13:3) as well as the human voice (1 QH 1:28 f.). However, not all of the relevant texts actually use the word רז or the like. What is more, the precise type of mystery intended is not everywhere plain; nor is a clear distinction between "cosmological" and "soteriological" mysteries always possible (cf. Chapter One above).

Of particular significance in this regard are the mystical *Songs of the Sabbath Sacrifice* with their intricate descriptions of the mysteries of heavenly worship; these texts appear to substantiate Gershom Scholem's claim of a continuum of tradition linking the esoteric *Hekhalot* literature of Rabbinic mysticism with the celestial visions of the earlier apocalypses. A study of the secrets of the heavenly doxologies reveals the author's keen awareness of the liturgical and theological significance of these celestial mysteries for the worshipping community on earth. Nevertheless, in the writer's description of the "incremental" worship of the seven exalted angelic princes, phrases like "his wonderful mysteries" (4 Q401 14.ii:1) or "seven mysteries of knowledge in the wondrous mystery of the seven [most] holy precincts" (4 Q403 1.ii:27) do not permit of a distinction between cosmological and soteriological concerns.[81] (We observed a similar overlap in many of the apocalyptic texts; cf. Chapter One above.) Revelation of both kinds of mysteries illustrates and derives from God's wisdom and understanding (דעת, שׂכל, חכמה etc.).[82]

4.4. The last kind of mystery, secrets of iniquity (רזי פשע: 1 Q27 [= Myst] 1:2–4; 1 QH frg. 50:5; 1 QapGen 1:2; cf. יסודי פשע, 4 Q402 1.5) or of Belial (1 QH 5:36; 1 QM 14:9), carries a more negative value.[83] Although the roots of

---

[80] Cf. Penna, *Mysterion*, 21. Note however that among the predicates of the psalmist of 1 QH are some which were at times applied to the Messiah: e.g. the speaker is afflicted (1 QH 4:8 f.); he (and God's Torah) is kept hidden until a final revelation (1 QH 5:11 f.; cf. 5:25 f.; 9:24; poss. 8:11); he is involved with labour pangs leading to the birth of a male child who is פלא יועץ עם גבורתו (1 QH 3:7–10; see Isa 9:5). Cf. the (Christian) messianic references in OdSol 17, 22, 36, 42, poems which often resemble 1 QH. Coppens is led to conclude that the Teacher of Righteousness is himself a "mystery" ("Mystère", 145).

[81] Cf. also 4 Q401 14 ii; 4 Q401 17.4–6; 4 Q402 4.11 (par. Masada ŠirŠabb i.1), 14 (par. Masada Šir Šabb i.4 f.); 4 Q403 1 i.18–20.

[82] See below, Chapter 9 on 1 Cor 2:6; also cf. Casciaro Ramirez, "Regla", 490–495; idem, "Himnos", 15, 29.

[83] Cf. further God's hatred of the סוד of the evil spirit (1 QS 4:1); the fellowship of de-

this notion must be seen in the Old Testament idea of secret counsels of evil,[84] its occurrence here is a function of Qumran's fundamentally dualistic cosmology: good and evil (or light/darkness, truth/falsehood, Melchizedek/Melchiresha', etc.) engage in universal conflict until God brings victory to the good.[85] The term "mysteries of evil", then, is simply an expression of the fact that the workings and devices of the evil one are equally real, and equally inscrutable to man, as the mysteries of God.[86]

To sum up: the DSS conceive of new revelation as received by the Teacher of Righteousness and a leading council of priests through a process of exegesis. Halakhic "hidden things" in the Torah have been disclosed only to the covenant community and enable it to live according to a full knowledge of the will of God. Similarly, the eschatological meaning (גמר הקץ) of the "mysteries of the prophets" has been revealed to the Teacher of Righteousness. This helps to explain the confident confession in the "Daily Prayers" that "God has made His design known to us by the counsel of His great understanding" (4 Q503 51.v:13).

---

ceit and counsel of Belial סוד שוא ועדת בליעל (1 QH 2:22); the סוד of violence (1 QH 6:5) or of vanity (1 QH 7:34); and the destruction of those who detain the wondrous mysteries of God (1 Q27 I 1:7).

[84] See e.g. Psa 1:1 מושב לצים/עצת רשעים; 2:2; 64:3 סוד מרעים; also 31:14; 83:4; specifically of evil powers in Job 1:7 ff.; 1 Chr 21:1; also Judg 9:23; 1 Sam 16:14; 1 Kgs 22:22). Cf. Sæbø, "סוד", 145. In the NT the scheming and plotting of evil powers occurs e.g. in Matt 13:19par, 39; Luke 22:31; John 8:44; esp. 2 Cor 2:11; 4:4; 11:3, 14 f.; 1 Thes 2:18 (?); Eph 2:2; 4:11; 6:11; also 1 Pet 5:8 f.; and cf. Rev 2:9 f; 17. See more especially on 2 Thes 2:7 below.

[85] Note the inscription on trumpets of the eschatological battle: "mysteries of God for the destruction of evil" (1 QM 3:9).

[86] Vogt, "Mysteria", 257: "Iniqua mysteria Belial sunt eius decreta atque consilia opposita consiliis divinis." Cf. Nötscher, *Terminologie*, 75. See further CD 4:15–17; 4 Q280 2:6; 4 Q286 [Berª] 10.ii.2–12 (N.B in Milik, "Milkî-ṣedeq", 127, 130 f.) on the evil plans and snares of Belial (also e.g. TDan 2:4); and cf. the idea of *interpretations* of evil/deception in 1 QH 2:31, 34; 4:7 ff., specifically in the context of the devices of Belial. Compare further Rev 2:24 (τὰ βαθέα τοῦ σατανᾶ: for βαθέα see below, Chapter 9, n. 38 on 1 Cor 2:10); and cf. esp. Chapter 11 below on 2 Thes 2:7.

Chapter Three

Wisdom Literature

1. Introduction

This chapter focuses on Sirach and the book of Wisdom, although it will also consider pertinent sections from the Letter of Aristeas, Baruch, Tobit, 4 Maccabees, the Testaments of Issachar and of Judah, and *Pirqe Abot*.[1]

We will begin with a look at the view of prophetic revelation in these writings; this will be followed by the treatment of a cluster of issues pertaining to the idea of scribal inspiration, including views of the cult, Torah, and the Spirit. The chapter concludes with a discussion of divine "mysteries" in relation to the preceding observations.

2. The View of Prophetic Revelation

2.1. No Present-Day Prophecy

"We did not heed the voice of the Lord our God in all the words of the prophets whom he sent to us." These words from Bar 1:21 indicate the essentially past-tense perspective of prophecy and prophetic revelation which prevails in the post-Biblical Jewish wisdom literature.[2] Although the current generation can refer to itself as "the sons of the prophets", there is no direct claim to con-

---

[1] N.B. this is the only non-halakhic Mishnah tractate; Davies ("Tradition", 27) describes it as "a miniature Book of Proverbs, designed especially for rabbis and their students".

[2] Even broader in its pessimism (at least on this score) is PrAzar: "And at this time there is no prince, or prophet, or leader..." (15). Cf. e.g. Sir 49:10 (and by implication the Prologue: cf. Frey, "Révélation", 480); further 1 Macc 4:46; 9:27; 14:41; Matt 23:35 (cf. VitProph 23:2); also SibOr 1:386 (post-apostolic Christian perspective).

temporary προφητεία.[3] After the δώδεκα προφῆται (49:10), Ben Sira names no other prophets.[4]

But is this really the last word on the matter? Perhaps not. The next three sections will deal with possible exceptions and alternatives.

2.2. Revelatory Experiences

At least some of the wisdom writings do occasionally speak of relevant contemporary phenomena, though the term "prophet" is sparingly used. The Letter of Aristeas mentions a dream revelation to warn one Theopompus against his meddlesome desire to disclose divine matters to the common man,[5] and Tobit allows for an extended angelophany in the form of Raphael.

2.3. Uses of "Prophet" and "Prophecy"

In fact the term "prophet" *does* occur now and then, though not always with favourable connotations. Clearly those who "prophesy" in the context of idolatrous Hellenistic (mystery) rites in Wisdom 14:28 are in fact *false* prophets at their worst.[6]

But even true prophets are sometimes mentioned at least in passing. Thus, TJud 18:5 describes the man given to fornication and money as one who "holds back the sacrifices due to God, and ignores his blessing, and pays no heed to a prophet when he speaks." Wisd 7:27 goes further in asserting about the figure of wisdom that "in every generation she passes into holy souls and makes them friends of God, and prophets." Wisdom herself, it is implied, can give to him who longs for experience and *savoir faire* (πολυπειρία) many of the privileges associated with prophets: "She knows the things of old, and infers the things to come; . . . she has foreknowledge of signs and wonders and the outcome of seasons and times" (Wisd 8:8). The book of Wisdom, then, does not subscribe to

---

[3] Tob 4:12 (υἱοί προφητῶν ἐσμέν). Note the pungent inversion of this claim in Jesus's remark to the Pharisees, υἱοί ἐστε τῶν φωνευσάντων τοὺς προφήτας (Matt 23:31).

[4] The otherwise glorious description of Simon son of Onias (c. 219–196 B.C.) in 50:1–21 no longer contains any reference to divine activity.

[5] EpArist 315 (cf. Josephus, *Ant* 12:112); cf. on Sir 3:23 below. See further Wisd 18:17–19; 2 Macc 15:11–16 regarding dreams. Note, however, that Sir 34:1 ff. decidedly repudiates dreams (as does e.g. Jer 23:25; cf. also EpArist 213–216 and Gen 37:19); see also Ehrlich, *Traum*, 166 and 168 n. 3.

[6] Cf. p. 85 below; also e.g. Zech 13:2. Fascher, *ΠΡΟΦΗΤΗΣ*, 146 f., writes, "Der Gebrauch dieser sonst für die eignen Offenbarungsträger vorbehaltenen Worte für Heiden bedeutet absolut keine Anerkennung ihrer Tätigkeit."

the view that prophecy has ended; but even where no contemporary prophets are known, at least a *notion* of prophecy appears to have been kept alive.

2.4. The Sages

Thirdly, and most importantly, we must ask whether prophecy may not to some extent have been subsumed or appropriated by another religious phenomenon, viz. the emergence of the scribal sages as the stewards of Torah. In Ben Sira, the scribe by the grace of God ("if the great Lord is willing")[7] can find himself the recipient of divine inspiration (39:6—8):

> He will be filled with the spirit (πνεύματι) of understanding; he will pour forth words of wisdom and give thanks to the Lord in prayer. He will direct his counsel and knowledge aright, and meditate on his secrets (ἀποκρύφοις). He will reveal (ἐκφανεῖ) instruction in his teaching, and will glory in the law of the Lord's covenant.

The activity of the sage here is certainly described in terminology which indicates a spiritual giftedness analogous to that of a prophet (cf. Matt 23:34). "The place of prophecy," writes Nickelsburg on this passage, "has been taken by the scribe's study and interpretation of the ancient writings, especially the Torah."[8] This suggestion of a prophetic analogy is explicitly confirmed elsewhere in Ben Sira. Chapter 24 gives what may best be understood as an expression of the author's view of himself and his legacy (24:32—34):

> I will again make instruction shine forth like the dawn, and will make it shine afar; I will again pour out teaching like prophecy (διδασκαλίαν ὡς προφητείαν), and leave it to all future generations. Observe that I have not laboured for myself alone, but for all who seek instruction.

In other words, Ben Sira maintains a conscious analogy, *mutatis mutandis*, between the gift of prophecy and his own inspired teaching of wisdom and Torah. Both are inspired, and both are channels of revelation — inasmuch as both convey Torah.[9]

At the same time, διδασκαλίαν ὡς προφητείαν (Sir 24:33) implies that at issue is no *more* than an analogy with prophecy.[10] Ben Sira studiously refrains from calling himself a prophet; his self-understanding may indeed be more sig-

---

[7] Cf. Wisd 8:21; 9:17; 3 Ezra 4:59; also Gen 41:16, 38 f. (Joseph); 1 Kgs 3:12, 28, etc. (Solomon); Dan 2:19—23 (Daniel), etc.

[8] Nickelsburg, *Jewish Literature*, 60. See further Chapter 7 below; cf. e.g. Hengel, *Judentum*, 246 ff.; Blenkinsopp, *Prophecy and Canon*, 128—132.

[9] Note Isaiah's charge, "Seal תורה among my disciples" (8:16). Ben Sira's grandson places him in the succession of the writers of Scripture: cf. προήχθη καὶ αὐτός, Prologue 12.

[10] Cf. the poetic parallelism with 24:32, παιδείαν ὡς ὄρθρον. Contrast, however, the Syriac *bnbywt*': cf. Marböck, "Sir., 38,24—39,11", 309.

nificantly characterized by his view of priests and sages.[11] As Stadelmann shows, another reason for this reluctance is Ben Sira's view of the *function* of Biblical prophecy: the Biblical prophets bridge the gap between on the one hand the union of spriritual and secular rule under the "trilogy of priests" in the desert (Moses, Aaron, Phinehas: Ch. 45), and on the other hand the restoration of this union after the exile (Zerubbabel, Jeshua, Nehemiah,[12] and ultimately Simon son of Onias (Ch. 50). The mission of the prophets was to guard the patriarchal heritage in the meantime.[13] Given this limited view of the function of the prophets, Stadelmann concludes, Ben Sira clearly no longer counts himself as one of their number.[14]

3. Sapiential Inspiration

3.1. Development

In the Old Testament, man was initially encouraged to "seek" wisdom actively; he was promised success in his search if it was conducted in the fear of the Lord.[15] But the history of later times brought to bear some of the complexities and problems of the moral world order. As we noted in the Introduction, stress was increasingly laid both on the elusiveness of wisdom (Eccl, Job, Prov 30:1−4) and on God's sovereign grace in bestowing it.[16] Wisdom is now prayed for (2 Chr 1:10; Wisd 7:7 ff.; Sir 51:13 ff., etc.) rather than independently sought; and she is bestowed as a special gift of grace rather than merely "found".[17] God's dispensation of wisdom is restricted ethnically by being

---

[11] Thus Stadelmann, *Ben Sira*, 265; cf. 237 f. *Pace* Maier, *Mensch*, 39 ("In Form und Bewußtsein lebt hier echtes Prophetentum weiter"); similarly Hengel, *Judentum*, 247 f.; van Imschoot, "*Sagesse*", 34; Peters, *Sirach*, 206. Note the importance of Simon son of Onias II in Sir 50, crowning the שבח אבות.

[12] Sir 49:11−13; cf. Ezra 3:2; Hag 1:12; 2:23; also 3 Ezra 6:1 f.

[13] Note also the idea of prophets as *sent* by wisdom (Luke 11:49). Bousset (*Religion*, 346) cites Luke 7:35 in support of the prophets as the *children* of wisdom.

[14] Stadelmann, Ben Sira, 265 f.; cf. also 214−216, 149−167. He argues specifically (215) against Snaith, "Importance", 68, who fails to recognize the continuity of the priestly motif; and (266) against Maier's claim (*Mensch*, 163) of a shared, living prophetic consciousness between Ben Sira and Qumran.

[15] Prov 1:20−23, 2:4, 8:17, 15:14, etc.

[16] E.g. Prov 1:23; 2:6, etc.; Job 32:7−9; 38−42. Note also Eccl 12:11 LXX: λόγοι σοφῶν ... ἐδόθησαν ἐκ ποίμενος ἑνός. Cf. e.g. Sir 1:6−10; EpArist 267, 270; Wisd 7:7, 8:21; 9:1 ff., esp. 9:4, 17, etc.

[17] Cf. Rylaarsdam, *Revelation*, 73. However, with that proviso, a search for God is still encouraged, e.g. Wisd 1:1 f.; Sir 14:22.

granted only to Jews (viz. in the Torah);[18] it is, moreover, only *some* Jews who receive it (viz. the inspired).[19]

In Sirach this last trend can be observed quite clearly e.g. in Chapter 39, where the author distinguishes between two types of scribes, the ordinary (39:1–5) and the inspired (39:6–8).[20] Wisdom, too, distinguishes between those who have received the divine dispensation of the Holy Spirit and those who have not (9:16f.): knowledge of the will of God is always a privileged gift of revelation, of inspired wisdom.[21] The Holy Spirit or spirit of understanding (πνεῦμα συνέσεως), then, is not simply a professional mark of the scribe but a sign of extraordinary divine giftedness.[22]

Three dimensions of such inspiration merit further reflection, viz. its relation to the cult, to the Law, and to the Spirit.

3.2. Liturgy and Revelation

This topic is of significance primarily in the book of Sirach. Two observations spring to mind: one, the relative emphasis placed on the priesthood; and the other, the apparent revelatory function of liturgical praise.

3.2.1. *Priesthood.* Sir 33:3 reads, "A man of understanding will trust in the law; for him the law is as dependable as an inquiry by means of Urim." It is particularly relevant that the Torah's significance for the scribe should here be compared with the Urim and Thummim, i.e. the Old Testament instrument of high-priestly divination and prophecy[23] (cf. 24:10f.: the Torah's original abode is the Temple in Jerusalem). This passage (cf. 45:10) need not imply that the Urim were still in use in Ben Sira's own day;[24] indeed a common view was that their operation ceased with the exile.[25] However, as e.g. Bammel and Stadelmann have argued, there are sufficient indications to show that at least some form of priestly or Levitical "prophecy" continued in the post-exilic age.[26]

---

[18] E.g. Bar 3:9–4:4; Sir 24:8; Wisd 18:4; EpArist 200; m. Abot 1:1 ff. See below.

[19] Fichtner, *Altorientalische Weisheit*, 121.

[20] Cf. Stadelmann, *Ben Sira*, 219 ff.

[21] Cf. Volz, *Geist*, 102 f.; Larcher, *Sagesse*, 2:602.

[22] Cf. Maier, *Mensch*, 37; also Stadelmann, *Ben Sira*, 234. For the relationship of Wisdom and Spirit in the book of Wisdom cf. Larcher, *Sagesse*, 2:602 f.; *Études*, 363 f.

[23] For the link with prophecy see Ezra 2:63; Neh 7:65; 3 Ezra 5:40 (with 1 Macc 4:46; 14:41); and see Chapter 5 below.

[24] *Pace* Perdue, *Wisdom*, 209.

[25] See Ezra 2:63; Neh 7:65; and cf. p. 85 n. 22 below.

[26] Bammel, "ΑΡΧΙΕΡΕΥΣ", 351 ff.; Stadelmann, *Ben Sira*, 260–262. Cf. Josephus, *Ant* 3:218; TLevi 8:2, 9 ff. Qumran's charismatically gifted Teacher of Righteousness was a priest, 1 QpHab 2:8. See also John 11:51.

Other indications of the importance of the priesthood occur in Sir 7:29–31 and esp. in the "praise of fathers" (Sir 44 ff.). Although Ben Sira was not a priest,[27] Stadelmann rightly argues that even as a scribe (indeed *qua* "inspired" scribe) Ben Sira must be understood in a liturgical setting: "Im vormakkabäischen Priesterstaat steht auch der Schriftgelehrte in der priesterlichen Tradition."[28]

3.2.2. *Liturgy.* Sir 15:9 f. introduces the idea of a wise man's hymn of praise as "sent from the Lord" (παρὰ κυρίου ἀπεστάλη).[29] In Chapter 24, Wisdom comes to earth at God's behest to make her dwelling in the cult at Jerusalem: "In the holy tabernacle I ministered before him, and so I was established in Zion" (24:10).[30] What is more, if the distinction between a charismatic and a non-charismatic scribe in 39:1–8 holds true, 15:9 f. would there be further corroborated: while the ordinary sage expresses a prayer of supplication (δεηθήσεται, 39:5), it is the *inspired* sage of 39:6 who brings forth independent[31] confessing praise (ἐξομολογήσεται).[32] This notion of "prophetic praise" is not new in Ben Sira but occurs already in the Chronicler: the sons of Asaph and others were to "prophesy [*Q*: הנבאים] with lyres, harps, and cymbals.... [They] prophesied under the direction of the king ... in giving thanks and praising the Lord."[33] Certainly the idea of liturgical praise as prophetic and revealed by God Himself sheds interesting light on the reasons for the inclusion of the Psalms in the Old Testament "canon", possibly as early as Ben Sira's own century.[34]

---

[27] Note the injunctions of Snaith, "Love", 167–174; and Marböck, "Sir., 38,24–39,11", 306.

[28] Stadelmann, *Ben Sira*, 267; cf. 259. See also 4 Macc 5:35, ἱερωσύνη καὶ νομοθεσίας ἐπιστήμη.

[29] Cf. Perdue *Wisdom*, 204; also Stadelmann, *Ben Sira*, 243; and cf. e.g. Psa 51:15. Noting the use of נחלקה in 15:9, Marböck, "Sir., 38,24–39,11", 305 observes that hymns of praise seem to be understood as the divinely appointed portion of the sage, whose task it is to teach them.

[30] Perdue (*Wisdom*, 190) actually deduces from this passage an identification of wisdom with cult.

[31] Note the repeated αὐτός (cf. Volz, *Geist*, 102 n. 1).

[32] Cf. Volz, *Geist*, 102.

[33] 1 Chr 25:1–3 (cf. also e.g. 2 Kgs 3:15; 2 Chr 29:30). Cf. Blenkinsopp, *History*, 254; also Stadelmann, *Ben Sira*, 261.

[34] Note the tripartite formula of Sir Prologue; also 47:8–10; and cf. p. 47 n. 29 f. above. Revealed praise is common in the apocalypses (note esp. 2 Bar 54:7); see also *LAB* 32:14; 11 QPsa 18:5 f. (Psa 154 = Syriac Psalm II); OdSol 6:1 f.; 14:8; 16:5; Luke 1:67–79 (N.B. προεφήτευσε λέγων, κτλ.); Acts 2:4; 10:44, 46; 1 Cor 14:26.

3.3. The Torah

An important part of the Jewish *nationalization* of wisdom theology was the latter's *concentration* on the Law.[35] Just as the wisdom tradition increasingly identified the God of creation with the God of Israel, so also the observable laws of the cosmos came to be seen as most perfectly expressed in the Torah. While no doubt the origins of this idea can be observed within the Old Testament,[36] its full development occurred in the post-canonical Jewish writings: the giving of the Torah now coincides with Wisdom's condescension to make her dwelling in Israel.[37] This increasing equation of Wisdom and Torah is today universally recognized as a formative trend in postbiblical wisdom literature.[38]

This phenomenon is admittedly less obvious in Wisd (as is the localization of wisdom in the cult[39]), possibly because of the apologetic concern to present the figure of Wisdom in opposition to Isis, the popular Hellenistic wisdom goddess.[40] The greater emphasis here is on God's Wisdom expressed in His redemptive *providence* for Israel (Chapters 10–19; e.g. 12:18; 16:21; 19:22). The history of Israel becomes the paradigm of God's provident presence; miracles serve as its didactic and parabolic illustrations (while also reminding Israel of the commandments, 16:6).[41]

---

[35] Fichtner, *Altorientalische Weisheit*, 94–96; Rylaarsdam, *Revelation*, 19 f.

[36] E.g. Psa 19; Job 28; Prov 29:18.

[37] Sir 1:15 (?), 17:11–14; 24:23; Bar 3:36–4:1. Cf. Bertram, "Wesen", 282: in Sir, Wisdom as Torah represents an embodiment of revelation.

[38] E.g. Bertholet, *Theologie,* 2:177; Fichtner, *Altorientalische Weisheit*, 94–96; Ringgren, Word, 110; Küchler, *Weisheitstraditionen*, 547 f.; Marböck, "Gesetz", 5 f.; Nickelsburg, *Jewish Literature*, 61. A summary list of references is offered by Schnabel, *Law*, 162 f. E. Jacob ("Wisdom", 256; cf. Stadelmann, *Ben Sira*, 250 n. 1) suggests that the identification of Wisdom and Torah may take its point of departure in Deut 4:6. Of particular interest in this regard is Gerald T. Sheppard's *Wisdom as a Hermeneutical Construct:* reversing earlier approaches, his model takes its *starting point* in Sir and Bar, and from there works its way back to an understanding of the purpose of canonical wisdom.

[39] Harrington, *"Wisdom"*, 182 f. contrasts Sir 24:10 f. with Wisd 7:24 etc. But note the cultic setting of 1 Kgs 3/2 Chr 1, on which Wisd 7:7 ff. is modelled.

[40] Knox, *"Wisdom"*; idem, *Gentiles*, 56 ff., 68 ff.; also Hengel, *Judentum*, 285 ff.; Reese, *Influence*, esp. 46–49; Mack, *Logos*, passim; Kloppenborg, "Isis". Partly for such apologetic reasons the picture of righteousness and the persecuted righteous man in Wisd 1–5 is painted in terms of wisdom and moral virtues (4:1 ff. ἀρετή) rather than of loyalty to Torah and halakhah: Reese, *Influence*, 110 and passim. But although "the Spirit of the Lord has filled the world" (1:7), even this description retains its Jewish traits: 2:12 f.; 4:10–15; 4:20 ff. And *ceteris paribus* the archetypal sage is of course *Solomon* (7:1 ff.; 9:1 ff.), while 2:12; 6:4, 18; 16:6; 18:4, 9 safeguard a firm connection with the Torah.

[41] Cf. Eising, "Geschichtsbetrachtung", 30; Heinisch, *Weisheit*, 345; Sweet, "Theory", 120 ff.; Maneschg, "Gott", 220 and passim; Heinemann, "Kontroverse", 190. A similar perspective on national providence prevails e.g. in Jdt 13:11, 14; 16:2 ff.

The climax of the trend to identify Wisdom and Torah is perhaps to be found in the Mishnah tractate *Abot*, where, so to speak, a complete *communicatio idiomatum* has taken place.[42] But a similar narrowing of creational wisdom to its focus in the Torah (and partly *vice versa*, an expansion of the breadth of the Law to include the cosmos) occurs in Sirach, Baruch, and other works.[43]

More specifically, for the inspired scribe the *locus* of present-day divine revelation is his exegesis of the Torah, as we saw. Ben Sira speaks of his teaching as a water channel irrigating a garden (Sirach 24:30f.). This is in fact the same image used of Qumran's Teacher of Righteousness and his inspired exegesis (see Chapter 2 on 1 QH 8; CD 6:3f.). Compared to its likely origin in Psalm 1, this simile represents a further development.[44] In that Psalm, the student of the Torah is "like a tree planted by water channels"; here, Ben Sira actually claims that his teaching is a water channel taking its source in the river of Torah (v. 30a), but then in turn becoming a river and ocean in itself (v. 31b). In other words, he asserts a derivative revelatory status for his exposition of the Torah.[45]

3.4. The Spirit

After the topics discussed so far, this issue may be dealt with in brief. Of the present material it is primarily the book of Wisdom which speaks of the Holy Spirit's activity as a present reality.[46] In a general sense "the Spirit of the Lord has filled the world" (1:7);[47] but it is only if and when God specifically sends forth His Spirit that a man may acquire wisdom (9:17). In Ben Sira, it is particularly the scholar of Torah who is filled with the "spirit of understanding" (39:6).[48]

---

[42] Cf. Fichtner, *Altorientalische Weisheit*, 96: "Alles, was die *Prov*[erbia] von der *Weisheit* gesagt haben, gilt für die Pirke Aboth von der *Thora*. . . ." See e.g. Prov 3:16/m.Abot 6:7, etc.

[43] Sir 24:3–29; Bar 3:29ff.; TNaph 3:2; 1 En 2:1–5:4, etc.

[44] Stadelmann (*Ben Sira*, 255f.) recognizes a break in the metaphor; but he does not address its significance for Ben Sira's understanding of revelation.

[45] *Pace* Snaith, "Importance", 69 who denies any claim to divine authority in Ben Sira. Cf. further m.Abot 6:1.

[46] See also Fichtner, *Weisheit*, 39.

[47] This notion may show a certain Stoic influence, but no direct dependence; cf. Gilbert, "Raisons", 160.

[48] In Num 11:16–30 the 70 elders receive of the Spirit which is on Moses, and prophesy; Deut 1:9–16 relates the same incident as the appointment of *sages* (v. 13: אנשים חכמים ונבנים וידעים). M.Abot 1:1 cites the זקנים as transmitters of Torah. Cf. also Davies, "Tradition", 31; and see Chapter 7 below.

It is widely recognized that the book of Wisdom maintains at least a functional, if not an absolute identity between the Spirit and the figure of Wisdom. This is clear from such passages as 1:4f. or 9:17, where most would agree that the two entities are interchangeable.[49] In this regard the close link between σοφία and δόξα[50] may be significant: the latter appears to approximate the divine *shekhinah*,[51] which in the Rabbinic period came in turn to be closely identified with the Holy Spirit.[52]

4. "Mysteries" and their Revelation

The key texts are again Wisdom and Sirach;[53] it is particularly the former which speaks of the "mysteries of God".

4.1. Wisdom

Having described the evil plotting of ungodly men against the righteous (1:16–2:20), the author writes,

> Thus they reasoned, but they were led astray,
> For their wickedness blinded them,
> And they did not know the mysteries of God [μυστήρια Θεοῦ],
> Nor hope for the wages of holiness,
> Nor discern the prize for blameless souls;
> For God created man for incorruption,
> And made him in the image of his own eternity. . . .

The syntactic parallelism indicates that the "mysteries" here denote eternal life as the reward of the righteous.[54] Elsewhere the mysteries which God (7:17)

---

[49] E.g. Bousset, *Religion*, 400; Deane, *Wisdom*, 161; Drummond, *Philo*, 1:215–217; Georgi, *Weisheit*, 403; Heinisch, *Weisheit*, 189; van Imschoot, "*Sagesse*", 37; Larcher, *Études*, 363ff.; idem, *Sagesse*, 2:602f.; Rylaarsdam, *Revelation*, 103; Schoemaker, "רוח", 40; Winston, *Wisdom*, 102 (he also refers to 1 Enoch 49:3).

[50] E.g. Wisd 7:25; 9:10f.; cf. Sir 4:13; 6:29, 31.

[51] See Raurell, "Doxa", 374f. He cites 3 En 5:4 to illustrate the link between "glory" and *shekhinah*; we might add the close similarity of the two terms in the Targums. Cf. already the function of God's glory in the OT.

[52] See Chapter 7 below; and e.g. Blenkinsopp, "Prophecy", 261 n. 105 (with references).

[53] Cf. also 2 Macc 2:7f.: the Temple furnishings, hidden by Jeremiah on Mt. Sinai [m.Shek 6:1f.: the Temple Mount; *Memar Marqah* 3:4 and Josephus, *Ant* 18:85: Mt. Gerizim], will at last be disclosed by God Himself. See M. Collins, "Hidden Vessels", 97–116; Böhl, "Legende", 63–80.

[54] Cf. 3:1ff., 4:20ff.; also e.g. 1 En 103:2[ff.] (with Winston, *Wisdom*, 120f.).

or wisdom (7:22) teaches can be the secrets of nature and cosmology (7:17–22). Both categories are familiar from our previous two chapters, and will repeatedly be encountered below.

Divine mysteries can be known only by revelation.[55] But in Wisdom there is no reason not to disclose them to others: the mysteries are hidden merely insofar as their present transcendence makes them hard to fathom, especially for the unrighteous. In Wisd 6:22 the author confirms this exoteric reading of "mystery": "I will tell you what wisdom is and how she came to be, and I will hide no secrets [μυστήρια] from you. ...."[56] Wisdom is both initiate (μύστις, 8:4) and mystagogue into this knowledge of God: she teaches both what is secret (κρυπτά) and what is manifest (ἐμφανῆ).[57] She is the source of the virtues (8:7) and exercises the function of prophecy (8:8): "She knows the things of old, and infers the things to come . . .; she has foreknowledge of signs and wonders and of the outcome of seasons and times."

On at least two occasions the book of Wisdom hints at the theme of the revelation of a hidden heavenly reality. Thus in 9:1–18 (cf. 7:7, 17–22) Solomon, the paradigmatic recipient of the divine gift, prays for God's wisdom: "Send her forth from the holy heavens, and from the throne of thy glory send her, that she may be with me and toil, and that I may learn what is pleasing" (9:10).[58] The second, even more striking text is 18:14f.: "For while gentle silence enveloped all things . . ., thy all-powerful word leaped from heaven, from the royal throne, into the midst of the land that was doomed. . . ." The theme of heavenly revelation out of silence is common in ancient Jewish thought and recurs e.g. in Rom 16:25f., a passage discussed more fully in Chapter Eleven below.

4.2. Sirach

Ben Sira's attitude seems somewhat different. "Wisdom is not manifest [φανερά] to many" (6:22), and the untrained (?) should not seek out hidden things (κρυπτά/נסתרות) too difficult for them (3:22; similar anti-esotericism prevails

---

[55] Cf. Larcher, *Sagesse*, 1:264f.

[56] The note of anti-pagan polemic is unmistakable; a negative allusion to the mystery religions is suggested e.g. by Deane, *Wisdom*, 143; Larcher, *Sagesse*, 2:435; also Brown, *Mystery*, 10. The author's liberal attitude also reflects earlier Israelite wisdom traditions (e.g. Prov 8; but also Isa 45:19; 48:6, 16): Larcher, *Sagesse*, 2:426.

[57] Wisd 7:21f.; cf. Deut 29:28 and our discussion of נגלות and נסתרות at Qumran. Overall the influence of Hellenistic mystery terminology is limited and superficial (cf. Larcher, *Sagesse*, 1:264). Only once (Wisd 14:15, 23) does the word μυστήριον (pl.) designate (and condemn) pagan ritual.

[58] Miranda, *Vater*, 93, compares Paul's notion of revealed mysteries. Cf. also 7:21f.

in 20:30; cf. 11:4).[59] To meddle in the mysteries of wisdom is strictly reserved for those who are skilled and qualified in the study of the proper channels of wisdom, viz. in Torah scholarship.[60]

However, Wisdom is nevertheless said to reveal her secrets (τὰ κρυπτὰ αὐτῆς, מסתרים: 4:18; cf. Job 11:6) to those who seek her, especially to the humble. Of special interest in this respect is 3:19, which in the Hebrew reads (Heb), רבים רחמי אלהים ולענוים יגלה סודו; this text, although absent from the major textual witnesses of the Septuagint, is also supported by the Peshitta and Sinaiticus *suppletor* (πολλοί εἰσιν ὑψηλοὶ καὶ ἐπίδοξοι, ἀλλὰ πράεσιν ἀποκαλύπτει τὰ μυστήρια[61] αὐτοῦ.[62] Wisdom's disclosure of divine mysteries occurs in the study of Torah, since that is where the scribe "meditates on the Lord's secrets [ἀποκρύφοις]" (39:7).[63] This position, too, is quite consistent e.g. with the DSS;[64] Stadelmann argues for a close proximity of sapiential, prophetic, and apocalyptic literature in this regard.[65]

The scribe's meditation on the mysteries of Torah probably points in the first place to revelation in the halakhic realm. But eschatological mysteries do occur e.g. in Sir 48:25: Isaiah "showed what was to occur to the end of time, and the hidden things (ἀπόκρυφα) before they came to pass" (cf. 42:18 f.). Sir 23:1−33 speaks of the unfathomable secrets (ἀπόκρυφα, v. 32; cf. 43:32; Job 26:14) of creation, and in 49:8 there is even a fleeting reference to Ezekiel's vision of the throne chariot. Thus, special divine revelation takes as its chief object the secrets of Torah, but it also includes the hidden plan of history and the unfathomable wonders of the cosmos.

Wisdom and Ben Sira both treat contemporary revelation in terms of national concerns such as the Torah as well as the history of Israel and its archetypal

---

[59] Lebram ("ΜΥΣΤΗΡΙΟΝ", 322−324) argues that Tob 12:7 ("It is good to guard the secret [μυστήριον] of a king, but gloriously to reveal [ἀποκαλύπτειν] the works of God") means that one must carefully guard the *secrets* of "speculative" wisdom teaching (as belonging to the king, viz. Solomon), while at the same time publicly praising and making known the works of God. Cf. Chapters 2, 4, 7 below.

[60] Cf. also Skehan/di Lella, *Ben Sira*, 160 f.

[61] Note that, despite the plural μυστήρια, סוד as always in the OT is singular. The DSS use the plural once (1 QS 4:6).

[62] On the significance of the different textual readings see Prato, "Lumière", 330−332. Skehan/di Lella, *Ben Sira*, 159 suggest that v. 19b underlies the sayings of Matt 11:25, 29. *Pace* Böhlig, *Mysterion*, 18, who asserts that Sir 3:19 is determined purely by Hellenistic ideas.

[63] Cf. 14:21; m.Abot 6:1. *Pace* Harrington, "Wisdom", 185, who denies an interest in mystery and interpretation in Sir. Cf. further Brown, *Mystery*, 9 f. (though the allusion to the study of oral tradition is perhaps not yet as clear as he would have it).

[64] N.B. the scribe studies the prophets (39:1), the subtleties (39:2 Peshitta *bd'myqn*; cf. below, Chapter 9, on 1 Cor 2:10) of parables, and the hidden meanings (39:3 ἀπόκρυφα: long before the DSS evidence Smend, *Weisheit*, 353 conjectured נסתרות) of proverbs.

saints. Ben Sira's view of revelation is more obviously Torah-centred, since he localizes a proper revelation of divine secrets in a qualified and inspired exposition of the Law (thus foreshadowing Rabbinic ideas). In the probably Alexandrian book of Wisdom, the disclosure of mysteries is received by righteous seekers of wisdom in every generation. This is a perspective not unlike that of Philo.

---

[65] Stadelmann, *Ben Sira*, 244 f.

Chapter Four

Philo

1. Introduction

"The complexities of Philo make a just estimate of his work hard to achieve."[1] Though strongly committed to his Jewish faith and opposed to religious syncretism (e.g. *Spec* 1:319 ff.), Philo of Alexandria (c. 15 B. C. – A. D. 45) was a man who liked to clothe even his Jewish religious discourse in the refined philosophical idiom of the Hellenistic age. At least in this respect, he may be the most thoroughly "Hellenized" of the Jewish writers under consideration; Eusebius (*HE* 2.4.3) cites reports that Philo surpassed his contemporaries μάλιστα τὴν κατὰ Πλάτωνα καὶ Πυθαγόραν ἐζηλωκὼς ἀγωγήν. His mother tongue was very likely Greek, and he does not seem to have known Hebrew.[2] What we hope to find in Philo (and later in Josephus), therefore, is a model of meaningful speech about revelation in a Hellenistic setting.

The following paragraphs discuss Philo's view of the knowledge of God, of inspiration and "prophecy", of the Torah, and of mysteries.

2. Epistemology and Knowledge of God

Philo, guided as he is by philosophical considerations, addresses himself to the question of revelation largely in an oblique fashion, in terms of the know-

---

[1] Thus Chadwick, "Philo", 154.
[2] Cf. Nikiprowetzky, *Commentaire*, 50–81; Rokeah, "Onomasticon", 81 f.; and see Schürer/Vermes, *HJPAJC*, 3:874 n. 12.

ledge of God.[3] In order to acquire a grasp of this complex idea, we must begin by looking at Philo's epistemology.[4]

Philo distinguishes sense perception from noumenal perception. Of these two, the latter is considered superior;[5] it, too, however, is in turn subdivided into a "lower" and a "higher" kind of knowledge. The "higher" knowledge, albeit still imperfect and dependent on information from the senses, permits the perception of God's existence by a rational inference from the observation of His created works, διὰ σκίας τὸν θεὸν καταλαμβάνουσι.[6]

However, since God is invisible and incorporeal, true knowledge of Him can only be attained by the third and highest category, "knowledge of the mind" achieved by contemplating the incorporeal without the agency of the senses.[7] The mind (διάνοια) apart from sense perception is able to survey

> the nature of things immaterial, which sense is unable to descry. For we may say that it achieves all the keenness of vision, which an eye can have, without needing any adventitious light, itself a star and, we may say, a copy and likeness of the heavenly company.[8]

So far, Philo's threefold division of epistemology into sensation, science, and knowledge of the incorporeal ideas hardly differs from the model espoused by Plato.[9] It is this third type of knowledge, the mind's knowledge of the ideas, which corresponds to what Philo calls "prophecy".[10]

Philo repeatedly stresses that God in His essence cannot be known by the human mind. Thus he puts these words in the mouth of Moses,

> But what Thou art in Thy essence (οὐσίαν) I desire to understand, yet find in no part of the All any to guide me to this knowledge. . . . For as knowledge of the light

---

[3] Sandmel in fact concludes that revelation has for Philo become an act of man, viz. in the ascent to God: "Philo", 24 f. This shift from "divine revelation" to "knowledge of God" is a general trait of Hellenistic thought: cf. Seckler, "Verbum", 222. On the other hand, of course, it is true that Philo might well have found himself encouraged by revelatory terminology of "knowing God" in the OT (Botterweck, "ידע", 500–510) and esp. LXX (Bultmann, "γινώσκω", 699 f.).

[4] For the following description cf. Wolfson 2:1–72; Mühlenberg, "Offenbarung", 1–18.

[5] E.g. *LG* 2 ("For the eyes of the body discern what is manifest and close at hand, but reason reaches to the unseen and the future"). Cf. Mühlenberg, "Offenbarung", 9–11.

[6] *LA* 3:99; cf. *Spec* 1:41. N.B. as *Praem* 39 shows, it is only God's existence (ὅτι ἐστιν), not His essence (ὅ ἐστιν) which can thus be perceived. Evident in creation are only God's Powers (δυνάμεις): e.g. *Post* 14; *QE* 2:51. Cf. Hegermann, "Philon", 361; Früchtel, *Vorstellungen*, 155; n. 37 below.

[7] Wolfson 2:5.

[8] Philo, *Virt* 12; cf. *Gig* 60 f., *QG* 1:40.

[9] E.g. *Timaeus* 37C, 52A; *Republic* 6:510Bff.; cf. Wolfson 2:59.

[10] *Mos* 2:6, 187; cf. Wolfson 2:10.

does not come by any other source but what itself supplies, so Thou alone canst tell me of Thyself.[11]

Even in contemplation unaided by sense perception, νοῦς cannot ascend to an immediate, direct knowledge of God Himself, God in His οὐσία.[12] Moreover, the limited perception which is possible must be initiated by God Himself (e.g. *Abr* 80; *Post* 15 f.).[13]

Since as "prophecy" this highest type of knowledge is often described as inspired and ecstatic in character,[14] it seems desirable now to investigate the relationship between divine revelation and Philo's notion of prophecy and inspiration.

3. Inspiration and Prophecy

Wolfson likens Philo's idea of prophetic ecstasy to Plato's "philosophic frenzy" (*Phaedrus* 244B ff.).[15] According to this view there are four kinds of frenzy (μανία): mantic or prophetic (divination), priestly (magic etc.), poetic or legislative (the Muses), and finally philosophical frenzy (the contemplation of ideas, which is achieved by way of "recollection", ἀνάμνησις). Unlike Plato, Philo does not confine his use of "prophecy" to mantic frenzy, but (like the LXX) applies it to all four of Plato's categories.[16] At least in this semantic respect, then, Philo's notion of "prophecy" as the highest kind of knowledge transcends the Platonic pattern.[17]

One special case of such prophetic knowledge can be discerned in Philo's description of "heaven-sent" dreams[18] in *De Somniis*. Following (in reversed or-

---

[11] *Spec* 1:41 f.; cf. e.g. *Mut* 7 ("we have in us no organ by which we can envisage it [sc. τὸ ὄν, i.e. God], neither in sense, for it is not perceptible by sense (αἴσθησιν), nor yet in mind (νοῦν)"); *LG* 6; *Post* 15.

[12] Cf. Chadwick, "Philo", 148, who refers to *Spec* 1:20; *Mut* 7; *Immut* 62; *QG* 4:26; *QE* 2:45.

[13] Cf. Mühlenberg, "Offenbarung", 16.

[14] Cf. esp. *Opif* 69 f.; *Spec* 4:49; and see Chadwick, "Philo", 151, who also cites *Her* 68, 249 ff.; *Mut* 139; *QG* 4:196; *Spec* 1:65; *LA* 1:82, 3:43 f. Note in this regard the potentially suggestive use of ἐξίστημι in Exod 19:18 LXX.

[15] Wolfson 2:10; cf. Lampe, *God*, 54 f.

[16] Thus Wolfson 2:14−16, 60. On magic and divination in Philo cf. further Berchman, "Arcana", 403−428.

[17] Hecht "Scripture", 148 ff., citing a then unpublished paper by D. Winston, endorses a distinction in Philo between "hermeneutical prophecy" (involving interpretation) and "ecstatic" prophecy (predicting the future). However, I cannot see how this is "fundamental to ... Philo's concept of revelation" (ibid., 149). Philo himself does not make this distinction: see esp. *Spec* 4:49 in context (interpretation as ecstatic). Cf. further Frey, "Révélation", 495−497.

[18] θεόπεμπτοι ὄνειροι: *Som* 1:1, 190; 2:1; cf. 1:133, 2:113.

der) the threefold distinction of Posidonius,[19] Philo speaks of the first type of dream as that by which God on His own initiative grants visions to man in his sleep.[20] Unfortunately this category of dreams is only fully treated in the lost first part of *De Somniis*;[21] the extant treatise deals with dreams initiated not by God but by the mind of man reaching out to become divinely inspired.[22]

Prophecy, then, is characterized e.g. as ὅσα μὴ λογισμῷ δύναται καταλαμβάνειν:[23] God takes over the mind of a person and (by His spirit) speaks to it what cannot be perceived by sensation or pure reason.[24] Although prophecy occurs "outside the mind",[25] nevertheless this divine takeover in inspiration need not always mean total passivity and the abdication of reason.[26]

---

[19] Cicero, *De Divinatione* 1:64: (i) the soul's clairvoyance because of its kinship with the Gods, (ii) contact with immortal souls (demons) in the air, and (iii) direct communication of the gods with the dreamer. Cf. Bréhier, *Idées*, 186; Wolfson 2:57; Delling, "Wunder", 125. Colson in *Philo*, 5:593f. rightly considers Philo's classification to be a significant modification of Posidonius.

[20] *Som* 1:1 (τὸ θεῖον ... κατὰ τὴν ἰδίαν ἐπιβολὴν τὰς ἐν τοῖς ὕπνοις ἐπιπέμπειν φαντασίας).

[21] See *Som* 1:1; cf. Wolfson 2:57f.; Delling, "Wunder", 125.

[22] Wolfson 2:58: such dreams are initiated by the Logos.

[23] *Mos* 2:6; and further, ibid.: "For prophecy finds its way to what the mind fails to reach." Cf. also *Mos* 2:187.

[24] Cf. e.g. *Her* 259ff.; *Spec* 1:65, 4:49; *QG* 3:9f., 4:90, etc. Wolfson 2:28: "a new kind of knowledge, entirely independent of sensation, a knowledge imported from another region by the divine spirit and instilled into the rational soul of man...." See also Sandmel, "Apocalypse", 385.

Another, very different notion of spirit takes its point of departure from Gen 2:7 (LXX?): at creation God's πνεῦμα is breathed into man, thus conferring on his soul the capacity of a conception (ἔννοιαν) of the divine nature (*LA* 1:37f.). God does not thereby reveal Himself to man, but stamps man's mind "with the impress of the powers that are within the scope of its understanding" (LA 1:38).

[25] ἐνθουσιᾷ γεγονὼς ἐν ἀγνοίᾳ, μετανισταμένου μὲν τοῦ λογισμοῦ καὶ παρακεχωρηκότος τὴν τῆς ψυχῆς ἀκρόπολιν (*Spec* 4:49). Cf. Delling, "Wunder", 123; *pace* Hecht, "Scripture", 149.

[26] This point is now carefully argued by Piñero-Sáenz, "Concepciones", 223–233; cf. also Burkhardt, *Inspiration*, esp. 211ff. Philo himself considers the phenomenon of "prophecy" to be something of a paradox: note esp. his use of the term "sober drunkenness" (μέθη νηφαλία/νηφοῦσα) in *Opif* 70, *Fug* 166, *LA* 3:82, *Prob* 13, *Mos* 1:187 etc. (an oxymoron apparently derived from a pre-Gnostic dualism, analogous (but unrelated) to certain Dionysiac ideas; see Lewy, *Sobria Ebrietas,* esp. 62f., 89f., 101–103; also Chadwick, "Philo", 150 n. 4).

I remain to be persuaded of Winston's neat distinction between "prophecy" (ecstatic) and "inner intuitive illumination" (which does not in the same way bypass the mind): "Was Philo a Mystic?", 23ff. The appearance of a fully systematic philosophy is perhaps deceptive: here as elsewhere the absence of any specifically philosophical orientation in Philo's *text* (Scripture) is bound to rupture any "system", and calls for due acknowledgement (cf. Morris in Schürer/Vermes, *HJPAJC*, 3.2:879f.). Drummond, *Philo*, 2:10, writes, "I have thought it better to retain Philo's own vagueness of treatment than to as-

On the occasion of the people's hearing the voice of God at Sinai (*Decal* 35), Philo explains that "the hearing of the mind possessed by God (ἐνθέου διανοίας) makes the first advance and goes out to meet the spoken words with the keenest rapidity." The whole passage stands out as an extraordinary description of God's empirically perceptible (miraculously audible: *Decal* 33−35; visible: *Decal* 46 f.; cf. Exod 20:18) revelation of the Decalogue. The "ten words", as in early Judaism elsewhere, are of singular significance as the only revelation given by God directly to all the people,[27] rather than to Moses or another spokesman (*Decal* 18 f.). Philo's treatment here shows at least a general inclination to concur with traditional Jewish beliefs about the revelation at Sinai.[28]

It is in theory every worthy man who can receive the ecstasy of the prophet. Philo gives the qualifications as ἀστεῖος, σοφός, and δίκαιος;[29] for all intents and purposes he seems to view himself as a prophet too.[30] "True" and "false" prophecy are distinguished primarily on the basis of whether or not they are given by the one true God,[31] though certain perpetrators of pagan practices are *ipso facto* ψευδοπροφῆται.[32]

The difference between this type of commonly available "prophecy" and that which inspired the Scriptures seems to lie mainly in the simple fact of the latter's canonicity. Wolfson asserts that Philo agrees with the Rabbinic view that prophecy ceased with the last of the canonical prophets − yet only "the kind of prophecy which inspired the teachings contained in the Hebrew Scripture came to an end, so that henceforth no other teachings will have been inspired by the same *kind* of prophecy."[33] But this is to ignore that the Rabbis did not normally refer to the revelatory experiences of their day as "prophecy": it was precisely that term (נבואה/נביא) which at least in its positive use designated the former age of the prophets. For Philo, on the other hand, "prophecy" seems to carry a more general and philosophical connotation, which allows no distinction in principle between canonical and post-canonical instances (cf. above on Wisd 7:27).

---

cribe to him a severity of reasoning which he nowhere attempts." Cf. also Macleod, Review, 219 f.

[27] The ἐκκλησία (*Decal* 32 etc.), but addressing in the second person singular each one individually (*Decal* 37).

[28] Compare e.g. *Decal* 35 with e.g. TN/TPsJ/FT Exod 20:2. Cf. Philo's commitment to the validity of the Torah (*Spec* 1:153 ff.); note further his pilgrimage to Jerusalem (*Prov* 2:64).

[29] *Her* 259 f. Cf. Wolfson 2:47 f. (N.B. he notes that at least revelation by the divine voice also requires the recipient to be of Jewish descent); and Sandmel, "Apocalypse", 385 f.

[30] E.g. *Mig* 34 f.; *Cher* 27; *Som* 2:252; cf. Chadwick, "Philo", 153; Aune, *Prophecy*, 147; Piñero-Sáenz, "Concepciones", 225.

[31] E.g. *Spec* 1:315, 4:48 f.; and see e.g. Delling, "Wunder", 123; Wolfson 1:23.

[32] *Spec* 4:51 (the term is *hapax legomenon* in Philo).

[33] Wolfson 2:52 f.; cf. 54.

Excursus: Philo on the Hiddenness of God

Philo's view of "prophecy" as a kind of mystical[34] communion of the mind with God is the closest we come to a notion of revelation.

But inherent in his idea of revelation as knowledge of God are intractable logical difficulties. Thus on the one hand Philo's Moses as ἀρχιπροφήτης[35] is the foremost example of one on whom the Spirit stays an exceedingly long time (Gig 47); he is even said to be deified in his ascent to Sinai — a type for the highest kind of mystical experience.[36] He enjoys the closest access of all to God. Nevertheless God's answer to Moses's plea for revelation is that He *cannot* reveal Himself to man, and hence His only advice is γνῶθι δὴ σαυτόν (Spec 1:42; cf. Post 13–16). Despite his notion of the Logos and other Powers as mediating forces, Philo cannot bring himself to speak of God's self-revelation.[37] Instead, the (inevitably unsuccessful) quest for God is itself recommended as sufficient.[38] God's hiddenness is of course an important theme in the OT itself (note Philo's text, Exod 33:17ff.). However, what one misses in Philo is the ability to speak *dialectically* about the possibility of a revelation of God — an ability which at least in some measure is still safeguarded in Scripture.[39] In Philo, God can be known, in ascending approximations, only according to His existence (κατὰ τὸ εἶναι), not according to His essence.[40]

---

[34] Thus e.g. Hagner, "Vision", 89–91; Sandmel, "Apocalypse", 386; Goodenough, *Light*, 64. N.B. Dean-Otting, *Journeys*, 106 includes passages like *LA* 3:27, 71, 100 in her discussion of heavenly ascent in Hellenistic Jewish literature. Note also e.g. *Opif* 69–71.

[35] *Mut* 103, 125f.; *Som* 2:189; cf. *Mos* 2:187, *Sac* 130.

[36] *QE* 2:29, 40; *Prob* 43. Cf. e.g. *Sac* 8–10; *Det* 161; *Praem* 43f. See further Goodenough, *Light*, 225–229; Lührmann, *Offenbarungsverständnis*, 53. Elsewhere Philo even addresses a prayer (or merely an invocation?) to Moses as the great hierophant and mystagogue (*Som* 1:164f.). Moses as hierophant (Cerfaux, "Influence", 78f. discerns Orphic influence) occurs also e.g. in *Cher* 49 (Moses and Jeremiah); cf. *Gig* 54; *Virt* 178; *Post* 173. Joseph is a mystic and mystagogue of dreams in *Som* 2:78.

[37] On the Logos and the Powers see e.g. Copleston, *History*, 1.2:20ff.; Sandmel, *Philo*, 94–99. Though definitely inferior to God (part of ὅσα γέγονε, Copleston p. 203), both Logos and Powers remain transcendent. Cf. e.g. *LA* 3:175f.

[38] Cf. esp. *Spec* 1:36ff. ("For nothing is better than to search for the true God, even if the discovery of Him eludes human capacity. . . . The very seeking, even without finding, is felicity in itself") and *LA* 3:47f.; and see Chadwick, "Philo", 149, who also cites *Post* 21 and *Det* 89. We may add as something of a counterbalance that Philo can on occasion sound more optimistic about the possibility of God's self-disclosure; an example would be *Abr* 79f. (where the only limitation is καθ' ὅσον οἷόν τε ἦν ἰδεῖν τὸν βλέποντα), though the issue is there not addressed in the same depth.

[39] E.g. Exod 24:9ff., 3:1ff.; and cultic theophanies such as Isa 6:1ff., etc. No doubt these are *partial* revelations of God: nevertheless they appear to go beyond the answer afforded to Moses by Philo. Cf. also the throne visions of apocalyptic literature.

[40] *Immut* 62; cf. *Praem* 44f.; also *QE* 2:37 (on Exod 24:10 LXX). See further Früchtel, *Vorstellungen*, 156–63; Lührmann, *Offenbarungsverständnis*, 32f.

In Philo, then, belief in revelation appears to be replaced (or at least augmented) by a largely noumenal idea of "knowledge of God". Revelation to a significant extent becomes the action of man.[41] But despite an admission that the deity must aid man's perception, this view of revelation seems handicapped by the denial of God's ability to reveal Himself to man, and man's ability to know God.[42]

4. Scripture

Contemporary Judaism was struggling with the problem of the apparent discontinuation of classical prophecy; nevertheless the DSS and other writings evince a belief that revelation may occur in the interpretation of the Torah and the prophets. Could it be that Philo's view of Scripture opens similar avenues of revelation?

For the rabbis, the Torah was given in its entirety by God to Moses; in the Talmud we read that whoever suspects even the slightest addition to it by Moses holds the Torah in contempt.[43] But for Philo, the author of the Pentateuch is in fact Moses (*Mos* 1:4, etc. — albeit a Moses of almost superhuman standing: cf. n. 36 above). What is more, a brief glance at an appropriate index will show that Philo exhibits little *prima facie* interest in the Prophets and the Writings: citations from the latter are almost negligible compared with the deluge of Pentateuchal references.

The Torah was more than a human book to Philo; he never questions its authority and importance. Its divine qualities are maintained by his elaborate doctrine of prophetic inspiration, and by such characterizations of Scripture as "the oracles which are both words of God and laws given by men whom God loves."[44] The Pentateuchal laws are often described as having the force of com-

---

[41] Thus Sandmel, "Philo", 25. Cf. also Otte, *Sprachverständnis*, 118: knowledge and revelation largely coincide.

[42] See also *LA* 3:206: "Nothing that can give assurance can give positive assurance touching God, for to none has He shown His nature, but He has rendered it invisible to our whole race." Cf. Chadwick, "Philo", 148; also Wolfson 2:110–126 on the unnamability and unknowability of God. Früchtel, *Vorstellungen*, 156–63 considers that in the conflict between the possibility of ecstatic vision and the impossibility of knowing God, the emphasis falls on the latter: "Die Gewichte sind so verteilt, daß die Waagschale der Erkenntnisunfähigkeit nach unten sinkt."

[43] B. Sanh 99a; cf. m. Sanh 10:1; see further Str-B 1:244 ff., 900 ff. N.B. this does not prevent the Rabbis from allowing that while Moses wrote "his own book" it was in fact Joshua who added the last eight verses of the Pentateuch (b. BB 14b); contrast Philo *Mos* 2:291; Josephus *Ant* 4:326.

[44] *Det* 13; cf. Amir, "Philo", 4; also J. Morris in Schürer/Vermes, *HJPAJC*, 3.2:875 f.

mands and charges of the divine word (e.g. *LA* 3:11, 110; *Congr* 85; *Som* 1:191; *Spec* 2:23).

The authority of Prophets and Writings in Philo is more difficult to establish; attempts to do so on the basis of the casual reference in *Cont* 25 ("laws and oracles delivered through the mouth of prophets and psalms, and anything else which fosters and perfects knowledge and piety") must remain conjectural. A number of books are not cited, most notably Daniel, the five *Megillot*, Ezra/Nehemiah, Chronicles.[45] The absence of these, where not simply related to length or content, might be due to a traditional Alexandrian pattern of exegesis[46] or synagogal reading cycle.[47] Nevertheless, Philo does attribute to his quotations from the prophets (incl. the Psalms) a divine authority not unlike that of the Pentateuch.[48]

5. Revelation of Mysteries and Allegorical Interpretation

Given the high authority of the Torah, Philo's exegetical and hermeneutical method merits further inquiry. "The exposition of the sacred scriptures treats the inner meaning conveyed in allegories" (*Cont* 78). Philo perceives two meanings in Scripture: the literal (ῥήτη/φανερὰ ἀπόδοσις: *Abr* 200, 236) and the allegorical, which he regards as the higher meaning suited for trained minds.[49] While he does not want to stress the latter to the exclusion of the former,[50] clearly it is this allegorical method which in his view affords true knowledge of the ideas as they are, "facts... in naked reality."[51]

The straightforward confidence with which Philo arrives at allegorical interpretations is at times reminiscent of the unabashed exegetical aplomb exhibited

---

[45] Not cited according to Leisegang's Index: 2 Sam; the minor prophets except Hos and Zech; the *Megillot*; Dan; Ezra, Neh, 1+2 Chr.

[46] Knox, "Note", 34 suggests an exegetical tradition dating back to a time when the LXX had only been completed for the Pentateuch.

[47] Thus Amir, "Philo", 1 f.

[48] E.g. *Cher* 49; *Plant* 138; *Ebr* 143; *Mig* 196; *Conf* 44, 166; *Mut* 139, 169; *Som* 2:172; *Agr* 50 on the Psalms. Possibly Sir 12:10 (μὴ πιστεύσῃς τῷ ἐχθρῷ σου) is cited in a fragment: λόγιον ἡμᾶς διδάσκει μὴ πιστεύειν ἐχθρῷ (Harris, *Fragments*, 104). But whether this has scriptural status is impossible to establish. Generally regarding the extent and authority of Philo's "canon" cf. Frey, "Révélation", 497 ff.; Schürer/Vermes, *HJPAJC*, 3.2:876 n. 17; and cf. Burkhardt, *Inspiration*, 73–146.

[49] E.g. *Abr* 200, 236; *Plant* 36. Cf. further Wolfson 1:115–138; Christiansen, *Technik*, 134 ff. and passim.

[50] See his famous scolding of purist allegorizers in *Mig* 89–93. Cf. Copleston, *History* 1.2:202; Christiansen, *Technik*, 134 ff.; Fishbane, "Jewish Exegesis", 101.

[51] *Abr* 236; cf. *Cont* 78. Amir, "Philo", 7: the allegorical interpretation is Philo's main concern.

by the Qumran sectarians.[52] Indeed he expresses unreserved admiration for the famous *Therapeutae* (*Cont* 21–39, 64–90), whose exegetical and ascetic practices have led some to regard them as "an Egyptian branch of the Palestinian Essene movement."[53] There is even a measure of correspondence in the terminology used to distinguish between the "obvious" (ῥήτη/φανερά: cf. נגלות at Qumran) and the "hidden" (ὑπόνοια/ἄδηλος:[54] cf. the נסתרות) meanings of Scripture, as well as in the emphasis on "mysteries" (μυστήρια/רזים)[55] which must be kept secret from outsiders (*LA* 1:104; *Sac* 60; *QG* 4:8) and from the unworthy (*LG* 56; *Spec* 1:323; *Fug* 85).

Philo's particular interest, the spiritualizing allegorical reading of Scripture, is referred to as the "greater mysteries" (τὰ μέγαλα μυστήρια, as opposed to the literal interpretation, τὰ μικρὰ μυστήρια).[56] The hidden meanings of Scripture are disclosed by allegory and the resulting mystical quest (*Som* 1:164); here too Philo explicitly agrees with the *Therapeutae* (*Cont* 28; cf. *Prob* 75 on the Essenes).

Phenomenologically, such "revelation" of mysteries of Torah is of course quite unlike that which is found in Palestinian Judaism. Philo's exalted view of allegorical exegesis does make for a close link between Scripture and inspired interpretation.[57] However, his chief interest is in Platonic metaphysical ideas rather than in Palestinian eschatology, cosmology, or halakhah.[58]

What is more, Philo's allegorical mysteries merely *facilitate* the sage's revelatory experience,[59] but are not in themselves the object of revelation. They are a way of enabling greater minds to ascend from the literal meaning, concerned with the physical world, to the noumenal realm of perfection: "He who has

---

[52] Like them, he knows no hermeneutical pluralism (but see perhaps *Spec* 1:214). On the other hand, Philo's interpretations lack a claim to divine authority. And although he refers to the legendary LXX translators as prophets (ἐνθουσιῶντες προεφήτευον, *Mos* 2:37), this does not place both them and Philo himself on the same level of privileged access to the divine truths with Moses (*pace* Hecht, "Scripture", 150 f.).

[53] Thus e.g. Schürer/Vermes *HJPAJC* 2:597. Eusebius *HE* 2.17.1 ff. was convinced the *Therapeutae* were Christians.

[54] E.g. *Abr* 52, 200; *Cont* 78.

[55] *LA* 3:3, 27, 71, 100; *Cher* 48 f.; *Sac* 62; *Immut* 61; *Cont* 25. Moses (*Mos* 2:71) was initiated into the mysteries (ἐμυσταγωγεῖτο) when he received the Torah (cf. the Teacher of Righteousness). See also Sandmel, *Philo*, 87 f., 143 f.; Knox, *Gentiles*, 29–32.

[56] *LA* 3:100; *Cher* 49; *Sac* [33], 62. The terminology is that of the (Eleusinian) mystery cult. Cf. esp. Riedweg, *Mysterienterminologie*, 87 ff. Ziegert's unrelated distinction ("Ansätze", 721) between ethical/exegetical and metaphysical/ontological mysteries seems ill-founded.

[57] Cf. Hecht "Scripture", esp. 152. Philo also uses some familiar *middot*: cf. e.g. Siegfried, *Philo*, esp. 168–77.

[58] Revelatory experiences thus are limited to private contemplation of God's existence as τὸ ὄν. Cf. also Vanderlinden, "Modes", 298 f.

[59] Cf. e.g. Sandmel, *Philo*, 24–27.

been inducted into the processes of allegory can move from the 'speech' of Aaron, that is, the literal sense of Scripture, into the 'thought' of Moses, who is the Logos."[60]

Other types of mysteries are of little account in Philo, and bear no relation to the question of revelation. Eschatological mysteries are apparently unknown to him;[61] evil mysteries are mentioned once or twice in passing.[62]

Thus, the question posed in section 4 is probably best answered in the negative: Philo's doctrine of Scripture and interpretation does not offer an alternative view of revelation.

6. Origin and Setting of Philo's Allegorical Mysteries

Because of certain parallels with Palestinian exegesis, a straight adoption of Philo's notion of "mystery" from the Hellenistic mystery cults (not to mention a *Sitz im Leben* in a literal Jewish Hellenistic mystery cult) is less clear than was once supposed.[63] Philo consciously employs the terminology of the pagan rites (as indeed other Jewish diaspora writers did before and after him: e.g. Aristobulus, Artapanus, *Orphica*, Pseudo-Phocylides). But because he combines this

---

[60] Sandmel, *Philo,* 96. On the allegorical meaning of Moses and Aaron see also *LA* 3:45, 103; *Det* 39, 126 f.; *Mut* 208, etc.; cf. Goodenough, *Light,* 95−120.

[61] Philo's eschatology is rather slanted towards the question of the immortality of the soul (cf. Chadwick, "Philo", 157 n. 3; Wolfson 1:395−413). However, occasional remarks suggest that at least in practice his doctrine of the last things may have been much closer to familiar Jewish expectations. See esp. the extended passage *Praem* 163 ff.; cf. 88 ff.; also his belief that Moses' blessings in Deut 33 are still to be fulfilled (*Virt* 77, cf. 75; *Mos* 2:288); and various citations of Messianic prophecies (e.g. *Praem* 95; *Mos* 1:290), though the expected terms Μεσσίας or indeed χριστός are absent. Cf. also Schürer/Vermes, *HJPAJC* 2:507− 509.

Certainly there is a distinct lack of historical urgency. Braun, "Vaterland", 323 f. is right to consider that Philo places eschatological hope largely outside the framework of salvation history: "... Hoffen richtet sich bei Philo immer auf die nächsten Punkte des innerweltlichen Zeitverlaufes, es eilt nicht einem apokalyptischen Abbruch der Zeit zu. ... So wird verständlich, daß es bei Philo um die Seele geht; alles Hoffen und Streben des philonischen Frommen vollzieht sich auf dem Boden einer zeitlosen, undrängerischen Beschaulichkeit."

[62] *Sac* 32 f. mysteries of vice; *Mos* 1:264 Balaam (N.B. cf. Num 25:5 σʹ). Cf. Schneider, "Mysterion", 260.

The description of the *Therapeutae's* "mysteries of the holy life" (*Cont* 25) uses an analogy from the ethical stringency of initiation into pagan mysteries: cf. Harvey, "Mystery Language", 323; also Ps-Phoc 229 ("mysteries of righteousness"). Virtue as a requirement for initiation into God's mysteries occurs e.g. in *LA* 3:3, 27; *Cher* 42, 48; *Fug* 85.

[63] Actual Jewish mysteries were supposed e.g. by Pascher, ΒΑΣΙΛΙΚΗ ΟΔΟΣ, 261−65 and esp. Goodenough, *Light,* 12 ff. and passim. Cf. Chadwick, "Philo", 152; Nock, "Jewish Mysteries", esp. 464−466, in criticism of Goodenough.

with an intense dislike of the very essence of these cults,[64] his use of the terminology can hardly be due to a fascinated desire to emulate them.[65]

The content and intellectual level of his writings suggest that Philo's interlocutors are the literati of his day: his treatment of Jewish beliefs and practices to some extent corresponds to that which Hellenistic apologists applied to their own inherited rites and myths before an educated public. Such literary criticism enabled enlightened intellectuals to affirm their ancestral religion without needing to be embarrassed by its gross and unsophisticated mythology.[66]

Philo's exegesis in physical, moral (incl. etymological), and mystical terms bears generic affinities with the popular Hellenistic practice of Homeric allegory.[67] This literary phenomenon, originally developed during the period of Classical Greek reaction to theologically objectionable passages in the great poet,[68] spans the period from Theagenes of Rhegium (fl. 525 B. C.) to the Byzantine commentaries of John Tzetzes (fl. A. D. 1145).[69]

The earliest allegorical explanations were of a "scientific" rationalizing character; thus e.g. the notorious *theomachia* of *Iliad* 20 became a battle of the elements.[70] The philosophical hermeneutic of pre-Socratic interpreters of the gods as forces in nature (Parmenides, Empedokles, Herakleitos etc.) was soon viewed in analogy to the mystery initiation rites, and became the conscious model for the later allegorists — including Philo.[71]

---

[64] See esp. *Spec* 1:319 f., where mysteries are explicitly declared to be forbidden by the Torah. The appeal may be to Deut 23:17(18), where LXX adds to the prohibition of prostitution and temple prostitution, οὐκ ἔσται τελέσφορος ἀπὸ θυγατέρων Ἰσραήλ, καὶ οὐκ ἔσται τελισκόμενος ἀπὸ υἱῶν Ἰσραήλ. Cf. Deden, "Mystère", 439; Colson in *Philo*, 7:285, n. "b". See further *Spec* 1:323; 3:40; *Cher* 94.

[65] Indeed Riedweg, *Mysterienterminologie*, 103 plausibly concludes that Philo himself was never an initiate in any mystery cults.

[66] Cf. MacMullen, *Paganism*, 77—79 and n. 19; and see p. 80 f. below.

[67] Cf. recently Riedweg, *Mysterienterminologie*, 90 f.; for a full treatment see Pépin, *Mythe*, 85—214. A pioneering work on the question of Homeric allegoresis is Fritz Wehrli, "Zur Geschichte der allegorischen Deutung Homers im Altertum", (Basel: Ph.D. Diss., 1928), which unfortunately I have been unable to see.

[68] Beginning as early as Xenophanes and Pythagoras. Plato's more radical criticism even of allegory led him to ban Homer and the poets altogether (e.g. *Republic* 377d—e); cf. Pépin, *Mythe*, 112—121.

[69] Pépin, *Mythe*, 97 f.; Grant, *Letter*, 2 ff.; Werner, "Dichtererklärung", 274; Schmitt, "Tzetzes", 1032. In imperial Rome the technique was transferred also to Vergil.

[70] See e.g. Werner, "Dichtererklärung", 274.

[71] Leisegang, "Philosophie", 1189—91; see esp. the fragment (from Diels 21 n. 23) quoted on p. 1189: the schools of Parmenides and Empedocles wrote φυσικοὶ ὕμνοι dealing with the nature (φύσις) of Apollo and of Zeus — καὶ οἱ πολλοὶ τῶν Ὀρφέως τούτου τοῦ τρόπου. In Philo see e.g. *Post* 7 (τὴν δι' ἀλληγορίας ὁδὸν φυσικοῖς ⟨φιλὴν⟩ ἄνδρασι τρέπεσθαι); *Abr* 99; *Mos* 2:103. The "greater mysteries" are sometimes referred to as φυσιολογία, e.g. *LA* 1:60; *Cher* 121, etc. Cf. Leisegang, "Philosophie", 1192 f. (he also refers to Aristobulus, Eusebius *PrEv* 8.10.2).

But moral and etymological expositions (e.g. Athene as wisdom or φρόνη-σις, Hermes as eloquent reason, Hera as hazy ignorance)[72] quickly gained in popularity as well and were firmly entrenched during Philo's lifetime in such famous contemporaries as Herakleitos[73] and Cornutus. Neo-Pythagorean and Neo-Platonic commentators favoured the mystical exegesis which sought to find in Homer knowledge about the quest of the soul. In this way various schools of thought uncovered in Homer marvellous disclosures about the secrets either of the natural world (e.g. its spherical shape) or of the mystical realms above.[74] In Jewish circles the moral allegorization of various portions of Torah dates back at least to Aristobulus and the Letter of Aristeas (e.g. 144 ff.), but it was known also e.g. to Josephus.[75]

The mystical technique appears not to have been practised before Plutarch (c. A. D. 45—120), but it went on to find rich development in the second and third centuries e.g. in Numenius and Porphyry.[76] If this estimation is correct, Philo's employment of all three types of allegory to Scripture would appear to show him on the cutting edge of literary criticism in his day.[77] While in his understanding of Homer (whom he cites over 50 times) he may not in fact transcend the levels of literal and moral (e.g. *Cont* 17; *QG* 1:76; 3:3) interpretations, his Scriptural exegesis at any rate falls not far short of the later Neo-Platonic interest in the mysteries of the higher life: there, the *Odyssey* became the poem of the soul on earth as a pilgrim far from its homeland; in Philo the soul sojourns with Abraham in search of the heavenly mother-city (e.g. *QG* 4:74, 178; cf. *Mig* passim).[78]

---

[72] Cf. Buffière in *Héraclite*, xxiii f. The moral allegory deals with "le secret de bien vivre" (idem, *Mythes*, 394).

[73] See Herakleitos 1:1 [Homer] πάντα ἠσέβησε, εἰ μηδὲν ἠλληγόρησεν. Some of his allegories are particularly akin to those of Philo: Homer is the great hierophant of heaven and the gods (100:9; cf. 85:8), and the reader may be initiated into the mystic wisdom of the Homeric rites (75:18 etc.). Cf. Grant, *Letter*, 130 f.; Pépin, *Mythe*, 159—167, 234.

[74] Cf. Buffière, *Mythes*, 2 f.; Lévêque, *Catena*, 10.

[75] Josephus variously criticizes allegory (*Ant* 1:18 ff.; Ap 2:255: cf. e.g. Dio Chrysostom 11:17 f.), but can on occasion freely engage in it himself (*Ant* 3:180 ff.; cf. *Ant* 1:24). Eusebius, *Praeparatio Evangelica* 8:10 assigns both Philo and Josephus to the more allegorical group of interpreters. Cf. van Unnik, "Flavius Josephus", 252 and n. 22; Pépin, *Mythe*, 242 f.; Poznanski, "Anschauungen", 31—37.

[76] Cf. Buffière in *Héraclite*, x, xxi, xxvi; idem, *Mythes*, 2 f.; though he allows that mystical allegories may have been privately employed in Pythagorean circles at an earlier date (*Mythes*, 394).

[77] This is perhaps not altogether surprising for the prominent Alexandrian intellectual he appears to be. Buffière, *Mythes*, 480 n. 68 (on the interpretation of the Sirens in *QG* 3:3) allows that Philo's mystical allegory here precedes that of Plutarch by three quarters of a century.

[78] Cf. Buffière, *Mythes*, 38 f. n. 27. We must bear in mind all the while Philo's objection to purist allegory (*Mig* 89—93), and e.g. his undeniable interest in the fate of his community in the here and now (*LG; Flacc*).

Thus, an important *Sitz im Leben* of Philo's allegorical "mystery" language must be the contemporary literary and *philosophical* idiom,[79] rather than popular religious observance, in which allegory appears to have played no great part.[80] At least in direct comparison to the practice of pagan religion, Philo's mystery language is indeed "pure metaphor".[81] Nevertheless, his exegesis of the Jewish Scriptures clearly does have a mystical and religious purpose;[82] in light of this it may be significant to note that Plutarch, himself a priest of the Delphic Apollo, discusses not only the ambiguity of the Pythia's oracles,[83] but also offers e.g. an allegorizing interpretation of the mystery cult and legends of Isis and Osiris.[84]

In sum, therefore, Philo's middle Platonism substantively dictates an understanding of revelation in terms of a philosophical-mystical knowledge of God as Being. This knowledge, also called "prophecy", is prompted by the allegorical interpretation of the Torah, a practice to which the term "mysteries" here applies as a metaphor from Hellenistic philosophy and religion.

---

[79] With Prümm, "Mystères", 177; Chadwick, "Philo", 152; Nock, "Jewish Mysteries", 467 f.; idem, "Hellenistic Mysteries", 802; and cf. Harvey, "Mystery Language", 324 f. and passim.

[80] Thus e.g. Grant, *Letter*, 131; Bréhier, *Idées*, 243. According to Origen, *Contra Celsum* 1:12, it is only the Egyptian σοφοί, not the ἰδιῶται, who comprehend and discuss the "philosophical" significance of traditional religion. Plutarch (*De Iside* 9) insists that allegorical interpretation is secret, being discussed only among the priests. See Merkelbach, *Roman*, 57 f.

[81] Thus Nock, "Jewish Mysteries", 464; cf. Cerfaux, "Influence", 87 (though he envisions a pre-Philonic period of more direct comparison with the mysteries). Riedweg, *Mysterienterminologie*, 115, rightly concludes, "Philon braucht Mysterienterminologie in erster Linie als rhetorisch-stilistisches Mittel, um an Feierlichkeit und 'Tiefe' im sprachlichen Ausdruck zu gewinnen."

Philo himself never applies the word μυστήρια (*plurale tantum*) to actual contemporary ritual: Nock, "Hellenistic Mysteries", 802. An exception may be the Passover; cf. the fragment from *Sacra Parallela* 782b cited by Knox, *Gentiles*, 29 f. (this seems not to be in Harris, *Fragments*).

[82] Thus also Chadwick, "Philo", 154.

[83] E.g. *De Pythiae Oraculis* 24–26 (406B–407E); cf. Pépin, *Mythe*, 179 f.

[84] *De Iside* 20 ff. (358E ff.), 56 ff. (374A ff.). Cf. Pépin, *Mythe*, 180–184; see further Merkelbach, *Roman*, 57 ff., 65 ff.

Chapter Five

Josephus

1. Introduction

Josephus was an upper-class Jewish priest (*Vita* 2) who grew up in Palestine speaking Aramaic (*BJ* 1:3), received training from the Pharisees, Sadducees, and Essenes in his youth (*Vita* 10), and became a Pharisee himself at age 19 (*Vita* 12). His cultural and educational background may thus have some things in common with that of Paul, for whom the New Testament claims a Pharisaic heritage and Palestinian education (Phil 3:5; Gal 1:14; Acts 22:3, 23:6).

We find in Josephus a wealth of historiographical material relating to God's interventions and disclosures of His will, both Biblical and post-Biblical, among Jews and even Gentiles. However, present purposes will be best served by an analysis specifically of Josephus's view of "prophetic" revelation.

2. Revelation as Prophecy

Josephus's notion of the Torah, while not without its own interest,[1] seems less obviously in the foreground of his view of revelation. Except in the case of the Decalogue (*Ant* 3:89–101), Josephus tends to emphasize the Torah's venerable antiquity and quality as well as Mosaic authorship more than its divine origin (e.g. *Ant* 1:18ff.; 3:273; *Ap* 2:154–189; but cf. *Ant* 4:196f.). Despite a certain familiarity with both haggadah and halakhah,[2] Josephus generally shows a lack of concern with legal stipulations regarding foods, purity, and the cult.[3]

Josephus presents the *Jewish Antiquities* as a historiographical "translation" of Scripture (*Ap* 1:54).[4] Unlike the Qumran sectarians or Ben Sira, Josephus

---

[1] For a good survey see Vermes, "Summary", 289–303.
[2] Goldenberg, "Halakha", 30–43; Kohler, "Halakik Portions", 69–85.
[3] Cf. Vermes, "Summary", 292.
[4] Thus *Ant* could be said, *mutatis mutandis*, to emulate the practice (since Livius Andronicus) of "Romanizing" translations of the Greek Classics. Cf. Mayer, "Geschichts-

makes no claim to divine revelation in this process — except insofar as for him true historiography is in fact prophecy.

2.1. Biblical Prophecy

Josephus consistently holds the view that the Biblical prophets spoke by a binding, overriding divine inspiration, as expressed by such terms as ὑπαγορεύειν[5] (denoting dictation), ἔνθεος [γίνομαι],[6] etc. Prophets like Balaam acknowledge that they speak unconsciously (οὐδὲν ἡμῶν εἰδότων) when God's Spirit takes possession of them (ὅταν ἡμᾶς τὸ τοῦ θεοῦ λάβῃ πνεῦμα), and they have no discretion to speak or remain silent.[7] Indeed, Balaam confesses, "nothing within us, once He has gained prior entry, is any more our own" (Ant 4:121). Thus, not unlike Philo (see Chapter Four above), Josephus sees prophets as essentially passive, "conquered" (Ant 4:118) by inspiration, speaking even against their own will and intention where this is necessary to accomplish God's purpose.[8]

"Prophecy" here applies to a fairly broad range of revelatory phenomena. Once again Moses is "the prophet" par excellence (Ant 5:20; Ap 2:218, 286, etc.); this shows that a prophet's task is not only to predict but also to speak concerning and on behalf of God.[9] Elsewhere we read explicitly that what the people desired to learn after the death of Joshua and Eleazar (Josh 24:29 ff., Judg 1:1 f.), and what the high priest Phineas "prophesied" (προφητεύει), was not the future but the will of God (κατὰ τὴν τοῦ θεοῦ βούλησιν/τί καὶ τῷ θεῷ δοκεῖ).[10]

---

erfahrung", 299, 323; Mariotti, "Livius Andronicus", 694. Less felicitous and persuasive seems A. Paul's suggestion ("Concept", 383) that Josephus treats Ant as his Bible.

[5] Cf. Ant [3:84]; 4:121, 183.

[6] Ant 6:56, 76; 8:346; 9:35; BJ 4:388. But cf. also BJ 3:353 (Josephus himself inspired); 4:33 (Vespasian compared to [ὡς] one inspired). Contrast the purely secular meaning of ἐνθουσιάω (BJ 1:443; 6:260) and ἐνθουσιαστικός (Ant 15:240).

[7] Ant 4:119 f., 122. Cf. 6:166, 222; 8:408; 10:239, 250.

[8] Cf. e.g. Delling, "Prophetie", 118; Schlatter, Theologie des Judentums, 58—60. Pace Dienstfertig, Prophetologie, 25 f.

[9] Cf. e.g. Ap 2:286, Ant 4:329. Cf. Delling, "Prophetie", 110 (the primary concern is not Vorhersagen but Hervorsagen of the divine message). Yet Moses, too, fulfills an important predictive function; see Ant 4:303, 320.

[10] Ant 5:120. N.B. in Judg 1:1 f. Phineas is not the mediator of the revelation (cf. Delling, "Prophetie", 110). Cf. further Dienstfertig, Prophetologie, 31. On priesthood and prophecy see below. Note, however, Ant 4:218, where Deut 17:8 is understood to mean that a superior court consisted of ὅ τε ἀρχιερεὺς καὶ ὁ προφήτης καὶ ἡ γερουσία. It is difficult to know whether for Josephus this office of a judiciary "prophet" still existed in the present (Blenkinsopp, "Prophecy", 257 appears to think so).

However, while Josephus's depiction of Biblical prophecy is not purely predictive in character, nevertheless his predominant interest seems to lie in this direction.[11] None can deny the pleasure he takes in lining up a long series of prophets who engaged in the forecasting of future events: among these are Adam,
Moses, Joshua, Samuel, Nathan, Elijah, Elisha, Daniel, *et al*[12]. Prophecy *does*
here seem to consist for the most part in prediction.[13]

Indeed, Josephus shows a recurring interest in the specific intervals which
elapsed between a prophet's prediction and its fulfilment.[14] This seems to be
motivated primarily by an apologetic desire to stress the antiquity and continuity of the Jewish faith (e.g. *Ap* 1:1 ff.; *Ant* 1:5 ff.) as well as God's providence
in history (esp. *Ant* 10:277, 280).[15] Perhaps for similar reasons men like Moses,
Isaiah, and Daniel seem to assume the familiar Hellenistic guise of θεῖοι ἄν-
δρες: men privileged to converse with God, and endowed with divine qualities.[16] Through them God spoke His Word to His people, and by fulfilling their
predictions He manifests His providential sovereignty in history.

2.2. Contemporary Prophecy

Unlike e.g. the Mishnah or 1 Maccabees, Josephus never offers a statement
of principle on the question of the end of prophecy.[17] Nevertheless, he speaks
of the Holy Spirit[18] — and indeed of "prophets" — only in respect to Biblical
events.[19] The boundaries of the "canon" (however vaguely defined) do seem to
mark a subtle shift of religious attitude regarding prophecy which, while perhaps most evident in terms of lexical statistics, implicitly pervades Josephus's
assessment of contemporary phenomena.[20]

The latest figure whose prophetic status Josephus asserts with any degree of
confidence is John Hyrcanus, high priest in the years 135 – 105 B. C., who united in himself "three of the highest privileges: the supreme command of the na-

---

[11] But N.B. *Ap* 1:37: prophetic knowledge of the distant past.

[12] E.g. *Ant* 3:60, 4:125, 303, 312, 320; 8:232, 407; 9:27, 74, 183. Cf. further Delling,
"Prophetie", 111 ff.

[13] Cf. Hill, *Prophecy*, 27. Russell, *Method*, 97, compares apocalyptic literature.

[14] *Ant* 9:242; 10:276; 11:5 f.; 12:322, etc. Cf. Delling, "Prophetie", 114 ff.

[15] Cf. Attridge, *Interpretation*, 100 ff.

[16] E.g. *Ant* 3:180; 10:35; 10:250, 267 f., 277. Cf. also 8:243; 18:64; 19:289 (Augustus);
Ap 1:279 (Moses, as seen by the Egyptians). See Schlatter, *Theologie des Judentums*, 60.

[17] See below on *Ap* 1:41.

[18] Normally θεῖον πνεῦμα: e.g. *Ant* 4:108; 6:166, 222; 8:408.

[19] Cf. also Best, "Pneuma", 221–225; Blenkinsopp, "Prophecy", 262; and Schlatter,
Theologie des Judentums, 58.

[20] Cf. Schlatter, *Wie sprach Josephus von Gott?*, 78; Blenkinsopp, "Prophecy", 262.

tion, the high priesthood, and the gift of prophecy (προφητείαν)."²¹ Upon his death, Urim and Thummim (which Josephus views as safeguards against false prophecy, *Ant* 3:214) ceased their luminescent indication of God's will.²²

After this, Josephus no longer speaks of "prophets". Exceptions to this rule include polemical references, e.g. to Theudas (*Ant* 20:97), to the Egyptian impostor (*Ant* 20:169), and to the men hired by the authorities to lull the people into deceptive hopes²³ — all of whom in Josephus' estimation are properly to be understood as *false* prophets.²⁴

Must we conclude, then, that Josephus discounts any and all prophetic phenomena in his own day? Apparently not: although no contemporary could legitimately claim to be a prophet or to possess the Holy Spirit, Josephus relates a sufficient number of relevant incidents to assure us that in his opinion at least

²¹ *BJ* 1:68 f.; *Ant* 13:299 f. Similarly TLevi 8:14 f. (reference to one of the Maccabean priest-kings?); for the same triad of attributes see further Philo *Mos* 2:187). Cf. the somewhat earlier High Priest Jaddus, who receives a dream revelation (*Ant* 11:327).

²² See *Ant* 3:218: cf. Thackeray in *Josephus*, 4:420 f., n. "b". See also Blenkinsopp, "Prophecy", 240; and Attridge, *Interpretation*, 99 n. 3. Josephus in this regard is at variance with Rabbinic Tradition: m. Sota 9:12 sees the end of Urim and Thummim at the death of the first prophets; b. Sota 48b, at the destruction of the Temple (586 B.C.). VitProph 23 cites as terminus the murder of Zechariah ben Jehoiada at the hands of Joash (cf. Matt 23:35). EpArist 97 appears to assume the undiminished function of Urim and Thummim; cf. possibly ProtJames 5:1 (see de Strycker, *Protévangile*, 85; also Lindblom, *Gesichte*, 16). In the DSS the Urim and Thummim, if not actually functional, are a theological symbol of ongoing revelation: 4Qtest 14, 17 f. (cf. Deut 33:10 LXX); 4QpIsaᵈ 4 f. (re the council of twelve?); 11QTemple 58:18—21; and poss. the neologism אורתום in 1QH 4:6, 23; 18:29 (cf. Licht, *Thanksgiving Scroll*, 91). The subject continued to fascinate Jewish religious thought after the fall of the temple: see esp. b. Yoma 73a—b; but cf. also the *piyyutim*: Yose b. Yose speaks of the outcome of a battle being revealed to the high priest, יגלה לו סוד במשפט האורים (*The Penguin Book of Hebrew Verse,* 211; cf. Num 27:21).

²³ *BJ* 6:286. The context (ψευδοπροφήτης, 6:285; the motive of instilling false hope, 6:286; and Josephus's reflections about the nature of deception in adversity) makes it clear that we are dealing with intentional false prophecy. The use of προφήτης here may be no more than a reflection of the accompanying publicity granted to these men: i.e. "numerous *so-called* 'prophets' were at this time set up by the tyrants to delude the people...." *Pace* Aune, "Use", 419.

²⁴ N.B. the parallel account *BJ* 2:261 calls the Egyptian γόης and ψευδοπροφήτης. Fascher (*ΠΡΟΦΗΤΗΣ*, 161) aptly summarizes: "Die Nachrichten des Josephus über Prophetie lassen sich in zwei Gruppen teilen. Er berichtet 1. von Sehern, denen er nicht den Prophetentitel zuerkennt, 2. von politischen Schwärmern, die er als Pseudopropheten hinstellt."

Josephus's source Cleodemus/Malchos "the prophet" (Ant 1:240 — quoting Polyhistor) is probably no exception (*pace* Aune, "Use", 419—21). Josephus knows this writer only indirectly, and cites him not as a prophet but as a historian; the term προφήτης is used by Polyhistor. Short of additional evidence to establish that for *Josephus* (rather than just for his source) Cleodemus was a "prophet", we cannot assume the title προφήτης to be instrumental to the argument in *Ant* 1.

the predictive element of prophecy is hardly extinct. Blenkinsopp's summary is quite correct:

> Henceforth none could claim the title *nâbî'* in the proper sense until God should bring in the Kingdom in his own way and at his own time. Despite this conviction, Josephus believed that God still made use of certain individuals as instruments for revealing the course of the future and guiding the destinies of his people. These could not be called prophets ..., though those who abusively claimed to be such could be called false prophets.[25]

When one surveys the passages in question, one particular aspect stands out and calls for attention: viz., the apparent abundance of *Essene* personalities credited with near prophetic gifts. Thus we find e.g. Judas with his disciples,[26] Menahem,[27] and Simon,[28] all of whom are introduced as Essenes, and whose predictions are concerned with developments in the political realm.[29] Josephus was generally critical of apocalyptic tendencies, particularly those promising political salvation for Israel (cf. esp *BJ* 6:285 ff.), since they stood in direct conflict with his own endorsement of the Romans.[30] But never, as Blenkinsopp keenly observes, "does he describe Essene prophecy as pseudo-prophecy or associate Essenes with the apocalyptic *Schwärmerei* that he never tires of condemning; and this despite the fact that they did take part in the war and were punished by the Romans."[31] Perhaps Josephus's sympathies are due in part to his own early Essene training (*Vita* 11; see below). An apparently non-Essene example of contemporary political (and ecstatic?) prophetic activity is Jesus son of Ananias, a peasant who for over seven years preceding the fall of Jerusalem publicly cried out his monotonous message of impending doom for the city.[32]

Dreams are one acknowledged source of prophetic revelation: in sleep "the soul ... holds converse with God ... and foretells many things that are to come" (*BJ* 7:349).[33] Similarly, we have occasional references to the equivalent

---

[25] Blenkinsopp, "Prophecy", 256 [Part of this paragraph reappears almost verbatim in Hill, *Prophecy*, 31, but without any acknowledgement.]

[26] *Ant* 13:311–313; *BJ* 1:78 ff. He predicted Antigonus's death.

[27] Μανάημος, *Ant* 15:373–378, who predicted that Herod would be king.

[28] *BJ* 2:113; *Ant* 17:346 f. He interpreted the (political) meaning of Archelaus's dream.

[29] Cf. also Blenkinsopp, "Prophecy", 242.

[30] Apart from his dramatic defection to Vespasian, one of Josephus's clearest expressions of support for the Romans is the statement (*BJ* 5:367, 412) that God has fled the Jewish sanctuary and is now on the side of the Romans. See further the glowing paean to the Roman army in *BJ* 3:70–109; cf. also Lindner, *Geschichtsauffassung*, 28 ff., 42 f.

[31] Blenkinsopp, "Prophecy", 259.

[32] *BJ* 6:300–309 (Poznanski, "Anschauungen", 25 compares b.BB 12b). Archelaus has a prophetic dream in *BJ* 2:112 f. (=*Ant* 17:345–348), but this is interpreted by Simon the Essene. Note also the passing comment in *Ant* 17:43 about Pharisaic predictions. In *BJ* 2:411 Josephus appears to render the traditional triad שרים, כהנים, נביאים by the Greek terms δυνατοί, ἀρχιερεῖς, Φαρισαῖοι (thus Plöger, "Prophetisches Erbe", 292).

[33] Cf. Zeitlin, "Dreams", 10–13; Schlatter, *Wie sprach Josephus von Gott?*, 49. Cf. fur-

of a *bat qôl*, a heavenly voice, perhaps most significantly in the departure of the divine presence from the temple (μεταβαίνομεν ἐντεῦθεν).[34] By and large, however, Josephus remains silent on the revelatory process resulting in the pronouncements of contemporary figures, stating only (in the case of the Essenes) their close familiarity with Scripture (see *BJ* 2:159). His lean descriptions of these prophetic phenomena tend to stress the irrational (and even portentous, esp. *BJ* 6:288 ff.) nature of the predictions.[35]

The only theological weight which Josephus attaches to these predictions seems once again to be in the area of God's providence, which is being ignored by the misguided Jewish people:

> Reflecting on these things one will find that God has a care for men, and by all kinds of premonitory signs (παντοίως προσημαίνοντα) shows His people the way of salvation, while they owe their destruction to folly and calamities of their own choosing. (*BJ* 6:310)

This view of prophecy is decidedly non-eschatological,[36] although it does affirm historical manifestations of divine providence. Michel considers the treatment of those Jerusalem portents to betray Josephus' belief that the fall of the city initiated a whole new paradigm of *Heilsgeschichte*: "Gemeint ist doch wohl, daß eine geschichtstheologische Wende durch den Plan Gottes planmäßig vorbereitet wird."[37]

2.3. Was Josephus a Prophet?

It is an interesting corollary to his Essene background that Josephus probably regarded his own vocation in life in prophetic terms. Neither at Qumran nor in Josephus do we find the term "prophecy" used to describe present-day reli-

---

ther *Ant* 17:345−48 (=*BJ* 2:112 f.), 351 f.; *Vita* 208−212; also Philo, *Som* 1:2. As an aside we might mention that Josephus does relate the use of the lot in decisionmaking, but like Philo (*Her* 179; *Spec* 4:151) he does not value it highly or attribute its verdicts to God's agency (see e.g. *BJ* 4:153−57 on the zealots' appointment of the High Priest by lot; note also the Slavonic version (LCL 3, p. 654 f.) which ascribes to the priests the fear that because of this misdeed prophecy might cease).

[34] *BJ* 6:300; cf. Tacitus, *Hist.* 5:13.

[35] Michel, "Prophetentum", 61: "Das irrationale Element innerhalb dieser Weissagung tritt stark heraus. . . . Ein klares Bild von der Entstehung dieser Gottessprüche hat Josephus sicherlich *nicht* gehabt."

[36] Cf. Aune, *Prophecy*, 143 (though I would question his contention that Josephus's view of Biblical prophecy is "nonmessianic" as well; cf. *BJ* 6:313). Note also Josephus's ignorance of apocalyptic literature outside Daniel, and his disparaging appraisal of the popular apocalyptic enthusiasts (on which see Barnett, "Sign Prophets", 679−697) as inexperienced (ἄπειροι), unskilled (ἰδιῶται), etc.: *BJ* 6:291, 295.

[37] Michel, "Studien", 243 f. N.B. see also *BJ* 5:367, 412; and similar statements.

gious phenomena, but in both cases there is a claim to authoritative knowledge of God's scheme of *Heilsgeschichte*, and hence of the order of fulfilment of the Biblical prophecies.[38]

Josephus supports the common Jewish view that the prophetic gift resides in the religious leadership,[39] and he places considerable stress on his own priestly status and pedigree.[40] Added to this is the significant number of accurate political prognostications by divine inspiration to which Josephus lays claim,[41] as well as his special angelic vision (*Vita* 208 f.). In particular, he becomes possessed of the spirit (ἔνθους γενόμενος, *BJ* 3:353) and speaks to Vespasian as a messenger of God (3:400). Blenkinsopp fairly comments, "However we evaluate the claim in itself, it makes perfectly good sense in the context of traditional and contemporary understandings of both prophecy and priesthood."[42]

He subtly compares his role with that of the Biblical prophets Elijah,[43] Jeremiah,[44] Ezekiel,[45] and Daniel.[46] Indeed a comparison of Josephus' own historiography with his description of the work of the prophets suggests implicit but definite parallels: the prophets wrote by inspiration an account of history past and present (*Ap* 1:37). They were faithful historiographers who recorded events up to the time of Artaxerxes (*Ap* 1:40). Now it has fallen to Josephus's lot to record the history since Artaxerxes, although this "has not been deemed worthy of equal credit with the earlier records, because of the failure of the ex-

---

[38] Cf. *BJ* 3:351–354. Cf. Volz, *Geist*, 133 f.; Aune, *Prophecy*, 139; Blenkinsopp, "Prophecy", 247; Johnson, "Josephus", 340.

[39] E.g. *Ant* 13:282, 299; *BJ* 1:68 f. (Hyrcanus); cf. John 11:51 (Caiaphas); and below, Chapter 7. On priesthood and prophecy in general see e.g. Aune, *Prophecy*, 138 ff.; Bammel, "ΑΡΧΙΕΡΕΥΣ", 351–356; Blenkinsopp, "Prophecy", esp. 250 ff.

[40] *Vita* 1 f.; *BJ* 1:3, 3:352 f.; cf. Volz, *Geist*, 134; Blenkinsopp, "*Prophecy*", 242.

[41] See *BJ* 3:351–353; 400 ff.; 4:625; 6:312 f.

[42] "Prophecy", 256.

[43] See n. 46; Betz, "Problem", 32 f.; idem, *Offenbarung*, 106 f.

[44] Cf. nn. 44 f.; van Unnik, "Prophetie", 52 f.

[45] *Ant* 10:79 f.: both Jeremiah and Ezekiel were priests and prophets who predicted Jerusalem's downfall.

[46] Elijah, Jeremiah and Daniel were at various stages of their careers all misunderstood and plotted against. Jeremiah and Daniel were rescued from a "cave", so to speak, while God spoke to Elijah at the cave on Mt. Horeb (cf. *BJ* 3:340 ff: the cave at Jotapata). Daniel, like Josephus, was later honoured by the king when his interpretation/prediction proved true. More importantly perhaps, Daniel specifically prophesied (*Ant* 10:276) that the Romans would capture Jerusalem — a vindication of Josephus's own view of history. See also Bruce, "Josephus", 159; Johnson, "Josephus", 340 ff., esp. 346; Aune, *Prophecy*, 139 ff. Other parallels have been drawn with the patriarch Joseph, the book of Esther, and John Hyrcanus (see Daube, "Typology", 27 ff.; Thackeray in *Josephus*, 2:674 f., n. "b"; Johnson, "Josephus", 339).

act succession of the prophets" (*Ap* 1:41).[47] We may note here that this failure of ἀκριβὴς διαδοχή need not imply the failure of prophecy as such.[48]

Josephus's political prophecy has been compared to that of Yoḥanan ben Zakkai.[49] There are significant differences between the two men's oracles (unlike Yoḥanan, Josephus appeals to dreams: *BJ* 3:351 ff.; *Vita* 208 ff.), but both are said to derive their inspired knowledge from exegesis: ARN 4:67 (12a, on Isa 10:34); *BJ* 3:352 f. Lindner contends that Josephus's experience in *BJ* 3:351—354 falls outside the Pharisaic tradition, since Scripture is adduced only as a secondary supplement to the charismatic experience.[50] But although the appeal to Scripture is logically and chronologically secondary to the dreams, Josephus apparently could not have properly *interpreted* the latter without the revealed interpretation of the meaning of the Biblical prophecies (*BJ* 3:352 f.).[51]

Finally, Josephus places perhaps his highest self-appraisal in the mouth of none other than Vespasian himself: "'It is disgraceful,' he said, that one who foretold my elevation to power and was a minister of the voice of God (διάκονον τῆς τοῦ θεοῦ φωνῆς) should still rank as a captive and endure a prisoner's fate'; and calling for Josephus, he ordered him to be liberated."[52] In other words, Josephus explicitly considers himself to serve as the minister of the *bat qôl*, i.e. precisely the mode of divine communication which in Rabbinic Judaism is said to have taken the place of the Biblical prophecy.[53]

3. Revelation of Mysteries

Not much need be said on this subject. Josephus rarely uses mystery language, and then almost never of divine secrets. Explicit references to the mystery religions are uncommon (*Ant* 19:30, 31, 104; *Ap* 2:266). Josephus is concerned on the one hand to contrast the open simplicity of Jewish temple ritual with the clandestine proceedings of Hellenistic mysteries (*Ap* 2:107); he in-

---

[47] Cf. Blenkinsopp, "Prophecy", 241. Cf. also Dienstfertig, *Prophetologie*, 27 f., who contrasts Philo's view of prophecy but compares m. Abot 1:1; b. BB 14b.

[48] Cf. van Unnik, "Prophetie", 48; R. Meyer, "Prophetentum", 817.

[49] ARN 4:64 (12a); b. Git 56a/b, etc.: see Michel, "Prophetentum", 63; Aune, *Prophecy*, 141.

[50] *Geschichtsauffassung*, 54.

[51] See further M. Smith, "Occult", 246.

[52] *BJ* 6:626. The historical facticity of Josephus's prediction receives support from Suetonius, *Vespasian* 5:6 ("Iosephus ... constantissime asseveravit fore ut ab eodem brevi solveretur, verum iam imperatore"); cf. also Tacitus, *Hist* 1:10; 2:1. Jewish dream interpretation was not unknown to the Romans: Juvenal, *Sat* 6:542—547.

[53] Cf. Schlatter, *Theologie des Judentums*, 55; Delling, "Josephus", 304. For *bat qôl* (θεῖα φωνή) in Josephus cf. e. g. *Ant* 1:185; 3:90 (?); 8:352; 13:282 (N. B. John Hyrcanus); 19:60 f. See further Chapter 7 below.

sists that the guiding precepts of Judaism are not kept secret (*Ant* 16:43; cf.
1:11).[54] Yet on the other hand he is not loath to describe the ethical life of Judaism metaphorically as a kind of perpetual rite of initiation (*Ap* 2:189).[55]

His general attitude acknowledges the eminent respect commanded by the
pagan mysteries among his Gentile audience; yet at the same time he attempts
to demonstrate that Judaism as the religion of revelation is not dependent on secret ritual but instead practises its truth openly before all. The wisest of the
Greeks may have shared some of Moses's views about God, but they restricted
their teaching to the few. Moses, however, spoke openly and without secrets
(*Ap* 2:168 ff.), ensuring that all should be thoroughly familiar with their laws
(*Ap* 2:178; cf. *Ant* 4:209–211). Van Unnik writes,

> It is a distinctive mark of superiority that the Jewish nation is not kept together by
> such a difference between esoteria and exoteria [*sic*], but is built on revelation of that
> true God whom the philosophers secretly confessed. Therefore it is the fulfilment of
> their ideas.[56]

Nevertheless, Josephus's attitude of unrestricted accessibility is not entirely
unequivocal[57] — even if there are but a few faint echoes of the familiar apocalyptic and Rabbinic concerns with secrets. Of course Josephus subscribes to Jewish commonplaces such as that God knows the secret sins of man (*BJ* 5:402,
413; *Ant* 9:3, etc). But he also declares it impermissible for him to speak about
(περί) the divine name revealed to Moses in Exod 3 (*Ant* 2:276) or, strangely,
to give an explicit quotation of the Decalogue (3:90).[58] This is quite in keeping
with the common concern not to communicate "mysteries" to the unworthy
(i.e. here: to Gentiles); Josephus himself on one occasion appeals to Plato (*sic*)
for the notion that God's truth must not be disclosed to the ignorant mob (*Ap*
2:224). In a similar vein we learn about a dream telling Theopompus that his

---

[54] The "secret law" (*legem ineffabilem*) of the Jews in *Ap* 2:94 is part of Apion's accusation (cf. Juvenal *Sat* 14:102 "arcano. . . . volumine Moyses"). In light of this and the context concerned to stress precisely the *absence* of secrecy from the Jewish cult, *Ap* 2:82
("purissimam pietatem, de qua nihil nobis est apud alios effabile") is probably to be
emended (with Thackeray in *Josephus*, 1:326 f. n. "b", following Reinach) to read *ineffa-
bile*.

[55] Cerfaux, "Influence", 82–86 compares this with EpArist and Alexandrian Judaism; he considers that the Jews saw themselves as constituting "un collge sacerdotal,
un peuple de mystes et de hirophantes" (p. 87).

[56] Van Unnik, "Josephus", 272; cf. 268 ff.

[57] *Pace* van Unnik, "Josephus", 277 ("no hidden truth"). Note also M. Smith's sharp
criticism of van Unnik: "Occult", 245.

[58] Perhaps because it contains the divine name? But cf. possibly y. Ber 1:8, 3c31–33:
the Decalogue is no longer read because of the Minim who say only this was given to
Moses on Sinai (cf. Vermes, "Decalogue", 232–240). Contrast m. Tam 5:1.

M. Smith's mention ("Occult", 245) of the hidden graves of the kings (*Ant* 7:394) in
this context would seem to be less apposite.

mental affliction was due to excessive curiosity about divine matters and to his desire to disclose them to the unworthy (εἰς κοινοὺς ανθρώπους, *Ant* 12:112; cf. EpArist 314 f.).[59]

One or two statements about enigmatic Scriptural prophecies are probably also pertinent here: e.g. *BJ* 3:352 (τὰ ἀμφιβόλως ὑπὸ τοῦ θείου λεγόμενα); 6:312 (χρησμὸς ἀμφίβολος). Such language is reminiscent of talk about the prophetic mysteries in the DSS or apocalyptic literature; yet it is phrased so as to remain intelligible to those more familiar with the oracles of Delphi. Josephus also reports the Essene vow to preserve (συντηρέω: and keep secret?) the books of the sect and the names of the angels (*BJ* 2:142). However, his own pre-occupation with this matter is doubtful.

Other items of interest are haggadic remarks made in passing about a number of Biblical characters. Thus Joseph's rather enigmatic Egyptian name צפנת פענח is, in keeping with traditional Jewish interpretation, rendered "he who finds secrets" (κρυπτῶν εὑρέτης, *Ant* 2:91).[60] Isaiah's Cyrus prophecy is described as a secret communication from God (*Ant* 11:5 ἐν ἀπόρρητῳ = בסוד?). Daniel was one of the greatest prophets (*Ant* 10:266 ff.), admired by God for his wisdom (*Ant* 10:200); he was devoted to the interpretation of dreams, knew God's supernatural truth, and God became manifest to him (τὸ θεῖον αὐτῷ φανερὸν ἐγίνετο, *Ant* 10:195; cf. 10:237, 239). And although he refuses to discuss this in his work, Josephus cryptically suggests that the reader may discover eschatological mysteries by studying the book of Daniel.[61]

In stark contrast to the apocalyptic tradition, however, Josephus does not develop the Enoch legend beyond the bare Scriptural minimum. Enoch "returned to the Deity" (*Ant* 1:85) and both he and Elijah became invisible (*Ant* 9:28, ἀφανεῖς); no one knows of their death.[62] Possibly related is Josephus's igno-

---

[59] Cf. also, perhaps, the Slavonic addition after *BJ* 2:110, where John the Baptist tells his detractors, "I will not disclose to you the mystery that is among you."

[60] "Zaphenath-Paneah" is linked with a revelation of secrets to Joseph in GenR 90:4 (R. Yoḥanan [A2?]); TPsJ/TN and Peshitta Gen 41:45 (but N.B. in TO this reading occurs only in Yemenite and Tiberian MSS, see Sperber ad loc.; *pace* Thackeray in *Josephus* 4:206 f., n. "b"; Franxman, *Genesis*, 245; and Vermes, "Haggadah", 162 f., who appear to follow the *Miqrâ'ôt Gedôlôt*). Cf. quite differently Philo, *Mut* 91.

[61] *Ant* 10:210: περὶ τῶν ἀδήλων τί γενήσεται. Cf. similarly *Ant* 4:125 about the oracles of Balaam.
M. Smith, "Occult", 245 also cites *Ant* 8:73: the cherubim in Solomon's temple were too wonderful to describe or imagine. But this passage may pertain to a conceptual difficulty rather than a religious secret.

[62] Cf. *Ant* 4:326 on the death of Moses (a cloud descends on him and he disappears [ἀφανίζεται]), presumably in conscious comparison (sympathetic or sardonic?) with Enoch: "But he has written of himself in the sacred books that he died, for fear lest they should venture to say that by reason of his surpassing virtue he had gone back to the Deity."
An agnostic or mildly skeptical attitude toward Enoch is shared in TPsJ/FT/TN Gen

rance or omission of apocalyptic evil mysteries, and for that matter of Satan.[63] He does, however, believe in the ability of ghosts to disclose human secrets (*BJ* 1:599).

Finally we also find the popular, metaphorical use of μυστήριον as an activity or process which is awesome and shrouded in secrecy, e.g. the habitual secret wickedness of Antipater (κακίας μυστήριον, *BJ* 1:470)[64] or the eerie silence of the Essenes (*BJ* 2:133).

Over all, then, Josephus's stated (though perhaps not his private) interest in the revelation of divine mysteries is minimal by comparison with that found in much contemporary Palestinian literature. His view of prophecy, however, despite a superficial reluctance and ambivalence, shows a considerable openness to accept various contemporary phenomena as genuine. Most prominent among these is his own prophecy to Vespasian which, while sparked by God-given dreams, is complemented by a revealed interpretation of the prophetic Scriptures.

5:24. More negative is GenR 25:1, in contention with the *Minim*: God took Enoch away because he was fickle and was becoming wicked (cf. already Wisd 4:10 f.). Himmelfarb ("Report", 259 ff., 266) concludes that there are no positive statements on Enoch in the Talmudic period; but note e.g. 3 En 4:2 f. and passim; DEZ 1 (end); PRE 7:40. Cf. also Asatir 2:32 f.: Enoch died.

[63] Cf. Schlatter, *Wie sprach Josephus von Gott?*, 41. Perhaps the absence of the story of Job is due to its mention of Satan (but see *Ant* 2:178).

[64] Harvey, "Mystery Language", 324: "a systematic discipline of evil". Antipater's life was a continual orgy of hidden wickedness. But that the analogy is specifically of the rigours of initiation, rather than of the ritual celebration in general, is perhaps not as self-evident as Harvey assumes.

Chapter Six

The Ancient Versions

1. Introduction

Vernacular renditions of the Bible accompanied the public reading of Scripture in the synagogues of both Palestine and the Diaspora.[1] A Greek version at least of the Pentateuch existed in Alexandria by the early third century B. C.[2] We also know of the existence of written Targums in the first century A. D.; a Pentateuchal Targumic tradition may be assumed to be earlier.[3] Jonathan b. Uzziel, a disciple of Hillel, is said to have produced a Targum to the prophets (b.Meg 3a). Because of their widespread use in synagogues the Targums, as a kind of first-hand reception of Scripture, can serve as useful indicators of the type of Jewish "theology" which would perhaps have been familiar on a wider basis.[4]

2. The Targums[5]

For our purposes the best approach to the ancient versions is through an examination of theologically significant translation patterns. The following remarks, then, will address (i) the Targumic use of אתגלי, especially with divine subject or object; (ii) the application of such revelation terminology to the subject of divine mysteries; (iii) the significance of divine titles; and (iv) Targumic notions of Torah and prophecy.

---

[1] Cf. Bowker, *Targums*, 12f.

[2] See esp. EpArist; Sir Prologue (late 2nd cent. B.C.) knows a translation of Torah, Prophets, and "the other books". Cf. Goodman in Schürer/Vermes, *HJPAJC* 3.1:476f.

[3] See esp. 11 QtgJob; cf. b.Shab 115a; m.Meg 2:1; m.Yad 4:5. The Targum, apparently unlike the Greek version, carried no authority of its own (m.Meg 1:8, 2:1; m.Yad 4:5).

[4] But for the current disarray of scholarly discussion about dating the Targums (*difficile est saturam non scribere!*) see e.g. Kaufman, "Methodology", 118.

[5] The following remarks are aided particularly by the informed and circumspect work of A. Chester, *Divine Revelation and Divine Titles in the Pentateuchal Targumim*.

2.1. Divine Revelation as Expressed by the Verb אתגלי

A. Chester gives the surprising count of 104 uses of אתלי with divine referent
in the Pentateuchal Targums. This indicates a distinctively Targumic development in the use of the verb.[6] Two different but compatible motives for this interesting shift can be recognized.

2.1.1. *Anti-Anthropomorphism.* On the negative side, we find the well-
known avoidance of anthropomorphic descriptions of God's activities, in order
to safeguard God's transcendence and otherness. Thus אתגלי frequently repla-
ces nifal ראה and (less consistently) verbs of motion with divine subject in the
Targums to the Pentateuch[7] and Prophets.[8]

2.1.2. *Theological Purpose.* But a corresponding positive use of אתגלי is
borne out e.g. by the treatment of the Sinai theophany.[9] Unlike some other Jewish documents, the Targums virtually pass over in silence the mediating role
of Moses in the giving of the Law;[10] their prime concern here is to emphasize
God's sovereign work in revelation.[11] The function of אתגלי is to indicate a
theologically consistent, orthodox, and yet relevant manner of speaking about
the crucial theme of divine theophanies in Scripture.[12] As a standardized exegetical device, it paradigmatically describes and liturgically "actualizes" times and
places by which and in which God has made Himself manifest to His people in
the course of salvation history.[13]

2.2. Revelation of "Mysteries"

The root גלא/גלה is also used in theologically significant contexts with subjects or objects other than the deity. Thus we find references to the eschatolog-

---

[6] Chester, *Revelation*, 238—240 and passim; cf. also the usage of the Peshitta (p. 239; in
this regard Brock, Review, 550f. suggests Targumic influence on the earliest stratum of
the Peshitta text). At Qumran and in the book of Daniel, too, the use of גלא/גלה is almost entirely theological, although אתגלי/נגלה with divine subject is not found.

[7] Chester, *Revelation*, 95—99, 151—155.

[8] Nifal ראה: e.g. TJ Isa 30:30, 60:2, 63:15; Zech 9:14. Verbs of motion: e.g. TJ Isa
26:21, 30:27, 31:4, 40:10; Hab 3:3; Zech 2:14, 14:3—5; Mal 4:24. Cf. also Potin, *Fête*,
1:67.

[9] Cf. Potin, *Fête*, 233 on the frequency of אתגלי.

[10] Potin, *Fête*, 233 cites as an exception only TgPsa 68:8 (*sic*: read 68:19?) — Moses the
prophet ascends the mountain to obtain the Law.

[11] Potin, *Fête*, 234.

[12] Cf. Chester, *Revelation*, 261 f.

[13] Cf. Chester, *Revelation*, 262—264. TNgl Exod 3:14: "and I am the one who will be
your help in every generation" בכל דר ודר ואנה הוא דעתיד להווי בסעדכון].

ical "revelation" e.g. of the Messiah[14] or the Kingdom of God.[15] Of particular significance is the interest in a "revelation of secrets"; while this is by no means ubiquitous in the Targums,[16] two Pentateuchal instances in particular deserve mention.

TN/TPsJ Gen 49:1 sees the sons of Jacob gathered around their father's deathbed "after the end had been revealed to him" [מן דאתגלי לי[17] קיצא], expecting him to tell them (as promised) about the redemption in the Messianic age: "the concealed secrets [רזייא סתימייא], the hidden ends [קיצייה גניזייא], the giving of the rewards of the just and the punishment of the wicked and what the happiness of Eden is." However, according to Talmudic tradition God then prevented Jacob from doing so.[18] This tradition must be what lies behind the enigmatic words, "When the time (קיצה) was revealed to him, the mystery (רזא) was hidden from him. . . . (But) when the mystery was revealed to him, it was hidden from him and when the door was open to him, it was closed from him."

This differentiation between קץ (a technical term for an age or epoch, esp. the appointed time of redemption)[19] and רז (apparently the actual events and circumstances ordained for that future time) can be compared with our findings

---

[14] E.g. TPsJ/FT Gen 35:21; TPsJ Exod 12:42; TJ Isa 28:16; Jer 30:21; Mic 4:8; Zech 3:8, 4:7, 6:12; TN Exod 12:42. See also Chapter 1 above; cf. McNamara, *New Testament*, 246—252.

[15] See TJ Isa 24:23, 31:4f., 40:9, 52:7; Ezek 7:7, 10; Obad 21; Mic 4:7; Zech 4:7; 14:9. Cf. above, Chapter 1. On the kingdom of God in TJ Isa ("God's strong action on behalf of his people") see Chilton, *Glory*, 81. Koch writes that in the Targums the eschatological *rule* (מלך) of Yahweh is replaced by the revelation of the Kingdom (מלכות) as the decisive turning point of the eons, previously not visible on earth ("Offenbaren", 161f.). [However, his distinction (163f.) between a "revealing" of God's kingdom and a "coming" of the Messiah's kingdom is made less likely by TJ Mic 4:7f. (synthetic parallelism).]

[16] TO uses רז only in Gen 49:6. Chester, *Revelation*, 213—216 considers that (with the exception of passages like Gen 49:1; Exod 12:42) it is only TPsJ of the Pentateuchal Targumim which widely develops apocalyptic themes of revelation — a fact which may well reflect Rabbinic reservations about the public discussion of esoterica.

Tg Eccl is pessimistic about the possibility of knowing mysteries. See e.g. TgEccl 1:8 ("a man cannot say what will be after him, nor can the eye see all that is to be in the world"); 3:11; 7:24 ("who can find out by his wisdom . . . the secret of the day when the King Messiah will come?"). For the Targumic notion of man's inability to know God intimately see e.g. Smolar/Aberbach, *Studies*, 137.

[17] *Sic*; i.e. ליה, as in the next two lines.

[18] See Aberbach/Grossfeld, *Genesis* 49, 1; cf. Chapter 7 below.

[19] Cf. Le Déaut, *Nuit*, 274: "temps fixé pour la rédemption"; "le début de l'ère messianique". In the OT קץ is more frequently applied to eschatological judgment; but see e.g. Hab 2:3; Dan 12:9, 13; and cf. אחרית הימים e.g. in Isa 2:2/Mic 4:1; Jer 23:20; Hos 3:5; Dan 10:14. For TN/TPsJ Gen 49:1 (and the NT) see Pérez Fernández, *Tradiciones*, 102—109. Cf. futher Delling, "τέλος", 53f.; and p. 47 n. 32 above.

on 1 QpHab 7: the prophets were told about the end times (הקץ האחרון[20]), but not about their consummation (גמר הקץ). Only the Teacher of Righteousness has been privy to divine revelation regarding the "mysteries" of the prophetic oracles (כול רזי עבדיו הנבאים, 1 QpHab 7:4 f.). In each case קץ defines the *Heilszeit* in which the רז (i.e. the *Heilsplan*, as it were) is to be actualized.[21]

Jacob is given the privilege of knowing the appointed age of Messianic redemption (i.e. "the giving of the rewards, etc."), but how this will come about (the actual "mystery", God's plan) is hidden from him.[22] This perspective again recalls the attitude to divine mysteries in Rabbinic literature.[23]

The other major reference is Balaam's prophetic oracle[24] in TN/FT/TPsJ Num 24:3 f. The passage extols his privileged status: "What has been hidden from all the prophets has been revealed to him. ... And the mysteries of prophecy were revealed to him ורזי נבואת מתגלין לה." Both here and in the virtually identical parallel 24:15 f. this mention of a revelation of prophetic mysteries is closely followed by descriptions of the future age (24:5 f.?) and the Messiah (24:7, 17[25]).[26] Balaam was a privileged recipient of divine mysteries because God granted him a close knowledge of the Messianic salvation in store for Israel.[27] Not unlike the Biblical Daniel or Qumran's Teacher of Righteousness, Balaam here receives revelation which was concealed from the prophets of Scripture.

---

[20] 1 QpHab 7:7, 12; cf. הדור האחרון, 7:1.

[21] Cf. e.g. 1 QS 3:23; CD 2:9 f. On the connection between TN Gen 49:1, Qumran, and Daniel cf. Le Déaut, *Nuit*, 274 f.

[22] Cf. also TPsJ Gen 49:1, "And after the Glory of the Shekhinah had been revealed [איתגלי] to him, the designated time the king Messiah would come was concealed from him קיצא דעתיד מלכא משיחא למיתי אתכסי מניה."

[23] See Chapter 7 below. Cf. Chester, *Revelation*, 188 f.; and 215 f. (revelation of mysteries is largely repressed in the Pentateuchal Targumim). But cf. also TJ Mic 4:12: the *enemies* of Israel have no knowledge of the mysteries of the Lord.

[24] MT נאם is rendered במתל נבן[י]ותה in TN/FT/TPsJ.

[25] The LXX also renders both these verses messianically. Cf. CD 7:19 f., 1 QM 11:6, 4 Qtest 9—13; TJud 24:1.

[26] N.B. in light of the Messianic context and of the use of רז elsewhere, the intervening statement about Balaam's prediction of his own death (v. 4, 16) is unlikely to be the intended point of reference.

[27] This positive evaluation of Balaam is not universally shared in Judaism. Indeed even in the Pentateuch his image in "J/E" may differ from that in "P": e.g. Num 31:16. Later writings sometimes designate him as "Balaam the wicked" (e.g. m.Abot 5:19, b.Sanh 106a), though he can also be seen as a prophet to the Gentiles (e.g. b.BB 15b), and perhaps in his own right even greater than Moses (SifDeut 357 [on 34:10]; ed. Finkelstein, p. 410). The NT casts a negative light on him: 2 Pet 2:15; Jude 11; Rev 2:14; cf. Philo *Mut* 202 f. See further Grintz, "Balaam", 123 f.; Vermes, *Scripture*, 127 ff. This image of Balaam in the Targums suggests that his reception of heavenly secrets was a widely popular and influential tradition; cf. Chester, *Revelation*, 202.

Other pertinent "divine mystery" passages could no doubt be cited;[28] a comprehensive treatment is unfortunately beyond the scope of this inquiry.

2.3. The Revelatory Significance of Divine Titles

This subject cannot be properly addressed here; it must suffice to indicate the relevance of the subject and to point out significant recent discussions.

2.3.1. *Memra*. This uniquely Targumic[29] term occurs over a thousand times as a replacement of (or in conjunction with) God or Yahweh.[30] Suggestions about its meaning have ranged from a theologically meaningless verbal buffer[31] to the creative, salvific and revealing Word of God in hypostatized form.[32] The two most recent studies have been offered by Hayward and Chester; the former substantially links it with the divine name,[33] while the latter sees it as a limited and inconsistently used exegetical device expressing in a general sense "the effective utterance and word of Y."[34]

2.3.2. *Shekhinah/Glory*. Glory, Shekhinah, and "Glory of the Shekhinah" similarly serve to safeguard the transcendence of God;[35] unlike Memra, they are common also in the Rabbinic writings.[36] Chester observes that both Memra and Shekinah are "used in an apparently colourless or stereotyped manner in a great many instances."[37] Nevertheless, both are characterizations of God enabl-

---

[28] E.g. TPsJ Exod 28:30a (Urim disclose the secrets [טמירן] of the house of Israel), b (secrets revealed by calling on the name of the Lord); TO/TN/TPsJ/FT Deut 33:19; TJ Ezek 13:9 (false prophets are not ברז טוב דגניז לעמי, and are not written in the book of eternal life). Cf. also TJ Ezek 28:3[f.] (Daniel).

[29] Chilton, *Glory*, 66; McNamara, *Targum*, 108–110; N.B. Hayward (*Name*, e.g. 136f.) nevertheless believes in an early origin of this notion. Cf. 1 QapGen 22:30f.; Jub 12:4; 36:7; 1 En 14:24; 4 Ezra 6:38; Psa 107:20. In the LXX cf. Wisd 16:10, 12; 18:15; possibly Deut 8:3 (see Brockington, "Septuagint", 80–86); Hab 3:5 (Thackeray, *Septuagint*, 53f.: the Logos shod in Perseus's winged sandals!). Cf. already 1 Sam 3:21; Isa 45:23, 55:11; Jer 23:29. (Cf. Aber, "Memra", 2 n. 22: comparable oblique references to God ("name", "glory") are common in the OT.)

[30] Hayward, "Memra of YHWH", 412 cites 338 occurrences in TN and 628 in TNgl alone. Cf. Sabourin, "MEMRA", 79.

[31] Moore, "Intermediaries", 53f.

[32] Muñoz León, *Dios-Palabra*, 139. Cf. Hayward, Review, 94–96; Chester, *Revelation*, 299ff.

[33] Hayward, *Name*, e.g. 147 (cf. TN Exod 3:12; 4:12).

[34] Chester, *Revelation*, 308–313.

[35] E.g. TO/TPsJ/TN/FT Exod 24:10; TO Exod 33:20; TN/TPsJ/FT Deut 33:16.

[36] Except for the phrase "Glory of the Shekhinah", which is rare outside the Targums; cf. Goldberg, "Verwendung", 61. For detailed discussion see e.g. Goldberg, *Untersuchungen*; idem, "Verwendung"; Chester, *Revelation*; also Muñoz León, *Gloria de la Shekina en los Targumim del Pentateuco*, Madrid 1977, which I have not seen.

[37] Chester, *Revelation*, 322.

ing the believing community reverently to affirm its faith in God's verbal and
visible involvement with the world throughout the unfolding of history.[38]

2.4. Torah, Spirit, Prophecy

Finally, the Targumic understanding of Torah and Prophecy shows itself to
be consistent with widespread Jewish belief.

2.4.1. The Torah. The Targums continue the traditional exalted view of the Torah as the word of God;[39] the traditions about the Sinaitic revelation are richly
developed.[40] Here it may be useful to single out two familiar images: Torah as
light and as a spring of water. We begin with the latter. TJ Zech 13:1 reads, "At
that time the teaching of the Law will be revealed (אולפן אוריתא גלי) like a
spring of water to the house of David. ..." A similar metaphor was earlier encountered in Sir 24:30f. and 1 QH 8, where it denoted the inspired exegesis of
the Torah.[41] Allusions to this motif recur on several other occasions in the Targums, e.g. when in TJ Isa 12:3 "you will joyously draw water from the springs
of salvation" becomes "you will joyously receive new teaching (אולפן) from
the righteous elect."[42] The idea has been sufficiently discussed above; its meaning here is that (at least in the eschaton) new revelation will be received from the
Torah.

The familiar metaphor of the Torah as a light (cf. above Ch. 1 n. 29) is exploited in numerous Biblical references.[43] Anticipated in the OT itself (Psa
119:105; Prov 6:23), this symbolic emphasis on the Torah as revelation is further encouraged by the suggestive similarity of the Aramaic words involved
(אוריתא and אורתא).[44]

---

[38] Cf. Chester, *Revelation*, 322–324.

[39] So literally TJ 2 Sam 22:31b, where אמרת יהוה צרפה becomes אוריתא דיוי
בחירא היא (cf. Smolar/Aberbach, *Studies*, 161 and n. 215). God Himself has taught Torah to the tribes of Israel (TJ Hos 5:9b בשבטיא דישראל הודעית אוריתא), and He spends
three hours each day studying Torah (TN/TPsJ Deut 32:4; cf. e.g. b.AZ 3b). The Torah
is written by God's right hand (TO Deut 33:2; cf. 9:10 – note the absence of anti-anthropomorphic circumscriptions).

[40] Cf. Potin, *Fête*, passim.

[41] Gordon, "Study", 373 points out that CD 6:3f. specifically equates the "well" of
Num 21:18 with the Torah. Note also OdSol 30. Teaching (אולפן) pertains to the Torah:
e.g. TJ Isa 2:3, 12:3; Mic 4:2, etc.

[42] Smolar/Aberbach, *Studies*, 160 n. 206: בחירי צדקא are "the greatest scholars". For
the motif of revealed new teaching cf. also e.g. TJ Isa 1:27–30; 12:3 (cf. MT); 30:14f.;
58:11f.

[43] E.g. TJ Isa 2:5; cf. TJ Isa 42:7; TgJob 29:13; TgPsa 89:16; etc. In the LXX cf. 2 Kgs
12:3, 17:28 (φωτίζω); cf. Gaster, "Qumran Reading", 218.

[44] Cf. Vermes, "Torah", 437. In TJ Isa אוריתא also frequently renders "knowledge",
דעת.

2.4.2. *Prophecy and the Holy Spirit.* In Targum Jonathan the use of the root
נבא fulfills a harmonizing function similar to that of אתגלי. Thus e.g. God's
"calling" (קרא) becomes the prophets' "prophesying" (אתנבי).[45] Other examples include the substitution of נבואה for חזון (and cognates);[46] or of "word of
prophecy from before Y" (פתגם נבואה מן קדם יוי) for דבר־יהוה.[47] The root נבא
appears to be restricted in its application to prophecies of the Biblical past and
the eschatological future.

The Holy Spirit in the Targums is often[48] seen as the source of prophecy,
very commonly by reference to the "Spirit of prophecy" (רוח נבואה, a phrase
not used in the OT).[49] The Spirit functions as a divinely given medium by
which the prophet can receive revelations;[50] as such it is not cited in the context
of "direct" Biblical revelations, e.g. at Sinai or the burning bush.[51] Though on
the whole the Spirit occurs frequently, in some cases a Biblical instance is in fact
removed in favour of God's Memra (TJ Zech 4:6, 8:12) or His prophets.[52]

As we have begun to see, there was no universal Jewish consensus about the
termination of the Spirit's activity in prophetic revelation. However, in the
Targums the departure of the Shekhinah, and the corresponding end of the
prophetic age, seem to be presupposed;[53] this is at the same time specifically accompanied by a belief in the restoration of prophecy in the eschaton.[54]

At the same time Chilton shrewdly discerns in TJ an "implicit claim to speak
with almost prophetic authority":[55] often the *meturgeman* will add the phrase

---

[45] E.g. TJ Isa 22:12, 40:12, 41:27; Jer 7:13, 35:17; Zech 1:14, 7:13. Also cf. Gordon,
"Study", 332.

[46] E.g. TJ Isa 1:1; 2:1; 13:1; 22:1, 5; 21:2; 29:11; Hab 1:1; 2:2f.

[47] E.g. TJ Isa 38:4; 51:16; 59:21; Hag 1:1, 3; 2:1, 10, 20; Zech 1:1, 7.

[48] Though not always; see Schäfer, "Termini", 313; Chilton, *Glory*, 50.

[49] Cf. Schäfer, *Vorstellung*, 23(ff.); Gordon, "Study", 299f. See also e.g. Rev 19:10;
Justin *Dial* 43, 91.

[50] Chilton, *Glory*, 51; cf. Schäfer, *Vorstellung*, 62.

[51] Chilton, *Glory*, 51; Schäfer, *Vorstellung*, 66.

[52] Hag 2:5 "My Spirit is standing in your midst" becomes "My prophets are teaching
(מלפין) among you": cf. n. 41 above on אולפן. (Cf. also Seeligmann, *Septuagint*, 109 on
LXX Amos 3:7.) Other unexpected references to prophets and prophecy include TO
Gen 49:24 (Joseph's dreams); TJ Judg 2:1, 4; 5:23; Hag 1:13 (cf. Smolar/Aberbach, *Studies*, 224f.); also TJ Isa 8:2 (Uriah the Priest). Conversely, "prophets" can also become
"scribes": cf. e.g. TJ 1 Sam 10:5−12; Jer 6:13; 8:10; 14:18; 18:18; 23:11, 33, 34; 26:7, 8, 11,
16; 29:1; and see Hayward, "Scribes", 210−221.

[53] E.g. TO/TPsJ Deut 31:17f.; TO 32:20; TJ Isa 8:17; 35:5 45:15; 54:8; 57:17; 59:2; Jer
33:5; Ezek 39:23f.; TgLam 2:9. However, this need not be the last word. Cf. Tg Ruth 1:1
(in allusion to Amos 8:11): in the days of Ruth, too, there was a famine "of hearing the
word of prophecy from before the Lord"; similarly TJ 1 Sam 3:1 לית נבואה גליא; and see
below.

[54] E.g. TJ Isa 5:4f., 29:10, 35:5; Ezek 39:29; TgPsa 45:3. Cf. also Chilton, *Glory*, 54.

[55] Chilton, *Glory*, 53.

"the prophet said" (אמר נביא) before introducing significant midrashic material reflecting his own theological concerns.[56] Thus the Targumist speaks to his own situation in the name of the Biblical prophet — rendering no doubt what he believed the prophet *would* have said to express his message for the contemporary synagogue congregation. In this way the speaker's words participate in the revelatory status of the words of prophecy.

3. The Greek Versions

The date and provenance of the Septuagint are nearly as problematical as in the case of the Targums.[57] But the Septuagint is a very different document from the Aramaic paraphrases; as a much more literal translation on the whole, its theological stance on specific issues is often difficult to determine. Nevertheless, the official use of the LXX reflects a high view of the authority of Torah: its function was to approximate as far as possible the very Torah itself,[58] so that it represents as it were the Alexandrian Authorized Version[59] — a status seemingly recognized even in Palestine.[60]

3.1. LXX Translation Patterns

Many of the Septuagint's relevant theological translations are well known[61] (though there would certainly appear to be room for further research in this area). Urim and Thummim are rendered by the phrase δήλωσις καὶ ἀλήθεια, which clearly indicates their revelatory significance for the translators.[62] The

---

[56] TJ Isa 5:1, 3; 21:12; 22:14; 24:16, and passim.

[57] Cf. recently Lust, "Messianism", 180.

[58] Cf. EpArist 302, 307, 310 f. Philo *Mos* 2:34, 37—41 considers the Septuagint to have been given as revelation: its translators were inspired, under divine dictation *Mos* 2:37; they were "prophets and priests of the mysteries, whose sincerity and singleness of thought has enabled them to go hand in hand with the purest of spirits, the spirit of Moses" (40). And "to this day" the Alexandrians celebrate an annual festival on the isle of Pharos, commemorating "the place in which the *light* of that version first *shone out* (ἐξέλαμψε)" (41).

[59] Cf. Schürer/Vermes *HJPAJC*, 3:474 f.

[60] See m.Meg 1:8 and cf. Schürer/Vermes, *HJPAJC* 3:496 f.; but cf. also LXX Esth 10:3*l*, giving Palestinian sanction (see Swete, *Introduction*, 25).

[61] Thus e.g. יהוה = κύριος, צבאות/שדי = παντοκράτωρ. The אהיה of Exodus 3:14 becomes ὁ ὤν (a favourite title for God in Philo). רוח = πνεῦμα, כבוד = δόξα: both Greek terms experienced a significant change of meaning over against secular usage (cf. Forster, "Δόξα", 312; Kittel, "δόξα", 245 f.).

[62] N.B. δηλόω translates ידע (qal, nifal [esp. Exod 6:3], hifil/afel), ירה (hifil), ראה

occasional use of the suggestive term λόγιον[63] for the words of God goes some way toward explaining the Jewish Hellenistic idea of Scripture as containing divine "oracles".[64] Anti-anthropomorphic concerns are also present.[65]

3.2. The Use of ἀποκαλύπτω[66]

This word is the main Septuagintal equivalent to גלה,[67] and like the latter it carries primarily secular connotations. But even where it is found with divine subject or object, ἀποκαλύπτω may still frequently convey a non-technical meaning, e.g. of uncovering something previously obscured from perception.[69] Where it does carry specifically theological weight, this is most often in keeping with the underlying גלה (and hence does not disclose any particular *Tendenz*).[70] It is particularly Theodotion's version of Daniel which (unlike LXX) makes frequent use of ἀποκαλύπτω in the sense of an "apocalyptic" (visionary) disclosure of transcendent realities;[71] this meaning of the word is also common in the New Testament. The rare noun ἀποκάλυψις[72] is not used with theological connations in the LXX.

(nifal), שמע (hifil), חוה (afel), גלא. Note also ψ 118:130 δήλωσις τῶν λόγων σου for פתח דבריך. Cf. further p. 85 n. 22 above.

[63] Note esp. Num 24:4, 16; Deut 33:9; ψ 118 passim; cf. Wisd 16:11.

[64] E.g. EpArist 177; Philo *Fuga* 60; *Cont* 25; *Congr* 134; Josephus *BJ* 6:311–313. Cf. Acts 7:38, Rom 3:1f., etc.

[65] E.g. Exod 4:16; 24:10; Deut 14:23, etc. Cf. Fritsch, *Anti- Anthropomorphisms*, 62–65 and passim; idem, "Study", 53–55 (on the treatment of the "seeing God" motif, e.g. Exod 3:6; 24:10f.; Num 12:8; 1 Sam 28:13; Isa 38:11).

[66] For the history of usage cf. Oepke ("καλύπτω", esp. 567ff.); Smith, "History", 9–20. N.B. φανερόω occurs only in Jer 33(40):6, where it appears to render גלה; however, the text here differs widely from MT. Also Codex Coislinianus ψ 50:8 (ed. Field, *Hexapla* 2:174).

[67] Cf. the frequency list in Zobel "גלה", 1020.

[68] Sexual uncovering: e.g. Exod 22:26; Lev 18:6ff.; 20:11ff.; Ezek 16:36, 57; 23:29. With τὸ ὦτιον, meaning to "inform, announce": 1 Sam 9:15; 20:2, 13; 22:8, 17; 2 Sam 7:27; Ruth 4:4. Similarly with τοὺς ὀφθαλμούς: e.g. Num 22:31; 24:4, 16; ψ 118:18. Cf. Gehman, "Adventures", 126. The usage in Philo and Josephus is similar.

[69] It is of course difficult to draw firm distinctions in this respect, but see e.g. 1 Sam 2:27; Isa 52:10; 53:1; Sir 1:6.

[70] Cf. e.g. Num 24:4, 16; 1 Sam 3:7, 21; Isa 56:1; ψ 118:18. Of course, once a more theological usage of גלה/ἀποκαλύπτω had been adopted (cf. already Sir), such passages would invite special attention.

[71] See Dan ϑ' 2:19, 22, 28f., 30, 47; 10:1 (all גלה/גלא). Note also e.g. Isa 40:5 α' σ' ϑ'; Hab 3:3 α' ϑ'. Cf. Oepke, "καλύπτω", 579; Lührmann, *Offenbarungsverständnis*, 75.

[72] Only 1 Sam 20:30 and Sir 11:27; 22:22; 42:1.

3.3. "Mystery" in the Greek Versions

The LXX is reluctant to join the Targums in venturing forth into the realm of divine mysteries. This is perhaps clearest in its use of the word μυστήριον: with the exception of Daniel[73] (where LXX *multum ab Hebraica veritate discordant*[74]), the term occurs only in apocryphal works.[75] In the earlier books the theme of a revelation of mysteries is only rarely exploited beyond the Hebrew *Vorlage*; passages where the Targums tend to exercise the Palestinian penchant for haggadah (Gen 49; Num 24; Deut 32 f., etc.) are here left without elaboration.[76]

Other versions make a little more frequent use of μυστήριον, though it is still quite rare. In addition to previously cited references, Theodotion uses it to translate רז in Dan 4:6. סוד is rendered μυστήριον in Job 15:8 (ϑ', σ'); Psa 24(25):14 (ϑ', Quinta); Prov 11:13 (σ'); Prov 20:19 (ϑ'). Another interesting case is Isa 24:16, where in certain versions[77] (as in some Jewish interpretations) the puzzling phrase רזי־לי רזי־לי. ("Woe is me, woe is me") is rendered τὸ μυστήριόν μου ἐμοί, κτλ. Relevant uses of other terms such as ἀπόρρητον (Amos 3:7 α', סוד), ἀπόκρυφον (Isa 45:3 LXX, מטמון) are also rare.

One reason for the reluctant use of mystery language esp. in the LXX could be that at the time of its completion such terminology was still felt to be too obviously tainted with unacceptable pagan overtones. The Septuagint betrays its abhorrence of contemporary mystery religions by bringing to bear upon them the Biblical prohibitions of Canaanite practices.[78]

Positive stress is placed instead on the revelatory sufficiency of the Torah.[79]

---

[73] Dan 2:18, 19, 27, 28, 29, 39, 47 (2x).

[74] Jerome on Dan 4:6 (Migne 5:514).

[75] Tob 12:7, 11; Jdt 2:2; Wisd 2:22; 6:22; 14:15; 14:23; Sir 3:18; 22:22; 27:16, 17, 21; 2 Macc 13:21. The same incidentally applies to the other words of the μυστ-root: μυστάϑεια/μυστής Wisd 12:6; μυστικῶς 3 Macc 3:10; also μυέω/μυέομαι 3 Macc 2:30 (cf. Phil 4:12, wholly metaphorical). See however e.g. Symmachus Num 25:5; Isa 3:3; 6:10.

[76] But see e.g. Isa 33:6; Psa 50(51):8 (τὰ ἄδηλα καὶ τὰ κρύφια τῆς σοφίας σου ἐδήλωσάς μοι). Haggadah and Halakhah are understandably rare, but for a well-known example of the latter see Gen 2:2 (ויכל אלהים ביום השביעי מלאכתו — LXX ἐν τῇ ἡμέρᾳ τῇ ἕκτῃ); familiar Palestinian Haggadah occurs e.g. in Gen 6:2 (οἱ ἄγγελοι θεοῦ); Num 24:17 (ἀναστήσεται ἄνθρωπος), etc. Cf. also Swete, *Introduction*, 327 f.; Frankel, *Einfluss*, passim.

[77] ϑ', σ' and a range of MSS (see the Göttingen LXX). Cf. p. 119 n. 97 below.

[78] See e.g. Num 25:3 ("Israel was initiated ἐτελέσϑη into Baal-Peor"), 5; ψ 105:28 (cf. Philo *Spec* 1:56); further Wisd 12:3−6; 14:15, 23 etc. See Schreiner, "Leitlinien", 377 on the apparent avoidance of mystical language in Isa 23:18 and 58:14; cf. further Bertram, "Praeparatio", 231; Hengel, *Judentum*, 368 n. 570; Horbury, "False Prophecy", 500. On the much more accommodating attitude to pagan thought in LXX Job (e.g. 9:9, 42:14) see Swete, *Introduction*, 316 and n. 1; Gerleman, *Job*, esp. 38 ff.

[79] See esp. Isa 33:6; also 8:16; 24:16; and Chapter 3 above on Ben Sira. Cf. Seeligmann, *Septuagint*, 105−107.

At the same time the very inclusion of additions (e.g. Psa 151; Job 42:17a—e; Add Esth) as well as Palestinian (e.g. Sir; PssSol) and Alexandrian (e.g. Wisd; 3—4 Macc) "deutero-canonical" writings suggests a degree of flexibility about the inspiration and authority of τὰ λοιπὰ τῶν βιβλίων (Sir Prologue), and hence about continued prophetic activity.

Wherever sufficient evidence was available, we have observed a basic continuity of thought about revelation and divine mysteries in the Ancient Versions. In the Targums, although the Shekhinah has departed, God's nearness to His people is frequently emphasized. Continuing revelation takes place through the scribal teaching of Torah and through the work of the *meturgeman* himself. The heavenly mysteries of the eschaton are perceived in a familiar mode, but their study is discouraged (cf. the Rabbis), since revelation appears to be virtually unattainable even for the ancient holy men.

The generally more conservative LXX and other Greek Versions gradually abandon their reluctance to use μυστήριον and other pagan religious terms in describing divine revelation. The theological use of ἀποκαλύπτω is still rare. Revelation is focused primarily in the Torah (this is also emphasized by a number of translation devices), though the understanding of the other sacred writings seems to allow for ongoing inspiration.

Chapter Seven

Early Rabbinic Literature

1. Introduction

This chapter deals primarily with the religious views reflected in the Rabbinic teachings of the Tannaitic period (c. A. D. 70—220). My sources will include a variety of documents clearly dating from a later period, but I propose to cite Amoraic evidence only in order to illustrate views akin at least in substance to those of the earliest Rabbinic period.[1]

By way of clarification, we must acknowledge that the halakhic and much of the haggadic material at hand reflects in the first instance the scholarly discussions of the academy, rather than a broadly representative pattern of mainstream popular piety. In order therefore to supplement this picture, occasional reference will be made where appropriate to homiletical midrashim (LevR, Tanḥ, PesR, etc.) as well as to the mystical *Hekhalot* literature. To some extent, this latter group of writings falls outside the period under purview, and outside my area of expertise; but it indicates one important domain of life and practice in which apocalyptic modes of thought enjoyed continued popularity in the Rabbinic period.[2] Another broadly contemporary but non-Rabbinic reflection of the widespread interpretive interest in our theme is the importance of "hidden things" and their disclosure in Samaritan texts.[3]

The inquiry will begin by asking about Rabbinic views on the possibility of present-day revelation. In this context I will offer some remarks on the revelatory status of the Torah — or rather, in this case, of the "two Torot". The second major section will then unfold the theme of a revelation of halakhic and other mysteries.

---

[1] My dating procedure (e.g. R. Meir T3 = third generation Tanna; Rab A1 = first generation Amora, etc.), follows for the most part the index of Rabbis in Strack/Stemberger, *Introduction*; occasionally M—L, 700—708 has been taken into account. Generally on this subject see Neusner's important remarks in *Rabbinic Traditions*, 3:180—185.

[2] Cf. n. 108 below.

[3] Cf. p. 115 below. See further Wieder, *Scrolls*, 57—62 on Karaite interpretation.

2. Rabbinic Views of Revelation

2.1. The Question of Contemporary Revelation

> When the first Temple was destroyed, the kingship was removed from the House of David. The Urim and Thummim ceased. ... When the latter prophets died, i.e. Haggai, Zechariah, and Malachi, the Holy Spirit ceased in Israel.

This quotation (t.Sot 13:2f.) is perhaps the best known of a considerable number of Rabbinic affirmations that divine revelation through the Holy Spirit or prophecy has come to an end in Israel,[4] at least for the time being.[5] Such reticence about contemporary prophetic activity is familiar from earlier chapters; as above, however, we would expect this trend to be mitigated or compensated in a number of ways.

2.1.1. Continuing Activity of the Spirit/Shekhinah/Prophecy[6]

"The Holy Spirit of the rabbinic literature is really almost synonymous with God as he addresses men through the scriptures."[7] Judgements like this suggest something of the substantial difference between Rabbinic references to the Spirit and those e.g. in the New Testament. Nevertheless, it is significant that a number of Rabbinic texts *do* speak of the continued activity of God's Spirit. Thus in a moving story we read that when Vespasian was having young Jewish men and women shipped to brothels in Rome, they all threw themselves overboard and drowned in order to avoid this fate; hereupon "the Holy Spirit wept and said, 'For these do I weep.'"[8]

By and large one can discern a dialectical belief in God's continuing nearness to His people despite a seemingly increased transcendence.[9] Complementing

---

[4] Cf. t.Sot 12:5; t.Sot 13:4 par. (Hillel); b.Sot 48b; y.Sot 9:14 (24b23–25); b.Yoma 9b, 21b; b.Sanh 11a (Hillel/Samuel); b.BB 12a; y.Taan 2:1 (65a60ff.); GenR 37:7; ExR 32:1; QohR 12:7 (end); CantR 8:9.3, etc. Also e.g. DeutR 6:14 on the Shekhinah (cf. Urbach, *Sages*, 1:54f.).

[5] Cf. e.g. NumR 15:10 (R. Levi b. Rabbi), 25 (R. Tanḥuma b. Abba A5); PesR 1:2, for the conviction that the Spirit would return upon all Israel in the eschaton. Cf. Schäfer, *Vorstellung*, 112–115 for additional references; see also Ezek 36:27, Joel 3:1f. and Acts 2:16ff., etc.

[6] For the close relation of Spirit and Shekhinah cf. e.g. b.Yoma 9b, 21b. See also Blenkinsopp, "Prophecy", 261 n.205. The Shekhinah is rare in the Mishnah (only m.Abot 3:2, 6): cf. Urbach, *Sages*, 1:42f. For the Spirit as the author of prophecy see the earlier chapters and cf. Str-B 2:129f.

[7] Lampe, *God*, 60.

[8] LamR 1.16.45. For the Holy Spirit as effectively applying Scripture see similarly m.Sot 9:6; and below on CantR 8.13.2.

[9] Kuhn, *Selbsterniedrigung*, 43 n.180, observes "wie für das rabbinische Judentum ei-

the notion of a departure of the Spirit or Shekhinah, there is after A. D. 70 a tradition of the Shekhinah's going into exile *with* Israel, שכינה גלחה עמהם.[10] God hears even the prayer which a man whispers behind a pillar in the synagogue,[11] and the one who sins in secret "crowds the feet of the Shekhinah".[12] Hence, the Jew must exercise כוונה (devotion) in prayer: man's prayer is not accepted unless he "puts his heart in his hands".[13] "In his prayer a man should think that the Shekhinah is before him" (b. Sanh 22a). Lack of devotion and concentration offends God's Spirit: when the *Shema'* is read inattentively, "then the Holy Spirit cries out, 'Make haste, my Beloved'" (CantR 8.13.2).

All this may be taken to indicate a belief in the continuing presence not just of God, but of divine revelation as well. That *prophecy* has not completely died out is also suggested by the fact that false prophets are still a concern in the Mishnah.[14]

Sometimes the discussion hinges not on the question of the Spirit's activity, but on the worthiness of people to receive him; thus the disciples of Hillel, among others, were worthy of the Holy Spirit.[15] Qualities such as saintliness and a closeness to God are cited as requirements;[16] the Shekhinah rests on those who are [sc. like Moses] rich, strong, tall,[17] wise, and humble.[18] If, on the other hand, a prophet is boastful or angry, "his prophecy departs from him" (b. Pes 66b Resh Lakish A2).

These affirmations of God's presence notwithstanding, one does gain the impression that the remaining traces of the Spirit's revelatory activity in contem-

---

nerseits Gott in eine größere Ferne gerückt ist, als sie das AT je kannte, wie aber andererseits auch seine *Nähe* stärker als im AT empfunden wurde."

[10] Mek *Pisḥa* 14 (Exod 12:41; ed. Lauterbach 1:114f., cf. p. 113); cf. SifNum 84; b. Meg 29a (R. Simeon b. Yoḥai T3). Cf. Cohen, "Shekhinta", esp. 150ff. However, the Shekhinah does not reveal itself outside Palestine: Mek *Pisḥa* 1 (R. Eleazar b. Zadok T2; ed. Lauterbach 1:7f.); cf. e.g. TJ Ezek 1:3 *contra* MT.

[11] Y. Ber 9:1 (13a25−27); cf. DeutR 7:2 (R. Aibu A4): "If you are in a synagogue *God* stands by your side."

[12] B. Ḥag 16a; b. Qid 31a (דוחק רגלי שכינה; R. Isaac T4 [?]).

[13] B. Taan 8a (Ammi A3); cf. MidrPsa 108.1.1 (R. Samuel b. Naḥmani A3); b. Erub 65a (Rab T6), etc.

[14] M. Sanh 1:5; 11:1, 5 (נביאי שקר; cf. נביאי כזב in 1 QH 4:16); see also 11 QTemple 54:8ff. Prophets occur in m. Shebu 2:2.

[15] B. Sukk 28a; b. BB 134a. Also Hillel and Samuel the Little T2 (t. Sot 13:3f.; b. Sot 48b; b. Sanh 11a; CantR 8:9.3). Cf. section 2.1.3 below.

[16] M. Sot 9:15 (R. Phineas b. Jair T4) par. b. AZ 20b; LevR 35:7 (R. Aha [A4?]: learning in order to practise). Cf. also Büchler, *Types*, 55−57; Cohen, *Talmud*, 121; Schäfer, *Vorstellung*, 127ff.

[17] *Sic*; cf. b. Bek 45b: "the Holy One, Blessed be He, takes pride in men of tall stature."

[18] B. Ned 38a (R. Yoḥanan A2); b. Shab 92a. Cf. SifNum 95; b. Sanh 17a (R. Simeon: the humility of Eldad and Medad was rewarded by the life-long gift of prophecy).

porary life were seen as different in kind from the manifestations of former times. Two expressions of this attitude merit further attention: one, the replacement of the Holy Spirit by the heavenly voice, בת קול; and secondly, the belief that the prophetic office has been transferred to the Rabbis.

2.1.2. The Holy Spirit Replaced by Bat Qôl

Some of the same texts which speak of the departure of the Spirit or Shekhinah also mention an apparent substitute which God has put in its place: the בת קול (aram. [א]ברת קל; lit. "daughter of a voice").[19] Its function is to give advice and direction in situations of reflection and dispute.[20] Occasionally it resolves exegetical questions[21] or such feuds as between the schools of Shammai and Hillel.[22] It can also declare God's will or sentiment in response to a situation — as reflected in the famous story of Aqiba's martyrdom: when he died reciting the *Shema'*, "a *bat qôl* went forth and proclaimed: Happy art thou, Aqiba, that thy soul has departed with the word אחד!"[23]

The *bat qôl*, however, which in some ways resembles divination,[24] is by no means an *equivalent* replacement of prophecy. The Rabbis themselves realized that, as a greatly inferior indicator of the divine will, it carried no independent authority. The best known illustration (b.BM 59b[25]) relates how R. Eliezer

---

[19] E.g. t.Sot 13:3—6; b.Sanh 11a; b.Yoma 9b, etc.

[20] Cf. b.AZ 17a (upon R. Elazar b. Durdaya's repentance); b.Taan 25b (R. Aqiba T3); cf. QohR 9:7.1 (upon Abba Taḥna's battle between good and evil impulse). Solomon discerned the mother of the disputed child (1 Kgs 3:16—27) by means of a *bat qôl* (GenR 85:12). Samuel the boy heard "a voice from the temple of the Lord" (קלא אשתמע מהיכלא דיוי) in TJ 1 Sam 3:3, and a "vox de caelo" in LAB 53:3. Cf. further Dan 4:31 LXX; Matt 3:17, 17:5 par.; Acts 9:4 (?); TAbr 10:15; ApAbr 9:1 f.; 10:1, 4; 2 Bar 13:1 f.; 22:1 f.; 4 Ezra 14:38; Art (Eusebius *PrEv* 9.27.21, 36); Josephus *Ant* 13:282; 19:60—61; *BJ* 6:300 (cf. Tacitus, *Hist* 5:13); SibOr 1:267 f., 275; HermVis 4.1.4, etc.

[21] B.Meg 29a (Bar Kappara T6); b.Sanh 94a (Bar Kappara T6); QohR 7:16 (R. Benaiah [T5?]). See also Str-B 1:130.

[22] B.Erub 13b; y.Ber 1:7 (3b67—74): both speak the words of the living God, but the halakhah is according to Hillel.

[23] B.Ber 61b. B.Ber 3a: Rabbi Yose (A4) heard a divine voice in the ruins of Jerusalem, "cooing like a dove and saying, 'Woe to the children on account of whose sins I destroyed My house and burnt My temple and exiled them among the nations of the world!'" See also on b.BM 59b below; and cf. Str-B 1:128 ff.

[24] Lieberman, *Hellenism*, 194 ff.; he also adduces the stories of St. Antony and St. Augustine, who took as divinely given "a voice or a word heard without seeing the person who uttered it, or a word heard from a person who was not conscious of the import of his saying." Cf. b.Meg 32a (R. Yoḥanan A2), and further in Str-B 1:134. Cf. also Fishbane, *Interpretation*, 456 on kledonomancy.

[25] Note that, although this text is introduced as a *baraita*, its parallel in y.MQ 3.1, 81c69 ff. is not. Cf. Stemberger, *Einleitung*, 192.

[T2], having exhausted his own arguments to prove a case, appealed to heaven. A heavenly voice endorsed his views on principle ("the halakhah is always with him"), but then

> R. Joshua got up and said, "It is not in heaven" [Deut 30:12]. What did he mean by this? R. Jeremiah said, "The Law was given us from Sinai. We pay no attention to a heavenly voice. For already from Sinai the Law said, 'By a majority you are to decide' [cf. Exod 23:2].

Thus, it was not considered improper to rule evidence of a *bat qôl* out of court where necessary — and especially where it conflicted with the established consensus of understanding the revelation at Sinai.[26]

Nevertheless, it would seem unwarranted to read this lack of authority as "a sure indication that it was not associated with any experience of God."[27] Sometimes halakhic decisionmaking *does* take into account the witness of a heavenly voice,[28] and a number of instances appear in fact to suppose a close personal identification of God with statements derived from such a source.[29] Perhaps it is best understood as an occasional, tentative disclosure of God's disposition on a particular matter, a disclosure which needs to be tested against rabbinic majority opinion.

2.1.3. The Holy Spirit / Prophecy Transferred to the Sages

Rabbinic literature continues the belief that at least some of the prophetic functions have been transferred to the sages or scribes (see Chapter Three above). Various early sages had a prophetic gift;[30] several Rabbis are, moreover, given special insights by the Holy Spirit in matters of human predicament.[31] The Shekhinah resides wherever Torah is studied.[32] Amoraic dicta,

---

[26] R. Reuben A4 tells the parable of a king who can be personally approached when He is in His province, but in whose absence only an ineffective statue remains (CantR 8:9.3). Cf. CantR 8:9.3 (R. Aibu A4); b.Yoma 9b (Abba A3[?]); b.Ber. 52a par. b.Erub 7a (R. Joshua T2); PesR 35:1 (on Cant. 8:9); t.Sheb 3:8; b.Yeb 122a (School of Hillel). See also Str-B 1:125 f.; M-L 16; Leivestad, "Dogma", 289 f.; Blenkinsopp, "Prophecy", 251.

[27] Thus Kadushin, *Rabbinic Mind*, 262.

[28] E.g. m.Yeb 16:6; cf. n. 22 above; Str-B 1:133, n. 29.

[29] See the continuation of the passage from b.BM 59b just quoted: God "laughed and said, 'My children have conquered Me'"; and cf. above on R. Yose in the ruins of Jerusalem (b.Ber 3a).

[30] Cf. e.g. R. Ḥanina b. Dosa T1 in b.Ber 34b; b.Yeb 121b; R. Aqiba T2 in LevR 21:8.

[31] Y.Sot 1:4 (16d50); LevR 9:9: the Holy Spirit (in DeutR 5:15 Elijah) grants R. Meir T3 insight into the distress of a woman disciple. Cf. LevR 21:8 (R. Aqiba T2). See also b.Kal 51a (R. Aqiba's ability to identify the child of a menstruating adulteress because "the secret of the Lord is with them that fear Him" [Psa 25:14]). Cf. also Tg Ruth 3:18; EcclR 10:16 for Solomon; and see Schäfer, *Vorstellung*, 121–123.

[32] E.g. m.Abot 3:3 (R. Hananiah b. Teradion T2). Baeck, "Offenbarung", 660 sees

therefore, compare Rabbinic activities with those of the prophets,[33] and sometimes even assert their superiority over the latter.[34] "Since the day when the
Temple was destroyed, prophecy has been taken from the prophets and given
to the wise";[35] a different and perhaps somewhat cynical view is that prophecy
has been taken from the prophets and "given to fools and children".[36] Anyone
who teaches Torah in public,[37] who receives a precept in faith,[38] or who studies
the Torah with the aim of fulfilling it,[39] will be privileged to receive the Holy
Spirit. Several texts, then, affirm a measure of continuity between the Spirit's
activity in the prophetic period and the present work of the sages.[40]

2.2. Torah and Torot

Fundamental to any and all Rabbinic talk of revelation is the Torah. The
study, love, and obedience of God as revealed in Torah is the heartbeat of Judaism.

2.2.1. The Primacy of Torah

2.2.1.1. The Torah is of divine origin. He who denies that the Torah is from
heaven has no share in the world to come (m. Sanh 10:1). "Upon three things

this conviction as basic to Rabbinic mysticism. Cf. Kadushin, *Rabbinic Mind*, 227,
194—272 passim; also Sanders, *PPJ*, 221 f.

[33] B.Shab 119b (R. Judah [A4?]); b.MQ 17a (Resh Lakish A2).

[34] B.BB 12a (R. Amemar A6: "a wise man is even superior to a prophet"); cf. y.Ber
1:7 (3b61; R. Tanḥum b. Ḥiyya A3: "the decisions of the elders are worth more than
those of the prophets").

[35] B.BB 12a (R. Abdimi of Haifa A2). Cf. y.Sanh 10:2 (28b65—68 R. Eleazar [T2]):
"Where there are no sages, there are no prophets; where there are no prophets, the Holy
Spirit no longer reveals Himself; and then there will be no more synagogues or acade-
mies. . . ." Cf. Neusner, "Authority", 375.

[36] B.BB 12b. Cohen, *Talmud*, 124 suggests this may be a thinly disguised reference to
prophetic pretenders (cf. e.g. Josephus *Ant* 20:97, 169; *BJ* 6:286, 300 ff.). Schäfer, *Vorstellung*, 99 f. sees here converse irony, since R. Yoḥanan in b.Yoma 9b speaks emphatically
for the cessation of prophecy. However, the illustrations cited in b.BB 12b include actual
instances of "prophetic" insight on the part of the children of Rabbis. Cf. possibly Matt
11:25; 21:15 ff. for similar statements.

[37] CantR 1:1.8 (R. Judan A4, on Eccl 12:9).

[38] Mek *Beshallaḥ* 7 (end; R. Nehemiah T3, on Exod 14:3); ed. Lauterbach 1:252.

[39] LevR 35:7 (R.Aḥa A2 [?]). Cf. b.Ber 64a; b.MQ 29a: "He that goes out of the synagogue and enters the House of Study (בית המדרש) . . . shall gain the privilege of being
admitted into the presence of the Shekhinah" (R. Levi b. Ḥiyya A3).

[40] Cf. further t.Eduy 1:1; m.Sheb 2:2. Schäfer, "Geist", 174 also cites y.AZ 2:8 and
SER 30. See m.Abot 1:1 on the seamless transition from the prophets to the men of the
"Great Synagogue" (כנסת הגדולה) and to the sages. In b.Ber 55b (R. Yoḥanan A2 [?]) the
spontaneous citation of a Scripture verse upon rising in the morning is called נבואה קטנה.

the world stands: upon Torah, upon Worship, and upon Deeds of Kindness" (m. Abot 1:2). The Torah as such can never be superseded,[41] since it is funda-mental to the knowledge of God. The Sinaitic מתן תורה is *Uroffenbarung*; in re-lation to this all else is but meta-revelation, revelation *about* Revelation. The Torah is the light of the world.[42]

2.2.1.2. Mt. Sinai is the main literary (as well as geographical) *topos* of re-velation. The Sinai event is the subject of considerable meditation and specula-tion, its reality frequently being accentuated by an appeal to the empirical sen-ses of sight, of hearing, and even of smell: "With every single word that went forth from the mouth of the Holy One, blessed be He, the whole world was fil-led with spices [i.e. fragrance]."[43] At the same time, this revelation at Sinai is seen by some as an anticipation of the eschaton. When God gave the Ten Com-mandments, the earth feared this might be the beginning of the resurrection[44] – the events of Sinai foreshadowing redemption and new creation.[45]

2.2.1.3. The Torah sustains the world (cf. above on m. Abot 1:2). The uni-verse was created according to the Torah, which existed before creation and holds the universe together. Without it, the world would revert to chaos.[46]

2.2.1.4. The Torah is canonically defined. By and large there is a consensus

---

[41] DeutR 8:6: "Moses said to Israel: 'Do not say: Another Moses will arise and bring us another Torah from heaven. I therefore warn you, 'It is not in heaven,' [Deut 30:12] that is to say, no part of it has remained in heaven." Despite a certain anti-Christian po-lemic, this excerpt expresses a genuine sentiment of rabbinic religion. But note e.g. Da-vies, *Torah*; Jervell, "Tora"; Schäfer, "*Torah*"; on the debate about "new" Torah in the World to Come.

[42] E.g. DeutR 7:3; ExR 36:3. Cf. above, Chapters 1, 2, 6. The term "light of the world" was also applied e.g. to Jerusalem (GenR 59:5), God (NumR 15:5), the Temple (b. BB 4a), the Rabbis (b. BB 4a).

[43] Thus b. Shab 88b (R. Joshua b. Levi A1); cf. ARN 11. See also e.g. *LAB* 32:8 (the fragrance of the fruits of Paradise was released at Mt. Sinai); Sir 24:15; and cf. above on Philo, *Decal*. Possibly an allusion to Cant (e.g. 2:3; 3:6; 4:6; 8:14) is here intended. See Horbury, "Suffering", 151 and n. 34; cf. further Lohmeyer, *Wohlgeruch*, 27 on 2 Bar 29:7 (concerning the revelation of the Messiah).

[44] PesR 21:4 (R. Yoḥanan A2 on Psa 76:9). Cf. also Ginzberg, *Legends* 3:91; Baeck, "Offenbarung", 661.

[45] Cf. esp. TJ Hab 3:3 f.; also *LAB* 32:8. See Potin, *Fête*, 238; and Chernus, *Mysticism*, 14 ("in rabbinic Judaism the moment of revelation plays a crucial role as a turning point in the movement of history from creation to redemption"); Heinemann, *Prayer*, 33 (he also points to Psa 19 as combining the same triad of creation, revelation, and redemp-tion: p. 230).

[46] E.g. b. Pes 68b (R. Sheshet A3); SifDeut 37 (ed. Finkelstein, p. 70 on Prov 8:22); GenR 1:1, 5, 14; 8:2 (Torah preceded creation by 2000 years: citing Prov 8:30); b. Shab 88a (Resh Lakish A2: if Israel had refused the Torah, creation would have returned to תוהו ובוהו); PesR 21:4 (R. Ḥiyya b. Abba T5; R. Aḥa [A4?]). Cf. e.g. Baeck, "Offenba-rung", 661; Cohen, *Talmud*, 29, 131 f.; Ehrlich, "Tora", 540.

on Scripture as consisting of the "twenty-four" books,[47] and from Tannaitic times there is strong condemnation of those who read in the "outside" (heretical) works.[48]

2.2.1.5. Prophets and Writings derive from Torah. Not only the non-canonical books take second place to the Torah. The Pentateuch is as it were the "canon within the canon": "All the prophets looked into a dim glass (אספקלריה = *specularia*), but Moses our teacher looked through a clear glass."[49] This view, however, need not in itself diminish the status of the prophets: they speak (only) what was already contained in the Sinaitic Torah.[50]

2.2.2. *The Presence of Torah*

> While we say of God that "He has given the Torah" [in the past], He can also be designated at the same time [in every present time] as "the One Who gives the Torah". At every hour and time the fountain gushes forth without interruption, and what He gives at any time was potentially contained in what He gave [sc. at Sinai].[51]

This quotation from a well-known 17th-century Jewish treatise beautifully summarizes what Scholem calls "the eternal present of the revelation at Sinai".[52]

---

[47] Cf. e.g. CantR 4:11 (R. Simeon b. Lakish A2); b.Taan 8a (R. Adda b. Abbahu A2?); and often. The canonicity of certain books was questioned at times: Prov, Cant, Eccl (e.g. ARN 1; b.Shab 30b). Ezek was accepted, albeit thought to contradict the Torah: b.Shab 13b, 30a (Hananiah b. Hezekiah T1).

Sir is occasionally cited, though not in the customary form of Scripture quotations (כאשר כתוב בספר בן סירא): b.Sanh 100b and b.Yeb 63b (numerous quotations); b.Ḥag 13a (Sir. 3:21f., R. Aḥa b. Jacob A4). Raba A4 explicitly includes Sir 13:15 in the Hagiographa (b.BQ 92b). On the other hand it is considered the earliest non-canonical work (t.Yad 2:13); b.Sanh 100b (R. Joseph A3 [?]) prohibits its reading; and QohR 12:12 forbids even having it in one's house. Cf. the fuller discussion in Smend, *Weisheit*, xlvi–lvi. As late as the 10th century (Saadya) Sir was (like Scripture) pointed, accented, and divided into verses (Smend, lv; Lévi in *Ecclesiasticus*, vi). None of the pertinent Genizah fragments I have seen (T−S. Glass 12.727, 863−4, 871; 16.312−315) are pointed; but they employ the refined square script normally used for biblical, liturgical, and talmudical codices (m.Meg 1:8, 2:2; Birnbaum, "Alphabet", 707), and are divided into verses (except 12.863−4).

[48] M.Sanh 10:1 (R. Aqiba T2); cf. e.g. NumR 14:4.

[49] B.Yeb 49b (anonymous); cf. Num 12:6−8. Also cf. m.Meg 3:1 and b.Meg 27a (one may sell prophetic books to buy a scroll of Torah but not vice versa); m.Meg 4:4 (one may leave out verses from the prophets, but not from the Law). See also e.g. Krüger, "Würdigung", 11 (though he may be overstating the point).

[50] E.g. b.Meg 14a; b.Taan 9a (R. Yoḥanan A2); ExR 28:6; ExR 42:8 (R. Joshua b. Levi A1). אלה המצות in Lev 27:34 was taken to mean that "a prophet may henceforth make no innovations" (b.Shab 104a: R. Ḥiyya b. Abba T5).

[51] Horovitz, שני לוחות 25b. Translation as given in Scholem, "Revelation", 301.

[52] Scholem, "Revelation", 289.

Having come to terms with the cessation (for all practical purposes) of both prophecy and of the Temple, the Rabbis formulated a Jewish orthodoxy based on a substitution of the (study and practice of) Torah for the Temple.[53] This included the notion of a continual presence of the Sinaitic revelation in the very teachings of the sages; indeed Neusner cannot be far off the mark in suggesting that the rabbi actually "represents and embodies the Torah."[54] "The Holy One, blessed be He, speaks tradition (שמעתא) out of the mouths of all the rabbis."[55]

Numerous authorities attest to the Sinaitic derivation[56] of this "oral law" of Rabbinic tradition (תורה שבעל פה). The Bible, Mishnah, Gemara, Midrashim, even the questions of Rabbinic discussion are all said to have been received by Moses;[57] and from the chain of tradition since Moses derive both their substance and their authority.[58] Sometimes the oral Torah extends even to first-person divine discourse not found in the Bible.[59] The sages unfold and develop the written Scripture to speak to the present-day believer, showing how each precept of oral Torah derives from the text.[60]

---

[53] See e.g. ARN 4 (9b): "The study of Torah is more beloved by God than burnt offerings. ... When a sage sits and expounds to the congregation, Scripture accounts it to him as though he had offered up fat and blood on the altar." Cf. b.Shab 30a; b.Ber 32b (R. Eleazar [ben Shammua T3] et al.); b.Ḥag (R. Yoḥanan A2); also 4QFlor 1:6f. (works of Torah). Similarly, *prayer* became עבודה, liturgical service. As a symbolic sacrifice it was offered at the same times at which the daily sacrifices had been appointed; after the Temple ritual became impossible, prayer thus took its place. See Heinemann/Petuchowski, *Literature*, 2f.; cf. b.Ber 32b; but already Philo *Plant* 126; *Mos* 2:108 (see Wolfson, 2:245f.); 11QPsª 154:10f.; note also the third century marble inscriptions of the 24 priestly courses from Caesarea (*Inscriptions Reveal*, No. 172). And thirdly, *works of kindness* (גמילות חסדים) were a means of atonement (כפרה) as effective as the temple sacrifice: ARN 4 (11a; R. Yoḥanan b. Zakkai, on Hos 6:6); cf. Jas 5:20 and 1 Pet 4:8 on Prov 10:12.

[54] Neusner, *Midrash*, 137.

[55] B.Ḥag 15b (Elijah to R. b. Shila A4). תורה also proceeded from the Great Sanhedrin, m.Sanh 11:2.

[56] Apparent exceptions include e.g. NumR 19:6 (R. Huna [T5?]); PesR 14:13 (R. Aḥa [A2?]): R. Aqiba had things revealed to him which Moses did not. Also Num.R. 14:4: the words of the sages are better than Torah because they are not ambiguous and one can derive proper decisions from them. Cf. Petuchowski, "Bibel", 108.

[57] See ExR 47:1; CantR 1:2.5 (R. Nehemiah T3); b.Ber 5a (R. Simeon b. Laqish A2), etc. Cf. also Ehrlich, "Tora", 542 ("jede gültige Lehre ist Tora und gehört als solche zur Sinaioffenbarung"). Although halakhic disputes between rabbis needed eventually to be decided one way or another, meanwhile the opinions of *both* sides were regarded as part of ongoing revelation: see the famous case of Hillel and Shammai, b.Erub 13b; cf. Num.R. 14:4.

[58] M.Abot 1:1ff.; cf. Bikerman, "Chaîne", esp. 51−54.

[59] E.g. b.Ber 32b; GenR 22:6; m.Abot 2:2, etc. Cf. on 11QTemple above, Chapter 2.

[60] The principle of derivation from Scripture is one of R. Aqiba's major contributions: cf. Sandmel, *Judaism*, 247f.; Scholem, "Revelation", 287. While the oral Torah

It is true that the doctrine of an oral Torah may not have been dominant prior to the events of A. D. 70. But the idea of a dynamic presence of revelation in both written Torah and oral tradition is present at least *in nuce* already prior to the fall of Jerusalem.[61] The revealed word of Scripture was complemented by the revealed word of tradition, which in turn served as the authenticated primary interpretation of Torah.[62]

2.2.3. The Study of Torah

We are thus naturally led to examine the relationship between interpretation and revelation. Interpretation is, in Scholem's words, "the translation of the inexhaustible word of God into the human and attainable sphere . . . the transcription of the voice from Sinai in an unending richness of sound."[63] Rabbinic "theology", indeed, is not system but commentary.[64]

But if this be so, then here too the exegesis of Torah becomes itself a revelatory event — as indeed the Shekhinah abides wherever the Torah is studied (m. Abot 3:3).

> Everyone who is occupied with Torah for its own sake obtains of many things; and not only so, but the whole world is his equivalent. He is called friend, beloved, one that loves God and that loves mankind, that makes glad both God and mankind. . . .
> *They reveal to him secrets of Torah, and he is made like a spring that increases and like a river that does not cease.*[65]

If, therefore, the exposition of Torah constitutes an event of revelation, it may not come as a great surprise that the Rabbis even employ language reminiscent of the fiery Sinai theophany in describing the study of Scripture. It was said of Jonathan b. Uzziel (the traditional author of the Targum to the pro-

---

may be necessary to understand the written, sometimes at any rate it is described as secondary and dependent: Torah sets aside what is instituted by the Rabbis (b. Shab 128b). Cf. also Mek *Baḥodesh* 2 Exod 19:4 (ed. Lauterbach, 2:198 f.).

[61] *Pace* Neusner, "Rabbinic Traditions", esp. 63 ff. Josephus confidently discusses what appears to be the generally accepted Pharisaic doctrine of an oral law (νόμιμα, *Ant* 13:297). Note also Matt 23:2 f.; Mark 7:3 f.; b. Shab 31a (Hillel/Shammai); similarly Sif-Deut 351 (R. Gamaliel T1; ed. Finkelstein, 408); ARN 15:10 ff. (31a); and cf. above, Chapter 1 on Jub, AssMos, 4 Ezra, etc. Cf. further Schäfer, "Dogma", 179–193.

[62] Cf. Hruby, "Concept", 185; Moore, *Judaism* 2:255. See also Molitor, *Philosophie*, 1:4, 46 f.

[63] Scholem, "Revelation", 297. Cf. Cohen, *Talmud*, 125; Molitor, *Philosophie*, 1:47. In the Kabbalah this is taken to its logical consequence, so that Scripture carries "infinite meaning" and is "infinitely interpretable" (Scholem, 295).

[64] Scholem, "Revelation", 289.

[65] M. Abot 6:1 (R. Meir T3). Note the recurrence of the revelatory motif of the spring or river (cf. Chapters 2, 3 above). A curious variation on m. Abot 6:2 occurs in TgEccl 10:20 (*bat qôl* replaced by Raziel, etc.).

phets) that when he was studying Torah, birds flying overhead were immediately burned up.[66]

Interpretation here provides the necessary context for the text of Scripture. Using the example of R. Aqiba's exegesis, A. M. Goldberg has shown how Scripture and tradition were understood to be in a relationship of (sc. God's) speech (*Rede*) and field of reference (*Zeigfeld*); *both* elements together constitute revelation,[67] and the intention is the divine instruction of the reader. "Die wiederkehrende Frage lautet: Warum sagt dies die Schrift? Und die Antwort darauf heißt: Um zu lehren; und gemeint ist immer auch: um *dich* zu lehren — ללמדך."[68]

3. Revelation of Mysteries

Interest in divine secrets and their revelation seems markedly less pronounced in the extant corpus of Rabbinic writings than e.g. at Qumran or in apocalyptic literature. It may be that after the disasters of A. D. 70 and 135 official consensus turned against the kind of esotericism frequently associated with apocalyptic "mysteries" prior to the loss of Jerusalem.[69] Thus e.g. Sifra, SifNum/Deut, and Mekhilta never use the word רז,[70] the Mishnah only once (m. Abot 6:1).

Four categories of revealed mysteries will be discussed: the secrets of Torah, of Israel, and of the eschaton, as well as illegitimately disclosed mysteries.[71]

---

[66] B. Sukk 28a; cf. e.g. b. Ḥag 13a (the story of the boy studying חשמל; see below); 15b (Rabbi T4); b. BM 85b (R. Zera A3 and R. Habiba b. Surmakia); also m. Abot 2:15; JosAsen 17:3, 6. Acts 2:3 may also be significant in this regard. See further Sanders, *PPJ*, 221 f. (citing Urbach).

[67] Goldberg, "Rede", 79.

[68] Goldberg, "Rede", 61. On the theological issue cf. also Tillich, "Idee", 403 and passim; Ricoeur, "Herméneutique", 15 ff., 45 ff.

[69] On the Rabbinic attitude to apocalyptic eschatology see the classic statement of Ginzberg, "Observations", 115–36; but contrast e.g. Rowland, *Open Heaven*, 32–37

[70] Uses of סוד in these documents are restricted to Biblical quotations: Mek *Shirata* 1 on Exod 15:1 (Psa 89:8; ed. Lauterbach, 2:10); 6 on 15:7 (Psa 83:4; ed. Lauterbach, 2:43); 8 on 15:11 (2x Psa 89:8; ed. Lauterbach, 2:61, 63); Sifra 89:1 (Prov 11:13); SifNum 84 (Psa 83:4); SifDeut 27, 357 (Amos 3:7).

[71] Cosmological mysteries, so prominent in the apocalyptic writings, are comparatively rare; but cf. e.g. b. Ḥag 12b (stores of snow and hail, harmful dews, etc.); 3 En 11:1; as well as other *Hekhalot* writings.

Sometimes a Rabbi's insight into a halakhic difficulty or human predicament is seen as a revealed secret: e.g. b. Ḥag 3b (R. Eliezer T2); b. Sot 4b (Ben Azzai T2); b. Sot 10a/ b. Sanh 48b; b. Sanh 106b; b. Nid 20b.

3.1. Mysteries of Torah

"Moses wrote many things in the Torah without explaining them" (ExR 15:22). It follows most naturally on our earlier remarks that we should begin with exegetical mysteries. Together with the (normally halakhic, hence related) "mysteries of Israel", this is certainly the most frequent class of mysteries in the Rabbinic literature. Given the Jewish belief in the completeness and sufficiency of the Torah, an interest in the latter's hidden secrets is only to be expected; *all* mysteries for the Rabbis in the end are mysteries of Torah.[72]

Such secrets of Torah are described in many different ways. They were disclosed first and foremost to Moses who, when he went up to Sinai, saw God tying crowns to the letters of Torah; these crowns were understood by R. Aqiba and others to be fraught with hidden meaning.[73] Moses in turn revealed the secret treasure of Torah to man (e.g. b.Shab 88b). (Exegetical mysteries (כסיאתה, רזין) revealed to Moses are an important feature also of the Samaritan *Memar Marqah*.)[74]

In the present day, these mysteries are accessible primarily to the students of Torah (cf. m.Abot 6:1, above). In addition to scholarship,[75] requirements for

---

[72] Indeed the Torah itself is a secret treasure hidden for 974 generations before the world was created: b.Shab 88b (R. Joshua b. Levi A1). Rowland, *Open Heaven*, 70 observes, "Knowledge of the divine secrets was still a possibility, but the focus of revelation was not the vision or audition but the Torah. In it were given all the treasures of divine wisdom which God had given to men."

[73] B.Shab 89a (R. Joshua b. Levi A1); b.Men 29b. On the common theme of God as "wise in secrets" חכם הרזים, see e.g. b.Ber 58a, b; also 1En 49:2; Asatir 12:26 (חכום וגליאתה כסיאתה); Memar Marqah 1:1 (חכם כל רזין); b.Hag 5b ("God has a place and its name is מסתרים"); HistRech 16:8c (the mystic throne of God knows secrets); *ADPB* p. 354 Yom Kippur (אתה יודע רזי עולם וכ'); *Sefer ha-Razim* 5:26f.; *AposCon* 8.7.1. Cf. also Job 12:22; Dan 2:22; 2Macc 12:41 (God as "revealer of secrets") and many similar texts.

[74] "Mysteries were unravelled for him into revelations [כסיאתה לה נפשו גליאתה]" (*MM* 2:9); God taught him secrets old and new [רזין עתיקין וחדתין] (1:1; 2:9); Moses was a priest of mysteries [כהן כסיאתה] (5:3); cf. 2:11f.; 3:6; 4:1, etc. See further Lowy, *Principles*, 473f.; Macdonald, *Theology*, 308–310.

[75] N.B. the word סוד in Psalm 25:14 ("the secret of the Lord is with them that fear Him") is variously applied by *ma'al* (paronomasia) to those who wear a סודרא, a scholar's turban: b.Shab 77b; b.Qid 8a; b.Pes 111b. In b.Qid 10b and t.Ket 5:1 (Yohanan b. Bag Bag/Yehuda b. Batyra T2) the "inner chambers" of Torah (חדרי תורה: identified as secrets, סתרי תורה, in b.Pes 119a) are known through study (esp. *qal wahomer*).

receiving the revelation of exegetical secrets include righteousness,[76] maturity,[77] soberness,[78] and abstention from idolatry (b.Ket 111a).[79]

Excursus:
Secrets of Torah and Early Mysticism

Interest in the revelation of the mysteries of Torah, which is present from the earliest period, leads in a natural progression to the concerns of *mysticism*:[80] mysticism, that is, which in its broadest definition is really no more than the experiential desire for communion with God, along with an awareness of man's own separation from Him.[81] With Scholem and others we may agree that no difference of *substance* separates early statements of divine throne,[82] chariot[83] or creation mysticism (e.g. b.Hag 14b), and certain passages from later works such as 3 Enoch or even the Zohar.[84]

---

[76] Cf. SifNum 69; NumR 3:13 (end), where the following explanation is given for the unusual dots over the last words of Deut 29:28a (אלהינו ליהוה הנסתרות ולבנינו לנו והנגלות): "If you keep the revealed things, I will also make known to you the hidden." This interpretation would seem to turn the meaning of the passage on its head; but it might imply a Rabbinic awareness that the dots, indicating uncertain authenticity, had their original position over ליהוה אלהינו (leaving 'וכ' לנו והנגלות והנסתרות as the *Urtext*; this is the reading actually offered by one codex, according to Kennicott, *Vetus Testamentum*, 1:427). Cf. Brown, *Mystery*, 6 n. 23.

[77] E.g. CantR 1.2.5 (R. Samuel b. Naḥman A3).

[78] NumR 10:4 (applied to Solomon/Lemuel).

[79] R. Ammi A3 stipulates the five predicates of Isa 3:3: "the captain of fifty and the man of rank, the counsellor and the skilful magician and the expert in charms" (b.Hag 13a) . . . Cf. also TPsJ Gen 49:1 regarding purification before the revelation of mysteries.

[80] *Pace* Moore, *Judaism* 2:243. Cf. Lagrange, *Judaïsme*, 427 f.: Moore's index entry for "mysticism" betrays a narrow identification with esotericism. Willi-Plein, "Geheimnis", 80 insightfully describes rabbinic exegesis as "eine Apokalyptik des Gesetzes, die Deutung der Geheimnisse der Torah".

[81] Cf. Scholem, *Major Trends*, 7 f.; Lagrange, *Judaïsme*, 429.

[82] E.g. b.Hag 13a (Yoḥanan b. Zakkai T1), 14a (R. Aqiba T2 et al.); but cf. also earlier passages such as 1 En 14:8−24, EzekTrag 68 ff.; Dan 7:9 f.; even Isa 6:1 ff.; 1 Kgs 22:19.

[83] Esp. m.Hag 2:1; b.Hag 13a−14b; but also Ezek 1:15−21; Dan 7:9 f.; and cf. 1 Chr 28:18 (on this see Zunz, *Vorträge*, 171 and n. "c"); Sir 49:8; also JosAsen 17:6; OdSol 38:1 ff.

[84] See e.g. Scholem, *Major Trends*, 44; cf. Lagrange, *Judaïsme*, 428 f.; Saldarini, "Apocalypses", 189 ff.; Rowland, *Open Heaven*, 282 ff., 309 ff.; Chernus, *Mysticism*, esp. 1−17; also Alexander in Charlesworth, *OTP* 1:223−253. Exceptions may be the later theurgic, magical, and demonological aspects of ascent (cf. Scholem, *Ursprünge*, 95).

Mysticism and mystical revelations in general were not set in contrast to the interpretation of Torah. Significantly, Chernus observes the close relationship in second-century Midrashim between the terminology used of the Sinaitic revelation and that found in Merkabah mysticism.[85] Much as in apocalyptic, even the visionary revelation of "mysteries" does not come "out of the blue", but is mediated by a meditative exegesis of Scripture passages — be it Gen 1, Ezek 1, or Isa 6.[86]

3.2. The Mysteries of Israel

One of the intriguing aspects of Rabbinic teaching about mysteries is the belief that certain divine secrets have been revealed and entrusted to Israel as a peculiar national property, not to be disclosed to outsiders.[87] We encountered a similar notion in the Dead Sea Scrolls, although at Qumran the "true Israel" was defined much more narrowly. For the Rabbis, the "mysteries of Israel" include such items as the Sabbath (e.g. b.Beṣa 16a), circumcision,[88] the system of ca-

---

[85] Chernus, *Mysticism*, 1; he sees this similarity as an anti-Gnostic device (p. 13). Cf. further b.Meg 31a (Exod 19 and Ezek 1 were the appointed readings for the feast of *Shabu'ot*); b.Ḥag 14b (R. Yoḥanan's dream about feasting at Sinai); also Halperin, *Merkabah*, 128−33; Goldberg, "Traum", 23−27 and passim.

[86] Cf. e.g. Rowland, *Open Heaven*, 226.
The famous *Baraita* about the four *Tanna'im* who entered Paradise (b.Ḥag 14b; y.Ḥag 2:1 (77b8 ff.); t.Ḥag 2:3 f.; Cant.R. 1:4) clearly mentions secrets not accessible to ordinary human knowledge. But Schäfer, "Journey", 26−32 argues that the specific connections of this narrative with merkabah mysticism are redactional. Nevertheless, the word פרדס *is* linked with the interpretation of Torah e.g. in DeutR 7:4 (R. Simeon b. Ḥalafta T5); ExR 30:9 (R. Jose b. Ḥanina A2); cf. below, Chapter 9 on 2 Cor 12:4; note the lifegiving honeycomb (cf. Psa 19:10) of Paradise which proceeds from the angel's mouth in JosAsen 16:1−8, revealing τὰ ἀπόρρητα τοῦ θεοῦ. In Kabbalistic thought פרדס later served as an acronym for the four types of exegesis (פשת "simple", i.e. literal; רמז "allusion", allegorical; דרש "exposition", homiletical; and סוד "secret", esoteric): cf. also Schürer/Vermes, *HJPAJC* 2:354 and n. 56.

[87] E.g. GenR 71:5 (Israel בעלי מסטירים, "keepers of mysteries"). Cf. b.Shab 88a (R. Eleazar [ben Shammua T3]): when Israel gave preference to "we will do" over "we will hear" (Exod 24:7), a *bat qôl* responded, "Who has revealed to my children this secret [מי גילה לבני רז זה] which is employed by the angels...?" Cf. further b.Ket 111a (R. Levi A3); and see below.

[88] E.g. Tanḥ לך לך 23 (ed. Buber p. 79); GenR 49:2 (Psa 25:14).

lendrical intercalation,[89] the Passover lamb,[90] but also the Mishnah[91] and the name of God.[92]

These mysteries of Israel are halakhic in nature and derive from Scripture and Rabbinic teaching.[93] J. Bowker comments about the use of מסטירין,

> ... It had a particular reference to that which constitutes or identifies Israel in its special relation to God ...; and in this way *misteyrin* is appropriately related both to *mishnah* and to circumcision as distinctive marks of Israel. Consequently, Israel stands inside the *misteyrin*, while others stand outside it and cannot participate in it. ..."[94]

The use of the Greek loan word מסטירין (albeit interchangeable with רז, etc.) in this context clearly represents the adoption of a commonplace analogy from the mystery cults.[95]

3.3. Eschatological Mysteries

After the national catastrophe of A. D. 70 (and with the ascendancy of Jewish Christian ideas), the cautiously anti-esoteric attitudes (cf. previously Sir; Josephus) of a school-oriented spiritual leadership won the day. The eschaton was no longer dawning, and it had suddenly become much more difficult to understand:

---

[89] E.g. b.RH 20b (R. Abba A3); ExR 15:27 ("God entrusted the secret of the moon to Israel"; cf. PesR 15:21); b.Ket 112a (R. Eleazar A3, referring to the *council* of intercalation).

[90] E.g. ExR 19:6 (on Exod 12:43): "No other nation shall mingle in it (sc. Israel), and it shall not know its (sc. Israel's) mysteries, but you shall be by yourselves in this world."

[91] E.g. PesR 5:1; Tanḥ וירא 6 (ed. Buber p. 88: on Psa 25:14). Cf. Petuchowski, "Judaism", 150f.; Ehrlich, "Tora", 541f.; Jeremias, *Jerusalem*, 274; Bowker, "Mystery", 304, 306f.
"Scrolls of secrets" [מגלות סתרים] in b.Shab 6b, 96b; b.BM 92a, etc. may refer to private collections of halakhic teachings. Cf. b.Shab 156a (notebooks of R. Ze'iri A1 and R. Levi A3); and Strack/Stemberger, *Einleitung*, 46.

[92] E.g. ExR 1:29: Moses killed the Egyptian "with the mystery" of Israel, i.e. by pronouncing over him the name of God. On this cf. LevR 32:4 (end); see already Artapanus (Eusebius *PrEv* 9.27.24ff.). Cf. further Petuchowski, "Judaism", 145–148; Stemberger, "Esoterik", 371; also the magical texts.

[93] See above; and possibly b.Ber 22a (R. Aqiba T2 received a secret rule of halakhic interpretation from Nahum of Gimzo T1); HistRech 12:9d ("be hemmed in by the secrets entrusted to you").

[94] Bowker, "Mystery", 307. On מסטירין cf. also Wewers, *Geheimnis*, 195f. Note, however, that none of these texts can be confidently assigned a pre-Amoraic date.

[95] Cf. e.g. Petuchowski, "Judaism", 148f. on circumcision as a "mystery". Note, too, however, that מסתרים, clearly *not* a loan word, is already used e.g. in Sir 4:18 of the secrets of wisdom; cf. also Dan 2:22 (מסתרתא).

All Israel gathered near Moses and said to Him, "Our master, Moses, tell us what goodness the Holy One, blessed be He, will give us in the World to Come." He replied to them, "I do not know what I shall say to you. Happy are you for what is prepared for you."[96]

3.3.1. *The Mystery Hidden from Biblical Saints*

This inability on the part of Moses indicates that a disclosure of the time and circumstances of the Messianic deliverance was not seemly or feasible. When it was suggested that Hezekiah should be the Messiah, a *bat qôl* went forth exclaiming, "The mystery is mine! The mystery is mine!" The time of the Messiah belongs to the eschatological mystery known only to God.[97] Similarly, here as in the Targums Gen 49:1 is taken to mean that Jacob (as Isaac before him[98]) wanted to disclose the "mystery of the end" to his sons, but was prevented by God from doing so[99] (and the Shekhinah left him[100]).

3.3.2. *Various Mysteries Disclosed to Biblical Saints*

Nevertheless, Rabbinic haggadah does recognize a number of Biblical cases of revealed eschatological mysteries. Thus God showed to Adam "all the generations destined to come forth from him."[101] The two angels sent to Sodom illegitimately revealed to Lot their mystery when they told him (Gen 19:13), "For we are about to destroy this place."[102] God said to Rebekah (cf. Gen 25:23), "I tell you this mystery: the 'first of the nations' will descend from you" (MidrPsa 9:6). Elisha "stood in the mysteries of God [עמדתא במסטורין של אלהים]" when he promised a son to the Shunammite woman.[103]

---

[96] SifDeut 356 (ed. Finkelstein p. 424). Cf. b. Ber 34b on Isaiah 64:4 (R. Yo. hanan A2); b. Shab 145b (R. Eleazar [ben Shammua T5]); also e.g. Tanḥ כי תשא 16 (ed. Buber p. 116; on Exod 33:20): Moses prevented from understanding the reward of the commandments and the prosperity of the wicked.

[97] B. Sanh 94a (Bar Kappara T5 on Isa 24:16 [רזי לי רזי לי]); cf. p. 102 above. On Hezekiah as Messiah cf. also Justin *Dial* 33; and see Ginzberg, *Legends* 6:366.

[98] GenR 96 New Version (beginning); GenR 99:5; Tanḥ ויחי 9 (ed. Buber p. 216).

[99] Cf. e.g. Tanḥ ויחי 9 (ed. Buber p. 216); full citation of rabbinic references in Wewers, *Geheimnis*, 69–75. Cf. the parable about a king and his dying slave: GenR 96 New Version (beginning); Tanḥ ויחי 9 (ed. Buber p. 217); cf. also GenR 98:2 (R. Eleazar b. Abina [= b. Rabina A6?]); PesR 21:13.

[100] E.g. b. Pes 56a; cf. Wewers, *Geheimnis*, 73.

[101] ARN 31 (R. Nehemiah T3). Cf. Ginzberg, *Legends* 1:91 f.; 5:117 f. on Adam in *Sefer Raziel*.

[102] וירא Tanḥ גילו לו (קלא) מסטירין שלהם 21 (end; ed. Buber p. 98). Cf. also GenR 50:9, 68:12; and see § 3.7 below.

[103] ExR 19:1 (2 Kgs 4:30). Cf. Amos 3:7, etc.; and see Wewers, *Geheimnis*, 84.

3.3.3. No Contemporary Disclosure?

But in the Rabbis' own day, disclosure of soteriological mysteries remains for the future: "The things that are concealed from you in this world, you will see in the World to Come, like a blind man who regains his sight."[104] A *Baraita* reads,

> Seven things are hidden from men, and these are they: the day of death, and the day of [sc. Messianic] comfort, and the depth of judgement; a man does not know what is in his fellow's heart, and a man does not know how he will profit,[105] and when the kingdom of the house of David will return, and when the wicked kingdom [sc. Rome] will end.[106]

One or two exceptions to this pattern do occur. The passage in *Numbers Rabbah*, just cited, which declares that the secrets will be revealed in the World to Come, goes on to say that these things — not revealed to Moses — have in fact *already been done* for R. Aqiba (T2) and his colleagues (though this revelation is perhaps primarily of exegetical secrets).[107] Occasionally a revelation of eschatological mysteries is encountered in the *Hekhalot* literature,[108] where however the visionary is usually only *told* about such revelations through an angelic mediator.[109] (The requirement of secrecy is here less apparent,[110] al-

---

[104] NumR 19:6 (R. Huna A2 [?]). This applies to some halakhic mysteries too: Tg Cant 5:10 says that God "delivers every day new exegetical decisions [שמעתן] which He will make known to His people on the Great Day."

[105] משתכר; Jastrow 2:1576 renders, "No man knows which of his enterprises will turn out profitable." But perhaps this means: a man does not know his future reward, שכר — cf. m. Abot 2:19 etc.

[106] B. Pes 54b; par. Mek *Wayassa'* 6.61−64. Cf. GenR 65:12; QohR 11.5.1.

[107] NumR 19:6. Cf. b. Hag 14a (R. Naḥman b. Isaac A4); R. Ḥiyya's (T5) marvellously efficacious prayer discloses an eschatological secret (b. BM 85b: N.B. like the Patriarchs he might "wax strong in prayer and bring the Messiah before his time").

[108] E.g. 3 En 26:12; 3 En 45; *Hekhalot Rabbati* 1:1 (*BHM* 3:83, l.5 f.); cf. also Schäfer's edition, § 136−38 (*Übersetzung*, 2:65 f.) and passim. [Scholem (*Ursprung*, 16, 19; *Jewish Gnosticism*, 20−30) dates the central ideas of *Hekhalot* literature to the 3rd cent. or earlier; once strongly contested, his view now appears to have been vindicated by the publication of the *Songs of the Sabbath Sacrifice* from Qumran.]

[109] But N.B. in 3 En 41−48 Metatron actually does show R. Ishmael the mysteries of heaven, both cosmological and eschatological. For heavenly mediators of mysteries see 3 En 18:16 (Gallitsur; cf. PesR 20:4); 3 En 48:7 (Metatron, as "lesser Yahweh" and Prince of the Presence; cf. Yaoel in ApocAbr 10); also *Sefer Eliyahu BHM* 3:65, l.2 f. (Michael); 3:78, ll. 18, 21 (Metatron); *Seder Gan Eden BHM* 3:135, l.1 f.; *Ma'yan Hokmah BHM* 1:60, l.10 f. (Raziel hears behind the curtain what is to come, and announces it in the world). In *Hekhalot Rabbati*, Schäfer § 279 (*Übersetzung*, 2:263 f.), Metatron reveals to R. Ishmael the mystery (מידה: cf. Schäfer, "Prolegomena", 78) of the Torah.

[110] Stemberger, "Esoterik", 371; Gruenwald, *Apocalyptic*, 121−123.

though as in apocalyptic high personal and ethical qualifications for the mystical ascent are maintained.[111])

By and large, the revelation of celestial mysteries is only promised, but not carried out.[112]

3.4. Unlawful Revelation of Mysteries

Rabbi Aqiba said, "Silence is a fence for wisdom" (m. Abot 3:17). Two reasons are usually given for denying man access to the divine mysteries: first, God's secrets are His alone to disclose; secondly, certain recipients may be personally unqualified. Let us look at each of these reasons in turn.

3.4.1. *The Mysteries Belong to God*. Not unlike Ben Sira, the Rabbis believe that man is not to meddle in affairs not meant for him; the *revealed* Torah is the only proper sphere of investigation.[113] "Just as the [letter] *bêth* is closed at the sides but open in the front, so you are not permitted to investigate what is above and what is below, what is before and what is behind."[114] When Jonathan b. Uzziel published the Targum to the prophets, a *bat qôl* went forth and asked, "Who is revealing my secrets [סתריי] to mankind?"[115]

Similar constrictions apply to Biblical figures; we mentioned earlier the two talkative angels at Sodom[116] and Jacob's unsuccessful attempt to disclose the קץ, knowledge of which properly belongs only to God.[117] Hezekiah's explanation of his childlessness as due to fear of evil offspring is rebuked with the words, "What have you to do with the secrets [בהדיכבשי[118]] of the All-merciful?" (b. Ber 10a: R. Hamnuna A3).

---

[111] Stemberger, "Esoterik", 371 f.; also p. 29 n. 38 above.

[112] Thus Scholem, *Major Trends*, 56. His statement relates to the *Hekhalot* tracts, but applies *a fortiori* to Rabbinic literature in general.

[113] Cf. Wewers, *Geheimnis*, 82.

[114] GenR 1:10 (R. Levi A3; cf. b. Kappara T5); similarly m. Ḥag 2:1; y. Ḥag 2:1 (77c41−43). See also GenR 9:1 (R. Ḥama b. Ḥanina A2); PesR 21:21; b. Ḥag 13a (R. Aḥa b. Jacob A4, quoting Sir 3:22).

[115] B. Meg 3a; when he wanted to publish the Targums to the Hagiographa as well, a *bat qôl* exclaimed (N.B. this time in Aramaic . . .), "Enough! For therein is contained the קץ of the Messiah." The reference may well be to Dan 9 (b. Meg 3a: Dan part of the Hagiographa). Cf. further B. BM 85b, cited above.

[116] N.B. in return for their indiscretion they were expelled from the divine presence for 138 years, until Jacob in his dream (Gen 28:12) saw them "ascending and descending": GenR 50:9; 68:12; cf. TPsJ Gen 28:12.

[117] Cf. Wewers, *Geheimnis*, 74 f.

[118] I.e. בהדי (ב + הדי) "in the presence of, with", prefixed to the passive ptc. of כבש "to hide, withhold" (hence "secret"). See Jastrow 1:332, 610 f.

3.4.2. *The Recipients Are Unworthy*. An exclusion even from legitimate study of divine mysteries applied to certain Jews conditionally, and to many others and all Gentiles *a priori*, on the grounds of insufficient qualification or personal demerit. Thus the exposition of the *merkabah* (Ezek 1) was explicitly permitted only to mature and experienced Rabbis working *in camera*; similar restrictions applied to other passages.[119] Young people in particular were to be kept from studying the "Chariot", as they might otherwise come to harm.[120] The dangers arising for *bereshit* mystics are similarly emphasized.[121]

It was commonly agreed, perhaps largely for pedagogical reasons,[122] that no secret expounded in the בית המדרש may be disclosed to uneducated laymen (עמי הארץ:[123] one man in fact was expelled from the Academy because "this one revealed the secrets [דין גלי רזיא]" (b. Sanh 31a: R. Ammi A3). Most especially, however, Israel must keep its mysteries from the Gentiles.[124]

We have received yet another confirmation that despite a certain ambivalence about continued activity of the Spirit and of prophecy, postbiblical Judaism had a richly developed idea of revelation as based upon previous revelation. In Rabbinic circles the key to this meta-revelation is centred in the scholastic enterprise

---

[119] M. Ḥag 2:1. Cf. t. Ḥag 2:1; m. Meg 4:10; b. Ḥag 13a; y. Ḥag 2:1 (77a42 ff.), etc.; and cf. Zunz, *Vorträge*, 172 f. Stemberger, "Esoterik", 369 f. considers such passages to be clear indications of a Rabbinic *Arkandisziplin* (cf. also above on Sir 3:21); but N. B. the Gemara seems rather less tongue-tied than the Mishnah!

[120] Note the repeated story (b. Ḥag 13a) about a certain boy suddenly consumed by fire. The minimum age for expounding the *merkabah* was 50 years (b. Shab 13a; b. Ḥag 13a; b. Men 45a; cf. Jerome, Preface to Ezekiel: 30 years [Migne 5:17]). See also b. Shab 80b (a Galilean wanting to lecture publicly on the chariot was fatally stung by a hornet); and cf. e. g. CantR 1.2.5.

[121] Cf. t. Ḥag 2:6; GenR 2:4: even Ben Zoma died as a result of contemplating the "upper and lower waters".

[122] Jeremias, *Jerusalem*, 272 f. In light of a tradition of similar sentiments (e. g. Ben Sira), a specific anti-Gnostic intention is unlikely and at best incidental (*pace* Jeremias p. 270 f.).

[123] B. Pes 49b (*Baraita*). Cf. also m. Abot 3:15, ... המגלה פנים בתורה [שלא כהלכה] אין לו חלק לעולם הבא.

[124] B. Ket 111a; ExR 19:6, etc.: see above. Somewhat different is the (6th cent. A.D.?) En-Gedi synagogue inscription (cf. *Inscriptions Reveal*, No. 185) invoking a curse of divine judgement on anyone who reveals "the mystery of the town [רזה דקרתה]" to the Gentiles. This would suggest treason, i.e. betraying the community's political or perhaps professional secrets (thus e. g. Weinfeld, *Pattern*, 58–64). However, Dotan's reading ("Secret", 3) of קרייה for קרתה is equally possible; the resulting prohibition of disclosing the "mystery of the Reading [or Script]" would agree with what was said earlier about "mysteries of Israel". More open attitudes to Gentile knowledge of mysteries are rare and seem restricted to Biblical incidents such as the story of Balaam; note further EzekTrag 83–89, where the Gentile Raguel/Jethro explains to Moses the meaning of his heavenly vision.

of transmitting and interpreting both written and oral Torah. In keeping with this perspective, Rabbinic interest in divine mysteries concentrates on the secrets accessible in the texts. Such "mysteries" constitute special knowledge, and the study of "what is above, beneath, before, and hereafter" is closely restricted. Eschatological mysteries in particular remain distinctly behind a veil.

Synthesis

Ancient Judaism

How, then, was God understood to speak and disclose His secrets in a situation where Torah and Prophets had become Scripture and where the problem of God's presence in history nevertheless remained one of vexing importance? Our examination of this question in the ancient Jewish sources is now complete. A brief synthetic statement is therefore in order; further conclusions will be spelled out at the end of Part Two.

A coincidence of two basic trends can already be discerned in the post-exilic literature of the Old Testament: one, the increasing concentration on the written Scriptures as the primary focus of revelation; and secondly, the growing interest in hidden wisdom, especially in relation to questions of personal and national theodicy. These emphases were further accentuated in the Graeco-Roman period, sometimes in response to stimuli from Hellenistic culture and religion.

1. Common Features

A number of features are common to all the writings surveyed. The Sinaitic Torah is the focus of all revelation. It is fully comprehensive and contains all things necessary for Israel's life before God as the chosen people. While accepting the prophets and writings as fully inspired and authoritative, all except Wisdom and Philo (who generally does not think in epochs of *Heilsgeschichte*) express a certain hesitancy in speaking about a prophetic activity of the Spirit in their own day.

Nevertheless, all go on to affirm at least a measure of continued divine revelation, and in all writers this further revelation is intimately connected with the Torah and/or the Prophets. Often the recipient seeks such revelation with prayerful and ascetic preparation. New and old stand in a reciprocal relationship: new revelation is always meta-revelation, given shape and texture by a charismatic reading of the old; yet once accepted and accorded its rightful status, this new disclosure becomes in turn instrumental for the understanding of the old, the "proto-revelation".

Often these new interpretations, revealed to inspired, skilled, and ethically qualified exegetes, are described in terms of divine "mysteries".[1] Although subject to considerable variation in emphasis, mysteries pertain essentially to the two main orders of redemption (eschatology, cosmology) and sanctification (halakhah). Both are God's property and prerogative (hence the recurring theme of illegitimate disclosure), and can be described as stored up in heaven. Halakhic secrets in particular are at the same time resident in the text of Torah, where they can be uncovered by inspired interpreters.

True to character, the soteriological order of mysteries serves to demonstrate the sovereignty of God in history and the cosmos, and is often set in a context of historical theodicy. Both eschatological and cosmological mysteries are on the one hand studied for their intrinsic theological interest. But because of their close dependence on the prophetic view of salvation and history, the writers are always aware that full revelation at least of the eschatological mysteries must await the empirical manifestation of the eschaton. Present disclosure, therefore, is restricted and affords at best a prescient glimpse of what is to come.

Together, these two classes of divine mysteries contribute vitally to a given community's theological and social "plausibility structure".[2] Indeed their combination of divine authorization and hermeneutical *Sitz im Leben* contributes elements of both stability and adaptability for the community's understanding of itself and the world outside, of divine sovereignty, and of human responsibility.[3]

2. Particularities

In treating the theme at hand, each of the traditions surveyed manifests certain individual peculiarities. Thus, at Qumran, the mediation of revelation assumes an unusual focus in being restricted to the Teacher of Righteousness and a small group of priests; mysteries and "hidden things" designate the frequent revelations on halakhic (Torah) and eschatological subjects (Prophets). Apocalyptic literature (and to some extent early Rabbinic mysticism) shares with Qumran a greatly heightened interest in divine mysteries. With few excep-

---

[1] Cf. in this regard the interesting remarks of Knox, *Gentiles*, 228: in his view, the notion of a divine disclosure of mysteries is of necessity required by the Jewish and Christian assumption of "progressive" revelation.

[2] This term is used by sociologists of knowledge in describing the social and individual legitimation of world views. See esp. Berger, *Imperative*, 15—20; idem, *Construction*, 92—128. Cf. further Meeks, "Function", 688, 701.

[3] Cf. also Patte, *Hermeneutic*, 227 on the relation of eschatological (רז) and halakhic (נסתרות) secrets at Qumran, viz. in terms of the community's eschatological identity and way of life.

tions, however, the writers' interest centres on secrets of the celestial world, where the privileged seer glimpses prepared storehouses of the eschatological *Heilsgüter* along with other furnishings of heaven which demonstrate God's universal saving sovereignty.

Philo in particular clothes his language of revelation in unfamiliar garb, offering an example of deep interaction between Jewish hermeneutics and pagan philosophy. While he shows no consciousness of any termination of the Spirit's activity, revelation here has been equated with the knowledge of God. Philo's use of the term μυστήριον is most profoundly indebted to contemporary Homeric allegoresis. Josephus, whose historiography similarly reflects an awareness of contemporary Hellenistic practice, shows little interest in divine mysteries. But he highly values predictive prophecy, and assigns considerable significance to his own prophetic stature.

The Rabbis developed sapiential and Pharisaic notions of the revelatory status of interpretation and tradition into the idea of an "Oral Torah" revealed at Sinai alongside the written Torah, while at the same time they endorsed a hermeneutical pluralism. Their generally cautious attitude towards the pursuit of divine mysteries follows that of Ben Sira in permitting only the most qualified to engage in such study. They also adopted Hellenistic usage in regarding certain religious practices as "mysteries" establishing the distinctiveness of Israel; this apparently proved a useful device in a period calling for clearer sociological definition and internal cohesion.

3. Outlook

Against the background of this survey, many of the principles and categories encountered in Part Two will be familiar. At the same time, Paul's christology will be found to lead in some ways to a decisive modification of existing views of revelation and divine mysteries.

Part Two

Pauline Christianity

Introduction

Part Two of this investigation brings us to the Apostle Paul, the great pioneer of Gentile Christianity, who spent many years in Greece and Asia Minor proclaiming Jesus of Nazareth as God's Redeemer for Gentiles as well as Jews. Although he was by far the most prolific and arguably the most erudite of the New Testament writers, it was his fate to be much maligned and misunderstood by both Christian and non-Christian Jews and Gentiles.

The following paragraphs are intended as a rough and ready outline of the problems and characteristics of Paul's letters in relation to the Jewish literature previously treated.

1. General Observations: The Nature of the Material

Two methodological considerations need to be stated at the outset.

1.1. Like much of the Jewish literature we have surveyed, Paul's letters were written in *Greek*. This creates no insurmountable problems, but as in many Jewish writings it does call for sensitivity to the possible use of Greek philosophical or religious idiom. Obviously the crucial question here as else where is to distinguish (e.g. for the meaning of μυστήριον) between a genuine fusion or revision of basic concepts and the mere clothing of Jewish belief in a more cosmopolitan *façon de parler*.

1.2. Even aside from thorny questions of authorship,[1] we know the extant corpus of Pauline writings to be only a partial and incomplete selection (see e.g. 1 Cor 5:9–11; 2 Cor 2:3f.; Col 4:16.). This problem is not *eo ipso* peculiar to Paul. But it is complicated by the fact that in contrast to most other works dealt with so far, Paul's writings are largely occasional in nature and purpose.[2] They do not on the whole present concise and synthetic treatments but offer apostolic

---

[1] Ephesians and the Pastoral Epistles, treated separately in Chapter 11, will not be cited as primary evidence, except insofar as they second positions already supported in undisputed letters. A brief argument for the authenticity of Colossians will be offered in Chapter 10 below.

[2] Cf. the classic statement of Deissmann, *Paul*, 8–14.

instruction and advice on matters of immediate concern[3] (some of which are not altogether obvious).

On the other hand, the occasional nature of these writings is partly offset by other factors. Paul's letters share a common *Sitz im Leben* in his apostolic ministry; moreover, they frequently employ highly patterned theological and liturgical language,[4] techniques borrowed from classical rhetoric,[5] as well as formulae and fragments received from primitive Christian tradition.[6] These factors, together with the repeated treatment of certain key topics, lend the Pauline letters a greater measure of internal cohesion than might be expected from ordinary correspondence. With due caution, therefore, a study of "Paul's view of revelation" will not be out of place.

2. Sectarian or Apostate?

The Jewish literature surveyed above, albeit doctrinally often heterogeneous, displays a common allegiance to the basic religious concerns of Judaism, which we earlier summarized as a) monotheism, b) revelation and orthopraxis, and c) election and redemption. According to the largely praxis-based criteria for an identification of apostasy (ritual unfitness for membership and unfaithfulness to the covenant), quite likely none of the literature discussed would have been considered apostate (see above).

Could the same be said about Paul? It certainly seems that in his own mind Paul was being faithful to his calling as a Jew whom God had conscripted to proclaim in the Messiah salvation to the Gentiles. His call experience on the road to Damascus is nowhere described in terms suggestive of a "conversion" (contrast e.g. 1 Thes 1:9);[7] indeed he considers that both he and Peter are "Jews by nature, and not sinners from among the Gentiles" (Gal 2:15). Despite the acknowledgement of his pre-Christian persecution of the church (1 Cor 15:9; Gal 1:13), he sees no need to confess or apologize for his Jewishness *as such*.[8] His notion of righteousness according to the Torah being "counted as loss" before the righteousness through faith in Christ derives not from an abandonment of his

---

[3] Possible exceptions are Ephesians (if genuine), which may be a circular letter (cf. Metzger, *Textual Commentary*, 601; and the commentaries); and Romans, which is probably an apologetic exposé of Paul's Gentile mission for his proposed Western "sending base", the mixed Jewish-Gentile congregation at Rome (cf. Stuhlmacher, e.g. in Lapide/ Stuhlmacher, *Paul,* 19 and n. 11).

[4] See recently e.g. White, "Formulae", 91—97; idem, "Apostolic Letter", 436—442.

[5] See esp. 1 Cor 2:1—5 in recent discussion; or Betz's *Galatians*.

[6] See e.g. Rom 1:3 f.; 3:25 f.; 4:25; 1 Cor 11:23—26; 15:3—7; etc.

[7] For this point cf. e.g. W. D. Davies, *PRJ*, xxxvi; Stuhlmacher, "Ende", 20 n. 15.

[8] See esp. Schlatter, *Theologie der Apostel*, 281 f.

Jewishness but from the recognition that "gain" has been supplanted by "surpassing greatness" (Phil 3:7 f.).[9] It is true that he could express this contrast in the form of remarks critical of the Torah itself. But despite what he considered to be the hard-heartedness and disobedience of his kinsmen according to the flesh (Rom 9–11, etc.), Paul was unperturbed and in his own mind continued to be a faithful Jew.[10]

However, external evidence suggests that some of Paul's contemporaries may have had a different view.[11] Apart from the apparent reaction to misguided or misinterpreted Paulinism in Jas 2, the clearest NT evidence deals with Paul's final return to Jerusalem in Acts 21. Here he is challenged to confute reports that he has taught Diaspora Jews (i.e. Jewish Christians?) to apostatize from "Moses" by abandoning circumcision and the halakhah (21:21): ἀποστασίαν διδάσκεις ἀπὸ Μωϋσέως τοὺς κατὰ τὰ ἔθνη πάντας Ἰουδαίους λέγων μὴ περιτέμνειν αὐτοὺς τὰ τέκνα μηδὲ τοῖς ἔθεσιν περιπατεῖν. The charge clearly implies a fundamental offence against the Torah and the Abrahamic covenant itself.[12] Naturally, unchecked rumour, *parva metu primo, mox sese attollit in auras*; yet even so, this Christian accusation is phrased more cautiously than some of the Jewish allegations which are also recorded in Acts.[13] After a seemingly polite if less than enthusiastic reception by the Jerusalem church (cf. 21:17 vs. 20 ff.) we hear of no further Jewish Christian support for Paul throughout the period of his arrest, detention and trial (but see 23:16). It is, therefore, at least plausible that influential circles in the Jerusalem church had a sustained antipathy to Paul and his teaching;[14] second-century Jewish Christian evidence

---

[9] Cf. Sanders, e.g. *PLJP*, 140 f., who speaks of Paul's "black or white" reasoning. If Sanders is right, then of course this position might suffice to put Paul beyond the pale of "mainstream" Judaism in the eyes of some of his contemporaries.

[10] See also Sandmel, *Judaism*, 312, 336.

[11] The only *clear* internal evidence, apart from telling references to synagogal punishment (2 Cor 11:24 f.), would appear to be in Gal (2:12; 4:17; 5:12), where Paul counters tenacious opposition on the part of conservative Palestinian Jewish Christians over the crucial question of circumcision (cf. below). Although sensitive halakhic issues are also addressed in Rom 14:2 ff., 15–23, these appear to pose no major threat to the integrity and authority of the Apostle's teaching; cf. Cranfield, *Romans*, esp. 2:694–697. (Rom 3:8; 6:1 f. would seem to repel a misinterpretation rather than a substantive charge.)

[12] Gen 17:11, 14; cf. Jub 15:11–14, 26–29, 33 f.; 1 Macc 1:15; *ADPB*, p. 402 (Blessing after Circumcision); also m. Abot 3:15 (R. Eleazar of Modiim T2). M. Smith, "Reason", 265–268 similarly argues that Paul's persecution is fundamentally due to his attitude to the Torah.

[13] Esp. 18:13; 21:28. Note the call for the death penalty in 22:22; 25:24: on apostasy and the death penalty see e.g. Horbury, "Extirpation", 28 and passim.

[14] Dunn, *Unity*, 256 f. However, his argument that the Jerusalem church refused Paul's collection (p. 257) is perhaps less convincing; cf. Acts 24:17.

firmly establishes the existence of such a view.[15] In the eyes of some influential
Jewish Christian (and, *a fortiori*, Jewish) opinion, Paul's teaching had begun to
be apostate, and no longer "belonged to the main stream of first-century Judaism".[16]

The implications for our study, however, are perhaps not as significant as
might be suspected. True, in understanding and charting his theology on the
map of first-century Judaism it will be inadequate to speak of Paul simply as "a
Rabbi become Christian":[17] Jews and Jewish Christians in the first century
would not have regarded this as an acceptably accurate expression of Paul's
theological shift.

However, there are one or two mitigating considerations. It appears that an
incisive change from tolerance to intolerance of dissent took place *after* the fall
of Jerusalem.[18] While of course the excommunication of heretics and apostates
was practised prior to A. D. 70,[19] that socio-religious debacle, together with
the ascendancy of Christianity, would have substantially increased the prevalence and necessity of internal measures of Jewish self-defence.[20] Finally, a
more pragmatic consideration also warrants the study of Paul alongside Judaism: despite paradigmatic differences no one would dispute that there is in
fact broad agreement about many important themes and their correlation.[21]

3. Preview

The following pages will set the stage for the discussion of revealed "mysteries" in Paul by means of an outline (i) of his general view of revelation, and
(ii) of the relation of this to the "old" dispensation of revelation, the Torah.
This will be followed, as above, by a more detailed look at the theme of divine
mysteries and their disclosure.

---

[15] Cf. Irenaeus *Haer.* 1.26.2: "Ebionaei ... apostolum Paulum recusant, apostatam
eum legis dicentes." Similarly Eusebius, *EH* 3.27.4.

[16] *Pace* Davies, PRJ, 1. Cf. Stuhlmacher in Lapide/Stuhlmacher, *Paul*, 27; also the
cautious remarks of Gaston, *Paul and the Torah*, 76–79.

[17] Thus Davies, *PRJ*, 16; cf. p. xxx ("We understand the Apostle as a Pharisee who accepted Jesus of Nazareth ... as the Messiah").

[18] See Urbach, "Self-Isolation", 289, 291 f.

[19] Cf. Horbury, "Extirpation", passim.

[20] Urbach, "Self-Isolation", 292.

[21] Cf. even Sanders, *PPJ*, 548, who speaks of "*substantial* agreements and a basic difference" (ital. his).

Chapter Eight

Revelation in Paul

Given Paul's significant departures from contemporary Jewish beliefs, what fundamentally constitutes revelation for him? How does he conveive of God's communication with man in redemption and history?

The answer to these questions is by no means straightforward. Paul employs foundational language of revelation in contexts not only of the work of Christ, but also of the apostolic mission, and of God's overall redemptive purpose.

An initial sorting of the relevant texts suggests that revelation may be profitably analysed and presented as occurring in the three temporal dimensions of the past, present and future.[1] This will be followed by a brief assessment of the remaining revelatory significance, if any, of the Old Testament.

1. Past: Revelation of the Gospel of Christ

Paul speaks about several aspects of revelation in the past. Among these are both revelation in creation (e.g. 2 Cor 4:6; Rom 1:19 f.; cf. pp. 141–142 below) and the Old Testament as divine utterance (see § 4 below). However, clearly the most central subject in this regard is the recent revelation of Christ and the gospel.

1.1. The Revelation in Christ

Rom 3:21 ff., located at a logical and theological turning point in the epistle, speaks in paradigmatic fashion about God's righteousness which has "now"

---

[1] Cf. e.g. Luz (below); Ladd, "Revelation", 228 f.; Wilckens, "Offenbarungsverständnis", 65, 69 f. Stuhlmacher ("Gegenwart", 435, 440 f.) sees three temporal dimensions of God's "coming" in Paul, although the Christ event is not included in the recent past but in the present (443). Note also EpBarn 5:3. *Pace* Bultmann, "Offenbarung", 22 (present only); Lührmann, *Offenbarungsverständnis*, 155 (present and future only); Kim, *Origin*, 99 (past and future only).

been manifested (3:21) through Christ's public sacrificial death (3:25 f.).[2] The striking constellation of evidential and demonstrative terminology in this passage (πεφανέρωται,[3] μαρτυρομένη, προέθετο,[4] εἰς ἔνδειξιν, πρὸς ἔνδειξιν) indicates that it occupies a crucial place in Paul's argument,[5] as indeed the redemptive events referred to are the fountainhead of Paul's gospel.[6] If it is true that Paul's theology is to a very considerable extent soteriology,[7] then no event carries greater foundational significance than the demonstration of God's righteousness in the saving death, resurrection and exaltation of Christ.[8]

Various other texts deal with this same original event of revelation;[9] suffice it to adduce one further pericope from Galatians. Gal 3:23—25 is often appealed to in discussions of Paul's view of the eclipse of the law by faith. More significant for the present, however, is the observation that what stands at the turn of the ages is nothing other than the *revelation* of faith — closely identified with Christ (v. 24) as both author and enabler of that faith.[10] That Paul refers back to the historical founding events of the gospel is apparent in his speaking in the aorist of both the time "before" and "after" the revelation of faith (vv. 23, 25).[11]

---

[2] Some identify ἱλαστήριον as the mercy seat (כפרת: e.g. Manson, "ΙΛΑΣ-ΤΗΡΙΟΝ", esp. 4—6; Stuhlmacher, "Exegese", 120—131; more recently B. F. Meyer, "Formula", 200, 202 f.; Olford, "Cultic Language", 154—178; Fryer, "Meaning", 104—111. If this be correct, it is significant that the כפרת in the OT serves specifically as a *locus* of revelation and theophany: Exod 25:22; Lev 16:2; Num 7:89; also e.g. Josephus *Ant* 3:212, 222, 312, etc; NumR 14:19. Cf. Weiser, "Beziehungen", 520.

[3] On this word (as *distinct* from ἀποκαλύπτεται in 1:17 f., *pace* numerous commentators) see further Bockmuehl, "φανερόω".

[4] *Pace* Cranfield, *Romans*, 1:208—210 (cf. Wilckens, *Römer*, 1:192 n. 537; Stuhlmacher, "Exegese", 130). However, the issue is complex: the translation of προτίθημι as "propose, intend" makes sense (without being required) only if with Cranfield 1:216—218 one rejects the reading of ἱλαστήριον as "mercy seat". On the latter question see Dunn's circumspect remarks: *Romans*, 1:170 f. ("medium of atonement").

[5] Many commentators observe Paul's use of language; only a few recognize its logical significance: see esp. Michel, *Römer*, 150 ("es kommt Paulus alles darauf an, den allgemeinen Zugang zu diesem historischen Ereignis zu sichern...: jeder Mensch muß auf den Anspruch hören, der in diesem Geschehnis liegt"); Nygren, *Romans*, 158.

[6] Cf. Cranfield, *Romans*, 1:199; Wilckens, *Römer*, 1:199.

[7] Thus e.g. Sanders, *PPJ*, 433 and passim.

[8] For the all-pervasive significance of this event see, among many other texts, Rom 1:4; 4:24 f.; 5:6—11; 8:3 f., 32—39; 1 Cor 2:2; 15:3 f. (ff.); 2 Cor 5:14—17; 13:4; Gal 1:1, 4; 3:13 f.; 4:4 f.; Phil 2:8 f.; Col 1:22.

[9] See Chapters 9—11 below. Cf. further Col 1:19 f. (and 2:9): the divine πλήρωμα dwelt in Christ at His reconciling crucifixion (v. 20): see Lightfoot, *Colossians*, 157 (and 180 on 2:9); Martin, *Colossians*, 60.

[10] Cf. Oepke, *Galater*, 120 (faith and Christ are "geradezu Wechselbegriffe"); Ridderbos, *Galatia*, 143, 145; Schlier, *Galater*, 167 (faith the means, Christ the ground of salvation). *Pace* Mussner, *Galaterbrief*, 254 f. and n. 54.

[11] Betz's comment (*Galatians*, 176 n. 120) is much to the point: πίστις here "describes

Short of agreeing with Käsemann's view of a "manifestation of faith in personified form" in this passage, we may at any rate see the revelation of πίστις here
as that of an objectified, almost hypostatized entity.[12]

Paul resumes his theme of the historically pivotal function of the Christ event
five verses later[13] in Gal 4:1–7. Especially 4:4 confirms the constitutive significance of the revelation in Jesus. Paul speaks of the "fulness of the time" in relation to God's sending of His Son. The πλήρωμα τοῦ χρόνου expresses the
apocalyptic notion of an *appointed time* (of eschatological redemption and/or
judgement), often linked with revelation.[14] In the light of 3:23, 25, God's "sending" of His Son (cf. Rom 8:3) becomes a revelatory event of foundational significance.[15]

The basis of the new Christian dispensation, then, lies in the revelation of
God's righteousness and of "faith". This took place historically in the Messianic
redeeming work of Jesus at the "fulness of time", the turn of the ages.[16] God's
work in Christ is the wellspring of Paul's understanding of revelation.

1.2. The Revelation to Paul

The disclosure in Christ of God's righteousness and of faith is complemented
by another central revelation in the past, given specially to the Apostle. Once
again two or three texts will serve to illustrate this.

---

the occurrence of a historical phenomenon, not the act of believing of an individual" (cf.
Gal 1:23; 3:25; 5:6; 6:10). On the close relation of πίστις with the revelatory Christ event
see also Rom 3:21 f., 25 f.

[12] Käsemann, *Perspectives*, 83; cited approvingly by Betz, *Galatians*, 176 n. 120. *Pace*
Lührmann (*Offenbarungsverständnis*, 80), who denies any reference to salvation history
but insists instead on a purely existential significance of πίστις.

[13] Gal 3:26–29 follows naturally on v. 25 and serves to define further the new status
of the Gentile Christians: πάντες γὰρ υἱοὶ θεοῦ ἐστε.

[14] The term is, as Schlier (*Galater*, 195) observes, related to συντέλεια τοῦ αἰῶνος in
Matt 13:39, 40, 49; 24:3; 28:20; Heb 9:26. Cf. also Mark 1:15; Luke 21:24; 1 Cor 10:11;
Eph 1:10; Heb 1:2 (= OT באחרית הימים). Cf. above on גמר הקץ (1 QpHab 7:2 etc.); note
the frequent link of קץ with the revelation of mysteries.

[15] Lührmann (*Offenbarungsverständnis*, 78), though he expressly links Gal 3:23 and
Rom 3:21, denies the revelatory value of the Christ event and prefers to speak of revelation only on the level of the subjective appropriation of that event (cf. 79). He insists
throughout (cf. 16, 80, 92, 121, 146, 152, 155, 162) that Paul never applies revelation terminology to Christ or His death and resurrection. But such a view requires a good deal
of special pleading in the case of Rom 3:21; Gal 3:23, 25; 4:4 and other instances of past,
present and future revelation treated below.

[16] N.B. in apocalyptic, a new (messianic) revelation ushers in the new age, redemption, and judgement: 2 Bar 29:3; 39:7; 73:1 ff.; 1 En 46:3; 48:6 f.; 91:14; 4 Ezra 7:26–28;
13:32. See also Lührmann, *Offenbarungsverständnis*, 99; McNamara, *New Testament*,
249–251; and cf. above on the revelation of the Messiah.

In Gal 1:11 ff. Paul presents an apologetic *tour de force* to vindicate his gospel against the suggestion that its origin is anything less than divine. The formal thesis statement in 1:11 (γνωρίζω δὲ ὑμῖν, κτλ.) indicates that Paul treats this issue with utmost seriousness.[17] And indeed this is not surprising, since the very legitimacy of his apostolic office and message is at stake. The origin of Paul's gospel is first stated in 1:12 (cf. 1:1): he received it δι' ἀποκαλύψεως Ἰησοῦ Χριστοῦ, by a revelation of Jesus Christ. It is moot to debate the nature of this genitive, since v. 16 (ἀποκαλύψαι τὸν υἱὸν αὐτοῦ ἐν ἐμοί) establishes that an objective genitive must be at least part of the intention.[18] Paul clearly dates the reception of his gospel from the time when God "revealed His Son to me",[19] i.e. on the road to Damascus. This revelation is the chief buttress of his argument against the Galatian opponents who questioned the independence of his apostolic standing and message from the founding church in Jerusalem (Gal 1:6–2:9).[20]

The same event occupies a critical position in Paul's thought elsewhere, too:

> Have I not seen Jesus our Lord?[21] (1 Cor 9:1)

> Now I would remind you (γνωρίζω δὲ ὑμῖν), brethren, ... the gospel, which you received, in which you stand, by which you are saved. ... I delivered to you as of first importance ... that he appeared (ὤφθη) to Cephas, then to the twelve. ... Last of all ... he appeared (ὤφθη) also to me. (1 Cor 15:1–8)

> God... has shone (ἔλαμψεν)[22] in our hearts to give the light of the knowledge of the glory of God in the face of Christ. (2 Cor 4:6)

> I was apprehended by Christ Jesus (κατελήμφθην ὑπὸ Χριστοῦ [Ἰησοῦ]). (Phil 3:12)

---

[17] Betz, *Galatians*, 56; cf. e.g. Mussner, *Galater*, 64; Oepke, *Galater*, 53 f.; Bruce, *Galatians*, 88. Stuhlmacher, *Evangelium*, 70 and n. 1 considers that γνωρίζω here is a term of revelation.

[18] E.g. Kertelge, "Apokalypsis", 269; Lührmann, *Offenbarungsverständnis*, 76; Bruce, *Galatians*, 89; Betz, *Galatians*, 63.

[19] Various scholars continue to translate ἐν εμοί as "in me" (e.g. Betz, *Galatians*, 64, 70 f.; cf. Benz, *Paulus*, 102 f.; Guillet, "Révélation", 606; M. Smith, "History", 15). However, by introducing this important revelation as subjective and internal in the context of Gal 1, Paul might well be thought to argue contrary to his purpose (elsewhere he explicitly refuses to set much store by personal ἀποκαλύψεις, 2 Cor 12:1–7). This is not to deny the profound personal relevance of this event (cf. esp. 2 Cor 4:6), nor even a potential allusion to this passage in Gal 2:20; 4:6. But in the immediate context of Gal 1:16 the reading of ἐν εμοί as a plain dative is to be preferred; indeed the very parallel with ἐν τοῖς ἔθνεσιν would appear to require this. Cf. e.g. BDF § 220:1; Moule, *Idiom Book*, 76 and n. 1; Baird, "Visions", 656; Oepke, *Galater*, 60 f; Rowland, *Open Heaven*, 376; Lindblom, *Gesichte*, 48; also Bengel, *Gnomon*, 718.

[20] Bruce, *Galatians*, 25 f.; Luck, "Bekehrung", 191 n. 21.

[21] Cf. 1 Cor 15:8; Acts 9:17; 22:14; 26:16; but also 22:18.

[22] For the light terminology in this verse cf. Acts 9:3; 22:6, 9; 26:13, 18 (!); also Eph 1:18; Col 1:13. Cf. further Michel, "Licht", passim; and see above on the Torah as light.

These texts (esp. 1 Cor 9:1; 15:8) may fairly be seen to allude to the Apostle's Damascus road experience.[23] Without being very specific about the content of the revelation,[24] Paul refers here to the turning point which constitutes both his new being in Christ and his God-given apostolic charge and message. He aligns the revelation of the gospel to himself with the appearances of the risen Christ to the original witnesses.[25]

This apostolic revelation is constitutive, authoritative, and on principle unrepeatable:[26] not even an angelic revelation from heaven can alter it (Gal 1:8). In this respect it differs significantly from other ἀποκαλύψεις which the Apostle received, but which are by no means foundational for his self-understanding.[27] Together, the redemptive revelation of God's righteousness *in Christ* and the apostolic revelation of the gospel *to Paul* make up the past dimension of revelation in his theology.[28] These two pillars are irreplaceable, unalterable, and basic to all of Pauline Christianity.

2. Present: Ongoing Revelation of the Gospel

Not only does the past revelation define Christian faith and life in the present, but it also entails and prompts an ongoing divine disclosure in the apostolic mission. One might well speak of a "kerygmatization" of the constitutive past dimension of revelation for the present.[29]

---

[23] See e.g. Bruce, *Galatians*, 92 f.; Stuhlmacher, *Evangelium*, 76, 81; Kim, *Origin*, 6 (on 2 Cor 4:6, citing many others), 72 (on Gal 1:12, 16; 1 Cor 15).

[24] Stuhlmacher, "Evangelium", 162 suggests that Paul saw Jesus exalted as "Son of God" and as "Lord"; cf. Rom 1:3; Gal 1:16; 1 Cor 9:1; Phil 2:9 ff. See also idem, *Evangelium*, 70 f., 74. Kim in addition sees Paul's appointment to the Gentile mission as part of this same revelation (*Origin*, 56−66).

[25] Cf. Stuhlmacher, *Evangelium*, 81; also Kim, *Origin*, 55. *Pace* Lührmann, *Offenbarungsverständnis*, 97. This close link between Paul's call vision and the resurrection appearances should temper one's eagerness to speak of the former as an anticipatory revelation of the Christ returning in glory (e.g. Kim, *Origin*, 56; Rowland, *Open Heaven*, 378). No doubt the eschatological component is implicit; but it is not developed in the context.

[26] Kertelge, "Apokalypsis", 275.

[27] See § 2.3 below; cf. also Baird, "Visions", passim.

[28] Although of course this revelation in turn is explained in terms of the preceding word of Scripture. See § 4 below.

[29] Cf. Penna, *Mysterion*, 38 on Rom 16:26 ("'missionarizzazione' del Mistero"); Ladd, "Revelation", 224.

2.1. Revelation of God's Righteousness and Wrath in the Gospel

One of the most powerful expressions of the continuing revelation of the
Gospel comes in Rom 1:16–18. Paul is here giving what is sometimes regarded
as the "theme" of the letter:[30] an apologetic but confident identification of the
Gospel of Christ as the continuing *locus* of the revelation of God's righteousness.

> I am not ashamed of the gospel, for it is the power of God for salvation. . . .
> For in it the righteousness of God is being revealed from faith to faith; as it is writ-
> ten: "But the righteous shall live by faith." [Hab 2:4]
> For the wrath of God is being revealed from heaven against all ungodliness and
> unrighteousness of men. . . .

The εὐαγγέλιον must here be understood as the content of Paul's preaching;[31] at the same time it functions as a divine power for salvation. God's righteousness – his saving and sovereign covenant faithfulness,[32] later said to have
been visibly demonstrated in Christ (3:21 ff.) – is in the present being revealed
through the ongoing preaching of this Pauline gospel.[33] The use of the passive
ἀποκαλύπτεται in vv. 17, 18 is doubtless an indication of divine agency: it is
God himself who brings about both the continuous revelation of His saving
righteousness in the Apostle's ministry,[34] and the sovereign heavenly declara-
tion of His righteous wrath over all human *un*righteousness.

Although it is ἀπ' οὐρανοῦ rather than ἐν αὐτῷ which qualifies the revelation of wrath in 1:18, the gospel is nevertheless linked with this as well. Many
commentators are confounded by the unexpected contextual and logical (γάρ)
juxtaposition of God's saving righteousness and His wrath, and either excise[35]
or divorce[36] the latter from the dispensation of the εὐαγγέλιον. This, however,
is to miss an important theological dimension of Paul's argument.

The close constellation of divine judgement and redemption, wrath and
righteousness is in fact firmly rooted in the OT, esp. in the prophets. Just as
Heilsgeschichte progresses between historically particular saving events leading
ultimately to God's consummate act of salvation, so also there is a corresponding movement of the expressions of Yahweh's righteous wrath against His

---

[30] Stuhlmacher, *Gerechtigkeit*, 78; Käsemann, *Römer*, 18.
[31] Wilckens, *Römer*, 1:82; cf. Schlatter, *Gerechtigkeit*, 32 ff.
[32] See esp. Dunn, *Romans*, 1:40–42.
[33] Cranfield, *Romans*, 1:91 f.
[34] Cf. esp. Cranfield, *Romans*, 1:103.
[35] O'Neill, *Romans*, 41, 43.
[36] E.g. Bengel, *Gnomon*, 530; Stuhlmacher, *Gerechtigkeit*, 80 f.; others cited in Cranfield, *Romans*, 1:106 and Wilckens, *Römer*, 1:101 n. 155. The commonplace separation or
opposition of Rom 1:16 f. and 1:18 ff. may well hail from the (Lutheran) conviction that
the wrath of God is no more than an *opus alienum*, the work of His left hand.

enemies as well as His disobedient people,[37] leading up to the final "day of the Lord". A necessary corollary of God's righteousness is its expression in the form of wrath against human *un*righteousness — especially where, as in 1:21 ff., that unrighteousness is in true Biblical tradition characterized first and foremost as *idolatry*.[38]

Although God's wrath is not actually identified with His righteousness,[39] there is nevertheless a close theological link between the two concepts.[40] This is expressed both in God's opposition to sin and breach of the covenant, and also in the language of Yahweh as holy Warrior.[41] There is also good precedent for the close coincidence of God's future wrath and salvation.[42] The Septuagint, in its tendency to render somewhat anthropopathic idioms of God's wrath in more theologically refined terms,[43] has on occasion rephrased such statements in terms of a *revelation* of divine wrath.[44]

In contemporary Jewish expectation, too, the revelation of God's righteousness in the form of His heavenly wrath[45] is no less an eschatological occurrence than God's righteousness revealed in salvation.[46] Thus a Qumran writer affirms, "You will destroy all wickedness and sin for ever, and Your righteousness will be revealed before the eyes of all Your creatures."[47]

---

[37] Such particular manifestations of wrath include heavenly acts of destruction, hostile invasion, exile, drought and famine, disease, etc. (see Num 11:1, 33; Deut 29:24−27; 1 Sam 6:19; 2 Sam 24:15 f.; Psa 11:6; etc.). They are inflicted against grave sins in Israel (e.g. Num 16:31−47 Korah; 25:3 Baal-Peor; Deut 9:18−20 the golden calf; Psa 78:59, 61; Isa 10:5−11; 2 Kgs 23:26 idolatry), and also against pagan opposition to God's redemptive design (esp. Exod 15:7; Psa 78:49 f. Pharaoh and the Egyptians).

[38] Cf. Dunn, *Romans*, 1:53. Antecedents include esp. Jeremiah 7−10 and Wisdom 11−15 (note the description of ἀδικία in 11:15).

[39] Fichtner, "ὀργή", 409.

[40] Esp. Herold, *Zorn*, 276−284.

[41] E.g. Exod 15:7 f.; Isa 63:1−6; Ps 7:7, 10, 12, 18; also Wisd 5:17−22; and see Herold, *Zorn*, 280 f.

[42] E.g. Isa 30:27−30; 63:4; 66:10−16; Jer 50:34; Psa 2:12.

[43] Bertram in *TWNT* 5:413 (and n. 211).

[44] E.g. Hab 3:5 (λόγος for דֶּבֶר); 3:12 (ἀπειλή for זעם); Isa 30:27 (μετὰ δόξης τὸ λόγιον τῶν χειλέων αὐτοῦ, τὸ λόγιον ὀργῆς πλῆρες for וכבד משאה שפתיו מלאו זעם). That these renderings are not accidental is shown by TJ, which at Isa 30:27 adduces a prophetic revelation of wrath, and in Hab 3:3−6 gives a midrash on God's revelation of the law to Israel and of wrath to the nations [sc. at Sinai]; cf. also 3:9−15.

[45] N.B. I take ἀπ' οὐρανοῦ in Rom 1:18 to qualify ὀργή cf. e.g. Wilckens, *Römer*, 1:102; Cranfield, *Romans*, 1:110 f.

[46] Cf. e.g. Barrett, *Romans*, 30, 34; Bornkamm, "Offenbarung", 30 f.; Käsemann, *Römer*, 27 f., 34; Lührmann, *Offenbarungsverständnis*, 146 f.; Ridderbos, *Paul*, 110; Wilckens, *Römer*, 1:87 f., 101 f.

[47] 1 QH 14:15 f. On the link of God's righteous judgement with salvation cf. e.g. CD 20:20; 1 Q27(Myst) 1.1.6; PssSol 8:8; 15:4−6; 1 En 91:7 f., 14; ApZeph 12:5,7; SibOr

Both contemporary Jewish thought and the close proximity and logical (γάρ)[48] connection between 1:17 and 1:18 indicate that God's righteousness and wrath in this context should indeed be seen as linked. With Cranfield and others, then, we must conclude that God's righteousness and wrath are in fact *both* being revealed by the gospel (i.e. in the current proclamation as well as previously in the gospel events).[49]

This reading receives support also from the quotation of Hab 2:4b in v. 17. Without tackling the difficult text critical and syntactical problems, it is clear that in its context Hab 2:4 is a promise of the vindication of the righteous and a threat of judgement for the wicked.[50] Arguably both Rom 1:17[51] and Heb 10:37, which also quotes Hab 2:4, show a similar context of vindication and historical theodicy. In Heb 10 as in LXX, Hab 2:3f. has Messianic overtones ([ὁ] ἐρχόμενος, ὁ δίκαιός [μου]). The Messiah according to Jewish expectation will bring judgement leading to both vindication of the righteous and punishment of the wicked.[52] In Paul and the NT, too, it is the Messiah's parousia which will bring salvation as well as wrath from heaven (esp. 2 Thess 1:7−10; cf. 2 Pet 3:3−13). The quotation of Hab 2:4 in Rom 1:17, therefore, introduces a complex of thought which closely affiliates Paul's gospel with Messianic ideas of vindication and judgement − thus forming a natural connection of v. 17 and 18.[53]

The gospel, then, decisively proclaims and inaugurates the revelation both of God's righteousness and of His wrath.[54] In light of Paul's generally eschatolog-

---

4:159−61; 11:311−14; Jub 24:30; Jer 11:20 LXX; Hos 6:5 LXX; also 2 Thes 1:5−8; Rev. 15:4; etc. In Rev 14:6 ff.; Luke 3:18 (context) note the εὐαγγέλιον of judgement. For the note of God's righteous *wrath* in particular cf. e.g. 4 Macc 4:21; PssSol 4:21, 24 f.; Wisd 11:9 f.; Sir 5:6; 16:11; also e.g. SifDeut 331 to 32:41 (ed. Finkelstein, p. 380 f.: "When retribution proceeds from before me it is quick as lightning; and yet my hand holds fast to justice"). See further Sjöberg/Stählin, "ὀργή", 414−16. A *revelation* of wrath occurs in TIsaac 4:54 Arabic [Charlesworth, *OTP*] = 7:11 Sahidic [Sparks]: God's wrath "will be manifested from heaven".

[48] Cf. Herold, *Zorn*, esp. 267−69 on the Biblical logic behind this γάρ.

[49] Thus Cranfield, *Romans*, 1:109 f. Similarly already Willet, *Hexapla*, 57 f. (referring to Matt 3; Luke 13:3; also citing Cajetan); Grotius (according to de Wette, *Römer*, 19); Wettstein, *Testamentum*, 2:22 ("Nam *Evangelium* docet, etc."); also Leenhardt, *Romans*, 62 f.; Wilckens, *Römer*, 1:102; and Herold, *Zorn*, 261, 302−306.

[50] See Hab 1:2−4, 5−11, 12−14, 15−17: 2:3 f. stands in a context of corporate lament and proclamation of vindicating judgement; similarly cf. 2:6−20; also 3:1 ff.

[51] Herold, *Zorn*, 185 and passim.

[52] See SibOr 3:654−6; 5:414−33; 4 Ezra 12:32−34; and cf. Schürer/Vermes, *HJPAJC*, 2:526−529.

[53] See further Strobel, *Verzögerungsproblem*, 173−202, esp. 181, 195.

[54] Cf. also Rom 2:16; 1 Thess 1:9 f.; 2 Cor 2:15 f.: judgement is a fully integral ingredient of Paul's gospel.

ical notion of the wrath of God[55] (and cf. esp. Rom 2:5, 8), the present tense ἀποκαλύπτεται suggests, not that the the final judgement is now actually under way, but that the heavenly disclosure of the ultimate wrath is already making itself felt (cf. 1 Cor 3:13: the day of the Lord ἀποκαλύπτεται in fire).[56] No doubt God has from time to time manifested His wrath in the past: but now in particular with the historical inauguration of the gospel,[57] and apparently with its subsequent proclamation,[58] the heavenly wrath of God has begun to come to its eschatological realization.

In sum: God's revelation of His righteousness in Christ has now in our time (νυνί, 3:21) inaugurated the time of eschatological judgement and redemption, *both* of which are currently being disclosed in the proclamation of the gospel.

Excursus: A Note on "Natural Revelation"

This judgement of God declared in Christ and in the gospel is levelled against the idolatry and debauchery which show that man has not given glory to his Creator. For God has already demonstrated (ἐφανέρωσεν) His invisible attributes in creation since its beginning (ἀπὸ κτίσεως κόσμου) (1:19 f.).

Clearly we find here the notion of a continuous "natural" revelation[59] which (unlike the Mosaic revelation) appears to exercise no distinct *heilgeschichtliche*

---

[55] Of sixteen Pauline passages using ὀργή, all but three speak of divine wrath. Six instances clearly refer to the future (Rom 2:5, 8; 5:9; Col 3:6; 1 Thess 1:10; 5:9); three seem to do so implicitly (Rom 3:5; 4:15; 12:19). The four remaining references include Rom 9:22 (twice), which speaks of past wrath postponed (sc. until the judgement?); and 1 Thess 2:16, which avers that God's "wrath has come upon them [sc. the Jews who killed Jesus] to the uttermost" (Bruce, *1&2 Thessalonians,* 48 sees this as a present anticipation of the eschatological wrath of 1:10.)

[56] Sanday/Headlam, *Romans,* 41 go further still in considering (with Euthymius Zigabenus) that the reference is in fact to the Day of Judgement, which is near at hand. Similarly other early commentators (cf. Poole, *Synopsis,* 4:19) and more recently Eckstein, "Zorn", 74–89.

[57] Cranfield, *Romans,* 1:110 recalls the events of our Lord's passion: "the reality of the wrath of God is only truly known when it is seen in its revelation in Gethsemane and on Golgotha."

[58] Michel, *Römer,* 97: "Gottes Gerichtsstunde ist angebrochen und wird im *Evangelium* proklamiert."

[59] Cf. Gärtner, *Areopagus,* 79. In view here is not indeed a "natural revelation" as somewhat narrowly defined (and then rightly rejected) e.g. by Hooker, "Adam", 299 ("a knowledge of God to which men have by their reasoning attained"): for 1:19 (ἐφανέρωσεν, aorist) does intend an actual divine revelation. Her observations (300 ff.) regarding parallels with Gen 1–3 and with the idea of an original revelation to Adam are certainly helpful. However, I am not persuaded that in order to affirm an allusion to Adam in this passage one must relinquish as incompatible the notion of an ongoing natural revelation.

function in regard to the the recent (νυνὶ δέ) revelation of God's righteousness in Christ (3:21) — except perhaps insofar as it applies to the period of God's patience preceding the incarnation.[60] Since it is therefore not essential to Paul's view of the central revelation,[61] it need not occupy a prominent place of its own in this study.

A "theology of creation", nevertheless, is not far removed from our theme. Paul repeatedly affirms significant links between Christology and cosmology: "Through Him are all things, and we through Him" (1 Cor 8:6; cf. e.g. Col 1:15—20; 2:2 f.). In 2 Cor 4:6, Paul affirms a continuity between "creational" and "evangelical" revelation: "God who said, 'Light shall shine out of darkness,' has shone in our hearts. . . ." Creation is even caught up in longing for the eschatological revelation of the children of God (Rom 8:19—22).

It may be tentatively suggested, therefore, that for Paul the immediate and primary function of "natural" revelation lies in its indictment of human idolatry and immorality (thus declaring even the Gentiles guilty before God).[62] In its broader setting, however, this revelation is summed up in Christ who is both head and author of creation and in whom all its secrets are hidden (cf. Col 2:3).

2.2. Manifestation of Truth in the Apostolic Ministry and Message

In addition to Rom 1:16—18, a number of other passages can be adduced to show that Paul believed God's revelation to be continuing in the preaching of the gospel, and more specifically in the apostolic ministry. Some of the clearest language in this respect is to be found in 2 Corinthians.

Thus Paul uses the image of the divine victory procession, in which the Apostles are led about as captives through whom God manifests "the sweet aroma of the knowledge of Him in every place" (2 Cor 2:14 f.).[63] Here it is, as Collange has noted, both the message (v. 14) and the person (v. 15) of the apostles which function as the *locus* of this divine manifestation.[64] The church

---

[60] In this respect the logical function of "natural" revelation for Paul is properly that of *praeparatio evangelica*. In Rom 1:19 ff. it is set in a contemporary Jewish form dependent on both OT and Stoic ideas; cf. esp. Wisd 13, and see Gärtner, *Areopagus*, 133—144.

[61] Cf. e.g. Lührmann, *Offenbarungsverständnis*, 26.

[62] Cf. Gärtner, *Areopagus*, 80: "the natural revelation is in some measure of only negative significance."

[63] On the disputed term θριαμβεύω see e.g. Collange, *Énigmes,* 24 f.; Furnish, *2 Corinthians*, 174 f.; most fully Hafemann, *Suffering*, 18—39.

[64] Collange, *Énigmes*, 28—33. Cf. e.g. Barrett, *2 Corinthians*, 99 f.; Hafemann, *Suffering*, 51—54; Plummer, *2 Corinthians*, 70; Schlier, "Parole", p. 133 f. On the use of the image cf. further Lohmeyer, *Wohlgeruch*, 26—34; Hafemann, *Suffering*, 43—51.

which he founded is manifested as a letter from Christ to all mankind, Paul being instrumental in its delivery (3:2 f.).[65] He conveys in his preaching "the light of the gospel of the glory of Christ" (4:4).[66] Paul (like all apostles)[67] acts as the ambassador of reconciliation on Christ's behalf (5:20); indeed it is none other than Christ who speaks through him (13:3), i.e. (as Allo nicely puts it) "qui parle par sa bouche".[68] Like a prophet, Paul speaks and acts on behalf of Christ:[69] his message carries the force of divine revelation, indeed of a divine *manifestation* (φανέρωσις) of the truth (2 Cor 4:2). In some aspects his self-understanding resembles the picture of Moses.[70]

However, it is at the same time with a distinct element of irony that Paul opposes his opponents' vainglorious boasts of letters of reference (2 Cor 3:1), of skilful speech (2 Cor 11:6), of heavenly ἀποκαλύψεις (2 Cor 12:1), etc. Instead (somewhat as he emphasizes the *cross* in 1 Cor, esp. 4:6—13) Paul stresses the image of revelation *through weakness*, a treasure of heavenly glory (cf. 2 Cor 3:7 ff., esp. 3:18; 4:6) concealed in earthen vessels (4:7 ff.): he is a prisoner of war in an imperial triumphal procession (2:14 f.); he carries the *death* of Jesus in his body (4:10 f.),[71] and his prayer for healing is met with an answer quite unbecoming to the Corinthian *theologia gloriae*.[72] In Damascus the apostle was made to act the fool, escaping only by being let down in a basket (11:32 f.)![73] Paul will only boast in his weakness (11:30; 12:5b, 9 f.) — and it is precisely in

---

[65] Cf. Bultmann, 2 Korinther, 74 f.; Plummer, *2 Corinthians*, 81; Allo, *2 Corinthiens*, 81; Hafemann, *Suffering*, 183—218. The idea of a heavenly letter need not be of Gnostic origin, *pace* Lührmann, *Offenbarungsverständnis*, 65: see Ezek 2:9 f.; Rev 2:1—3:20; also Exod 32:15 f.; poss. OdSol 23:5—10, 21 f.

[66] Cf. Allo, *2 Corinthiens*, 100; Collange, *Énigmes*, 135; Barrett, *2 Corinthians*, 131 f.

[67] Thus Allo, *2 Corinthiens*, 172; cf. Barrett, *2 Corinthians*, 176 on 5:18.

[68] Allo, *2 Corinthiens*, 338.

[69] Cf. Exod 4:12, 15; Jer 1:9; Ezek 3:27; Hab 2:1; Mal 2:7; 2 Chr 36:21 f., etc. See also Matt 10:20. Aune (*Prophecy*, 202 f., 248 f.) speaks of a functional equivalence with OT prophecy; cf. Cerfaux, *Christian*, 85—88; Myers/Freed, "Paul", 40—53. Note, however, that Paul (like Josephus!) never directly refers to himself as a prophet.

[70] E.g. the willingness to be cut off for Israel's sake (Rom 9:3; Exod 32:32); communing with the glory of God face to face (2 Cor 3:18; 4:6; Exod 33:11; Deut 34:10; Num 12:8); pleading with God and receiving the answer "my grace is sufficient for thee" (2 Cor 12:9; cf. DeutR 11:10 on Deut 3:26). See further Bammel, "Paulus", esp. 406; also Hafemann, *Suffering*, 216—218 (with specific reference to 2 Cor 2:14—17; 3:2 f.).

[71] Cf. possibly Gal 3:1 — in Paul's message and person (?) Christ was portrayed to the *Galatians* as crucified; cf. Gal 2:20; 6:14, 17.

[72] But Lincoln's suggestion (partly following Betz), that we have here "a miracle story where there is no miracle" ("Paul", 209), seems infelicitous. A parody on miracles would serve Paul badly in his quite contrary assertion three verses later (12:12).

[73] A comical scene; and indeed a *reductio ad absurdum* of his opponents' pursuit of self-glorification, as Lincoln ("Paul", 208) suggests.

his *weakness* that Christ is revealed.[74] The Apostle embodies and manifests his own proclamation.[75]

2.3. A Note on Occasional Revelations

Paul repeatedly employs revelation terminology in reference to a variety of contemporary disclosures. Examples include prophetic and other manifestations of the Spirit in the course of congregational worship (1 Cor 12:7—11; 14:6, 26, 30) as well as heavenly visions (2 Cor 12:1—4). Their function may be to convict of sin (1 Cor 14:24 f.) or of an improper disposition of life (Phil 3:15). The ἀποκάλυψις in Gal 2:2 (which may correspond to Acts 11:28—30) clearly consists of a concrete instruction pertaining to Paul's visit to Jerusalem. A somewhat different example may be the Spirit's special prompting of Christian prayer (Rom 8:15 f., 26 f.; cf. Gal 4:6).[76]

Here is not the time or place to enter into a full discussion of the phenomenon of occasional revelations and the role of prophecy in Paul.[77] This type of divine disclosure was certainly important and recurrent in the experience of Paul and his churches;[78] indeed at least in the Corinthian correspondence it would appear to be regarded as one manifestation (φανέρωσις, 1 Cor 12:7) among several of the Holy Spirit's presence in communal worship.[79]

However, there are good reasons to suspect that the logical place which such contemporary prophetic disclosures occupied in Paul's theology of revelation is not foundational or constitutive. His appraisal of this phenomenon, even in the Corinthian correspondence, is relatively restrained (1 Cor 12:31—13:2; 13:8 10). He esteems it highly (1 Cor 14:1 ff.), but it does not carry the full and immediate authority of the divine word, as Grudem has demonstrated on the basis of 1 Cor 14:29 f., 36, 37 f.[80] Even with regard to his own heavenly visions Paul

---

[74] Cf. Lührmann, *Offenbarungsverständnis,* 61; Lincoln, "Paul", 209.

[75] An idea also explicitly present in Ps-Philo, *De Jona* (26) 101 (= Siegert, *Predigten,* 26). Cf. e.g. Isa 20:3 f.; Jer 32:6—15; Hos 1:2 ff.; also Acts 21:10 f.

[76] Cf. Cranfield, *Romans* 1:398 f.; Goppelt, *Theologie,* 449 f.

[77] Several full-scale treatments have appeared over the last decade. Note particularly Aune, *Prophecy* (esp. 248—262); Hill, *Prophecy;* Grudem, *Gift;* Müller, *Prophetie.*

[78] Cf. esp. 2 Cor 12:7; but note also the frequency of such phenomena in Acts (13:2; 16:6—10; 18:9—11; 22:17—21; 23:11; 27:23 f.).

[79] A conviction not without significance against a background of Jewish and Old Testament eschatology: see above on the perceived presence or absence of the Spirit, Shekhinah, etc. in Judaism; and cf. Joel 3:1 f. (Heb).

[80] Grudem, *Gift,* 66—74. Grudem envisions (67 and passim) a distinction between authority of "actual words" (as in the OT prophets) and of "general content" (as here), the latter being subject to critical scrutiny on the part of the congregation. But this argument is somewhat infelicitous. I am not aware of any Biblical or Jewish precedent for a

shows considerable reluctance (2 Cor 12:1—10; see below), since this was a bone of contention for his Corinthian opponents — and one which he himself ultimately regards as incidental to the foundation of his faith.

Occasional revelations are, *sub specie aeternitatis*, only of temporary value (1 Cor 13:8—10). The abiding and truly foundational experience for the church is the work of the Spirit of Christ in faith, hope, and love (13:13):[81] "God has sent forth the Spirit of His Son into our hearts, crying, 'Abba! Father!'" (Gal 4:6).[82] The significance of contemporary revelations in the larger pattern of God's saving design is in the final analysis theologically secondary and transient. Nonetheless, in the message and apostolic ministry of the gospel the present dimension of revelation remains essential for Paul.[83]

3. Future: The Revelation of the Saviour Jesus Christ

Given the preceding observations, it may be something of a surprise to find that the revelation of Jesus Christ, and with it redemption and judgement, is still to come. Thus e.g. a number of references of ἀποκαλύπτω / ἀποκάλυψις and φανερόω clearly refer to the future consummation.[84] It is difficult to present in a few lines an adequate picture of the future dimension of revelation in Paul, since (in a manner of speaking) *all* eschatology could be contained under this heading. The following will merely outline the relevant statements in their direct bearing upon the question at hand.

Having declared the eschatological revelation of God's wrath in the current preaching of the gospel in Rom 1:18 (see above), Paul nevertheless continues to hold that there is a final judgement (or "wrath to come") still to be revealed (Rom 2:5; 1 Thes 1:10; 2 Thes 1:7 f.; cf. 1 Cor 3:13, etc.). Similarly, despite the

---

distinction along these lines; and I fail to understand (in the terms of early Judaism as well as of common sense) the practical difference in authority between revealed *content* and revealed *words*. Moreover (*pace* Grudem 19 f., 66 f.) the scrutiny to which prophets were subjected in the Deuteronomic tradition applied not only to the person of the prophet but also to his *words* (Deut 13:2 [omitted by Grudem]; 18:20, 22; 1 Kgs 13:18; Jer 14:13—16; 23:9—15 with 16—22; etc.): in this respect they differ little from their NT counterparts.

All the same, Grudem is clearly justified in distinguishing between the authority of OT and NT prophets. I would venture to suggest, however, that the causes and criteria of distinction are rather to be found in the religious atmosphere of contemporary Judaism, where the Scriptural prophets *ex hypothesi* had a standing of prior authority.

[81] Cf. Gal 5:5 f., 22 f. The Spirit is also the "down payment" (ἀρραβών: 2 Cor 1:22 and 5:5; ἀπαρχή: Rom 8:23) of the salvation that is to come.

[82] Note the proximity to 4:4, discussed above. Cf. Rom 5:5; 8:15.

[83] Sandmel, *Genius*, 53, compares the emphasis on present revelation in Philo.

[84] E.g. Rom 2:5; 8:18 f.; 1 Cor 1:7; 4:5; Col 3:4; 2 Thes 1:7.

past manifestation of God's righteousness in Christ and the apostolic proclamation of the gospel, Paul is still "awaiting eagerly the revelation (ἀποκάλυψις) of our Lord Jesus Christ" (1 Cor 1:7; cf. Phil 3:20 f.; 1 Thes 1:9 f.; 2 Thes 1:7; 2:8). Revelation of faith and the adoption of sonship in Christ have been given (Gal 3:23 f.; 4:4—7), but the present heavenly citizenship still awaits its full consummation at the coming of the Saviour (Phil 3:20 f.). The Christians' participation in the new creation (2 Cor 5:17; cf. Gal 6:15; Col 3:10; etc.) does not obviate the need for a future revelation of their state of glory (Rom 8:19; 1 Cor 15:42, 49; Col 3:4).

The incompleteness of the revelation given so far, even as it relates to the standing of the Christian, is expressed in a variety of other terms as well. Thus justification and reconciliation with God are chiefly grounded in the past (Rom 4:2; 5:1, 9 f.; 8:30; 1 Cor 6:11; 2 Cor 5:18; Col 1:22, etc.) and the present (Rom 3:24, 26, 28; 4:5; 8:33; Gal 3:8, 11; 2 Cor 5:19 f., etc.), whereas *salvation* appears to be implemented largely in the future (Rom 5:9 f.; 10:9; 11:26; 1 Cor 3:15; 5:5; 1 Thes 5:8 f.; contrast Eph 2:5, 8; 2 Tim 1:9; Tit 3:5).[85]

For Paul, then, the crowning revelation of salvation in Christ is still to come.[86] Without for a moment denying the eschatological significance of revelation past and present (which against its Jewish background must be understood to inaugurate the world to come), we can see that in relation to their future consummation in glory these two dimensions are only precursors.[87]

In this respect Beker is certainly right to point out the crucial function of

---

[85] The only occasion of a past tense of σῴζω in the accepted corpus of eight letters serves to prove the rule, for it clearly stresses the future dimension of salvation: "In hope we have been saved (ἐσώθημεν). . . . But if we hope for what we do not see, with perseverance we wait eagerly for it" (Rom 8:24 f.). Instances of σῴζω with divine subject in the *present* tense are also best understood to refer to a future event: 1 Cor 1:18; 15:2; 2 Cor 2:15. Cf. Fohrer/Foerster, "σῴζω", esp. 992—994; Cranfield, *Romans*, 1:88 f.

[86] Cf. also Oepke, "καλύπτω", 586; Ladd, *Theology*, 386.

[87] I am consciously wary of the somewhat overloaded and abused term "proleptic". In Stuhlmacher (*Evangelium*, 71, 77) and Rowland (*Open Heaven*, 377) it seems to apply to apocalyptic visions, viz. as disclosures of heavenly realities. Both writers see this phenomenon in Gal 1:12. However, this is not properly prolepsis but the foresight of (e.g.) saving events which are and remain in the future. Consistent with his own usage, Stuhlmacher (78 n. 1) contrasts *proleptic* and *anticipatory* revelations: the former *refer* to future events; the latter mediate actual *participation* (Stuhlmacher denies the presence of this in Paul, in my opinion rightly).

Kim, on the other hand, is inconsistent in his use of the term. Convinced that in Gal 1:12 Paul does claim actual participation in the future reality (*Origin*, 56: "Christ was revealed to Paul in the form in which he will come at the End-time"), he sees here "a proleptic realization or an anticipation of the parousia". But elsewhere Kim seems to follow the more limited usage of Stuhlmacher and Rowland, as when "Paul's gospel . . . bursts the apocalyptic schema in which the revelation to a seer through a vision is merely a prolepsis of the eschatological revelation" (73 f., ital. removed).

hope (ἔλπις) in Paul's theology as the element which bridges the apocalyptic tension between the "already" and the "not yet", both of the Christian life in general and of revelation in particular:

> Paul speaks not about the fulfillment of the promises but about their confirmation in Christ (Rom 4:16, *bebaios*). Indeed, the Christ-event ratifies the Old Testament promises, but it is not a closure event, because it reactivates the hope of his Parousia in glory (1 Cor 1:7, 8). And it seems that the hope entails the expectation of new revelation and new acts of God.[88]

If, then, revelation for Paul is not complete until its consummation in the future, the most appropriate description of the two dimensions of revelation currently accessible must surely be that these revelations (both past and present) are indeed partial incursions of the new age into this age.[89] In the coming of the Messiah Son of David, crucified and then resurrected as Son of God in power (Rom 1:3f.), this new world of salvation has unquestionably dawned, and in the proclamation of the gospel the eschatological righteousness of God is now being revealed. But the consummation of God's promises of salvation and vindication (and thereby the conclusive answer to the question of historical theodicy) still awaits its revelation.

4. Τί οὖν ὁ νόμος; The Old Testament in Paul's View of Revelation

Our analysis of constitutive revelation in Paul suggests that without doubt the key to Paul's understanding of revelation is the εὐαγγέλιον τοῦ Χριστοῦ (or τοῦ θεοῦ), which pertains to the work of God in Christ as revealed and manifested in the three temporal dimensions of past, present, and future.

But despite a number of conceptual parallels with Judaism, one item of central importance in the Jewish texts did not immediately suggest itself in our study of Paul, viz. the notion that revelation occurs through the interpretation of Scripture. What is the role of "Torah" in the apostle's understanding of revelation?

Obviously in view of the complexity of the issue and of the sea of publications on related topics such as "Paul and the Law", "Paul and the Old Testament", etc. these few paragraphs must of necessity remain incomplete and inadequate. But keeping in mind that our interest is neither in the "law" (whether in its role for justification or for Christian ethics) nor indeed in Paul's technique of OT exegesis, it may be possible to narrow the field down sufficiently to be able to make one or two apposite suggestions.

---

[88] Beker, *Paul*, 148; cf. 146–149.
[89] Cf. Beker, *Paul*, 145.

4.1. Paul's Use of the Scriptures

The empirical facts about Paul's use of the Old Testament are well known.
Paul cites the Scriptures as his authority more than 100 times, without distinguishing between Torah and Prophets.[90] They amount to the "oracles of
God" (Rom 3:1 f.) and are holy, prophetic, and πνευματικός (e.g. Rom 1:2;
4:3; 7:12, 14a). The authority Paul attributes to his Old Testament quotations is
unquestioned, and at least implicitly divine.[91] He speaks highly of the Sinaitic
מתן תורה, the priestly service and the prophetic promises (Rom 9:4), and repeatedly affirms that God's word is unchangeable (Rom 9:6; 11:29). Scripture enables the Jew to know and discern the will of God (Rom 2:18). Whatever else
Paul may say, it would seem that he continues to hold the Old Testament as
containing authoritative disclosure of the will of God; the prevalence of arguments from Scripture in his discourse indicates that Paul still sees himself irre-
versibly committed to the Scriptures as his "holy book" and theological under-
pinning.[92] D. M. Smith writes, "While Paul vests his letters with his own
apostolic authority, by citing Scripture he appeals to a higher authority, a word
that is divine revelation in a sense that he does not take his own words to be."[93]

We would expect, therefore, to find some attempt to redress the possible logical and theological friction between this previous disclosure of God's will and
Paul's view of the centrality of the revelation in the gospel. A cursory overview
of the relevant material may be given from two different perspectives: (i) the
"new" and "old" revelation in contrast; and (ii) the "new" as intention (consummation) of the "old".[94] It will not be possible in this short section fully to
resolve the evident tension between (i) and (ii);[95] but in my opinion the latter
aspect of Paul's thinking may in itself go some distance toward a moderation of
the conflict.

4.2. "New" vs. "Old" in Revelation

It is clear that Paul's own faith and religious system must have been shaken to
its foundations on the Damascus Road. Given Jewish convictions about the
centrality of Torah, it would indeed have been, as W. D. Davies writes, only "a

---

[90] See D. M. Smith, "Pauline Literature", 272; Siegert, *Argumentation*, 162–164.
[91] Ellis, *Use*, 20 f., 23 ff; Bonsirven, *Exégèse*, 345; Cranfield, "Law", 45.
[92] Vielhauer, "Paulus", 208; Michel, *Paulus*, 136 f.; Conzelmann, *Theologie*, 182 f.
[93] D. M. Smith, "Pauline Literature", 265.
[94] Cf. also Luz, *Geschichtsverständnis*, 93 f., 132–134.
[95] Luz argues that Paul does *not* have a systematic, integrative pattern (e.g. of prede-
stination) by which to harmonize the two motifs of continuity and of discontinuity with
the past: *Geschichtsverständnis*, e.g. 263, 267; cf. idem, "Bund", 322, 326.

messianic event of revelatory and cosmic significance"[96] which could have induced Paul to re-evaluate the role of the "old" revealed dispensation as in fact he did. There would need to be new revelation beyond, *outside* the Torah (cf. Rom 3:21 χωρὶς νόμου).[97]

In the event that messianic encounter did occur, and Paul's thought changed profoundly. The revelation of Jesus as the exalted Son of God, and Paul's own divine calling to the Gentile mission, introduce an authority which equals that of Scripture. From now on the revelation of the gospel, the "Law of Christ" (Gal 6:2; cf. 1 Cor 9:21), and the "words of the Lord" (1 Thes 4:15; 1 Cor 7:10; 9:14; 11:23; cf. 2 Cor 12:9) have become the highest court of appeal.[98] Indeed this new revelation enables Paul to think in terms of two distinct, even contrary dispensations: viz., of death and life (2 Cor 3:6), Moses and Christ (2 Cor 3:7 ff.), or of Sinai and Zion (Gal 4:24; cf. Heb 12:18−24).

It is perhaps E. P. Sanders who in recent scholarship has most strongly emphasized the element of *dis*continuity in Paul's view of the old covenant in relation to the new. Sanders considers that Christ has replaced the Torah at the centre of Paul's theology, and that the two dispensations are mutually exclusive.[99] Paul now, in Sanders's view, denies the very fundamentals of Judaism: election, covenant, and Torah;[100] in his thinking about the old dispensation Paul moves "from solution [i.e., salvation and participation in Christ] to plight [i.e., insufficiency of Judaism]."[101] H. Räisänen, who sees Paul's approach to the Torah as rather more incoherent,[102] suggests that in fact Paul's view of the "law" is subject to the psychological principle of "secondary rationalization": having come to faith in Christ, Paul now looks for arguments for the inferiority of the Torah.[103] Without following Sanders and Räisänen in some of their more sweeping conclusions, their view of a rationalizing logic of "solution to plight" may be accepted as helpful in understanding the origin of

---

[96] Davies, "Law", 101−3; cf. Blank, "Schriftverständnis", 51 f.

[97] Blank, "Schriftverständnis", 52.

[98] Cf. Michel, *Paulus*, 162: "Hier wächst eine autoritative Größe heran, welche dem A.T. überlegen ist. Das A.T. muß ausgelegt werden; das Herrenwort richtet sich an alle." But as Michel points out (159 f.), Paul also appeals to other non-scriptural sources of authority such as nature (1 Cor 11:14 ff.), rhetorical devices like analogy (1 Cor 9:7; 14:7 ff.; 15:35 ff.); and (we might add) Christian tradition (1 Cor 11:23 ff.; 15:3 ff.).

[99] Sanders, *PLJP*, 151 f. Cf. e.g. *PLJP*, 138−140 (on 2 Cor 3 and Phil 3).

[100] Sanders, *PPJ*, 551 f.

[101] E.g. Sanders, *PPJ*, 442−447; *PLJP*, 150 (though Sanders applies this primarily to Paul's soteriology).

[102] E.g. Räisänen *Paul*, 199 f. Hübner (*Law*, 5 f. and passim) also affirms inconsistencies, but he postulates a development in Paul's thought between Gal and Rom. Sanders, *PLJP*, 147 f. (cf. *PPJ*, 518) sees Paul as "coherent" but not "systematic" (agreeing with J. C. Beker on the hermeneutical principle of Paul's thought as having a "coherent centre" with potentially differing "contingent interpretations").

[103] Räisänen, *Paul*, 201.

some of Paul's more antithetical language about the role of the Torah[104] — especially in situations of dispute with those who wished to return to that old dispensation.[105]

In short: in one recurring facet of his thought Paul lays store by the decisively new character of God's eschatological work in Christ.[106] And because God has acted decisively in Christ, what precedes is necessarily "old" and at least relativized by the word of the gospel: in a sense it might well be said of Paul that ἐν τῷ λέγειν καινὴν πεπαλαίωκεν τὴν πρώτην.[107]

4.3. The "New" Intended in the "Old"

The logical conclusion of the preceding paragraph might well be the complete displacement without remainder of the old revelation ("Sinai") by the new ("Zion"). *Prima facie* this would appear to be the position of Sanders,[108] and it has at any rate been suggested by a multitude of scholars for the interpretation of Rom 10:4: Christ as the "end" (termination) of the "law". It is to this passage as of paradigmatic significance that we will now for a moment turn our attention.

4.3.1. The End of the Torah? Rom 10:4

"Τέλος γὰρ νόμου Χριστὸς εἰς δικαιοσύνην παντὶ τῷ πιστεύοντι." These words of Paul constitute a particularly knotty *crux interpretum* in the history of exegesis. For present purposes I must simply refer to the discussion of plentiful secondary literature in the commentaries,[109] and limit my remarks to one or two immediate observations.

---

[104] Note that it is the "faith-righteousness" which exposes Israel's failure in Rom 10:5—8: the "zeal not according to knowledge" is perhaps recognizable only from within the fold of "faith".

[105] A sociological interpretation of this trend (full disengagement from the Jewish community, legitimation of law-free Gentile Christianity as constituted by "faith" vs. "works") is now argued by Watson, *Paul*, 177—179 and passim.

[106] Cf. e.g. "new covenant" 1 Cor 11:25; 2 Cor 3:6 (but N.B. only there); "new creation" 2 Cor 5:17; Gal 6:15; also Eph 2:15; 4:24.

[107] But N.B. neither Paul nor the writer to the Hebrews would agree to the application of Heb 8:13 in its entirety to the OT as such.

[108] See e.g. *PPJ*, 550—552; *PLJP*, 140f., 151f. [However, it may be that Sanders makes these general statements about the function of the "law" for Paul only in regard to *justification*. At times he does allow e.g. for Paul's application of OT promises to believers (*PPJ*, 551), or for a continuing role of the Torah in Pauline ethics (*PLJP*, 153).]

[109] For a condensed overview of common views see Räisänen, *Paul*, 53 and nn. 47—49. A definitive new study (1985), also for the history of exegesis, is R. Badenas,

Even a cursory word study quickly demonstrates that the meaning of Rom 10:4 cannot be derived from any prior considerations about the semantic value of τέλος; for this ranges widely between "end", "termination", "goal", "outcome", "fulfilment", etc. (not to mention "tax" in Rom 13:7).

The idea that Christ is the "termination" of the law, although it cannot be strictly ruled out on semantic grounds, is made quite unlikely by contextual considerations.[110] Rom 9–11 should be consistently understood as answering the question, Have God's design and His promises failed with regard to Israel? (see esp. 9:6). Just as the answer to this larger question stresses not the termination but the fulfilment of the former promises in Christ, so we would expect Paul to argue similarly regarding the "old" revelation. And indeed, as we saw above, he affirms the irrevocability of the gifts and the promises to Israel (cf. Rom 9:4; 11:29).[111] Thus an understanding of Christ as the "termination" of the law would appear to be more than a little counterproductive to the thrust of these chapters.[112]

Without being able to examine all the arguments in detail at this point, I would like to consider a reading of τέλος in this context as *prophetic fulfilment* or *consummation*. While this is not the primary meaning of τέλος, it is nevertheless one which is well and widely attested.[113] The notion of a prophetic function of

---

Christ the End of the Law (though unfortunately he has not seen either Räisänen or Sanders [1983]).

[110] Unlikely, too, is the understanding of νόμος here not as Torah but in the narrow sense as "law", since in the context this would do little to buttress Paul's argument. Cf. Badenas, *Christ*, 113 f. The idea of Christ as "termination" of the Law has sometimes (wrongly) been linked with a supposed first-century expectation of a complete cancellation or replacement of the Torah in the Messianic age. Cf. also Bammel, "Νόμος", 121–123; and see above, p. 110 n. 41.

[111] On χαρίσματα as an expression specifically of God's revelation in the Torah see Horbury, "δωρήματα", 47 f.

[112] Cf. Badenas, *Christ*, 114; Cranfield, *Romans*, 2:519. This would apply even if, as is sometimes suggested (e.g. by Hübner, *Law*, 138; Lapide in *Paul*, 37; Luck, "Bekehrung", 200 n. 63), Christ were to be the end only of the misuse of the law (viz. for justification: εἰς δικαιοσύνην), and only for the believer (παντὶ τῷ πιστεύοντι). This latter reading falters also on grammatical grounds: see e.g. Cranfield, *Romans*, 2:519 f. n. 2; Badenas, *Christ*, 116; Sanders, *PLJP*, 40.

[113] Josephus BJ 4:387; Ant 2:73; 4:125; 8:218; 10:35 (all of the fulfilment of prophecy). Similarly cf. HermVis 3.3.2 (link of τέλος with πληρόω); SibOr 3:211; VitProph 2:10, 19; also 4Ezra 6:12; 9:6 (*finis*). In the NT cf. 1 Pet 1:9. Eusebius, *Demonstratio Evangelica* 8.2.33 specifically links Rom 10:4 and Matt 5:17 under the heading of fulfilled prophecy; καὶ πᾶσαί γε αἱ περὶ αὐτοῦ προφητεῖαι ἀπλήρωτοι καὶ ἀτέλεις ἔμενον, εἰς ὅτε αὐτὸς ἐπιστὰς ἐπιτέθεικεν ἅπασι τέλος τοῖς περὶ αὐτοῦ προαναπεφωνημένοις. Similarly cf. Clem. Alex. *Strom* 2:9; 4:21. As a possible Semitic equivalent cf. (not קץ – pace e.g. Luz, *Geschichtsverständnis*, 141 –, but) גמר: cf. above on Gal 4:4; also 1 Cor 10:11 (τὰ τέλη τῶν αἰώνων).

the Torah was suggested by the Pentateuch itself[114] and consequently became quite widely accepted in ancient Judaism.[115] The Jesus of the Gospels speaks of the prophetic function of the Torah (cf. Matt 11:13; also 5:17); he considers himself and his ministry to be in fulfilment of the Scriptures,[116] and both his followers[117] and opponents[118] agree that the Messiah is promised in the Torah. Paul, too, gives expression to his belief that the revelation of Jesus the Messiah as God's righteousness is in fulfilment of that which was attested by the Torah and the prophets.[119]

The same theme, then, may profitably be understood as carrying on in the context of Rom 10:4. The Jews, pursuing the "Torah of righteousness", nonetheless have not attained to that true Torah, since they pursued it as though God's faith-based righteousness was to be achieved on the ethnically particular basis of works of Law (ὡς ἐξ ἔργων, 9:30; cf. 10:6 f.).[120] Hence they stumble over the issue of faith (9:31), viz. over the Messiah who is himself that true meaning and fulfilment of Torah: despite their admirable zeal they fail to recognize (10:2) God's righteousness (as revealed in Christ: cf. 3:21 etc.). But it is in fact the Messiah who is the fulfilment of Torah (10:4).

Appropriating the Bible's own revelatory language to describe the new revelation,[121] Paul uses Deut 30:12 f. to present Christ as the fulfilment of the Torah.[122] Life-giving righteousness, as defined in the Torah, is *doing* (10:5; Lev 18:5). But this doing applies to something (ῥῆμα, 10:8) which is simple and near at hand (Deut 30:12 f.).[123] It is precisely *not* a matter of exertion to heaven

---

[114] Esp. Gen 12:2 f.; 13:15 f., etc.; 49:1 ff.; Num 24:15−24 etc.; Deut 18:15, 18 f.; 28 ff. passim; and passages which stress Moses' prophetic status (Num 12:6−8; Deut 18:15, 18; 34:10).

[115] See e.g. the image of Moses as a prophet and visionary in the apocrypha (Sir 46:1; 2 Macc 2:4; [7:6]) and pseudepigrapha (e.g. Jub 1:4, 26; 2 Bar 3:9; 4:5; 59:4−11; AssMos 1:17 f. and passim; EzekTrag 68−89). Also Josephus, *Ant* 5:20 and passim; Philo *Mut* 103, 125 f.; *Somn* 2:189; *Mos* 2:187; *Sacr* 130. See also Lührmann, *Offenbarungsverständnis*, 102 on Jub 1:1−4.

[116] See esp. Luke 4:21. Cf. John 5:45−47; also 14:6, 15.

[117] See e.g. John 1:45 ("we have found him of whom Moses in the Law and also the Prophets wrote"). Cf. Luke 24:27, 44; Acts 28:23.

[118] E.g. John 12:34 ("we have heard out of the Law that the Messiah will remain forever").

[119] Esp. Rom 3:21; 10:5−8. Cf. 1 Cor 14:21 (prophecy from the νόμος); also e.g. Heb 10:1.

[120] Cf. Dunn, e.g. *Romans*, 1:lxix−lxxii.

[121] Thus D. M. Smith, "Pauline Literature", 266; cf. also Eckstein, "Nahe", 212 ff.

[122] For Rom 10:6−8 cf. also the role of the divine Memra in TN to this passage. Cf. also Eph 4:7−10, where the reference to Psa 68:19 is applied to "Moses the prophet" in the Targum; also MidrPsa 68:11; cf. Bietenhard, *Welt*, 236 f.

[123] A logic of *progression* rather than of antithesis in 10:5, 6−8 (*contra* many commentators) is ably defended by Badenas, *Christ*, 121−125. Yet *pace* Badenas I would still hold

or the abyss[124] as though this could bring the Messiah (10:6 f.):[125] instead it calls for simple confessing faith in Jesus (10:9−13).[126] "So then faith arises from the message heard, namely the message which comes through the word about Christ" (10:17).

No doubt many other issues would need to be addressed.[127] Suffice it for present purposes to suggest that rather than espousing the termination of the Torah, Paul in Rom 10:4 considers Christ to be its eschatological consummation and fulfilment.

4.3.2. Paul's Hermeneutical Key

A similar view of prophecy and christological fulfilment is borne out elsewhere in Paul's writings, and virtually becomes his hermeneutical ground rule.

Christ appears to be for Paul the functional equivalent of the wisdom of God,[128] and thus he becomes the key for the understanding of all revelation: whether in the gospel, in Scripture, or in creation. On at least four occasions, each following an interpreted Scripture passage, Paul states very clearly and explicitly his conviction that the Torah and the Prophets must now be read as pointing forward to the new dispensation of the Christ:

---

to a measure of contrast: not indeed between legalism (10:5) and faith (10:6−8), but between the true righteousness of "doing" the Messianic word of faith which is near (10:5, 8 ff.), and the human exertion as though to produce the Messiah from heaven or from the dead (10:6 f.). In the background of this understanding may lie the view, later attested in various forms, that God would send the Messiah as soon as Israel repented and at least once perfectly kept the Torah (or part of it): e.g. b.Sanh 97b−98a passim (R. Jonathan T3; Rab A1; R. Eliezer T2 vs. R. Joshua T2; R. Joshua b. Levi A1); b.Shab 118b (R. Simeon b. Yohai T3); y.Taan 1:1, 64a29−34 (R. Tanḥum b. Ḥiyya A3; R. Levi A3: par. ExR 25:12/MidrPsa 95:2). Cf. Badenas, *Christ*, 131.

[124] Cf. Moses and Jonah: FT Deut 30:12 f. Goldberg, "Torah", 131 regards Paul's remarks (like those of the Targum) as subtly anti-mystical in intention. But cf. also 4 Ezra 4:8.

[125] The τοῦτ' ἔστιν here does not technically signify a *midrash pesher* (pace e.g. recently Eckstein, "Nahe", 211), but is a simple literary device of explanation, equivalent to "*i.e.*" (cf. [ה]איה, e.g. 1 QS 8:14 f.; 1 QpHab 12:7, etc.). See further Aageson, "Scripture", 276; Cranfield, *Romans*, 2:524. Siegert, *Argumentation*, 162 denies that Paul employs *pesher* at all.

[126] Cf. also Badenas, *Christ,* 131.

[127] E.g. Suggs, "Word", esp. 309−311: Rom 10:6−10 is a midrash on Wisdom and Deut 30:12 f. (similar to Bar 3:29 f.) in which Paul identifies *Christ,* the Torah, and the hidden heavenly Wisdom. However (pace Suggs), Bar 3:29 f. deals with the inaccessibility to human reason of the wisdom and knowledge of Torah, while Paul deals in 10:5−8 with the supposed elusiveness not of wisdom and knowledge but of righteousness and "life" (i.e. salvation: 10:10). Nevertheless it is conceivable that a (vaguely satirical, 10:6 f.?) undercurrent of "hidden wisdom now made manifest" is indeed present in the argument of 9:30−10:8.

[128] 1 Cor 1:24, 30; 2:6 f.; 8:6; cf. Col 1:15−18; 2:3.

Now not for his [Abraham's] sake only was it written . . ., but for our sake also . . ., as those who believe in Him who raised Jesus our Lord from the dead. (Rom 4:23 f.)

For whatever was written in earlier times was written for our instruction (εἰς τὴν ἡμέτεραν διδασκαλίαν[129]), that through perseverance and the encouragement of the Scriptures we might have hope. (Rom 15:4)[130]

Or is He speaking altogether for our sake? Yes, for our sake it was written. . . . (1 Cor 9:10)

Now these things happened to them as an example (τυπικῶς), and they were written for our instruction (πρὸς νουθεσίαν ἡμῶν), upon whom the ends of the ages (τὰ τέλη τῶν αἰώνων) have come. (1 Cor 10:11)

Paul does not deny that the original reference of the Scriptures may have been literal and not allegorical.[131] But in the new dispensation and for his gospel he takes their function to be deictic and prophetic: his axiom is that in the post-Messianic situation the Old Testament exercises an important function as pointer to the Christ and the gospel.[132] Indeed Paul can go so far as to attribute the functions of the Torah to Christ.[133] This is not so much the adoption of an eclectic "canon within the canon",[134] but a complete *relecture* of the Old Testament.[135] Given the advent of the Messiah, Scripture itself now makes the gospel clear:[136] "For as many as are the promises of God, in Him they are Yes'."[137]

---

[129] Luz, *Geschichtsverständnis*, 111 n. 357 points out the similarity of this term with the Rabbinic ללמדך. Cf. 1 Cor 10:11 below.

[130] Cf. also 2 Tim 3:15.

[131] See Rom 4:23; 1 Cor 10:11a; cf. Hanson, *Studies*, 151.

[132] Cf. Duganzic, "Ja", 247: the OT now has "heilspädagogische Bedeutung"; also Hooker, "Beyond", 305; Vielhauer, "Paulus", 213. Cf. also D. M. Smith, "Pauline Literature", 277 f.; he writes, "It is an oversimplification to say that the rabbis regarded Scripture as law, while for Paul it was fundamentally prophecy. Yet that generalisation does not badly mislead us." Koch, *Schrift*, 347–350 grounds Paul's approach in the hermeneutical presupposition of the fundamental "sameness" (*Selbigkeit*) of God's action in the OT and in the gospel.

[133] See e.g. Rom 8:3; 10:5–8. Cf. also below on Christ as the "mystery"; and cf. Hooker, "Beyond", 303; Davies, *PRJ*, 149 and passim. However, D. M. Smith is probably wise to restrict the equation of Christ and the Torah to "the general sense of God's revelation of his righteousness" ("Pauline Literature", 266).

[134] Thus Sanders, *PLJP*, 161.

[135] Cf. Bonsirven, *Exégèse*, 268 f. ("lecture du palimpseste biblique"). 2 Cor 3:14 indicates the removal of the veil from the understanding of the OT (with Duganzic, "Ja", 121 f.; cf. Hooker, "Beyond", 304 f.). Of course the pattern of reapplying Biblical texts to new situations is as such formally parallel to early Jewish exegesis: see above, e.g. Chapter 2; Chapter 6, § 2.4.2. Note also the principle of Acts 8:34, and already 2 Kgs 22:13: כל הכתוב עלינו. The difference is that Paul's exegesis revolves around an axis of Messianic fulfilment. Cf. generally Koch, *Schrift*, 322 ff., 344 f.

[136] Cf. D. M. Smith, "Pauline Literature", 281.

[137] 2 Cor 1:20. Stuhlmacher ("Gegenwart", 434) specifically links this verse with

In the ethical realm, it may be an overstatement to say that Paul consciously shifted away from the *halakhah* aspect of Torah to maintain only its *haggadah* aspect.[138] Nevertheless, according to the "gospel of uncircumcision" the halakhic sphere of Torah is no longer applicable as a requirement for converting Gentiles: for Christ has already taken upon himself the curse attached to the non-observance of Torah (Gal 3:10, 13; cf. Deut 27:26; 28:15−68).[139] What remains as the "halakhic" will of God for converted Gentiles, then, is the "law of the Christ".[140] This might perhaps be seen as consisting of the "words of the Lord" (see above, § 4.2) as filled out by a body of Torah-based ethical teaching related in some way to the notion of Noachide commandments[141] (which in common Jewish tradition applied to *all* the nations).[142]

To conclude: Paul (not unlike some of his Jewish contemporaries) believes that the interpretation of the Scriptures is sealed and concealed until the time of their prophetic realization, i.e. (in his case) in Christ and the gospel. For the

---

Paul's OT hermeneutics. Cf. Rom 15:8, where Christ's ministry is specifically εἰς τὸ βεβαιῶσαι τὰς ἐπαγγελίας τῶν πατέρων.

[138] Thus Vielhauer, "Paulus", 220; cf. J. A. Sanders, "Torah and Christ", 373 f.

[139] Note also Westerholm, "Fulfilling", 232: "Paul never derives appropriate Christian conduct *simply and directly* by applying pertinent commands in Torah ..." (ital. mine).

[140] Gal 6:2; cf. Rom 8:2; and see Reinmuth, *Geist*, 63−65; also Styler, "Basis", 183−187. Cf. further n. 110 above.

[141] N.B. as developed e.g. in Jub 7:20 f.; t. AZ 8:4; GenR 16:6 (R. Levi A3); 34:8, 13 f.; DeutR 1:21 (R. Levi A3; R. Jose b. Hanina A2); b. Sanh 56a; also Acts 15:20, 29. Cf. by implication Jonah; Lev 17: 8, 10, 12 f.; Amos 1; Rom 2:14 f.; etc. See further Urbach, "Self-Isolation", 275−278; Wyschogrod, "Law", 12 f.; idem, "New Stage", 360 f.; more generally Novak, "*Origin*", 302−309.

[142] Related to this is the observation that Paul's ethical summaries (e.g. Rom 1:26−31; 13:13; 1 Cor 5:1, 9−11; 6:9 f.; 2 Cor 12:20 f.; Gal 5:19−21; Col 3:5, 8; 1 Thess 4:1−8) follow a common Hellenistic Jewish custom of summarizing the demands of the Torah by moral stipulations regarding idolatry, sexual misconduct, murder, avarice, etc. (e.g. Ps-Phoc; Ps-Heraclitus 7; T12Patr passim; cf. Wisd 14:12−27; SibOr 3:8−45; 4:31−34; etc.; but conversely EpArist 144−170 on the symbolic meaning of food laws *literally* observed) − thereby emphasizing the more "congenial" aspects of the Torah. Central concerns of the Law are expressed in terms which are substantially equivalent to these so-called Noachide commandments − and which also overlap significantly with the concerns of the three cardinal sins of Judaism, שפיכות דמים, עבודה זרה, and גילוי עריות (b. Yoma 85b; b. Sanh 74a; Acts 15:29; cf. also Tertullian *De Pudicitia* 12, 19). It is almost certainly in this sense that Paul speaks of Christians "keeping the commandments of God" (1 Cor 7:19, etc.); cf. Reinmuth, *Geist*, 12−22, 22−47, 61−65; Holtz, "Weisungen", 391−395; also see Siegert, *Argumentation*, 158 and passim on the generally Hellenistic, "common sense" character of the Pauline style of argumentation (though he almost certainly overstates his case). Possibly this νόμος Χριστοῦ, so defined, may even reflect a trend in the attitude of Jesus e.g. regarding טהורות and Sabbath legislation (Holtz, "Weisungen", 394; cf. Riches, *Jesus*, 112−144; but see Sanders, *Jesus*, 267−269, 325).

Christian interpreter[143] the true meaning of the OT has only now been uncovered in Christ (2 Cor 3:12–18, etc.). In this way, although the "new" is explained and defined by appeal to the "old", revelation in the Torah must now be read altogether in light of the revelation in Christ.[144]

From here the discussion naturally leads on to the Pauline idea of revealed mysteries of God, which will occupy us for the remainder of this study.

---

[143] N.B. such exposition seems to be a special χάρισμα, viz. that of διδασκαλία, the authoritative interpretation of Scripture: Bonsirven, *Exégèse*, 272 f.; Michel, *Paulus*, 115, 154; Aune, *Prophecy*, 345; Rengstorf, "διδάσκω", 164; *pace* Luz, *Geschichtsverständnis*, 107. Cf. Rom 12:7; 1 Cor 12:28 f.; also Eph 4:11.

[144] Note in this respect the virtual absence of explicit Scripture quotations from 1 and 2 Thes, Phil, Col/Phm, Eph; fully half of Paul's OT quotations are found in Rom alone (cf. D. M. Smith, "Pauline Literature", 274). These facts led Harnack ("Das Alte Testament", 137 f. and passim) to the somewhat drastic conclusion that in Paul's catechesis the OT played only a minor and secondary role.

Chapter Nine

The Letters to Corinth and Rome

In the next two chapters, the major Pauline passages on revealed mysteries will be addressed individually. The intention is not to offer a complete exegesis of the texts concerned, but rather to sketch possible directions for interpretation in light of previous results.

The Corinthian Letters, though incomplete, are the longest extant collection of Pauline correspondence. This, along with their repeated use of the theme at hand, makes them a suitable starting point.

1. "We Speak God's Wisdom in a Mystery"
(1 Cor 2:6–10)

1.1. Introduction

Our first and in some ways most significant text offers important insights into Paul's view of revelation and of heavenly secrets. Much ink has been spilt over the interpretation of this passage, and scholars have propounded and sometimes retracted theories and counter-theories in the attempt to understand its intention. My only purpose here can be to determine what light, if any, may be shed on the motif of a revealed mystery in view of its widespread use in contemporary Judaism.

Paul writes in the face of Corinthian factionalism and the desire on the part of some of the church members that the Apostle and his gospel should be vindicated by argument and persuasion. Side-stepping their demands for human credentials of polished rhetoric and scholarly wisdom of argument (1:20; 2:1–5),[1] Paul avers that his own message ever since his first arrival in Corinth has offered precisely the opposite. The only knowledge displayed in his proclamation of "the mystery of God"[2] at Corinth was that of Jesus as the crucified

---

[1] See most recently Lim, "Words", esp. 146–148.

[2] Arguments about the text of 2:1 tend to remain somewhat inconclusive. Evidence

Messiah; the only proof (ἀπόδειξις) supplied was that of the Spirit[3] and of the gospel's power of salvation (2:4 f. with 1:18; cf. Rom 1:16).

It is in the context of this dispute that Paul arrives at 2:6. Having virtually denied *any* use of σοφία in his preaching, he now stops to guard against a misunderstanding which his preceding remarks might appear to suggest (cf. the similar logical function of 1:16). "In fact we actually *do* speak wisdom among those who are qualified [ἐν τοῖς τελείοις], but it is not the wisdom of this world or of those who have power in this world, who are being eliminated [καταργουμένων]."[4] The bridge between this statement and the preceding denial, and with it the integrity and aim of the whole context, lies in Paul's affirmation of the wisdom of God over against the wisdom of man.[5]

1.2. V. 6: The τέλειοι

Who are these τέλειοι, the mature ones who share in Paul's heavenly wisdom? They would appear to be those who manifest a spiritual rather than a carnal disposition and way of life.[6] Attitudinal and *ethical* connotations of "maturity" seem clearly implied by 3:1−3 and other passages.[7]

---

for μαρτύριον is more plentiful but that for μυστήριον is early. Cf. Metzger, *Textual Commentary*, 545. The criterion of *lectio difficilior* might suggest that the introduction of μυστήριον was felt to be too abrupt, whereas the use of μαρτύριον for the gospel has precedent in 1:6.

[3] Though perhaps including miracles: see the comprehensive claims of 2 Cor 12:12; Rom 15:19; 1 Thes 1:5; and cf. the Paul of Acts 13:11; 14:8−10; 16:18; 19:11 f.; 20:9 f.; 28:3−5, 8. See also Horbury, "False Prophecy", 506 f. and n. 1.

[4] On the demise of the powers cf. 15:24; Col 2:14 f.; Phil 2:10, etc. But also N. B. Bar 3:16−23, of *earthly* rulers who perish without finding wisdom (cf. Wilckens, "1 Kor 2,6−16", 508, following Feuillet); cf. Job 4:21LXX. See further below on 2:8.

[5] The integrity and continuity of the passage is safeguarded by the sustained antithesis of human vs. divine wisdom (manifested in the crucified Christ): cf. 1:30; 2:1 f. with 7 f.; see also Wilckens, "1 Kor 2,1−16", 503 f., 506. It is therefore not necessary with Barrett (in Wilckens, "Kreuz", 86; cf. Wilckens's own earlier view in *Weisheit*, 60) and others to regard 2:6 ff. as a partial *retraction* of Paul's preceding argument. Further *contra* Widmann ("Einspruch", 46 and passim), who considers 1 Cor 2:6−16 an interpolated gloss by the Corinthian enthusiasts.

Some have postulated here a dominance of the language and ideas of Paul's opponents: e.g. Bornkamm, "μυστήριον", 825; Lührmann, *Offenbarungsverständnis*, 113; Ellis, "Gifts", 130; etc. It is true that Paul's talk of σοφία in 1:18 ff. appears to address a Corinthian preoccupation. But with Wilckens (recently) and earlier Conzelmann, "Weisheit", 239 f. I am on the whole not persuaded that 2:6−10 in particular is entirely dominated by alien elements polemically or otherwise derived from Paul's opponents, be they Gnostic (see below) or not; the passage could reflect an ethos very like 2 Cor 12:1−4.

[6] Barrett 69; Rigaux, "Révélation", 249−52.

[7] See 14:20; Rom 12:1 f.; Phil 3:15; Col 4:12; cf. Matt 5:48; 19:21. With Baumann,

At Qumran, too, knowledge and ethical/ritual "perfection" (תום) were expected of full initiates[8] and especially of leaders;[9] there as in 1 Cor 2:6 only the τέλειοι (תמימים) had access to the mysteries of deeper knowledge.[10] After one year initiates were evaluated and then graduated to a status of full ritual purity and provisional acceptance into the community (1QS 6:16f., 19f.); then after a second year and a further examination full membership was granted (6:20–23). But it would appear that only such full initiates, after an *additional* two-year period of testing for "perfection of way" (בתמים דרך) could be "set apart as holy within the [12-member] Council of the men of the Community" and gain *unrestricted* access to the exegetical secrets (1QS 8:1–12; cf. CD 15:10f.).

Philo similarly sustains high ethical requirements for his τέλειοι (Philo *LA* 3:100; *Sacr* 60; cf. *Cher* 42, 48, etc.), initiates into the lesser and greater mysteries; in his case the influence from the mystery religions is unmistakable.[11]

Certainly Paul does not affirm a *disciplina arcani* as in the DSS or the mystery religions. Therefore we also do not find here the language and ideas of a Corinthian Gnosticism: though once fashionable in New Testament scholarship, this view has recently been debunked in a surprising aboutface by Ulrich Wilckens, who in his own book *Weisheit und Torheit* (1959) had been one of its staunchest defenders.[12] At the same time the passage remains consistent with a commonplace of both pagan and Jewish religion in antiquity: secret divine wisdom is properly reserved for those who are qualified. With Conzelmann and Rigaux I am inclined to see this disposition in Paul as a pedagogical measure and as a matter of straightforward common sense (cf. 3:1ff.):

> Die Nicht-Pneumatiker *können* ja gar nicht verstehen. So erklärt Paulus, daß er den Korinthern die Weisheit noch nicht mitteilen konnte. Er vertritt aber keine Arkandisziplin, sondern erklärt sein Schweigen als bloße Pädagogik.[13]

Mitte, 194f.; Winter, *Pneumatiker,* 91. *Pace* Stählin, "Verständnis", 99 (merely cognitive); Reitzenstein, *Mysterienreligionen,* 338f. (initiation).

[8] 1QS 1:8; 2:2; 3:3, 9; 5:24; 8:20f.; 9:2, 8f., 19, etc.

[9] 1QS 8:1f., 9f.; 9:5f.; 1QSa 1:17; 1QSb 5:22, etc.

[10] 1QS 4:22; 8:10–12, 15–18. *Pace* Winter, *Pneumatiker,* 66, 91: probably not *all* members of the community had access to these revelations. (For internal differentiations at Qumran cf. also Baumann, *Mitte,* 181f.) Kuhn's idea (*Enderwartung,* esp. 160ff.) that at initiation the essence of the sectarian "revelation" was at once disclosed to all new members derives mainly from his reading of 1QH, esp. the belief that salvation is actualized at initiation (p. 31 and passim).

[11] Cf. further Winter, *Pneumatiker,* 96–157; also Harvey, "Mystery Language", 323f. on the metaphor of the gravity and discipline of initiation.

[12] Against the Gnostic view (in emphatic *methodological* criticism of his own earlier position) see esp. Wilckens, "1 Kor 2,1–16", 520, 524–37; also his programmatic statement in "Kreuz", 93.

[13] Conzelmann 77 (ital. his); Rigaux, "Révélation", 250f. Cf. also Prümm, "Phänomenologie", 152f.; Klöpper, "Offenbarung", 531. While Matt 11:25/Luke 10:21 also describes the revelation as hidden from the σοφοί (N.B.!), a different attitude is taken re-

The *difference* between Paul's view and that e.g. of Qumran or the mystery religions is that the apostle preaches the "word of the cross" to *all*, both to σωζόμενοι and to ἀπολλύμενοι (1:18).[14] All Corinthian Christians are κλητοὶ ἅγιοι (1:2); all have λόγος and γνῶσις (1:5); indeed all are meant to be recipients of the benefits of Christ, the wisdom of God (1:24, 30). This is one side of the coin, and according to the flow of Paul's argument the more important one. Paul's message, which he calls in general terms the "mystery of God",[15] is intended for everyone. But at the same time not all at Corinth are mature and ready for "solid food" (3:2), i.e. deeper instruction in the full hidden dimensions of that divine wisdom.[16]

1.3. V. 7—10: The Revelation of God's Hidden Wisdom

Verses 7—10 stand in logical apposition to 2:6, offering a further qualification of the nature of this wisdom which Paul affirms. Instead of human argument, the apostles speak

> God's wisdom in a μυστήριον : viz. a wisdom having been concealed, which God foreordained before the ages for our glory, which none of the rulers of this world knew (for if they had known it, they would not have crucified the Lord of glory), but as it is written: "what eye has not seen and ear has not heard, and what has not entered the heart of man — what God has prepared for those who love Him." Now to us God has revealed it through the Spirit.

1.3.1. V. 7: "God's Wisdom in a Mystery"

God's wisdom which the apostles speak is a wisdom ἐν μυστηρίῳ,[17] recalling the application of the term "mystery of God" to the Apostolic message in 2:1.

---

garding the νήπιοι. Cf. also Heb 5:1 ff. However, Feuillet, "L'Énigme", 74 surmises that Paul may in fact betray here a knowledge of dominical logia related to Matt 11:25—27.

[14] Cf. Winter, *Pneumatiker*, 89 f. This also confirms Baumann's observation (*Mitte*, 195) that for Paul the "mature" are not *on principle* different from the "immature": "keine besondere, von den übrigen Gläubigen streng bzw. metaphysisch geschiedene Klasse oder Kaste".

[15] Note the difference in substance between the general use of "mystery of God" in 2:1 (cf. Col 1, 2, 4; Eph 3), and the more specific reference to the deeper dimensions of that mystery in 2:6.

[16] Note the absence in 1:1—9 of a blanket thanksgiving for God-given σοφία amongst the church at Corinth; and cf. the *selective* revelation by the Spirit of λόγος σοφίας even in 12:8. Special instruction to a smaller group may also be present in 1 Thes 5:14—22, 26 f. (so Chrysostom, Homily 10 *ad loc.*; Theodore of Mopsuestia [ed. Swete 2:36 f.]; also Findlay 124; Masson 73; well-balanced Rigaux 581 f.); and cf. the Pastorals.

[17] Ἐν μυστηρίῳ with σοφία rather than with λαλοῦμεν (cf. Bornkamm, "μυσ-

More particularly, Paul's talk of "God's wisdom in a mystery" (as such hardly intelligible to the modern reader[18]) may perhaps be profitably interpreted as God's (gen. poss.) חכמה ברז, "wisdom in the/a mystery"), i.e. His wisdom displayed in His saving design. Similar language occurs at Qumran:[19] God has opened to the worshipper "knowledge in the mystery of Thy understanding" דעת ברז שכלכה (1QH 12:13); He has "admonished me by the mystery of Thy wisdom" ברז חכמתכה (1QH 9:23).[20] Our study of Jewish literature showed that the constellation of mysteries and divine wisdom belongs to the very heart of the notion of revealed secrets of heaven (whether pertaining to eschatology or to cosmology).[21]

Paul's idea of God's wisdom in a mystery (2:7), therefore, is quite akin to contemporary Jewish terms used to speak of God's eschatological design for the salvation of His people. This design has been "foreordained before the ages for our glory" (cf. esp. Rom 9:23), i.e. set apart in God's counsel to effect for the believer the glory, *olim revelandam*,[22] which will be his in the world to come. So with Hamerton-Kelly I am inclined to see God's σοφία in this passage as referring by synecdoche both to the overall plan of salvation and to the individual contents of that plan — what in v. 9 is called "the things that God has prepared for those who love Him."[23]

τήριον", 826 and others). On merely intratextual grounds the issue cannot be resolved, as Conzelmann 72f. n. 1 recognizes. However, additional weight is lent to this interpretation by the traditional link between wisdom and mystery; cf. Brown, *Mystery*, 41—44; and see below.

[18] And perhaps equivocal for Corinthian Gentiles too?

[19] I am not aware of this connection having been drawn elsewhere; though for a related understanding of the phrase cf. e.g. Wilckens, "1 Kor 2,6—16", 510f. (wisdom pertaining to God's saving design). The idiom is admittedly difficult, and renderings such as "wisdom by a mystery" [i.e. not humanly accessible but only in this revealed secret] (cf. Heinrici 67) or "mysterious" wisdom (Barrett 70; Prümm, "Mystères", 193) are not impossible, though necessarily paraphrastic. Dautzenberg's epexegetical "Weisheit, die Geheimnis ist" ("Botschaft", 142; cf. Eph 2:15 τὸν νόμον τῶν ἐντολῶν ἐν δόγμασιν) is also conceivable. At any rate we are dealing with the familiar factors of divine "mystery", hidden wisdom, and revelation.

[20] Similarly e.g. 1 QS 4:18; 1 QpHab 7:15; [מריא ידע אנה ברזי in 4 QEn^c 5 ii:26 (ed. Milik, p. 209); also Dan 2:29f.; ψ 50:8; EpBarn 6:10.

For σοφός with ἐν in *Greek* cf. 1 Clem 48:5 (ἐν διακρίσει λόγων); 60:1 (ἐν τῷ κτίζειν); also Euripides *Iph.Taur.* 1238 (ἐν κιθάρᾳ); Maximus Tyrius (125—185 A.D.) 24:6b (ἐν πολέμῳ), 6c (ἐν γεωργίᾳ).

[21] See further Job 28:12 ff. (esp. v. 20: חכמה נסתרה); Dan 2:19—23; Sir 43:31—33; Wisd 9:13—17; also 1 En 49:2f. (combining wisdom, spirit, and the secrets of righteousness); 51:3. See Ch. 10 on Col 2:3; and note Eph 1:8 f., ἐν πάσῃ σοφίᾳ καὶ φρονήσει γνωρίσας ἡμῖν τὸ μυστήριον τοῦ θελήματος αὐτοῦ.

[22] Bengel, *Gnomon*, 614.

[23] Hamerton-Kelly, *Pre-Existence*, 115 f. It is true that the relative clause of v. 7c refers not to the mystery itself but to God's *wisdom* in the mystery as having been "fore-

1.3.2. V. 8: Mystery and the Cross

After v. 7 Paul interposes a parenthesis intended to clarify further the contrast between this wisdom of God and the one demanded by the opponents. The former remained unrecognized even when expressed in human history, because it is the paradox "wisdom" of a crucified Messiah (2:1 f., 7).[24]

Verse 8 is sometimes thought to indicate a straightforward identification of the mystery with "the cross". Certainly 2:1 f., 8 suggest a close connection between "mystery" and crucified Christ; and the σοφία τοῦ θεοῦ carries a clearly christological focus in 1:24, 30. In this respect Lührmann is almost certainly wrong to deny that Paul's talk of mystery relates to the Christ event.[25] However, v. 9 suggests that what Paul has in view is *more* than strictly the *theologia crucis* (or even than "the event of the life, death, and resurrection of Christ").[26] At issue is, rather, the whole gamut of the believer's eschatological inheritance — i.e. as it were the wider *implications* of the work of God in Christ.[27] God's hidden wisdom pertains not only to the past history of Christ, but also and very significantly (as v. 9 shows) to his future purpose, viz. the things which are yet to be revealed. Sellin aptly describes v. 9 as the "*meta-language* of the word of the cross"; Allo, as a deeper understanding of these same truths.[28]

Such divine wisdom is unknown to the "rulers" of this world: for only ignorance of the mystery can explain their crucifixion of the "Lord of glory" (cf. Jas 2:1; and esp. 1 En 63:3 f.[29] and passim). One is reminded of other Pauline passages (e.g. 1 Cor 1:18; 2 Cor 4:3 f.; cf. Eph 4:17—19) and also of Wisd 2:22, where the wickedness and blindness of the ungodly is due to the fact that they did not know the μυστήρια of God.

---

ordained" (and "revealed", v. 10). That wisdom could be seen as an eschatological *Heilsgut* is clear from 4 Ezra 8:52; cf. 1 En 5:8; 32:3; 48:1; 91:10, etc.; cf. Kuhn, *Enderwartung*, 174, 150 f.; Wilckens, *Weisheit*, 70 f.; idem, "1 Kor 2,6—16", 510; also Baumann, *Mitte*, 216 f. n. 38. Beyond that, however, it seems fair to see here a reference also to the object of that foreordained wisdom, i.e. the *Heilsplan* (note the function of ἃ ἡτοίμασεν ὁ θεός [v. 9]).

[24] V. 8 is reminiscent of the motif of the hidden and revealed Messiah (cf. above). Von Soden, "ΜΥΣΤΗΡΙΟΝ", 192 further compares the "messianic secret" of the synoptic gospels.

[25] *Offenbarungsverständnis*, 113 ff., 131. Cf. the critique of Penna, *Mysterion*, 57 f.

[26] Thus Hanson, "Midrash", 28. In this respect the views of the "new Wilckens", too, are in danger of remaining a little myopic.

[27] Schlatter 108. Here too Barrett's timely reminder (*Adam*, 92) applies: "Paul is interested in nothing less than the whole story of mankind from beginning to end, for the whole story stands under the righteous and merciful design of God."

[28] Sellin, "Geheimnis", 81; Allo 40; cf. Deden, "Mystère", 415; Ladd, *Theology*, 385; also Schlatter 109. At issue is not merely the past history of the cross, but the mystery of God which for Paul sustains an important future dimension.

[29] Cf. Hamerton-Kelly, *Pre-Existence*, 114.

Whether these ἄρχοντες are political powers or the angelic beings in charge
of human affairs (or both) is a question which exceeds the scope of this study;
scholarly debate of this issue has been long and protracted.[30] On balance, there
is probably better and more tangible evidence in favour of *human* ἄρχοντες —
even if this were to be closely linked in Paul's mind with the spiritual forces of
the old world order: "The god of this world blinded the minds of the unbeliev-
ing, that they might not see the light of the glorious gospel of Christ" (2 Cor
4:4).[31]

1.3.3. Content: The Inheritance of the Saints (V. 9)

The traditional quotation in 2:9[32] serves Paul well in illustrating just this
point about the hiddenness of the divine wisdom: the mystery of God's salvific

---

[30] For a history of research see Pesce, *Arconti*, 19—235. Several early commentators
including Theodore of Mopsuestia (Staab, *Pauluskommentare*, 174) already held the "demonological" view; Hanson, "Midrash", 24 supposes IgnEph 19:1 to be the earliest example. Various NT texts affirm the hiddenness of the Mystery (though N.B. not of
Christ himself) from angelic powers: 1 Pet 1:12 [cf. 1 Cor 11:10?]; Eph 3:10; Mark 13:32;
cf. 2 En 24:3. Demonic guilt or implication in the crucifixion of Jesus is affirmed e.g. in
John 8:44; 13:2; 14:30; AscIsa 11:19 — but Wilckens, "1 Kor 2,6—16", 508 f. points out
that even in Gnostic texts the demons are never actually (as here) said to *crucify* Christ
(note also Carr, "Rulers", 23: the NT only uses the singular ὁ ἄρχων [= Satan] in the demonic sense). Though angelic ignorance also recurs in the myth of the heavenly redeemer descending in disguise (AscIsa 10:8 ff.; EpApost 13; and Gnostic texts), vital ingredients of this notion are missing here: See Hanson, "Midrash", 30—38.
    The interpretation of the mystery's inaccessibility to *earthly* rulers (sc. of Jerusalem,
v. 8 being more specific than v. 6) would seem *prima facie* to have little immediate bearing
on the situation in Corinth which Paul is trying to address (viz. the flaunting of human
wisdom). However, Carr and others (following Schniewind) have argued that since the
contrast in 1:20—2:16 is between divine and human wisdom rather than between God
and the angels, the ignorance must be that of human rulers (as e.g. in Acts 3:17; 13:27):
Carr, *Angels*, 119; Sellin, "Geheimnis", 84; Wilckens, "1 Kor 2,1—16", 508 f. (*contra* his
Weisheit, 70 f.). The specific reference to the crucifixion is clearly significant (cf. Riesner,
"Christus-Offenbarung", 418): Paul may indeed be betraying a quite particular familiarity with the synoptic passion narrative, which similarly exhibits the "wise" and the
powerful as protagonists of the opposition to Christ: esp. Mark [3:22; 7:1 ff.; 9:14 (N.B.
γραμματεῖς συζητοῦντας πρὸς αὐτούς, cf. 1 Cor 1:20); 10:33; 11:18, 27; 12:28, 35, 38]
14:1, 43, 53; 15:1, 31; and parallels. See also 1:22 with Mark 8:11 f. par. The underlying
theme is clearly the failure of the religious and political authorities to *recognize* who Jesus
is (cf. Mark 4:11 f. par.; and e.g. Acts 13:27). That 2:8 indicates a familiarity with the trial
of Jesus has also been affirmed e.g. by Stuhlmacher, "Jesustradition", 245 (with reference to Luke 23:13, 35; 24:20); cf. Wilckens, "1 Kor 2,6—16", 508 f.

[31] Caird, Review, 544: "Neither theory can stand unless it is so framed as to be closely
assimilated to the other. If we take the rulers to be human, we must grant . . . that they
are treated as representative types of the old world order." See also Allo 41; Cullmann,
Christ and Time, 195 f.

[32] This is apparently a haggadic weaving together of Isa 64:3 with other motifs (Isa

design (ἃ ἡτοίμασεν ... τοῖς ἀγαπῶσιν αὐτόν) completely escapes human thought and perception. But according to His plan God has prepared it for all who "love" Him, i.e. who long for His redemption (cf. also Rom 8:28−30).[33]

The content of the hidden wisdom, then, is a deeper knowledge of the inheritance which is in store for those who love God.

1.3.4. V. 10: Revelation to the Apostles by the Spirit

Having described the nature and content of this hidden divine wisdom, Paul now goes on to describe its source:[34] the revelation is given ἡμῖν (v. 10), i.e. probably to the apostles and prophets (cf. 2:1−5 and below on 4:1; 13:2).[35]

65:16; Psa 31:20; Sir 1:10; etc.); no simple derivation is feasible. Cf. *LAB* 26:13 (first noted by Philonenko, "Oculus", 51 f.) and early Christian texts: esp. *Coptic* TJac 8:8 (cf. the debate about Christian recension of this text in von Nordheim, "Zitat"; Hofius, "Zitat"; Sparks, "Quotation"); AscIsa 11:34 [L2, Slav.]; 1 Clem 34:8 (as Scripture: the text differs sufficiently from 1 Cor 2:9 to be an independent citation); 2 Clem 11:7; MartPol 2:3; GThom 17; etc. Rabbinic "parallels" (see Str-B 3:328 f.; also *Seder Gan 'Eden BHM* 2:53.19 f.; Version B *BHM* 3:133.21; 139.16 f.) tend to follow the MT of Isa 64:3 rather more closely; but ExR 45:6 and SifNum 27:12 do combine with Psa 31:20. Cf. further the Gnostic Apocalypse of Paul, I A 25−29 (*NHL*, p. 28): "Grant what no angel-eye has [seen] and no archon-ear ⟨has⟩ heard and what [has not] entered into the human heart . . .

Origen (Comm. on Matt 27:9, Migne 5:29) found the quotation in ApEl. But Jerome (Comm. on Isa 64:3, Migne 4:622; cf. Letter 57 to Pammachius, Migne 1:576), while acknowledging the presence of the quotation both in that source and in AscIsa, emphatically denies that Paul derived it from there: it comes, rather, from Isa 64:3, developed paraphrastically, "eumdem sensum aliis sermonibus indicavit" (Migne 1:576). His considered opposition to Origen's view on the grounds that Paul would not cite an apocryphon as Scripture is shared among modern commentators e.g. by Allo 44.

Recent discussion most fully in Berger, "Herkunft", 270−283; Hanson, "Midrash", 43−69; cf. also Ponsot, "D'Isaïe", 229−242; and earlier Prigent, "L'oeil", 416−29. Berger (280 f.) argues for an origin of 2:9 in an established, eclectically used apocalyptic tradition; cf. similarly Fee 109. Its *Sitz im Leben* may have been liturgical: cf. Hanson, "Midrash", 62; following Prigent and Feuillet.

[33] N.B. the verb חכה piel ("to wait, yearn, be anxious for") is in Isa 64:3 applied to waiting for redemption: cf. e.g. Hab 2:3; Zeph 3:8; Dan 12:12; b.Sanh 97b. In this respect 2 Tim 4:8 τοῖς ἠγαπηκόσι τὴν ἐπιφανείαν αὐτοῦ is another interesting parallel to 1 Cor 2:9c; similarly Jas 1:12. But cf. also Exod 20:6 LXX (ποιῶν ἔλεον τοῖς ἀγαπῶσίν με) with Isa 64:3 LXX.

[34] Thus rightly Davis, *Wisdom*, 87.

[35] Debate on this issue shows few signs of abating: on one hand the apostolic "we" could plausibly and consistently be maintained throughout 2:6−16. This would follow on from 2:1−5, remain true to a past tense of ἀπεκάλυψεν (2:10), and provide continuity with 4:1. On the other hand 1:18, 23 show inclusive and exclusive "we" in close proximity; further examples of the former might conceivably be 2:7c, 12, 16. Moreover e.g. Robertson/Plummer 43; Senft 51 suggest that ἡμῖν in 2:10 takes up τοῖς ἀγαπῶσιν. Perhaps on balance we may allow for Paul's tacit inclusion of those τέλειοι at Corinth who

The DSS, too, speak of a special revelation of "wisdom hidden from man": הביטה עיני תושיה אשר נסתרה מאנוש (1QS 11:6).[36] More specifically, we are told that this revelation has occurred through the Spirit (v. 10–12)[37] — for the Spirit has leave to inquire even into the mysteries of God.[38]

Paul describes himself as having God's "wisdom" (v. 6f.) and Spirit-given "knowledge" (v. 12f.) of the saving gift of God. He "speaks" (v. 6f., 13) and "preaches" (v. 1) this God-given, Spirit-revealed mystery "not in words taught by human wisdom, but in those taught by the Spirit" (v. 13). As a recipient of the revelation of divine mysteries, Paul communicates this wisdom to the "mature". The same kerygmatic orientation[39] of the revelation of mysteries occurs in other NT texts (cf. below; also Eph 3:2–9).

1.4. Summary

In sum, then, we are dealing in 1 Cor 2:6–10 with Paul's affirmation, over against all human claims, of God's wisdom in His salvific purposes. This hidden divine wisdom is expressed chiefly (but, as we saw, not exclusively) in the cross; and Paul's message about Christ crucified is called the mystery of God. Instruction in its deeper dimensions seems here (*pace* many commentators) reserved for mature believers, who are ready for "solid food" — though Paul evidently wants all the Corinthians to attain to that level (3:1 ff.).

Moreover God's wisdom and His corresponding plan of salvation are concealed from the "wise" and the "rulers" of this world. Indeed this hiddenness continues in the present era: contrary to the opinion of some critics, the "wisdom in a mystery" is not simply "a divine secret, hitherto concealed, but now revealed."[40] The eschatological realization of God's mystery of salvation

---

are also λαλοῦντες (and καταγγέλλοντες), i.e. apostles and prophets? Thus Heinrici 71 ("die berufenen Verkünder des Evangeliums"); Schlatter 107; Baumann, *Mitte*, 205f.; Lindblom, *Gesichte*, 155; Fee 101 n. 13 (with modification).

[36] That 1 QS 11:5–9 is parallel to 1 Cor 2:9 is also suggested by Feuillet, "L'Énigme", 57f., following S. E. Johnson.

[37] Cf. e.g. Sir 48:24f.; Dan 4:6(9); see above (Part I) on the mediating role of the Spirit in revelation. Penna, *Mysterion*, 44 speaks of the Spirit's "funzione gnoseologica" in regard to the revelation of mysteries; he compares Eph 3:5b ἐν πνεύματι and 1 QS 8:16 וכאשר גלו הנביאים ברוח קודשו.

[38] τὰ βάθη τοῦ θεοῦ is cognate with divine mysteries: Dan 2:22; 1 QM 10:11; Job 12:22 (cf. 11:7 f.); also 1 Clem 40:1; 2 Bar 14:8; and contrast Rev 2:24 with its *v.l.* in MS 2329. Cf. Dautzenberg, "Botschaft", 143 n. 30; 153; idem, *Prophecy*, 212f.; van Roon, "Wisdom", 216 n. 46.

[39] Noted also by Lührmann, *Offenbarungsverständnis*, 125 f.; Penna, *Mysterion*, 34.

[40] Thus Knox, *Gentiles*, 115.

through Christ's work at the cross is still to occur (v. 9).[41] Nevertheless, this wisdom has been disclosed by the Spirit to the spokesmen of the gospel, who proclaim it among the mature.

2. The Rest of the Corinthian Correspondence

We may now move rather more quickly through a number of related texts in the Corinthian correspondence and in Romans.

2.1. 1 Cor 4:1 "Stewards of God's Mysteries"

Paul sees the apostolic ministry (his own as much as that of Cephas or Apollos, 3:22) summarized in the function of "servants of Christ and stewards of the mysteries of God." While the word οἰκονόμος[42] may be unusual for this context, its function is clear and fully consistent with that of the recipient of secret revelation in the texts we discussed earlier (including of course 2:7, 13): Paul is the responsible mediator and dispenser of the divine mysteries[43] to those who are worthy to receive them. Moreover, this metaphor fits perfectly with the function of Paul's ministry as a source of revelation (see Chapter Eight above).[44] A comparison with the אנשי משמרת לרזיכה of 1 Q36 16:2 is not out of place.[45]

---

[41] Cf. also Rom 8:18−25. *Pace* Davis, *Wisdom*, 95 f.; Schmithals, *Gnosis*, 131; et al., who deny that the reference is to future blessings. Note the absence of a νῦν from v. 10: unlike e.g. Col 1:26 f., 1 Cor 2:6−10 does *not* compare a past era of hiddenness with a present era of disclosure. At least in this respect Paul here remains well within the scope of Jewish apocalyptic thought. Cf. Luz, *Geschichtsverständnis*, 259.

[42] Reumann, "Stewards", 349: use of a secular term from Greco-Roman life (of a slave who arranges his master's resources) with existing religious connotations. Rabbinic literature uses the loan word איקונומוס of a steward or town clerk (y.BM 9 [12a.25]; corrupt e.g. y.BB 4 [14c.57]). Reumann (*"Oikonomia-Terms"*, 160) considers this to be a "straightforward metaphor"; although the term was appropriated in popular Hellenistic religion (and a vague association in the minds of Paul's Gentile readers cannot be excluded), no precise Greek parallel seems to exist. See also Brown, *Mystery*, 44.

[43] The use of the plural is probably of little consequence; on the other hand it may point back to the plural *Heilsgüter* described in 2:9 (thus Penna, *Mysterion*, 15 n. 7, following Kümmel). Prümm, "Phänomenologie", 139 considers that Paul's henceforth exclusively singular use of μυστήριον may reflect a primary interest in the *unity* of the concept. That eschatological mysteries are in view is clearly affirmed (with ref. to 4:5) by von Soden, "ΜΥΣΤΗΡΙΟΝ", 192.

[44] Dautzenberg, "Botschaft", 157 sees here Paul's assertion of his office as that of a *prophet*, receiving and dispensing the divine secrets.

[45] Cf. Coppens, "Mystère", 148; Brown, *Mystery*, 45; further EpDiogn 7:1. Weiss 94 also compares Matt 13:52; Luke 12:42 ff.

As a commonplace, the metaphor of stewardship would of course remain intelligible to a Gentile audience, albeit perhaps with pagan overtones.[46]

2.2. 1 Cor 13:2 Love and the Limits of Prophecy

In this context Paul points out the futility of even the greatest spiritual gifts and privileges in the absence of Christian love: "If I have prophecy, and know all mysteries[47] and knowledge... but do not have love, I am nothing." He is not critical of these gifts in themselves, but merely exposes their emptiness without love. That a truly Christian way of life is required for the proper reception of revelation comes as no surprise after what was learned about the τέλειοι in 2:6. If the knowledge of mysteries is here linked with prophecy, it is once again clear that Paul esteems it very highly (cf. 14:1 ff.), and that it must carry strong eschatological overtones.[48] However, even the privileged knowledge of "all the mysteries" of the world to come remains dim in relation to their future realization: now we see in a mirror dimly, but then face to face (v. 12).[49]

---

[46] See Harvey, "Mystery Language", 331; cf. also Fee 160.

[47] For the phrase "all the mysteries" cf. e.g. 1 QpHab 7:5; [1 QM 14:9]; 1 QH 12:20; 1 En 41:1; and esp. 4 QEnGiants[a] 9:3 (ed. Milik, p. 316): כול רזיא יד[ע אנתה. This last reference together with 1 QH 12:20 suggests that Paul may be speaking hyperbolically of ideal rather than real prophecy: for the knowledge of *all* mysteries belongs only to God (see also Schlatter 354 f.; Brown, *Mystery*, 46; and cf. Chapter 7 above).

[48] A fact which points against Penna's otherwise not impossible suggestion (*Mysterion*, 16) of a secular, non-technical meaning of "mystery"; similarly Caragounis, *Mysterion*, 27 ("all that is a riddle to man..."). Robinson (*Ephesians*, 237) rightly muses that the "connexion with prophecy is noteworthy"; similarly Weiss 314; Grudem, *Prophecy*, 177 f.; Aune, *Prophecy*, 333; and cf. Dautzenberg, "Botschaft", 138 and Fee 632 f. (link with the mysteries of Jewish Apocalyptic). This same connection also intimates that Harvey's assumed "overtones from ... the mystery cults" ("Mystery Language", 332) are probably minimal or non-existent in the author's (though perhaps not the readers') mind.

[49] Cf. e.g. 2 Bar 55:8 (present revelation surpassed "when the event reveals marvels"). Seaford's conclusion ("1 Corinthians xiii.12", 120) that the mirror imagery betrays its derivation from an analogous use in the mystery religions ("confusing and stimulating the initiand as a prelude to the final revelation") is hardly convincing: cf. also Barrett 307. The metaphor would have been commonplace in an age of imperfect reflectors (cf. Knox, *Gentiles*, 121 n. 4); but if a source of Paul's thought must be suggested, an *'al tiqrē'* midrash on Num 12:8 (מַרְאָה = מֵרְאָה) seems at least possible (cf. אספקלריה in b. Yeb 49b, discussed earlier; LevR 1:14; etc.); *pace* Conzelmann 268.

2.3. 1 Cor 14:2: Heavenly Worship and Church Edification

Desirable though it is,[50] a full understanding of this verse obviously eludes the present study: one would require a detailed inquiry into the nature and function of glossolalia in Pauline Christianity, and of 1 Cor 14 in particular. However, short of such a study it is possible to observe one or two relevant pointers for our theme.

Paul's argument has progressed one step since Chapter 13. Having ensured the prior necessity of Christian love, he now goes on to encourage the Corinthians to seek also τὰ πνευματικά. Apparently the Corinthians had failed to distinguish between prophecy and tongues.[51] The aim of v. 2 ff., therefore, is to indicate the superiority of the former over the latter for purposes of communal worship and edification. Paul's reasoning is that the one who "speaks in a tongue" speaks not to men but to God: and no one understands (ἀκούει), since he speaks μυστήρια in his spirit.[52]

Yet in this case these μυστήρια are in no way identified as God's saving designs; they seem rather to designate in a general sense the envisioned "furniture" of the heavenly world.[53] Another obvious difference from the soteriological "wisdom in a mystery" of 2:6–10 is the unintelligibility of these mysteries without proper "interpretation" (better: articulation[54]).

Paul's hesitance about tongues in corporate worship is linked to his view that glossolalia, unlike prophecy, presents in a sense an "unfinished" revelation. Prophecy falls into the category of ἀποκάλυψις (14:6, 26, 30)[55] — but tongues without articulation remain indistinct (14:7–9), providing only *unrevealed* mysteries.[56] In other words, where a partaker of heavenly secrets does not also receive and express their meaning and content, such revelation remains abortive. Both prophecy and tongues are eschatological "signs" (14:21 f.) and manifestations of the Spirit (12:7 ff.; 14:1 ff.); more particularly, both pertain to μυστήρια (13:2; 14:2) and appear to transpire in the company of angels (11:10; 13:1[57]). But the charismatic's ecstatic (πνεύματι) participation in angelic prai-

---

[50] *Pace* Brown, *Mysterion*, 47, who considers this passage to be "very difficult" but also "not very important".

[51] Callan, "Prophecy", 136 f., following Bornkamm. Cf. n. 64 below.

[52] Various commentators take πνεύματι as referring to the Holy Spirit; but see 14:14–16 as well as e.g. Rev. 21:10. Cf. also Allo 355.

[53] Cf. Senft 174. Contrast 2:7 and quite likely 4:1, 13:2.

[54] Thiselton, "Interpretation", 23 f. and passim.

[55] Kosmala, *Hebräer*, 264 compares Qumran's משכילים.

[56] Cf. Robertson/Plummer 306; Weiss 322.

[57] The identification of 13:1 "tongues of angels" with glossolalia in Ch. 14 is widely accepted.

ses,[58] as such by all means desirable (14:18), must earn its place in the worship of the church by being "interpreted", i.e. articulated τῷ νοΐ (cf. 14:13–15, 19).

Quite possibly this is all we can learn about the "mysteries" of 1 Cor 14:2.[59] On the other hand, one or two interesting observations arise from an examination of ancient Jewish mysticism. Part and parcel of the ascent through the heavens was the visionary's observation of and sometimes *participation in* the angelic hymns before the throne of God,[60] the praises of the heavenly beings being viewed as the model and example for earthly worship.[61] In a seminal article on early merkabah mysticism, A. Altmann showed that the visionary who ascends to the palaces beholds there the bands of angels serving before the throne of glory and imitates them, speaking in the diction (לשון[62]) appropriate to the level of ascent.[63] Even the studies of the great first-century mystic Yoḥanan b. Zakkai were said to have included *inter alia* the conversation (שיחה) of the ministering angels (b.BB 134a; b.Sukk 28a).

Certainty on this matter is probably not to be had. But if Paul in 1 Cor 14:2 refers to the charismatic worshipper conversant in "tongues of angels" (13:1) as

---

[58] That it is in fact an act of *worship* in which the charismatic engages is suggested not only by 13:1; 14:2, but by the fact that the phenomenon in view includes ecstatic praying, singing, blessing, and thanksgiving (14:15–17).

[59] Indeed the matter could be insoluble if, as Allo 356 suggests, we are dealing with a whole cluster of related phenomena (γένη γλωσσῶν = "les divers genres de glossolalie").

[60] Esp. ApAbr 17:4–6; AscIsa 9:31–33; ApZeph 8:4; TJob 48:3; 49:2; 50:1 f.; Hist-Rech 16:8a–b; but note also *Poimandres* 24–26. Gruenwald (*Apocalyptic*, 45) considers 1 En 71:11 to be one of the earliest references. Related notions may also be reflected in Luke 2:13f. (cf. v. 20); Col 2:18; Heb 12:22f. Note further Qumran's "Angelic Liturgy" (4 QŠirŠabb) and the belief in a liturgical fellowship with the angels (e.g. 1 QH 3:21–23; 11:14; 1 QSb 4:22–26; cf. Kuhn, *Enderwartung*, 72 and passim; Schäfer, *Rivalität*, 36–40; Weinfeld, "Praise", 429–432). In the NT see esp. Rev passim; but cf. already Isa 6:3; Ezek 3:12; Gen 28:12(?); Psa 29:1; 148:2; etc.

[61] See Grözinger, "Singen", 77; but N.B. idem, *Musik*, 76, 86 ff.; Schäfer, *Rivalität*, 230–232: non-mystical rabbinic literature stresses that God prefers the hymns of Israel over those of the angels. Grözinger notes ("Singen", 66 n. 1) that in this context of heavenly worship singing and ecstatic speech are probably not to be distinguished; cf. also 1 Cor 14:15.

[62] לשון frequently means "expression, phraseology, parlance" (Jastrow 720), as does γλῶσσα (BAG 162). Hence angelic "tongues" are probably best understood not as "languages" but as types of speech. Moreover Thiselton, "Interpretation", 27–30 argues on exegetical grounds that the glossolalia of 1 Cor 12–14 cannot refer to identifiable "languages" (contrast Acts 2).

[63] Altmann, "שירי־הקודש", 2. Cf. further the ascending order of praises, voices, and words in AscIsa 7:15, 20, 27, 30, 36; 8:3, 16–20; also Rev 14:3 (no one could learn the song except the 144,000). Grözinger, *Musik*, 311f.; idem, "Singen", 75 discusses the motif of a transformation of the tongue to enable participation in the heavenly exultation. He also cites an intriguing text from *Merkabah Shelema* 4a to the effect that this celestial hymning of God's name reveals mysteries of wisdom: Grözinger, "Singen", 73 n. 26.

one who "speaks mysteries" to God in his spirit, it seems a reasonable working hypothesis to locate such notions — at least in Paul's mind[64] — in the realm of Jewish apocalyptic and early mysticism (cf. on 2 Cor 12:1 ff. below).[65] The apostle is asking those who gaze upon the heavenly mysteries to respect the edification of the church and to limit their use of this gift in corporate worship to those instances when the meaning can be intelligibly communicated (and thus fully revealed) to all the congregation.

It may be a bit of poetic hyperbole to conclude that (despite certain concessions) Paul essentially "pours a douche of ice-cold water over the whole practice" of glossolalia.[66] Nevertheless his reluctance, as indeed in the probably related cases of 2 Cor 12:4; Col 2:18, is beyond doubt. What is more, it would seem to be quite consistent with the concern e.g. of the Rabbis to restrict the study of esoterica to private contemplation or individual instruction (m. Ḥag 2:1; see Chapter Seven above).

2.4. 1 Cor 15:51 f. / Rom 11:25 f.: New Doctrine as μυστήριον

Only on these two occasions does Paul explicitly disclose to his readers an element of new teaching which he calls a μυστήριον. Though differing in content, 1 Cor 15:51—55 and Rom 11:25—27 exhibit a number of interesting formal similarities, as the synoptic arrangement on Table 1 shows. (Since 1 Thes 4:13—18 shares some of these features,[67] it is included as a third column.)

In both cases, Paul's disclosure of the mystery immediately follows on the summary statement (1) of a lengthy preceding argument about the resurrection and about Israel's salvation, respectively. The mystery is then specifically announced (2.1[68]) and its content briefly stated (2.2). And finally, Paul proceeds

---

[64] Gentiles might well have thought instead of the Pythia's incoherent utterances and of "prophetic" ἐκστάσις; cf. 14:23 ὅτι μαίνεσθε. See further Dautzenberg, "Glossolalie", 229— 232, 235 f.

[65] *Pace* many commentators. Penna, *Mysterion*, 16 and n. 9, sees μυστήριον here in a negative sense as a slur on the *cognitive* inaccessibility of the charismatic's utterance; similarly Caragounis, *Mysterion*, 27; Bruce 130 ("riddles with no solution"); Hill, *Prophecy*, 130.

[66] H. Chadwick, "All Things", 268; quoted approvingly by Thiselton, "Interpretation", 30.

[67] Cf. Zeller, *Juden*, 246 f.; Siegert, *Argumentation*, 171.

[68] Cf. e.g. 1 En 103:2; 104:10, 12; also Rom 1:13; 1 Cor 10:1; 12:1; 2 Cor 1:8; 1 Thes 4:13; and further Nag Hammadi *Asclepius* VI 8.70.10 ff. [*NHL*, 303], 78.22 ff. [*NHL*, 306]; *Poimandres* 1:16. See also Siegert, *Argumentation*, 172.

Table 1: Synopsis

A. 1 Cor 15:50–55	*B. Rom 11:25–27*	*C. [1 Thess 4:13–17]*
1. Now I say this, brethren, that flesh and blood cannot inherit the kingdom of God; nor does the perishable inherit the imperishable.	1. For if you were cut off from what is by nature a wild olive tree, and were grafted contrary to nature into a cultivated olive tree, how much more shall these who are the natural branches be grafted into their own olive tree?	1.0. [follows 2.1.2] For if we believe that Jesus died and rose again, even so God will bring with Him those who have fallen asleep in Jesus.
2.1. Behold, I tell you	2.1. For I do not want you, brethren, to be uniformed of	2.1. But we do not want you to be uniformed, brethren, about those who are asleep,
2.1.1. a mystery:	2.1.1. this mystery,	2.1.1. [follows 2.1.1.] For this we say to you by the word of the Lord,
	2.1.2. –lest you be wise in your own estimation––,	2.1.2. –that you may not grieve, as do the rest who have no hope––,
2.2. We shall not all sleep, but we shall all be changed, in a moment, in the twinkling of an eye,	2.2. that a partial hardening has happened to Israel	2.2. that we who are alive and remain until the coming of the Lord shall not precede those who have fallen asleep.
3.1 at the last trumpet; for the trumpet will sound, and the dead will be raised imperishable, and we shall be changed.	3.1. until the fulness of Gentiles has come in; and thus all Israel will be saved;	3.1. For the Lord Himself will descend from heaven with a shout, with the voice of the archangel, and with the trumptet of God; and the dead in Christ shall rise first. Then we who are alive and remain shall be caught up together with them in the clouds to meet the Lord in the air.
3.2 For this perishable must put on the imperishable, an this mortal mut put on immortality. . . .		
4.1. Then will come about the saying that is written,	4.1. Just as it is written,	4.0.1. And thus we shall always be with the Lord.
4.2 "Death is swallowed up in victory;" –– "O death, where is your victory? O death, where is your sting?"	4.2. "The Deliverer will come from Zion; He will remove ungodliness from Jacob. And this is my covenant with them" "when I take away their sins."	4.0.2. [cf. 2.1.1] Therefore comfort one another with these words.

to situate this disclosure within the context of familiar eschatological tradition[69] (3.1, 2[70]) and of Scripture (4.1–2, composite quotations).[71]

2.4.1. *1 Cor 15:51* comes near the end of Paul's extended argument (15:1 ff., esp. 12 ff.) against the apparent Corinthian disregard for his view of the resurrection (15:12). The importance of the subject (essentially the future dimension of the gospel, 15:32) makes his tone quite forceful throughout (cf. 15:1–3a, 12–19, 29–32, etc.).

V. 51 is no exception in this regard: it offers the "emphatic introduction of information of great moment."[72] This is not the place to discuss the *content* of the mystery (i.e. the sudden transformation of believers alive at the parousia), which may owe something to Paul's Pharisaic background.[73] The point of interest for the present context is that the Apostle here discloses publicly a teaching of the kind which in 2:6 ff. seemed reserved for the τέλειοι.

Why should Paul have taken this unexpected measure? Several considerations come to mind. The communication of an "authentic" mystery known to the Apostle would surely have been thought to boost his argument, and would leave an appropriate impression on his audience.[74] The Apostle really needs to score a victory on this point: he is convinced that the resurrection, judgement, and world to come are *articulus stantis et cadentis ecclesiae* (cf. m.Sanh 10:1, etc.).[75] It is therefore worth employing all the argumentative artillery at his disposal to keep the fledgling Corinthian church safe from competing views in this matter.

We may suppose then that the seriousness of the matter, perhaps together with the earnest efforts which the Corinthians had obviously expended on this

---

[69] In addition to commonplace apocalyptic expectations, dominical sayings tradition has been suspected in all three cases. Regarding 1 Cor 15:52 see esp. Matt 24:31; also 1 Thes 4:15–17; Did 16:6–8; 10:5; and cf. e.g. Wenham, *Rediscovery*, 306 n. 1, 367; Hill, *Prophecy*, 130 f. For Rom 11:25 f. see Mark 13:10; Luke 21:24; also 1 Thes 2:16; and cf. Stuhlmacher, "Evangelium", 178; Wenham, *Rediscovery*, 200, 283 f.; Refoulé, *Israël*, 266 f. See also Stuhlmacher, "Jesustradition", 243 and n. 15 on 1 Thes 4:15–17.

[70] The latter (1 Cor 15:53 f.) being a didactic restatement of the former; cf. Conzelmann 348: "Erläuterung im Lehrstil".

[71] 1 Thes 4:13, while obviously comparable in a number of features, is in other respects quite different — a fact *not* noted by Zeller or Siegert. The short statement does not come at the end of a lengthy discourse, but seems to be occasioned by a Thessalonian query regarding the timing of the resurrection and the fate of the deceased. Appeal is here made not to a revealed "mystery", but to an equally authoritative "word of the Lord"; no supporting Scripture quotation is offered. Cf. Chapter 8, above, on the revelatory authority of dominical tradition (cf. 1 Cor 7:10).

[72] Thus Robertson/Plummer 376.

[73] Cf. 2 Bar 50:1–51:5; see Stemberger, *Leib*, 86–91; Harris, *Raised*, 214–219.

[74] The cumulative effect of the use of μυστήριον in 2:1, 7; 4:1; 13:2; 14:2; 15:51 may also be significant in this regard.

[75] Brown, *Mystery*, 48 f.: at stake is nothing less than the future reward, the inheritance of the saints in the life to come.

issue, will in Paul's mind have merited the uncommon step of a public statement of theological intricacy otherwise studied only *in camera*.

2.4.2. Most of these considerations apply to *Rom 11:25–27* as well. Paul introduces the "mystery" at the end of his extensive argument for the irrevocability of God's promises and against His rejection of Israel (9–11). Once again a detailed analysis of his views about the substance and meaning of Israel's πώρωσις ἀπὸ μέρους would unfortunately lead too far afield.[76] However, here too what Paul is meting out must belong to the category of the eschatological mysteries of God.[77]

In Jewish literature motifs of salvation and/or the Messiah coming to the Gentiles (and even of a temporary rejection of the Jews), while admittedly not abundant, stretch from the Old Testament to the Rabbinic period.[78] These together with statements like "all Israel will be saved" (m. Sanh 10:1) would have been familiar territory to the Roman Christians. New was the idea that according to the plan of God Israel was first to be hardened and the Gentiles converted, before "all Israel"[79] could be saved.[80] The composite Scripture quotation linking the nation's "conversion" with the (N. B. future) coming of the Messiah may indicate that Paul understands the "mystery" to imply the salvation of Israel at the parousia.[81] Only this revealed piece of divine wisdom could provide the answer to a question of theodicy[82] which otherwise eluded human reason.

---

[76] For a full study see most recently Refoulé, *Israël* .

[77] *Pace* Sänger, "Rettung", 115, who argues that Paul discloses no "mystery" in the accustomed sense at all: everything he says is already known from the preceding argument. While this may to some extent be true for the separate elements (Israel's partial hardening, Israel's salvation), it is precisely the logic of the οὕτως which supplies what is new.

[78] For the idea of salvation (and/or the Messiah) coming to the [Jews and] Gentiles see Amos 9:11 f. LXX; Zech 12:3 LXX; Tob 14:5–7; TBenj 9:2; 11:2 (cf. Luke 2:32); TZeb 9:8 f. (incl. poss. the idea of a temporary rejection of the Jews in favour of Gentiles); 4 Ezra [1:35 f.; 2:40 f.;] 4:35 f.; TO Gen 49:10 (cf. Rashi); the words of Jesus in Mark 13:10 par. Matt 24:14 (cf. Kim, *Origin*, 91 and n. 1); Matt 21:43; Luke 21:24 (cf. Zech 12:3 LXX). In the OT cf. already Isa 11:10; 19:19–25; 42:1–4; 55:4, etc. See further Refoulé, *Israël*, 88–92.

[79] This term continues to be disputed. See Refoulé, *Israël*, 25–45, 135–189: intended is the righteous and elect remnant of Israel (and that only), which is still hardened: "C'est bien seulement le Reste qui sera sauvé, mais *tout le Reste*, celui qui est déjà dans l'Eglise, et celui encore présentement endurci" (181, ital. his).

[80] That the hardening forms part of God's design for Israel's salvation is clear from the emphatic use of καὶ οὕτως as well as from 11:31 f. See Bengel 588: "non dicit, *et tunc*, sed majore vi, *et sic*, quo ipso τὸ *tunc* includitur"; similarly Cranfield 2:575 f.; Hübner, *Gottes Ich*, 110 f.; Lübking, *Paulus*, 123; cf. Luz, *Geschichtsverständnis*, 293 f.

[81] Thus e.g. Cranfield 2:577 f., citing among others Chrysostom (ed. Migne, 585); cf. Hübner, *Gottes Ich*, 118.

[82] Note 9:1–6, 14 (ff.); 11:1 ff. Zeller (*Juden*, 249 f.) considers that the phrase ἄχρι οὖ

Here too Paul's disclosure is motivated by the conviction, not that all Christians may know all mysteries, but that this particular mystery will serve the Roman church's οἰκοδομή as it strives to come to terms with its relation to the Jews. He is concerned to avert among the Gentile believers a myopic and arrogant view of their incorporation into the people of God.[83]

2.4.3. *Nature of the Revelation.* It remains to ask, finally, how Paul obtained knowledge of these mysteries in Rom 11 and 1 Cor 15. This is of course a disputed issue, with scholarly views ranging widely from an experience of direct oracular revelation[84] through "speculative imagination"[85] to a straightforward exegesis of "the OT seen in the light of the gospel events":[86] a poll of critical opinion will do little to clarify the issue. Perhaps this is yet another instance where less is known than is confidently asserted. The fact is simply that here as in other doctrinal issues, Paul gives no palpable indication of basing the authority of doctrine on a private vision (cf. below on 2 Cor 12; Col 2:18).[87] Here in 1 Cor 15:51 f./Rom 11:25−27, as we have seen, he takes pains instead to introduce this hitherto unreleased piece of eschatological intelligence against a background of familiar terms and concepts. He exercises his stewardship of the divine mysteries by couching new disclosures in fully traditional language and Biblical reasoning. It seems likely, therefore, that we are dealing with "revelation by exegesis": a dynamic inter-reaction of Scripture, [exegetical] tradition, and religious experience (which may or may not *include* a vision). The catalyst (as in many Jewish examples) is a Biblical meditation sparked by a problem of

---

(11:25) matches the recurring question of apocalyptic, "How long?" (e.g. Dan 9:24 ff.; 2 Bar 81:3; Tob 14:4−7; Rev 6:10 f., etc.; cf. Isa 6:10 f.; Jer 12:4; Zech 1:12; Psa 13:1; Psa 89:46; 90:13; and often), and that this forms part of the traditional form critical constitution of revealed [sc. eschatological] mysteries, its concern being the "Befristung des Unheilszustandes" (p. 250).

[83] Note the specific reason for Paul's disbursement of this mystery: ἵνα μὴ ἦτε [παρ'] ἑαυτοῖς φρόνιμοι (11:25; cf. 11:18, 20; further 1 Thes 4:13b; Rom 3:27). Cranfield 2:574 and Schlatter 326 f. both recognize this qualifying clause as indicative of Paul's intention; cf. Glombitza, "Sorge", esp. 314, 318; Luz, *Geschichtsverständnis*, 278.

[84] E.g. Michel 354 f.; Bruce 221.

[85] Bultmann, *Theologie*, 484 ("spekulierende[n] Phantasie").

[86] Cranfield 2:574; cf. Pallis 131.

[87] Cf. Chapter 8, above, on this point; Phil 3:15 should not be seen as an exception. Luz, *Geschichtsverständnis*, 289 considers Paul's argument from Scripture a clear indication against a disclosure of the mystery in a "vision". Cf. further Bornkamm, "μυστήριον", 829; Conzelmann, *Theologie*, 270 on 1 Cor 2:6−16; Schlatter, *Theologie der Apostel*, 261 f.

Gal 1:6, 12; 1 Cor 9:1; 15:8; are not to be confused with the occasional revelations here in view: for Paul classes his call with the resurrection appearances, which are constitutive not only to his ministry but to the faith. Note also the absence of vision terminology where he does appeal to a λόγος κυρίου or the like for a point of doctrine: see esp. 1 Cor 14:37; also 7:10; 9:14; 11:23; 14:37; 15:3; 1 Thes 4:15.

current concern: and the answer thus obtained is described as a mystery, i.e. a gift of revelation.[88]

2.5. 2 Cor 12:1—4: Paul in the Third Heaven

In the two instances where Paul explicitly dispenses a "mystery" to his readers he fails to appeal to any visionary or ecstatic experience; but on one occasion,[89] at the instigation of his Corinthian detractors, he reluctantly reports an intensely mystical revelation of heavenly realities which he received a good many years earlier.[90]

Paul in 2 Cor 12:1—4 takes great care to show that he himself does not regard this experience as an apostolic or doctrinal credential (12:1, 6, etc.). Indeed his "boast" (12:1, 5—7) is described in well-nigh embarrassed impersonal terms,[91] and "tempered and framed" by two illustrations of weakness: viz. his humiliating, comical departure from Damascus (11:32 f.) and his unhealed "thorn in the flesh".[92] (At the same time, however, he supplies his critics with an impressive claim that his apparent weaknesses are in fact the channels of hidden divine power: 12:7—10.)

Paul's public attitude to his visionary experience, and his view of its significance for his apostolic status, once again exhibits the same kind of restraint about esoterica which we found e.g. in the Rabbis.[93] Indeed earlier on he has already reminded his readers of his principle in this regard: εἴτε γὰρ ἐξέστημεν, θεῷ· εἴτε σωφρονοῦμεν, ὑμῖν (2 Cor 5:13).[94]

But what can we learn about the nature of this vision? Since Scholem a number of scholars have favoured a *Sitz im Leben* of this vision in the practices re-

---

[88] See also Hall, "Paul", 207—211 on Rom 11:25 f./1 Cor 15:51 as a prophetic claim based on "charismatic exegesis"; he considers Rom 11:33—36 to be a thanksgiving for received revelation (p. 159: cf. 2 Chr 20:18—23; Matt 11:25 ff. etc.). Cf. esp. Hübner, *Gottes Ich*, 120 f., also 127 ff.; Schmidt, *Römer*, 198; Dunn, *Romans*, 2:678; Hofius, "Evangelium", 311—324; Aune, *Prophecy*, 342. But N.B. Aune, Hall's mentor, argues (339—345) *against* the idea that charismatic exegesis was the domain of Christian prophets, *contra* Ellis et al.

[89] Acts implies Paul to be less taciturn in this regard: 16:9 f.; 18:9 f.; 22:17—21; 23:11; 27:23 f.

[90] With Martin 399 f. it is best to admit that any attempt to reconstruct or identify the event of 14 years earlier must remain conjectural.

[91] Martin 396. Benz, *Paulus*, 108 f. aptly describes the syntax as faltering, stuttering, and inhibited.

[92] Martin 392 f.; cf. Furnish 544, following Käsemann et al.; Lincoln, *Paradise*, 84 f.

[93] Rowland, *Open Heaven*, 375; Furnish 543 f. Note also v. 1 οὐ σύμφερόν μεν: cf. 1 Cor 14:5, 12, etc. on οἰκοδομή.

[94] Lindblom, *Gesichte*, 41; Bultmann, "Probleme", 14 f.

flected in early *Hekhalot* literature;[95] however, this thesis has recently been called into question.[96] What does seem clear is that Paul experienced a vivid visionary ascent to paradise in the third heaven, where he heard "inexpressible things which cannot be told to man." The debate over whether Paul ascended to the highest of three or the third of seven heavens is interesting but ultimately contributes little to our understanding of his view of the revelation of mysteries.[97] And while many have speculated about the specific content of his vision, Paul does *not* actually tell his readers what he saw or heard. An introductory announcement of a μυστήριον is conspicuously *absent*: we only learn that he heard ineffable things (ἄρρητα[98] ῥήματα) which must not be disclosed to man.[99]

However, given the apostle's secretiveness and our knowledge of the traditional conception of the place he visited, it is not implausible to suppose that he glimpsed — perhaps *inter alia* — the eschatological inheritance of the saints. In that case he would have been privileged to perceive the "things that eye has not seen and ear has not heard" (1 Cor 2:9),[100] and of which he can only speak to the τέλειοι. Furthermore, Paul's claim to have *heard* ineffable heavenly sounds may possibly allude to the inexpressible heavenly worship of saints and angels;[101] this is a matter which was referred to earlier.

We are also not told about the purpose of this vision, or indeed about its particular function in Paul's ministry. It seems to be the prime example of regular mystical experiences in his private spiritual life (cf. ὑπερβολή v. 7; also 1 Cor

---

[95] Scholem, *Jewish Gnosticism*, 14−19; cf. e.g. Bowker, "Merkabah- Visions".

[96] Schäfer, "Journey", 32−34 and passim.

[97] On the evidence largely of TLevi 2:6 ff. (where an earlier threefold pattern of uranography may have been overlaid with a later sevenfold one), some have argued that Paul still knew only three heavens. Others have supposed that "it would seem illogical for Paul to write of such blessedness if he were not in the ultimate heaven" (Martin 402; cf. e.g. Plummer 343 f.; Tasker 171).

However, there are clearly other examples of visionaries ascending to less than the highest heaven: e.g. 3 Bar 11:1; cf. 14:1; 15:1; 3 SlavBar 11:3; 14:1; (*contra* Martin 402, who claims 3 Bar knows only five heavens); there is also no indication that e.g. for the seer of ApZeph (Clem. Alex. *Strom.* 5:11.77) the fifth heaven is the highest. There are also examples of paradise located in less than the highest heaven (e.g. 2 En 8:1; cf. 1 En 32:3 (Greek); ApMos 37:5, etc.). Nevertheless, Dupont's comment that there are *no* texts of either the tripartite or the sevenfold uranology which locate paradise in the highest heaven (*Gnosis*, 189 f. n. 1) cannot be sustained in the light e.g. of VitAd 25:3; cf. AscIsa 9:7; b.Ḥag 12b [Resh Laqish A2].

[98] Caragounis, *Mysterion*, 11: ἄρρητον (as distinct from ἀπόρρητον) means something "ineffable". Cf. Krämer, "Wortbedeutung", 125 on ἄρρητον and μυστήριον.

[99] For this reading of οὐκ ἔξον, κτλ. see e.g. Furnish 527, 545; Martin 405; Lincoln, "Paul", 216.

[100] So Dupont, *Gnosis*, 189 f.; Bultmann 224.

[101] E.g. 2 En 17; Rev. 14:3; and see above on 1 Cor 13:1; 14:2. Also Bietenhard, *Himmlische Welt*, 167.

14:18), though we know little more than that. Even here Paul is being kept from boastfulness by his much-debated σκόλοψ τῇ σαρκί, which caused him so much vexation as to require in turn a word of reassurance from the Lord (12:9). This additional revelation, however, betrays none of the characteristics of a "mystery".

This last pertinent passage in the Corinthian correspondence, therefore, indicates how in his private meditative life Paul has been granted mystical access to the eschatological inheritance which is stored up for believers in paradise. At the same time we have noted his hesitance to share such experiences openly with his church, and in particular to derive and publish teachings declared as "mysteries" on this basis. He speaks of his vision only in answering his opponents' charges, and not because he thinks it can benefit the church or be an authority for new teaching (although the overall effect of his description can be seen to strengthen his own position).

Chapter Ten

Colossians

1. Introduction

The authenticity of this letter has been questioned on the basis of differences of style and vocabulary as well as of theology (esp. a more explicitly developed Christology and reduced emphasis on eschatology).[1] Enormous efforts have been expended on this question, but the case seems far from closed. Obviously the arguments cannot here be rehearsed: I can only state my awareness of the basic considerations against authenticity, and perhaps to confess that I am not yet persuaded of their cogency.

In light of J. C. Beker's recently proposed heuristic model for Paul's thought (a coherent centre, but with contingent interpretations)[2] a number of items of external evidence must in my view be weighted rather more heavily than is generally acknowledged; for we know from other letters how much Paul's style and approach to various issues (e.g. the Law) can differ depending on the contingent situation.

The relevance of Beker's model for the question of authorship in Colossians has perhaps not been fully appreciated. This letter is directed to a church which Paul has never seen (2:1, cf. 1:4) and about whose current situation he seems to have learned only through its founding missionary Epaphras (1:7f.). The church's problems with an elitist brand of ascetic[3] and perhaps mystical religion by their very nature call for a treatment which unleashes Paul's most fully ma-

---

[1] In addition to various commentaries and New Testament Introductions see esp. Bujard, *Untersuchungen*; recently Kiley, *Colossians*; but also (in favour of Pauline authorship) Percy, *Probleme*, esp. 16–66.

[2] See e.g. Beker, *Paul*, 11 (N.B. he himself regards Col as pseudepigraphical, p. 3 n.) This emphasis is of course not new; see also e.g. Moule, "Influence", 1 and passim.

[3] N.B. commandments about food and drink, festivals, new moons, and Sabbaths (2:16) as well as "Do not handle, do not taste, do not touch" (2:20; cf. EpArist 142: God πάντοθεν ἡμᾶς περιέφραξεν ἁγνείαις καὶ διὰ βρωτῶν καὶ πότῶν καὶ ἁφῶν καὶ ἀκοῆς καὶ ὁράσεως νομικῶς) are of course all found in the Torah, though they appear here to be subject to a harsh, ascetic interpretation (2:23).

tured, "untamed" Christology, and in which eschatology perhaps necessarily plays a minor role.[4]

Other, more basic external criteria might be cited. The letter's claim to be co-authored by Paul and Timothy (1:1; N. B. cf. Phlm 1), is a fact which would make arguments based largely or exclusively on stylistic analysis seem rather precarious.[5] Then too the list of greetings in Colossians is an external criterion of significant importance, since it bears a close and yet complex relationship to that in the letter to Philemon — whose authenticity is universally accepted.[6]

The debate on these issues must obviously continue. Here I can do no more than to acknowledge the important critical difficulties, and in the absence of conclusive evidence to identify with the arguments of those who have spoken for the letter's origin within the ministry of Paul (in the Roman or Caesarean[7] imprisonment).

2. Col 1:26f.; 2,2f.

The most significant use of our motif occurs in the context of 1:24—2:5. The investigation takes us into the first main section of the body of the epistle (1:13—2:5): this is a rousing, panoramic summary of the universal dimensions of the work of Christ, which lays the groundwork for Paul's ensuing attack on the heterodox incursion at Colossae.

2.1. The Colossian Situation

As in the case of the Corinthian correspondence, the apostle is addressing a situation in which the cohesion and body life of a church is threatened by an (ultimately doctrinal) aberration. It is due to the pressures exerted by a particular, probably local, brand of Judaism or Jewish Christianity which promoted ascetic practices and esoteric worship in the Colossian church (2:16, 18, 21, 23b).

The meaning of θρησκεία τῶν ἀγγέλων (2:18) is hotly disputed. The view of "worship of angels" as a *subjective* genitive (with resulting mystical connotat-

---

[4] Cf. Lincoln, *Paradise*, 182. It is interesting that in combatting an error chiefly of soteriology and ecclesiology Paul's main recourse is to Christology (on this cf. e.g. Francis, "Argument", 206f.). Cf. below on the close link between "Christ" and "the Gospel".

[5] Ellis, "Dating", 499: "Any conclusions about the authorship of the letters on the basis of their language, style and theological idiom are questionable at best."

[6] Robinson, *Redating*, 61.

[7] See esp. the lucid arguments of Robinson, *Redating*, 65—67, correlating the names of Phil and Col with the account in Acts.

ions) was proposed by Francis and has recently been taken up by others.[8] It is true that interesting Palestinian texts (Qumran, apocalyptic, *Hekhalot* literature) can be adduced as a viable foil for Col 2. However, against this stand a number of other arguments, not the least of which is the question why Paul should find an interest in angelic worship reprehensible.[9] The natural reading of θρησκεία is with objective genitive;[10] ταπεινοφροσύνη is easily (though not necessarily) detached from this genitive construction.[11] Given the apparently thorough Hellenization of Jews in the Lycus Valley[12] and plenty of inscriptional and literary evidence for a popular (pagan, Jewish, and Christian) devotion to angels,[13] the objective reading further gains in probability. We might then be dealing not with an exotic mysticism imported from Palestine but with the hodge-podge of practices (some conventional, some heterodox, some mystical) encountered in the local synagogue.[14]

The issue need not be decided here, and does not in fact fundamentally affect my argument.[15] Either way we can say that in the face of elitist preoccupation with an ascetic lifestyle and esotericism about the heavenly world, Paul in Colossians affirms *every* Christian's birthright of participation in the heavenly realities.

---

[8] Francis, "Humility", 183–185 and passim; Bandstra, "Errorists", 331 ff.; Evans, "Mystics", 196 f.; O'Brien xxxvii f.; Rowland, "Exaltation", 77; Yates, "Worship", 14. This proposal also makes excellent sense of ἃ ἑόρακεν ἐμβατεύων (2:18), although a visionary understanding of this phrase does not depend on it.

[9] With Bruce, "Heresy", 204.

[10] BAG 363; LSJ 806.

[11] *Pace* Rowland, "Exaltation", 75. See esp. his reference to *ARN* 12 (23a), which nicely demonstrates the motif of angelic humility (cf. also 3 En 18). (His other references illustrate the different (and indeed much more common) motif of angelic prostration before God's throne and power, not *eo ipso* a mark of humility [cf. Phil 2:10]).

[12] Cf. Hemer, *Letters*, 183 f., following Ramsay; more cautiously Bruce, "Jews", 7.

[13] Cf. magical texts, epitaphs; and see Wettstein, *Novum Testamentum*, 2:288 f.; Lueken, *Michael*, 4–12, 62–91; Ramsay, *Phrygia*, 2:541, 741 f.; Williams, "Cult", 420–438. Various Jewish texts inveigh against the practice (t. Ḥul 2:18; b. AZ 42b; b. Ḥul 40a; b. RH 24a; y. Ber 9, 13a70; TPsJ Exod 20:20), and the Samaritan *Asatir* 10:8 (ff.) condemns Balaam for angel worship.

[14] This — influence from the local synagogue — may also account for the relative composure with which Paul seems to address the whole matter. Cf. Hooker, "False Teachers", 316 (though to speak of Paul's "extraordinary calm" may in view of 2:8, 18, 23 be a slight overstatement). True, there is no evidence that the Colossians have already submitted to these advances (ibid., 317 f.), but Paul's tone is concerned enough to indicate a genuine threat (cf. Lightfoot 176 on 2:8). Some measure of what Lampe terms Jewish "counter- evangelism" is plausible at Colossae ("Grievous Wolves", 254 f., 259 ff.), and forms a likely backdrop for Gal, Phil (3:2 f.), and Heb. Cf. similarly Wright 24–27; see further Justin *Dial* 17; 108.

[15] Perhaps modern scholarly perplexity is due in part to the fact that Paul's own knowledge of the situation was limited?

As in earlier letters (see Chapter Nine above), Paul does not deny the legitimacy of an interest in heavenly matters as such; indeed he affirms that all Christians should "seek what is above" (3:1 ff.). But he is convinced that the benefits accruing to believers from extraneous exploits and practices must not be required for the full life in Christ. Being at best *epiphenomenal* upon the "word of the Cross", they cannot surpass what has already been revealed in the gospel (see above; cf. 1:19−22; 2:14 f.); nor may they be admitted as criteria of apostolic or Christian pedigree (cf. 2 Cor 12:1, etc.). What Paul wishes to counter in the Colossian situation, therefore, is the heretics' disturbing claim of exclusiveness, viz. that there are in fact esoteric benefits and requirements of salvation to which believers have not already attained in the gospel and by virtue of baptism (2:11 ff.).[16] For it is a deeper maturity and understanding *in this same gospel of Christ* which Paul desires for the believer (1:28, 2:2).

2.2. The Argument of Col 1:24−2:5

The structure of the passage is difficult to ascertain. Obvious syntactical breaks occur only at the beginning of 1:21 and 1:24: but even these provide no real intermittence in the argument. The topic throughout is the exalted and the crucified Christ as Son of God, though subthemes are his reception by the Colossians (vv. 21−23) and Paul's apostolic ministry in relation to this Christ (1:23b−29). The verses 2:1−3 and 4 f. then specifically apply Paul's responsibility for the "mystery of God" to the Colossian and Laodicean situation and explain the intent of the whole section (2:4).

Paul in v. 24 describes his own present afflictions as the "topping-off" (ἀνταναπληρῶ) in his person of the θλίψεις τοῦ Χριστοῦ, i.e. most plausibly the Messianic birth-pangs (חבלו של המשיח), in which the church participates as the Messianic community at the ushering in of the new age.[17] Although he does not know the Colossian Christians, his suffering is for their sake as for the sake of the body of Christ at large (ὑπέρ here as e.g. 1:7; 2 Cor 12:10). For his ministry to the church in "fulfilling [i.e. fully carrying out[18]] the word of God" is a direct

---

[16] Lona, *Eschatologie,* 208 rightly speaks of the opponents' "christological deficit".

[17] See e.g. Zeilinger, *Erstgeborene,* 93; Moule 76; O'Brien 78−80; also cf. Yates, "Note", 88−92; Bauckham, "Colossians 1:24", 169 f. − though the contemporary Jewish commonplace has here been adapted to the Christian perspective. Cf. Gal 4:19; also 2 Cor 1:5; 4:10 f.; Phil 3:10. See on the other hand Flemington's revival of the alternative view, viz. that of Christian sharing in the passion of Jesus ("Colossians 1:24", 87 f.); cf. earlier e.g. Kremer (*Leiden,* 202), who also offers a history of interpretation to 1956 (pp. 5−154); and Schneider, *Passionsmystik,* 48−61. Note further the belief that Christ suffers in the martyrs, Eusebius *EH* 5.1.23 (Sanctus of Lyons).

[18] See Rom 15:19; cf. O'Brien 82. An eschatological overtone of this expression is probably implied; de Wette 25 compares גמר.

corollary of his God-given οἰκονομία[19] (cf. above on 1 Cor 4:1; also 1 Cor 9:7) on behalf of the churches.

This λόγος τοῦ θεοῦ[20] is in v. 26 f. further described in by now familiar terms as

> the mystery which, having been hidden
>> from the ages and generations,
> was recently manifested to His saints,
>> those to whom God wished to make known
>>> what is the glorious richness of this mystery
>>> among the Gentiles,
>>> viz. Christ among you, the hope of glory.

The use of the demonstrative pronoun τούτου qualifying μυστήριον in v. 27 reflects the fact that a *specific* mystery is in view: viz., regarding Paul's Gentile ministry in "the word of God". This is further explained as "Christ among you" — i.e. the fact of the Gospel's proclamation among the Gentiles.[21] At the same time the present mystery's close link with the gospel gives it greater import than some others we have discussed; indeed it could be regarded as substantially overlapping with the μυστήριον Paul uses to designate his kerygma (4:3; 1 Cor 2:1).

2.3. "Hidden from ages and generations"

This mystery was hidden ἀπὸ τῶν αἰώνων καὶ ἀπὸ τῶν γενεῶν. Lightfoot and most other commentators favour a temporal reading of ἀπό: "a mystery hidden *since* past ages and generations". Certainly Paul's use of ἀπό supports this possibility: e.g. Col 1:6,9; Rom 1:20; 2 Cor 8:10; 9:2. However, a mystery (in the accustomed sense) is by definition hidden with God until its disclosure, whereas temporal ἀπό supposes a *terminus a quo* of concealment. Where Paul refers to a point in protological time, he tends to speak with greater precision.[22]

---

[19] On the problem of whether οἰκονομία here takes the notion of a human administration of God's designs (as in earlier letters and perhaps Eph 3:2) or of the divine plan itself (as e.g. in Eph 1:10; 3:9 f.), see esp. O'Brien 81 f. Reumann, "OIKONOMIA-Terms", 162 f. points out possible Hellenistic philosophical connotations which the term may have had for Paul's readers.

[20] Lohmeyer 80 considers this term to be the "Inbegriff aller göttlichen Offenbarung"; cf. Merklein, *Amt*, 175.

[21] Cf. τὸ μυστήριον τοῦτο (Rom 11:25). On the functional interchangeability of "Christ" and "gospel" see below.

[22] E.g. 1 Cor 2:7 πρὸ τῶν αἰώνων; cf. Eph 1:4 πρὸ καταβολῆς κόσμου; 2 Tim 1:9/Tit 1:2 πρὸ χρόνων αἰωνίων. With ἀπό as "since", a more precise protological terminus is chosen: e.g. Rom 1:20 ἀπὸ κτίσεως κόσμου. Similarly Matt 25:34 ἀπὸ καταβολῆς κόσμου; Mark 10:6 ἀπὸ δὲ ἀρχῆς κτίσεως.

Some have suggested a personal (angelic) reading of αἰῶνες.[23] However, given the plentiful LXX antecedents both for the combination of αἰῶνες and γενεαί[24] and for ἀπό with αἰών designating an indefinite period of the past,[25] a more generally temporal meaning of αἰῶνες is here to be preferred.[26] At the same time, the established usage suggests a nonspecific reading of the phrase at hand: "hidden from [RSV: for] ages and generations".[27]

2.4. "Now Manifested to His Saints"

The predicate is straightforward: the eschatological mystery pertaining to the word of God — to wit, Christ preached among Gentiles (Χριστὸς ἐν ὑμῖν) — has now been manifested and demonstrated to the saints.[28] The empirical dimension of this "demonstration" may be suggested by the historical references in the context: Christ "made peace through the blood of His cross" (1:20), "through death in his fleshly body" (1:22).

The revelation is granted τοῖς ἁγίοις. This indirect object probably includes elements of a *dativus commodi*,[29] not just a *dativus comitativus*, so that the mystery of the word of God was made manifest *to* the saints as much as *for* their sake or benefit. More vexing, however, is the question: Who are these "saints"? *Prima facie* (i.e. semantically), there would appear to be no difficulty: God has revealed the mystery to the ἅγιοι, a group which from 1:2, 4, 12, 22; 3:12 seems coextensive with the body of all believers. Yet the identification of οἱ ἅγιοι with all believers is perhaps less neat than is sometimes assumed.[30] It is conceivable that the "saints" here constitute the body of those who exercise ecclesial authority or leadership.

---

[23] E.g. Bengel, *Gnomon*, 786; Dibelius 17; also BAG 28. Cf. IgnEph 19:2 (ἐφανερώθη τοῖς αἰῶσιν); 8:1; 1 En 9:4 (Greek).

[24] Gen 9:12; Exod 27:21; 30:21; Lev 6:18; 7:26; 10:9; 17:7; 23:14, 21, 31, 41; 24:3; Num 10:8; 15:15; 18:23; cf. Isa 58:12.

[25] Gen 6:4; 1 Chr 16:36; 29:10; Neh 9:5; ψ 24:6; 40:13; 89:2; 92:2; 102:17; 105:48; 118:52; Isa 46:9; 64:4; Jer 2:20; 25:5; 35(28):8; Ezek 32:27; Mic 5:2; Sir 14:17; 39:20; 44:2; 51:8; 3 Macc 5:11; Tob 4:12; 6:17; also Dan 2:20 ϑ'; Luke 1:70; Acts 3:21; 15:18. Cf. the Hebrew מן העולם, מעולם, etc.

[26] Cf. however the notion of a plurality of עולמים/עולמות: God rules many worlds (MidrPsa 18:15; CantR 1:9); cf. b.Sanh 100a; LevR 4:7. See further Str-B 3:672; also 1 QapGen 2:7, 21:2, etc. The plural עולמים is common in the OT and e.g. at Qumran.

[27] Moule, *Idiom-Book*, 73 on John 9:32 ἐκ τοῦ αἰῶνος: "from time immemorial".

[28] See above on φανερόω. Cf. also de Wette 26: "ἐφανερώθη ist nicht = ἀπεκαλύφϑη, ... sondern bezeichnet die geschichtliche Verwirklichung".

[29] The two uses often overlap and can be difficult to distinguish. Cf. Robertson, *Grammar*, 538; also BDF § 188:2.

[30] See D. W. B. Robinson, "Saints", 45–47; and passim.

While no absolute case can be established and sufficient exceptions can be found, in many cases a *plausible* reading of the definite οἱ ἅγιοι is in reference to a specific group of people within the body of believers. This is perhaps clearest in reference to the collection and the ministry to the mother church in Jerusalem: Rom 15:25, 31; 1 Cor 16:1; 2 Cor 8:4; 9:5; etc).[31]

But other instances also seem to imply a distinction: thus Phoebe is to be received ἀξίως τῶν ἁγίων (Rom 16:1) — does this mean only "receive her as a Christian"? The "saints" may include heavenly figures, as perhaps in Col 1:12[32] (cf. Eph 1:18) or 1 Thes 3:13.

Ephesians offers additional examples of the saints as a distinct group: Eph 2:19 stresses that the [sc. Gentile] Christians are now συμπολῖται τῶν ἁγίων, and the statement (3:8) that Paul is the ἐλαχιστότερος πάντων ἁγίων is not dissimilar from the ἐλάχιστος τῶν ἀποστόλων in 1 Cor 15:9. In 3:18 the Christians are to apprehend the full dimensions of salvation with the saints (who apparently have done so already).[33]

Three specific arguments can be brought in favour of a reading of "the saints" in Col 1:26 as those to whom the Gospel was first revealed and entrusted. First, it is consistent with Paul's view of revelation as spelled out above: apostles and prophets as the chosen vehicles and stewards of the Gospel.[34] This is more than could be said for the alternative view of a blanket revelation of the mystery given indiscriminately to *all* Christians. Secondly, it preserves the logical distinction in 1:26 f. between the ἅγιοι (*recipients* of revelation) on the one hand and the parallel ἔθνη / ὑμεῖς (modifying the *subject matter* of that revelation) on the other.[35] And thirdly, v. 28 (like v. 25) clearly speaks of the apostolic ministry, so that the logical sequence would seem to be once again that of (i) revelation to the apostles, (ii) proclamation to the Gentiles (cf. 1 Thes 2:4, and see Chapter Eight above).

The trend of modern commentators is to opt for the inclusive reading of οἱ ἅγιοι. But others, including e.g. Cerfaux and Penna, adopt a narrower reading of "the saints" as the leading ministers of the Gospel;[36] the present study lends a cautious endorsement to this interpretation.

---

[31] See esp. Holl, "Kirchenbegriff", 58—60.

[32] On this passage as referring to angels see recently Benoit, "Ἅγιοι", 94 f. and passim.

[33] See further e.g. Jude 3 (recipients of the "faith once for all delivered"); 1 Clem 46:2 (outstanding examples of faith and discipleship); IgnPhld 5:2 (the Christian prophets).

[34] *Contra* Lührmann, *Offenbarungsverständnis*, 121 and passim, who denies the presence in the Pauline *homologoumena* of this view of apostleship as mediating revelation.

[35] Cf. rigthly Bengel, *Gnomon*, 786, 750 (on Col 1:26 par. Eph 3:8): "*Sancti hîc opponuntur gentibus.*"

[36] Cerfaux, *Christian*, 488 f.; Penna, *Mysterion*, 31 f.; also Theodore of Mopsuestia (ed. Swete, 1:281); further Percy, *Probleme*, 346 f. Cerfaux, "Saints", 515 f. argues for an identification of the "saints" in the first instance with the believers of the Jerusalem

2.5. "Those to Whom God Wished to Make Known the Mystery"

Further support for the ἅγιοι as a limited group of leaders may come from v. 27a. The saints are evidently those "to whom[37] God wished to make known the richness of the glory of this mystery among the Gentiles": not, it would seem, all Christians, but those specifically appointed to receive this mystery's full dimensions, in order then (v. 28) to apply and dispense it to their flock. Penna rightly points to the interesting conceptual parallel in Acts 10:41: God manifested the risen Christ "not to all the people, but to previously chosen witnesses, i.e. to us who ate and drank with him after he rose from the dead."[38]

2.6. "Christ Among You, the Hope of Glory"

If the word μυστήριον in 1:26 is in close syntactic alignment with the λόγος τοῦ θεοῦ of v. 25, its second occurrence in 1:27 is more specifically linked with the phrase Χριστὸς ἐν ὑμῖν, ἡ ἐλπὶς τῆς δόξης.

The debate over whether to translate "Christ *in* you"[39] or "Christ *among* you"[40] has been long and protracted. Although one rendering tends to bear out a more mystical and the other a more objective slant, the question is perhaps less important than is sometimes assumed: each of the two emphases is consistent with Paul's thought[41] and in light of the other can be said to obtain at least by implication. *Ceteris paribus* the reading "Christ among you" is probably to be preferred on contextual grounds (see n. 41).

---

mother church, who are apostles and witnesses of the resurrection. A similar view is already assumed in Codices F and G (omitted from *NTG*[26] but see Tischendorf, *Novum Testamentum*, 2:732: τοῖς ἁγίοις ἀποστόλοις αὐτοῦ), and of course in Eph 3:5.

[37] Bowers, "Note", 110–114 makes the interesting and plausible proposal of reading the relative οἷς as an *accusative* pronoun by attraction to τοῖς ἁγίοις, thus making it the *subject* of γνωρίσαι. However, failing more cogent considerations, the less fanciful *prima facie* reading of οἷς as a regular dative is to be preferred in view of the lack of any real NT parallels.

[38] Penna, *Mysterion*, 32.

[39] Thus e.g. AV, RV, RSV, NASB, NEB, NIV; Bornkamm, "μυστήριον", 827; Schneider, "Mysterion", 270; Caragounis, *Mysterion*, 30; Schmithals, Gnosis, 63; Lightfoot 167; O'Brien 87; Schlier, *Epheser*, 61.

[40] Thus e.g. JB/NJB; Abbott 235; Lohse 121 f.; Moule 83; Gnilka 102; Martin 72; Schweizer 88; Best, "Revelation", 23; Rigaux, "Révélation", 250; Schnackenburg, *Epheser*, 138; Meuzelaar, *Leib*, 44 n. 3; Wolter, "Weisheit", 307. Poole, *Synopsis*, 4:902 cites Estius and Zanchius.

[41] Thus also Bruce 86. "Christ among you": cf. the parallel ἐν τοῖς ἔθνεσιν; adducing further Pauline proof passages would be superfluous. "Christ in you": see 3:11, 15 f.; and cf. Rom 8:10; Gal 2:20; 2 Cor 13:5; Eph 3:17, though N.B. all (except Eph 3:17?) could also be read as *dativus modi* (BDF § 198).

There would appear to be *two* levels of meaning to which the "mystery" here corresponds: (i) "the word of God", i.e. the gospel and its proclamation (cf. 1 Cor 14:36; 2 Cor 2:17; 4:2; Phil 1:14; 1 Thes 2:13); and (ii) by metonymy a particular *aspect* of that Gospel, viz. here its bearing upon the Gentiles, which became the hub and centre of Paul's ministry. (N. B. a similar twofold distinction was suggested earlier for 1 Cor 2:1, 7. A closely related aspect of the gospel is called a μυστήριον in Rom 11:25−27.) "Christ preached among the Gentiles" is the mystery here in view, and it is given eschatological prominence by its identification as "the hope of glory" (cf. 1:5; 3:3 f., 24).[42] What is more, this shows that despite the emphasis on the mystery's decisive revelation to the saints, there is in Paul's mind even now a dimension of residual hiddenness, an awareness of that which is yet to be revealed (cf. below on 2:3; 3:3 f.; and p. 165 above).[43]

2.7. "Everyone Mature in Christ"

Paul goes on to describe the apostolic[44] labour in the οἰκονομία entrusted to him as an act of proclaiming, correcting, and teaching "everyone in all wisdom", in order to present "everyone mature in Christ". This is evidently a statement of general principle, not of particular pedagogical application − and so it would be inappropriate to postulate a fundamental difference between this and the argument of 1 Cor 2:6 ff. Indeed one might almost regard Col 1:28 f. as the rationale on the basis of which the Corinthian pattern is formulated: in both cases Paul's desire is for all believers to become τέλειοι[45] and to attain to a full and deep understanding of the salvific wisdom of God.

---

[42] Cf. 1 Tim 1:1; hope in God as Saviour: cf.PssSol 17:3; 8:31; 9:19; 15:1; TAsh 7:7; 2 Macc 2:18; 4 Macc 11:7; Sir 34:13, etc.; hope in God for the resurrection: 2 Macc 7:11, 14, 20; 1 En 40:9; Acts 23:6; 24:15; 26:6 f.; 28:20, etc. NEB appropriately paraphrases "the hope of a glory to come"; cf. also von Soden, "ΜΥΣΤΗΡΙΟΝ", 193; Schweizer 89 ("Vorgabe der Herrlichkeit"); Penna, *Mysterion*, 46 f. *Contra* O'Brien 84, who denies the future dimension of the mystery.

[43] On this see esp. Penna, *Mysterion*, 46 f.: the mystery is still *in fieri*; "il Mistero oggi noto alla Chiesa racchiude ancora in sé qualcosa di inedito, un aspetto di sorpresa non ancora svelata."

[44] N.B. ἡμεῖς, i.e. presumably the ἅγιοι to whom the mystery has been revealed.

[45] O'Brien 89 f. (following Bruce, Pfitzner) suspects that this term here has an eschatological orientation, i.e. that this "perfection" will be fully realized only at the Parousia.

2.8. "Full Knowledge of the Mystery of God, i.e. of Christ"

In Col 2:1–5 the apostle applies this principle of ministry to the situation of the Laodiceans and Colossians. His labour for them is

> that your hearts may be encouraged
> having been knitted together in love,
> and [attain] to the wealth of fully assured understanding,
> > to the knowledge of the mystery of God,
> viz. of Christ in whom all the treasures of wisdom
> > and knowledge are hidden.

The syntactical function of Χριστοῦ in the phrase τοῦ μυστηρίου τοῦ θεοῦ Χριστοῦ has baffled interpreters for a long time.

Proposed solutions range from the adoption of one of the numerous textual variants, to a possessive genitive ("the mystery of Christ's God")[46] or an apposition ("the mystery of God, i.e. Christ").[47] The textual problem, albeit obstinate and intractable, is probably to be settled in favour of the UBS text.[48] As for the option of a possessive genitive, it has only marginal support among scholars; and though the idea is possibly Pauline, its closest parallels are formulated differently (Rom 15:6; 2 Cor 1:3; Col 1:3; Eph 1:3, 17). Despite its popularity, the third option of a straightforward apposition seems to lack contextual plausibility and grace of syntax: "If this is the apostle's meaning, he has expressed himself very obscurely."[49]

We find ourselves without an obvious explanation; not impossibly the text is corrupt.[50] Certainly Benoit's shorter reading τοῦ θεοῦ is the smoothest and makes reasonable sense of the context; but its limited MS support makes this option unadvisable. Given τοῦ θεοῦ Χριστοῦ as the best *available* reading, it is in the end difficult to avoid the somewhat inelegant conclusion that Χριστοῦ κτλ. must be loosely appositional to τοῦ μυστηρίου τοῦ θεοῦ; so that the desired "full knowledge" of God's mystery stands in parallelism with the "full knowledge" of Christ.

We seem at any rate to witness a development (or at least a hitherto unattested tenet) in Paul's thought at this point: for nowhere previously are "mys-

---

[46] Von Soden 41.

[47] The objective genitive asserted by Zeilinger, *Erstgeborene*, 110 n. 132 and Meuzelaar, *Leib*, 45 f. ("the mystery of God as revealed in Christ") amounts to much the same thing. "Mystery of God" is gen. *auctoris* (with Penna, *Mysterion*, 55).

[48] *Pace* Benoit's recent erudite argument for the reading τοῦ θεοῦ (D[1] H P 1881.2464 *pc* sa[ms]), "Colossiens 2:2–3", 46–49. This would indeed remove the difficulty most elegantly, but it lacks early MS support; and the UBS reading can *also* explain the other variants. See further Metzger, *Text*, 236–238.

[49] Abbott 239.

[50] Thus Beare 185.

tery" and "Christ" linked quite so immediately. Yet at the same time some commentators would appear to have read into the text certain conclusions about this connection which Paul himself does not draw. Thus Penna sees this "mysteriological" passage as *ontologically* linking Christ and mystery. Others infer from the seemingly "grander" use of mystery here a major difference between this letter and the Pauline *homologoumena*.[51] But a glance at the syntax should suffice to demonstrate that the author's concern is not ontological but epistemological:[52] ἐπίγνωσις of the mystery of God. We expect the term μυστήριον τοῦ θεοῦ to be synonymous with Paul's gospel message: and if this identification holds, the appositional Χριστοῦ comes as much less of an innovation. Paul can use the terms εὐαγγέλιον and Χριστός almost interchangeably.[53] And just as "preaching the gospel *about* Christ" can be elliptically rendered "preaching Christ", so Paul is introducing no theological *res novae* by equating full knowledge of God's mystery with full knowledge of the Christ who has manifested it.[54] Seen in this light, the occurrence in 4:3 of τὸ μυστήριον τοῦ Χριστοῦ (clearly to designate the gospel) also comes as no surprise.

2.9. "In Whom Are Hidden All the Treasures..."

The antecedent of ἐν ᾧ in v. 3a must be Χριστοῦ, both on grammatical and conceptual grounds. For if, as it were, a comma of apposition separates Χριστοῦ from what precedes (thus the UBS text), the immediately subsequent relative clause cannot very well modify the μυστήριον τοῦ θεοῦ.[55] What is more, to take ἐν ᾧ with the mystery of God would effect a malapropism: our earlier results suggest that "treasures" [of wisdom and knowledge] can hardly be hidden in a "mystery", since the former are instances of the latter.[56]

Instead, the thrust of v. 2 f. is that every mystery of heaven, every treasure of wisdom is already hidden in Christ.[57] Hence there is no need for the Colossians

---

[51] E.g. Schenk, "Christus", 155 and passim; Steinmetz, *Heils- Zuversicht,* 108.

[52] Though Theodore of Mopsuestia is undoubtedly correct in linking *cognitio* and *participatio* (Latin ed. Swete, 1:283).

[53] See esp. 1 Cor 1:23, 15:12; Gal 2:2; Phil 1:15; Col 1:23; etc. − and, not implausibly, 1:27. Cf. e.g. Stuhlmacher, *Evangelium*, 277; Friedrich, "εὐαγγελίζομαι", 730.

[54] Cf. also Zeilinger, *Erstgeborene*, 110 and n. 132.

[55] With O'Brien 95; Martin 75; Gnilka 111; Penna, *Mysterion*, 64. *Pace* von Soden 41; Abbott 241; de Wette 31.

[56] See esp. 1 En 41:1−7. Regarding treasures of wisdom see also 2 Bar 44:14; 54:13; Sir 1:25; cf. Isa 33:6 LXX; Philo *Fug* 79; *Her* 76; *LA* 3:104 f.; b.Ḥag 12b (on this cf. Bietenhard, *Himmlische Welt*, 222, 228).

[57] These treasures of wisdom presumably include on an equal footing with eschatological mysteries the secrets of Scripture as well as of cosmology (note e.g. the

and Laodiceans to be beguiled "through philosophy and vain deceit" (2:8). In other words: what the Colossian opponents are claiming to be their privilege is in fact the rightful property of *all* Christians by virtue both of their incorporation in the Christ (in whom God's fulness is already manifest: 1:19 f.; 2:9; etc.), and of their assured share in the "inheritance of the saints in light" (1:12). Paul's concentration of hidden treasures in Christ may well be a polemical[58] appropriation and extrapolation of Jewish views about the Torah for his purposes of expressing full revelation in Christ.[59]

And yet, how can it be maintained that all the treasures of wisdom are *still hidden* in Christ (εἰσιν ἀπόκρυφοι) — not least after what has just been said in 1:26 f.? It is important to remember that the revelation of 1:26 f. is given specifically to the ἅγιοι; neither this reference nor our knowledge of Paul's general view of revelation (see Chapter Eight above) allows us to assume that the celestial mysteries and treasures of wisdom have in the Christ event already been openly disclosed.[60] The universal public *revelation* of Christ, as we saw earlier, is an event which is yet to come at His parousia. He is still hidden, and the believer's life is stored up with Him in God (3:3 f.); Paul too might have said, οὔπω ἐφανερώθη τί ἐσόμεθα (1 John 3:2). And so also the mysteries of God's wise purposes are treasured up in Christ who subsumes and crowns them all.

A most interesting parallel to Paul's statement exists in the Messianic expectation of the Similitudes of Enoch. For there the Messianic Son of Man, hidden in heaven, is revealed by the "wisdom of the Lord of Spirits" to the holy and the righteous (48:6 f.; cf. 62:7). This too takes place before the eschaton (cf. 48:7b), apparently in order to comfort the righteous who will be saved in the name of the Lord of Spirits. In the eschaton (cf. 51:1) the Messiah (Chosen One) will "sit on his throne, and all the secrets of wisdom will flow out from the counsel of his mouth" (51:3); he will "reveal all the treasures of that which is secret" (46:3).

Paul's desire, then, is for the Laodicean and Colossian Christians to be presented as τέλειοι in Christ. In the course of such maturing he wants them to be

---

scope of 1:15−20). At issue is not a reduction of cosmology to theology and christology (*pace* Bietenhard, *Himmlische Welt*, 253 f.), but an expansion of christology to encompass cosmology.

[58] The polemical force of 2:1−3 is indicated by 2:4; cf. Bandstra, "Errorists", 339 f.

[59] Cf. e.g. LXX Isa 33:6 (ἐν νόμῳ παραδοθήσονται, ἐν θησαυροῖς ἡ σωτηρία ἡμῶν, ἐκεῖ σοφία καὶ ἐπιστήμη καὶ εὐσέβεια πρὸς τὸν κύριον· οὗτοί εἰσιν θησαυροὶ δικαιοσύνης); 45:3 (note MT מסתרים; cf. Knox, *Gentiles*, 228); and above, Chapters 2, 7, passim. Occupation with Torah results in revelation of secrets (m. Abot 6:1; b. Ḥag 14a), enables one "to see the face of the Shekhinah in this world" (MidrPsa 105:1), etc. See further Lightfoot 172; Zeilinger, *Erstgeborene*, 115; Davis, "Wisdom", 92; also O'Neill ("Source", 87−100), who argues that the christological passages of Col use excerpts of Jewish thought to show that Christ fulfils the hope of Judaism.

[60] Cf. Chrysostom *Hom.* 5: it is still hidden inasmuch as it was only manifested to the saints.

"knitted together in love" (the ethical component of τελείωσις)[61] and to come to an ever deeper knowledge and appreciation of the salvific mystery of God as summed up in Christ.

3. Other Passages in Colossians

While 1:26 f. and 2:2 f. are clearly the most important occurrences of our motif, two other passages were mentioned in passing above and ought briefly to be acknowledged.

3.1. Col 3:1—4

In Col 3:1—4, immediately following on his refutation of the Colossian error, and as a transition to the ethical section which follows in 3:5—4:6,[62] Paul encourages the church at Colossae to "keep seeking the things above". That τὰ ἄνω is indeed a reference to the heavenly world and its contents[63] is made clear by the modifying clause, "where Christ is, etc." But this clause at the same time sets the *agenda* of any quest for the heavenly world: the "things" above are of relevant interest insofar as they relate to the enthroned Christ; anyone lacking this perspective misses the point altogether. V. 2 reiterates the call to an "upward orientation", but here an ethical component is added (φρονέω).[64] The relevance of the heaven-earth dualism for ethics is that Paul affirms two opposing dispositions, the way of life of the heavenly sphere vs. the earthly way of life.[65] In v. 3 Paul cites the reason (γάρ) for this call to the lifestyle of the world above: in baptism the believer has already died (ἀπεθάνετε) to the things of earth, and has been raised with Christ (v. 1). The new life is, however, still "hidden with Christ in God", and so the Christian's orientation must clearly be to the mode of life appropriate to the heavenly world (3:5—4:6 goes on to spell this out).[66] Its future dimension, i.e. manifestation with Christ in glory at the parousia

---

[61] Cf. Brown, *Mystery*, 54, who compares 1 Cor 2:7—10.

[62] See O'Brien 157 f. and others cited there.

[63] Cf. 2:3 (the treasures); 1:5 (the hope stored up); and most importantly 3:3 (Christ/your life).

[64] Lincoln, *Paradise*, 125 (comparing Rom 8:5 f.); O'Brien 163 f. (Phil 2:5 etc.).

[65] In Phil 3:19 f. the contrast is between τὰ ἐπίγεια φρονοῦντες and Christians whose πολίτευμα is ἐν τοῖς οὐρανοῖς. Cf. O'Brien 164; Lincoln, *Paradise*, 126.

[66] The argument here as elsewhere can be summarized as "be what you are" (see the classic statement of Bultmann, *Theologie*, 334): you have died with Christ and been raised with him so that your life is hidden in the heavenly world — therefore now "put to death" your earthly nature (3:5).

(v. 4), is a central aspect of Paul's view of the drama of salvation (see esp. Rom 8:18–25; 1 Cor 15:43; 2 Cor 5:1–10; Phil 3:20 f.); he therefore does not suppress it even where circumstances call for a reduced emphasis on eschatology.[67] We have in Col 3:3 f., then, another clear confirmation of the idea of a continuing residual hiddenness of God's mysteries which was encountered in 1 Cor 2:6–10; Col 2:3.[68]

3.2. Col 4:3 f.

The general exhortation to pray (4:2) is followed by a request of prayer for Paul himself (and for his fellow labourers). His specific desire is that God might open a door for "the word", i.e. the preaching of the gospel,

> λαλῆσαι τὸ μυστήριον τοῦ Χριστοῦ·
> διὸ καὶ δέδεμαι,
> ἵνα φανερώσω αὐτό,
> ὡς δεῖ με λαλῆσαι.[69]

The use of μυστήριον here is now familiar, and no different e.g. from 1 Cor 2:1. We saw earlier (2:2 f.) that the link of Paul's abstracting use of "the mystery of God" with the gospel naturally lends itself to a connection with Χριστός as well. And this is here carried out: the mystery of Christ is his work of redemption announced in the gospel.[70] Paul's desire and intention to "manifest" and to "speak" this mystery is fully consistent with his understanding of the apostolic ministry elsewhere (e.g. 1:28; cf. Eph 3:5 f., 9 f.; Rom 16:25 f.).[71]

Some have taken Paul's application of φανερόω to his ministry as indicative of a bold claim that he himself performs the act of revealing, which is elsewhere reserved for God.[72] This I believe to be quite unthinkable. While Paul can indeed freely acknowledge his ministry — even his apostolic weakness and suffer-

---

[67] *Pace* e.g. Bornkamm, "Hoffnung", 206–13; Grässer, "Kol 3,1–4", 165, who argue that in this (post-Pauline) letter eschatology has given way to an otherworldly existential "hope". See O'Brien 168 f.

[68] Note the close link of the believer's hidden life with the heavenly Christ; Wright 132 even considers that it is part of the central "mystery".

[69] For arguments in favour of this textual layout over against Nestle-Aland see Bockmuehl, "Note", 484–489.

[70] Cf. del Páramo, "Misterio", 253; Bruce 173.

[71] The notion of proclaiming mysteries, although rare (and in Paul clearly dependent on his eschatological perspective), recurs in various forms e.g. in SibOr 3:812 (προφητεῦσαί με βρότοις αἰνίγματα θεῖα); TLevi 2:10 (μυστήρια αὐτοῦ ἐθαγγελεῖς τοῖς ἀνθρώποις); 3 SlavBar 17:1. Cf. also Hollander/de Jonge, *Testaments*, 135 (but several of their examples appear to be incorrect).

[72] E.g. Lohse 234; O'Brien 240; Best, "Revelation", 23; esp. Lohmeyer 162.

ing — to be an *instrument* of God's revelation (see above, Chapter Eight), never does he go so far as to describe himself as the *subject* of the revelation of the gospel.

The answer must be sought elsewhere. Despite repeated claims to this effect,[73] the word φανερόω is *not* in the first instance synonymous with ἀποκαλύπτω; it means rather "to demonstrate" or "to manifest" (in the empirical or logical sense).[74] This is surely what is meant here: Paul desires to make the gospel manifest, as indeed he is bound to. Obvious parallels to this notion are his φανέρωσις of the truth in 2 Cor 4:2, or of the death of Christ in 2 Cor 4:10 f. (see above, Chapter Nine).

A further trail is worth pursuing in this regard. Von Soden and Abbott follow Chrysostom in linking φανερώσω in some fashion with Paul's imprisonment.[75] Both are wrong in claiming that the verb is never used of Paul's kerygmatic activity, and therefore cannot be so employed here. Furthermore they assume without further argument that αὐτό can refer to Paul's being bound, rather than to the μυστήριον. However, what seems to me of abiding value in their interpretation is the observation that Paul's chains may in this passage be seen as illustrative, indeed as symbolic of his ministry: he is *bound* to speak.[76] This suggestion may be strengthened by the observation, not noted by Abbott or von Soden, of an apparent chiastic substructure of the verbs λαλέω, δέω, δέω, λαλέω (4:3 b—4).

Far from appropriating for himself the divine predicate of revelation — in any case a blasphemous thought for a Jew — , Paul speaks here of a *demonstration* of the "mystery of Christ" by way of his own bonds. He proposes a manifestation of the *theologia crucis* in his own person, as it were: and this is fully in keeping with earlier statements in 1:24 and especially 2 Cor 4 (see above).

Summing up, the treatment of divine mysteries and their revelation in Colossians agrees well with Paul's overall view of revelation and with his use of the divine mystery motif in other major passages. Against a background of

---

[73] See esp. Bultmann/Lührmann, "φαίνω κτλ.", 4 f., Müller, "φανερόω", 988 and Lührmann, *Offenbarungsverständnis*, 11, 148, 160, followed by many others.

[74] See further Bockmuehl, "φανερόω".

[75] Von Soden 67; Abbott 297 f.; Chrysostom, *Hom.* 10. Cf. further Wright 152.

[76] The same idea is expressed in Phil 1:7, 12 f.: Paul's "chains in Christ" have become evident (φανεροί) throughout the praetorium, so that most of his fellow Christians have been encouraged because of his imprisonment to trust in the Lord and to preach more boldly the word of God. What has become known is clearly the fact that his imprisonment is for Christ; and hence the symbolic, *demonstrative* function of his chains has been recognized. Cf. further Phlm 9, 13; also Eph 3:1; 4:1; 6:20; 2 Tim 2:9 (ὁ λόγος τοῦ θεοῦ οὐ δέδεται); Acts 28:20. That the thought of being under divine coercion and *bound* to speak the gospel occupied Paul even before his imprisonment is clear from 1 Cor 9:16; Acts 20:22; as well as implicitly from his descriptions of his sufferings.

Jewish encroachments on the Colossian church, the apostle categorically affirms the centrality and sufficiency of Christ as the one in whom all the heavenly mysteries are stored up. Full knowledge of "the mystery of God", i.e. the sum of God's salvific purposes, is equivalent to full knowledge of Christ who resides in heaven and with whom the believer's future life of glory is already stored up. In his labour in the gospel Paul prays that he may demonstrate the "mystery of Christ" by the very fact that he is a prisoner on its behalf.

Chapter Eleven

Postscript to Paul

(Remaining Uses in Paul and "Deutero-Pauline" Writings; Outlook to the Post-Apostolic Period)

The chosen mandate of this enquiry is now virtually complete. Additional Pauline references to revealed mysteries are few and have for the most part been treated in the earlier discussion of the major passages. Ephesians and the Pastoral Epistles are not adduced as primary evidence for the purposes of this study, since without extensive arguments in their support such a methodological step would lack credibility in the current critical consensus.[1] For the sake of completeness, however, I propose to give a rapid survey of relevant passages in these letters as well as in a sampling of early Patristic writings, showing their relation to the Pauline texts discussed above. This should help to sketch the early church's reception and further development of our motif in the wake of the Apostle's teaching.

---

[1] My own opinion of the matter is that while Eph is perhaps not from the hand of Paul himself (or of him alone), the case against a date in his lifetime and within the precincts of his ministry is by no means clear-cut. Recent votes *for* authenticity include the commentaries of Caird, Barth, and Bruce; van Roon, *Authenticity*; Guthrie, *Introduction*; L. T. Johnson, *Writings*, 367–372; Robinson, *Redating*, 62–64; cf. Lincoln, *Paradise*, 135–139; and of course Chadwick, Schlier, and Percy, *Probleme*. As for the Pastorals: while no doubt much continues to speak against Pauline authorship, here too the full implications of an epistemological approach such as Beker's (see p. 178 above) have yet to be studied. Works in favour of an origin within the ministry of Paul include e.g. the commentaries of Spicq, Jeremias, Kelly, Ridderbos, Ward, Fee; Guthrie, *Pastoral Epistles*; de Lestapis, *Énigme*; van Bruggen, *Einordnung*; Robinson, *Redating*, 67 ff.; Reicke, "Chronologie", 81–94. Lucan [co-]authorship during Paul's lifetime – an important alternative – is suggested by Strobel, "Lukas", 191–208; Moule, "Problem", 117 and passim; see also idem, *Birth*, 281 f. for further literature; Wilson, *Luke*, holds the same hypothesis but favours a date of AD 90–95.

1. "The Mystery of Lawlessness" (2 Thes 2:7)

First, however, there remains one significant Pauline reference: 2 Thes 2:7. There we read,

> For the mystery of lawlessness is already at work (τὸ γὰρ μυστήριον ἤδη ἐνεργεῖται τῆς ἀνομίας); only he who now restrains it (ὁ κατέχων) will do so until he is out of the way.

Both syntax and subject matter make it difficult to understand what Paul is exactly intending to say; many have found him to be less than clear.[3]

1.1. The κατέχον / κατέχων (v. 6 f.): An Insoluble Puzzle?

Unfortunately time and space do not permit a proper discussion of the old and much-debated question of the identity of ὁ κατέχων here and τὸ κατέχον in v. 6. A full survey of the various options, and arguments *pro* and *contra*, can be derived from the recent commentaries;[4] here we will give merely the briefest of summaries.

One widespread view at least since Tertullian has been the "restraining" function of the Roman government.[5] In the New Testament, government is seen as a restrainer of political and moral evil: cf. Rom 13:1−4; 1 Pet 2:14; and esp. 1 Tim 2:2. A common view is that the world to come can only begin after the downfall of the Roman empire.[6] On balance, the Roman government as the

---

[2] The authorship of 2 Thes has long been disputed, esp. in Germany. However, the overall majority view would still seem to support its authenticity. Indeed, the suggestion that the two letters were sent in rapid succession, Paul in 1 Thes being buoyed by recent good news (3:6 f.) and in 2 Thes anxious about apparent misunderstandings (2:1−3), seems to me a viable explanation, not least in view of the recent sociological approach of R. Jewett (*Thessalonian Correspondence*, esp. pp. 1−30). Harnack's not incompatible case ("Problem", 564 ff.) for a more Jewish audience of the second letter may also merit reconsideration.

[3] Marxsen 84 f. holds that the meaning of the passage is *intentionally* enigmatic and unintelligible in order to dissuade speculation. But if so, the author surely is a poor psychologist.

[4] Most fully Trilling 88−105.

[5] Tertullian, *Apologeticum* 32. Von Dobschütz 283 traces the notion of Roman protection from destruction to Maccabean times (1 Macc 8, etc.). But note also the neglected parallel m. Abot 3:2 [par. b. AZ 4a]: "Pray for the peace of the government; if it were not for the fear of that, we would have swallowed each other alive" (R. Ḥanina T1). Might this be a reflection on the murderous internecine fighting of the years leading up to A.D. 70? Cf. Josephus *BJ* 5:376 ff., 395 ff., and esp. 404−412.

[6] E.g. AssMos 10:8; 2 Bar 39:1−8; Luke 21:24. Although both Judaism and Christianity could regard Rome as the enemy of God's purposes, they nevertheless encouraged prayer for the government. Cf. Trilling 96 f.

κατέχων is a credible possibility; but given the text's ambiguity, this option rather suffers from the lack of explicit parallels.[7] An alternative view in light of passages like Rev 7:1; 9:14 f. etc. is that God or an angelic restraining force might be intended;[8] something to this effect appears to be the view of Justin.[9] In the end, however, probably no completely cogent answer can be had; as Morris writes, "The plain fact is that Paul and his readers knew what he was talking about, and we do not. ... It is best that we frankly acknowledge our ignorance."[10]

It is at any rate clear that the "mystery of lawlessness" culminates in the appearance of the eschatological antichrist just before the parousia. Paul's interest is not to provide a detailed schedule of the last things, but to encourage soberness and realism in these matters.

1.2. The Notion of a Mystery of Evil

"Mysteries" of evil, as we saw in Chapter Two, are the designs and devices of Satan and the powers of darkness.[11] Overall, the specific link of Satanic designs with the notion of "mystery" is comparatively rare in ancient Judaism,[12] although much light is shed on this concept by the "mysteries of iniquity",

---

[7] Cf. also Best 296.

[8] Cf. the frequent idea of the binding and subsequent release of Satan: Jude 6; Rev 20:1–10; cf. e.g. 1 En 10:4 f., 11 f. [Gk.]; 18:16; 21:6; TLevi 18:12; Jub 48:15 f.; Tob 8:3, etc. See also the binding of the Watchers, e.g. 1 Pet 3:19, etc. For the opposition of angels, esp. of Michael, to Antichrist, Satan, demons, the beast, etc. see Lueken, *Michael*, 24–30, 106–109.

[9] *Apol* 1:45: καὶ κατέχειν [sc. τὸν Χριστὸν] ἕως ἂν πατάξῃ τοὺς ἐχθραίνοντας αὐτῷ δαίμονας.

[10] Morris 227; cf. already Augustine, *Civ. Dei* 20:19E: "Nescimus quod illi sciebant. ... Ego prorsus quid dixerit me fateor ignorare." This may speak in Harnack's favour (above, n. 2); he stresses that this paragraph is written only for "experts" ("Problem", 569).

[11] Whether the genitive is adjectival or epexegetical does not ultimately affect the meaning, which signifies neither a cognitive riddle "to be solved" (*pace* Caragounis, *Mysterion*, 27) nor the modern "problem of evil" (*pace* Mitton *Epistle*, 87).

[12] The wicked mysteries of 1 Enoch are "evil" by virtue of being illegitimately revealed. They are also of a generally "scientific" character (related to our "cosmological" category), rather than eschatological. The κακίας μυστήριον of Josephus *BJ* 1:470 is probably also unrelated (pace Marshall 195), since there the analogy seems to be taken from the Hellenistic mystery rites — i.e.: Antipater's life was a continual orgy of secret wickedness. Rev 17:5, 7, though in the context of Antichrist, is also in a different (viz., mantic) category. A possible exception is SibOr 8:58 (in context).

רזי פשע[13] etc., in the Dead Sea Scrolls.[14] The reference to malicious designs of Satan which are opposed to the mysteries of God is unmistakable: Vogt is surely justified to conclude, "Iniqua mysteria Belial sunt eius decreta atque consilia opposita consiliis divinis."[15] There seems, moreover, to be a close link between such supernatural devices of evil and the human powers who are their agents on earth (cf. 2 Thes 2:3–10 and see the remarks on 1 Cor 2:8 above).

1.3. Distinctives of the Pauline "Mystery of Lawlessness"

What is interesting about the "mystery of lawlessness" in our text is that Paul envisions a clandestine present activity in the world, even prior to its eschatological manifestation in the antichrist. The idea of a present anticipation of the eschatological evil is not without parallel in the Qumran texts (see 1 QH 5:36 ff.; 1 QM 14:9 with 15:2 f.; cf. 1 QS 3:20–24).

At first sight this notion seems to contradict Paul's conception of his own central mystery of the gospel, which had for all practical purposes not been manifested until its revelation in Christ. Indeed, evidence of a secret activity of "the mystery of God" before the coming of Christ is rare in Paul: examples might include 1 Cor 10:4; Gal 3:8 (προευηγγελίσατο τῷ ᾿Αβραάμ); the anticipating presence of saving faith in Rom 4, and possibly the announcement of the gospel in the prophets (Rom 1:2; cf. Rom 16:26).[16] The idea is more fully developed in Justin Martyr.[17]

Presumably the mystery of lawlessness, though already active, is at present still hidden from men; it is known to Paul as part of his God-given insight into the eschatological mysteries.[18] The following is a functional analysis of three possible modes of the revelation of such mysteries:[19]

---

[13] See above, Chapter 2. N.B. that ἀνομία in 2 Thes 2:7 represents פשע is strongly favoured by Brown, *Mystery*, 39 f., who points out that this correpondence is supported 20 times in the LXX.

[14] *Pace* Marshall 195, who denies the parallel. The fact that Qumran tends to use the plural (except in 1 QGenAp 1:2) need not be an obstacle, since Paul uses both the singular and plural of μυστήριον (see above).

[15] Vogt, "Mysteria", 257.

[16] Cf. the "mysteries of the prophets" at Qumran; also 1 Pet 1:12.

[17] *Dial* 128; also John 8:56–58; 12:41; Heb 3:5 f.; 4:8 f. and passim. In Eph, certainly, the opposite seems assumed, as Barth 1:354 points out: "In Ephesians revelation is treated as an unheard-of novelty which goes beyond the gifts given to men like Abraham, Moses, David, Isaiah." Cf. Gnilka 167.

[18] Thus also Schneider, "Mysterion", 274. That Paul knows this mystery by revelation is not explicitly stated; Trilling 93 for one thinks instead that the mystery is self-evident. However, to the Thessalonians at any rate the mystery is *not* self-evident but needs to be disclosed by Paul (v. 5) like other mysteries of which he has received knowledge by revelation.

[19] "General": the eschatological mysteries of apocalyptic, including Rom 11:25 f.;

General	*Christ / Gospel*	*Lawlessness*
1. Now hidden in Heaven;	1. Once hidden in Heaven;	1. Now hidden;
2.1 now disclosed in anticipation to the seer;	2.1 now decisively enacted and revealed to the apostles,	2.1 now [secretly] at work, though restrained;
2.2 to be manifested at the eschaton.	2.2 though its full manifestation remains for the parousia.	2.2 to be manifested in the Antichrist just before the eschaton.
3.1 The seer communicates it to the righteous	3.1 The apostles preach it to all	3.1 Paul discloses it to the Thessalonians
3.2 for their encouragement.	3.2 and specially equip Christians to become τέλειοι.	3.2 lest they be deceived.

In keeping with the dualistic traditions of apocalyptic thought, the first two columns must be treated as functional and theological opposites of the third:[20] the mystery of lawlessness is the destructive master plan of the prince of darkness, set in terminal hostility against the salvific designs of God.[21] Just as in the ongoing preaching of the gospel the mystery of Christ is being manifested (see Chapter Eight above), so also the evil mystery is working itself out. It will ultimately be personified in the revelation of the antichrist,[22] and in this figure in turn the counsels of Satan will be overcome at the final confrontation (2:8).

---

1 Cor 15:51 etc.; "Christ/Gospel": Paul's abstracting, inclusive use of mystery for God's plan of salvation in Christ (incl. the incorporation of the Gentiles); "Lawlessness": 2 Thes 2:7, but similarly Jewish parallels.

[20] Furfey, "Mystery", 189; and Bruce 170 also note the formal antithesis between the μυστήριον τῆς ἀνομίας here and the τῆς εὐσέβειας μυστήριον in 1 Tim 3:16.

[21] Cf. Furfey, "Mystery", 189: "Satan's malign plan to frustrate as far as possible the redemptive work of Christ."

[22] Indeed the implication may be that the antichrist himself is already secretly present, but still to be publicly manifested: cf. 1 John 4:3; also John 1:31; 7:3 f., and the hidden Messiah motif in Rabbinic literature.

2. Ephesians

We will now deal in rather more cursory fashion with some relevant material which, if not authentic, nevertheless in many ways continues Pauline perspectives and emphases. This will include Ephesians (including special reference to the doxology of Romans 16:25—27) and the Pastoral Epistles. The chapter then concludes with a sampling of the earliest Fathers, with one or two interesting observations about the Patristic reception of Paul's thought about revealed mysteries.

The theology of the mystery and revelation in Ephesians differs from Colossians in its further reduced interest in eschatology, and in its increased ecclesiological emphasis. The term μυστήριον occurs only in the singular, in the abstracted sense corresponding to Paul's "mystery of Christ" etc.[23] Without treating the relevant passages in detail, the following remarks will be in order.

2.1. Eph 1:9 f.

Eph 1:9 explicitly places the mystery revealed to the apostle[24] in relation to God's will (θέλημα: v. 5, 9, 11), purpose (πρόθεσις: 1:11; N. B. cf. 3:11), counsel (βουλή: 1:11) and good pleasure (εὐδοκία: 1:5, 9).[25] We expect therefore to find once again a salvation historical orientation of the mystery. While the familiar elements of such a perspective are indeed present, a more cosmic and universal dimension is introduced in 1:9 f.[26] The mystery of God's will is this: that His intention for the fullness of the times has been to gather up everything (ἀνακεφαλαιώσασθαι) in Christ — i.e. to subject the cosmos (v. 10b) under his sovereignty (cf. 1:21 f.; 4:10; cf. Col 1:19 f.).[27] This formulation of the central mystery is equally eschatological in intent, for the ἀνακεφαλαίωσις of all the cosmos in Christ is specifically linked with the fullness of the times.[28] R. E. Brown writes,

---

[23] The only exception is 5:32, on which see below.

[24] ἡμεῖς might seem in light of 1:3—8 to extend to all Christians, but v. 12 at least suggests it may be otherwise. Eph 3:3 ff., at any rate, shows that the apostles are in view.

[25] Cf. רזי חפצו in 1 QH fr. 3:7.; also רזי ערמתו in 1 QpHab 7:14. The often quoted parallel Jdt 2:2 (καὶ ἔθετο μετ' αὐτῶν τὸ μυστήριον τῆς βουλῆς αὐτοῦ) should not be adduced here (*pace* e.g. Penna, *Mysterion*, 54 n. 90), since it speaks of a secret *human* counsel and is equivalent to סוד rather than רז, rather like 2 Macc 13:21; Tob 12:7 (cf. further ψ 24:14 θ';/Quinta; Prov 11:13 σ' 20:19 θ'; in all likelihood Sir 22:22; 27:16—21).

[26] Cf. Gnilka 79; also Lincoln, *Paradise*, 144.

[27] Similarly Mussner, "Contributions", 162; Caragounis, *Mysterion*, 117; Penna, *Mysterion*, 60; Brown, *Mystery*, 59 f.; Bieder, "Geheimnis", 342.

[28] It is difficult to know to what extent the ἀνακεφαλαίωσις is still to be implemented; see 1:21b, and cf. 3:10; also 4:27 (the devil still schemes against believers) 5:16b (the

... The mystery of the divine will in Eph. 1:9—10 is a picture of the final stage of the divine *oikonomia*: the fullness of time wherein men on earth and the angels are all subject to Christ. From the eternal point of view, this mystery of complete subjection to Christ exists already, for Christ has come and evil is vanquished; from the temporal view, the Christians are locked in struggle with the forces of evil to bring about the perfect headship of Christ.[29]

Without addressing in full the difficult problems of this passage, we may say that the "mystery of God's will" corresponds well with the (equally eschatological) "abstract" use of mystery encountered in Paul. And as Penna rightly notes,[30] the instrumentality of the cross in this context continues to be maintained (1:6b —7). However, the notion of a universal, *cosmic* encompassment in Christ, while not entirely alien to Pauline theology (1 Cor 15:28; Col 1:15—20, etc.) has not hitherto been a part of the Pauline μυστήριον.[31]

2.2. Eph 1:17—19

Another apparent departure from the pattern encountered earlier follows in 1:17—19: the author expresses his prayer that God will give the readers the (or a) "spirit of wisdom and revelation in the knowledge [ἐπίγνωσις: cf. Col 2:2] of Him". This is achieved by enlightening their moral vision (τοὺς ὀφθαλμοὺς τῆς καρδίας) and thus enabling them to understand the content of their hope, the glory of their inheritance, and the power of God towards believers. Schnackenburg distinguishes this, perhaps rightly, from the revelation of the mystery in 3:3 ff.;[32] and certainly this revelation cannot be interpreted as in any way replacing or duplicating that granted to the apostles.[33] But whatever one may think on this issue, it seems clear that here the intended recipients of ἀποκάλυψις on the subject of the heavenly inheritance are *all* Christians, rather than merely apostles and prophets. This would appear to go one step beyond the Pauline letters.

---

days are evil). Barth 355 considers that "the 'days of fulfillment' (1:10) are not just the end of time but the extended end- time in which the church lives."

[29] Brown, *Mystery*, 59 f.; cf. Penna, *Mysterion*, 55. For the future dimension cf. also 2:7.

[30] Penna, *Mysterion*, 61.

[31] Another interesting innovation is the explicitly doxological intention of the saving purpose of God, v. 11 f. This is no more than implicit in Paul, though it recurs in Rom 16:25—27.

[32] Schnackenburg 73; Merklein, Amt, 186 and n. 158. Contrast Abbott 28.

[33] Robinson 39 puts it nicely: a mystery once revealed becomes in a sense an "open secret". "But it is no less true that the Christian 'mystery' demands for its unveiling the perpetual intervention of the 'Spirit of apocalypse'."

[If on the other hand, as Schlier suggests, the ἀποκάλυψις in view is the charisma mentioned in 1 Cor 14:6, 26, 30,[34] then the closest parallel to Paul's prayer may be 1 Cor 14:1, 5, 24; and cf. Phil 3:15. However, this hypothesis is impossible to verify. Cerfaux has argued, perhaps rather more felicitously, that what this "spirit of wisdom and revelation" mediates is in fact knowledge and understanding of the mystery (1:18−23; cf. 3:14−19), and not necessarily revelation *per se*.[35] Nevertheless, whether such "mystical"[36] activity of the Spirit can be ultimately distinguished from ἀποκάλυψις proper remains to be shown.]

2.3. Eph 3:3−10

In chapter 3 we are initially on more familiar ground: Paul is a steward of God's grace to the Ephesians (3:2) and has received his knowledge (σύνεσις) of the central mystery of God by (κατά[37]) revelation.[38] This mystery's previous hiddenness from mankind and recent revelation to apostles and prophets (3:5)[39] is also familiar (in broad outline) from 1 Cor 2:7−10; Col 1:26, and compatible with Paul's general view of revelation − though the ambivalence of Col 1:26 τοῖς ἁγίοις αὐτοῦ has here been replaced by the unmistakable "holy apostles and prophets".[40] That its revelation must be ἐν πνεύματι comes as no surprise after 1 Cor 2:10.[41]

---

[34] Schlier 78 f. He also speaks of the "Geist der Inspiration" (seconded by Merklein, *Amt*, 220).

[35] Cerfaux, *Christian*, 507.

[36] Thus Cerfaux, *Christian*, 511 f.

[37] N.B. indicating not means but *mode* of the disclosure. See Schlier 148; Merklein, *Amt*, 198; Caragounis, *Mysterion*, 99.

[38] Cf. e.g. Ezek 28:3 f.; Dan 1:17; 2:21 f. (in context); 10:1 ϑ'; 1 QH 2:13; 12:13, 20; 1 QS 9:18; etc. for knowledge/understanding in the mysteries. See also Brown, *Mystery*, 61. There is no need to regard this as an un-Pauline redactional insertion (*pace* e.g. Merklein, *Amt*, 217 f.): 1 Cor 2:10−16 speaks in very similar terms. And while it is true that Eph/Col tend to multiply terms of knowledge in relation to the μυστήριον, the evidence of the DSS and other early Jewish texts assures us that it would be wrong to drive a wedge between "apocalyptic" and "epistemic" language about mysteries (*pace* e.g. Cerfaux, *Christian*, 474, who is disturbed by the presence in the captivity epistles of apocalyptic language alongside the preference for 'knowledge' over eschatology).

[39] N.B. ὡς νῦν should not be read comparatively, *pace* Caragounis, 102 f. and n. 24. The point is not one of degrees of revelation.

[40] This special antithesis ("hidden from the sons of men" − "now revealed to His holy apostles and prophets") is unparalleled in its emphasis on the apostolic recipients/mediators of the revelation, as Merklein, *Amt*, 167−70 argues.

[41] N.B. Merklein, *Amt*, 189 wishes to take ἐν πνεύματι only with καὶ προφήταις. This would seem to be quite unlikely, since an appeal to the spirit is only to be expected in the context.

However, v. 6 brings to completion a certain "gentilizing" and ecclesiological trend in the development of the Pauline "mystery of God". While Paul always confesses that his mission is especially a mission to the Gentiles (Gal 2:9), the respective reception of the gospel and of salvation in Christ by both Jews and Gentiles is at first only one aspect of the comprehensive use of μυστήριον (Rom 11:25–27). By the time of Col 1:26f. the idea of the Messiah preached among Gentiles is beginning substantially to overlap with the broader mystery of the gospel (and/or λόγος τοῦ θεοῦ, 1:25), as we saw. Here in Eph 3:6 the central mystery of Christ is now the fact "that the Gentiles are fellow heirs and fellow members of the body, and fellow partakers of the promise in Christ Jesus through the gospel."[42] This of course is by no means to deny that the salvation of both Gentiles and Jews was a central feature of Paul's gospel from the beginning;[43] but simply to point out that it seems here to have become a fully acceptable *definition* of the "mystery of Christ".[44] Nevertheless, it would not be correct to consider that this notion of the incorporation of the Gentiles is an innovation which in Ephesians completely displaces the more comprehensive idea of the mystery:[45] the latter seems present e.g. in 3:8 τὸ ἀνεξιχνίαστον πλοῦτος τοῦ Χριστοῦ (cf. Rom 11:33); 3:10 ἡ πολυποίκιλος σοφία τοῦ θεοῦ; and 1:9f. (see above). We are merely dealing with a change in emphasis, seconded by a concomitant shift (noted by Kim et al.) in the presentation of the gospel, viz. from a christological (Gal 1:12, 15) to an ecclesiological focus.[46] It is this shift which lends the Ephesian μυστήριον, despite its continuing christological dimension (1:9f.; 3:4), a somewhat unfamiliar look.[47]

The grace of the revelation[48] of this mystery was given to Paul in order that

---

[42] The infinitive εἶναι is epexegetical; cf. Abbott 83; Schlier 151.

[43] See esp. Kim, *Origin,* 59 and passim.

[44] A point also raised by Kamlah, "Untersuchungen", 100. Of course we must allow for the possibility that the incorporation of the Gentiles here stands for the mystery of Christ more as *pars pro toto* than as an actual definition.

[45] *Pace* e.g. Mitton, *Epistle,* 89f.

[46] Kim, *Origin,* 24; cf. 82; further Merklein, *Amt,* 202–209. (The absence of the *theologia crucis* from this context (cf. e.g. Steinmetz, *Heils-Zuversicht,* 107) might be relevant in this respect; but cf. on 1:7 above.) However, Merklein (208f.) also clarifies the "logical connection" between Paul and Eph: Paul's christological gospel has a *missiological* intent, while the Ephesian *ecclesiological* emphasis is still fundamentally centred in christology. Merklein sees the ecclesiological "mystery" of Eph 3 as the interpretation, on the basis of Col 1:26f., of the christological "gospel" of Gal 1.

[47] But whether this makes for a mystery "of a more Hellenistic type" (Knox, *Gentiles,* 190) I am not certain. Merklein, *Amt,* 214 and n. 316 is right to point out that at Qumran the closest parallel to the eschatological *community* as a "mystery" is in the use of סוד. And of course the function of סוד is not primarily *heilsgeschichtlich* (a fact not noted by Merklein). Nevertheless, the eschatological manifestation of the Messiah and his community does appear e.g. in 1 En 38:1; 53:6; and cf. Rom 8:19; Col 3:4; 1 John 3:2.

[48] Merklein, *Amt,* 181, 189 supposes a basic difference between the specifically *aposto-*

he should preach it to the Gentiles (3:8). His task is to shed light on (φωτίσαι)[49] the administration (οἰκονομία) of the mystery, hidden since eternity in God who created heaven and earth (cf. 1:9 f.).[50]

Expressed in this mystery is the multi-faceted (πολυποίκιλος) wisdom of God (v. 10b; surely an indication that the writer still recognizes various specific *aspects* of the abstract mystery).[51] The purpose (ἵνα, v. 10a) of Paul's enlightening preaching, however — and herein lies one of the novelties of Ephesians — is that this rich wisdom should now be made known through the church to the heavenly powers.[52] *Pace* certain commentators,[53] there is here no hint that the church is itself the central mystery.[54] However, as the visible evidence of the mystery of Gentile incorporation into the Messianic community it is well suited to serve as a manifestation of God's inscrutable saving wisdom to the hitherto ignorant angelic powers.[55] God uses the church as an instrument (διά) of revelation to the spiritual "rulers", i.e. presumably the heavenly forces and their earthly (political, cf. on 1 Cor 2:8 above) counterparts.[56] The church functions as the visible testimony to God's wisdom victorious over "all things in heaven and on earth".[57] Her role in God's disclosure of the mystery to the powers would seem to be primarily understood as that of acclamation: viz., the acclamation of His wisdom in the universal ἀνακεφαλαίωσις (1:9; cf. 1:21; 4:10) accomplished in Christ (cf. also Rev. 4:11; 5:9, 10, 12; etc.).

---

lic revelation here and the open manifestation to the saints in Col 1:26. But much depends on one's reading of ἁγίοις in Col 1:26 (see above).

[49] Here probably not in a properly revelatory sense (*pace* Barth 342; Lona, *Eschatologie*, 279, 281 on 3:3, 8) but in that of "publish, shed light on, bring to light", as in 1 Cor 4:5 (cf. Psa 90:8); but cf. also Eph 1:18 (N.B. pass.). This of course is not to deny the claim of a revelatory function for Paul's ministry, which was amply demonstrated above.

[50] According to Gnilka 173 this reference to creation stresses that God also has the wherewithal to implement His mystery. Cf. also the theological function of "cosmological" mysteries in apocalyptic literature; and Eph 1:10; Col 1:16.

[51] Cf. Penna, *Mysterion*, 53: "cosa assai variegata".

[52] Perhaps both good *and* evil angels are intended, with Bengel, *Gnomon*, 750; Bruce 321 n. 68; *pace* Schlier 155 et al. Hiddenness of the mystery from angelic powers is a motif encountered earlier.

[53] E.g. Schlier 157; idem, "Kirche", 307 and passim; Schnackenburg 142. Gnilka 174 comes a little closer when he sees the church as the *realized* mystery of Christ (see below).

[54] So rightly Barth 356.

[55] The divine passive γνωρίσθη shows that the church is not itself an agent of revelation (with Merklein, *Amt*, 214; *pace* some commentators). Barth 356 speaks of the church's "servant role in the public manifestation of God's secret and wisdom."

[56] Barth 365 describes the church's "assignment among intangible powers that make their spiritual dominion felt from their 'heavenly' places." In a graphic analogy, Bieder ("Geheimnis", 343) speaks of the responsibility of the saints, as citizens of the kingdom of Christ (2:19; cf. 5:5), to pursue not only its "domestic" but also its "foreign policy".

[57] Cf. Gnilka 175: In the church "hat sich Gottes Weisheit vor dem Forum der kosmischen Mächte durchgesetzt."

2.4. Eph 5:31 f.

Eph 5:8, 11—13 assigns to Christians as "children of light" the function of exposing human sin, bringing to light the secret deeds of darkness.[58] This is a task which in Paul is assigned to Christ (1 Cor 4:5), but also to the prophesying community (1 Cor 14:24 f.).

Of greater significance as a *divine* secret is Eph 5:31, which stands without parallel in the Pauline corpus. Having adduced Gen 2:24 (LXX) to his famous analogy of a husband's love for his wife in Christ's love for the church, the author tersely remarks, τὸ μυστήριον τοῦτο μέγα εστιν· ἐγὼ δὲ λέγω εἰς Χριστὸν καὶ εἰς τὴν ἐκκλησίαν — before moving on almost immediately to another subject. This is not the place to adjudicate between a host of available elucidations of this passage. However, in light of our previous results any explanation concerned with a *cognitive* notion of "mystery" (i.e. something primarily to be "solved" or "understood") is unlikely to be sufficient.[59] Better, but still rather questionable (and imprecise), are suggestions to the effect that μυστήριον here denotes a religious "symbol".[60] Most plausible, and consistent with the practice not only of the New Testament, but also e.g. of Qumran, Philo, and the Rabbis, would seem to be the idea that we are dealing here with an *exegetical* mystery: a deeper (in this case either allegorical or prophetic) meaning of a Scriptural text which has been elicited by means of some form of inspired exegesis.[61] In other words, the deeper meaning of Gen 2:24 points typologically to Christ and the church. This idea is familiar and closely related to Paul's view of the revelatory value of the Old Testament, as discussed earlier. It may be, as Born-

---

[58] Cf. 4 Q'Amram[e] 9 f.: חשוכא חשיכין להוון [וכל בני] נהירין להוון [כל בני נהורא], etc.

[59] *Pace* Caragounis, *Mysterion*, 30 ("unsearchable and inexplicable"). Similarly the proposal of Harvey ("*Mystery* Language", 326) remains doubtful. He considers that the background is in Hellenistic rather than in Jewish religion; so that "the analogy in question, because of its sexual overtones, was felt to be a dangerous one to use in the company of any but 'initiates'."

[60] Thus e.g. Robinson 209; Hatch, *Essays*, 60 f.; Kennedy, *Paul*, 127; Deden, "Mystère", 411; Steinmetz, *Heils-Zuversicht*, 107; similarly Abbott 175; Schlier 262 f.; Gnilka 288; Schnackenburg 261; Bieder, "Geheimnis", 336. Several speak of the "mystery of the conjugal union": e.g. Westcott 86; de Wette 153; Mitton 207; Coppens, "*Mystery*", 147; also Cambier, "Mystère", 231; and perhaps Lincoln, *Paradise*, 164. Cf. earlier commentators cited in Schlier 262, n. 5. De Wette 153 also [implausibly] cites the use of סוד for marriage in *Yalkut Re'ubeni* 171.4b.

[61] Various forms of this view are held by Zunz, *Vorträge*, 174 n."a)"; Bornkamm, "μυστήριον", 830; Bonsirven, *Exégèse*, 270; Luz, *Geschichtsverständnis*, 287 n. 92; Brown, *Mystery*, 65 f.; Merklein, *Amt*, 215; Mussner, "Contributions", 162 [?]; Sjöberg, *Der verborgene Menschensohn*, 16; Barth 2:641—646; Bruce 394; also TEV; and cf. earlier commentators cited in Schlier 262, n. 4. *Pace* Cambier, "Mystère", 84, 88, who emphatically denies that μυστήριον could ever be so used in Pauline writings: see above on Rom 11:25—27; 1 Cor 15:51.

kamm suggests, that through the application of this exegetical mystery to Christ and the church (5:32b) the central ecclesiological mystery of Ephesians is implicitly reintroduced as well.[62]

2.5. Eph 6:19f.

This reference needs little explanation; once again the apostle's stewardship of the mystery is at stake. The epexegetical genitive μυστήριον τοῦ εὐαγγελίου, albeit hitherto unparalleled, expresses the familiar notion of 1 Cor 2:1; Col 4:3.

Eph 6:19f.	Col 4:3f.
δεήσει . . . ὑπὲρ ἐμοῦ,	προσευχόμενοι . . . περὶ ἡμῶν,
ἵνα μοι δοθῇ λόγος ἐν ἀνοίξει τοῦ στόματός μου	ἵνα ὁ θεὸς ἀνοίξῃ ἡμῖν θύραν τοῦ λόγου
ἐν παρρησίᾳ γνωρίσαι τὸ μυστήριον τοῦ εὐαγγελίου·	λαλῆσαι τὸ μυστήριον τοῦ Χριστοῦ·
ὑπὲρ οὗ πρεσβεύω ἐν ἁλύσει	διὸ καὶ δέδεμαι
ἵνα ἐν αὐτῷ παρρησιάσωμαι, ὡς δεῖ με λαλῆσαι.	ἵνα φανερώσω αὐτό, ὡς δεῖ με λαλῆσαι.

If (as seems plausible) the writer's point of departure parallels Col 4, he has taken slight liberties with the rendering of θύραν τοῦ λόγου; and with the expansion of λαλῆσαι to ἐν παρρησίᾳ γνωρίσαι. The thought introduced by ὑπὲρ οὗ, though a little more ornate, overlaps with that of the parallel: the apostle serves in chains so that in regard to the gospel [ἐν αὐτῷ] he may speak boldly, as indeed he must. If, as was argued earlier, Paul's external bonds and his speaking the gospel are in some way related in Col 4:3, a similar idea may be present here. The apostle is "an ambassador in chains" (a jolting image on any reckoning)[63] *in order that* he should speak the gospel boldly,[64] as he is bound to do. His chains manifest that he is under obligation.

---

[62] Bornkamm, "μυστήριον", 829f.; Merklein, *Amt*, 215. In the absence of more specific arguments Knox's claim (*Gentiles*, 183f.) that this use of μυστήριον derives (in any real sense) from the Hellenistic cults is less than convincing. However, in the light of Philo (Chapter 4 above) a link with Hellenistic allegoresis is not implausible.

[63] Westcott 98 calls it an oxymoron; Bengel 765 and Gnilka 319, a paradox. (Barth 2:782 uses both.) Cf. Phlm 9.

[64] Note the double emphasis on παρρησία. Boldness in the word of Christ is a recur-

3. Romans 16:25—27

Since the "revealed mystery" in the concluding doxology of Romans is often compared with that in Ephesians, this may be an appropriate moment to discuss it.

Because of the familiar textual problems, the doxology is today not usually considered to be part of the original epistle. However, in view of the fact that of the major MSS only F and G lack it altogether, discussion on the matter should not perhaps be closed. Its relocation in some texts (to 14:23 or 15:33) may possibly be due to the letter's use in public reading, in which the one or two last chapters were thought to be unsuitable and an appropriate conclusion needed to be supplied.[65] However, Marcionite influence on the textual history also cannot be ruled out.[66] On balance, the author may or may not be Paul: at any rate he shows a thorough familiarity with major motifs of the letter.[67] The issue need not here be firmly resolved.

These verses contain several points of interest:

> according to the revelation of the mystery which has been kept in silence [σεσιγημέ-νου] for eternal ages, but now is manifested; and through prophetic Scriptures, according to the command of the eternal God, has been made known for obedience of faith among all the nations.

No indication of the *content* of the mystery is in fact given. However, the two κατά-clauses in v. 25 closely correlate the eschatological disclosure of the mystery with Paul's preaching of Jesus Christ.[68] While this use of "mystery" is not found in Rom, it was applied earlier in 1 Cor 2:1 (cf. 4:1); moreover, the revelatory effect of the apostolic preaching is affirmed in Rom 1:16—18, as we saw. The use of σεσιγημένος is odd;[69] we might have expected ἀποκεκρυμμένος or

---

rent mark of the early Martyrs' Acts: note esp. παρρησιά[ζομαι] in Eus. *EH* 5.1.18, 49 (Blandina & Alexander of Lyons); 6.3.4 f. (Alexandrians). Cf. Wisd 5:1; 4 Macc 10:5.

[65] Thus perhaps esp. p46; cf. Prümm, "Mystères", 203; Penna, *Mysterion*, 25; Cranfield 1:9 and Wilckens 3:147 also consider a liturgical *Sitz im Leben*. But the question arises why the doxology should not have been placed after 15:13 or 21 rather than 14:23.

[66] See Metzger, *Textual Commentary*, 536.

[67] For a recent, even-handed review of the *status quaestionis* see Hurtado, "Doxology".

[68] Cf. Wilckens 3:149. Cranfield 2:810; Michel 487 and n. 14; and Herold, *Zorn*, 266 regard the second κατά as explaining and supplementing the first.

[69] Indeed its transitive use is *hapax legomenon* in the NT. But cf. Josephus *Vita* 338 ἐρῶ τὰ μέχρι νῦν σεσιωπημένα. For the (cultic?) idea of silence before revelation cf. Job 4:16; 1 Kgs 19:12; Hab 2:20; Zeph 1:7; Zech 2:13; esp. Wisd 18:14—16; Rev 8:1; also EpArist 95; and see below on IgnEph 19:1; Magn 8:2. Wilckens 3:148 f. is right to question those (like Käsemann 407 or Penna, *Mysterion*, 25 n. 31) who appeal to the Jewish notion specifically of silence before *creation* (e.g. 2 Bar 3:7; 4 Ezra 6:38 f.; 7:30; *LAB* 60:2). The point here is *heilsgeschichtlich*. [In mystery religions silence forms an important part of the secret proceedings, as just before the climactic *epopteia*. Cf. Penna, *Mysterion*, 25 n. 32.]

the like. The silence at any rate must surely be *God's* silence of keeping the mystery to himself.[70]

The mystery is here simply described as "manifested" (φανερωθέντος), with no specification of the recipients (contrast 1 Cor 2; Col 1; Eph 3). But this might well be related to the forensic emphasis of Rom 3:21 (see above), where φανερόω is also used. The two steps of the mystery's manifestation and then dissemination through prophetic scriptures are distinguished by the insertion of τε.[71] Interesting for our purposes, however, is that the act of γνωρίζειν for obedience of faith[72] is seen not as an ongoing but a completed action (aorist).[73]

Another significant departure from the accustomed pattern of revealed mysteries consists in the statement that the disclosure of the mystery occurs "through prophetic scriptures".[74] The identity of these writings is debated. On the one hand it is possible that reference is made to Christian scriptures, prominent among which would presumably be the letters of Paul himself (cf. 2 Pet 3:16).[75] But it would seem an odd understanding of the apostolic mission to suppose that the evangelization of the Gentiles had taken place through apostolic *writings* rather than through preaching. However, if (with most commentators) OT prophets are in view, a similar problem besets us[76] — unless διά be taken not instrumentally but as signifying *environment* or related *circumstances*.[77] What is meant in this case, then, is perhaps very similar to the μαρτυρουμένη ὑπὸ τοῦ νόμου καὶ τῶν προφητῶν of Rom 3:21,[78] leaving us with an implicit connection between apostolic preaching and the familiar idea of charismatic exegesis of the prophets.[79] The doxology, therefore, appeals to the notion that the

---

[70] Thus Dewailly, "Mystère", 116. Whether the perfect participle *eo ipso* implies the idea of a continued hiddenness (thus Dewailly 116 f.) must remain doubtful. Certainly πεφανερωμένη in Rom 3:21, taken in context, would seem to refer unequivocally to the past Christ event.

[71] On this see e.g. Cranfield 2:811 f.; Wilckens 3:150 n. 708. For the distinction of these two steps of disclosure (revelation proper; missionary propagation) see also Penna, *Mysterion*, 42.

[72] Cranfield 2:812 and nn. 2, 5: εἰς πάντα τὰ ἔθνη with εἰς ὑπακοὴν πιστεώς, not with γνωρισθέντος.

[73] A fact which, incidentally, may also militate against Pauline authorship (contrast 1:14—18; 15:19, 23 f.; and e.g. 1 Cor 2:13; Col 1:28 f.; 4:3; Eph 6:19).

[74] γραφῶν προφητικῶν: an odd phrase, unique in the NT. The gloss καὶ τῆς ἐπιφανείας κτλ. in Or Hier^{mss} is clearly secondary.

[75] Thus e.g. Lührmann, *Offenbarungsverständnis*, 123 f. (citing also Holtzmann, Godet, Jülicher, and Corssen); Wolters, "Weisheit", 310 f. n. 57; and cf. Wilckens 3:150.

[76] Käsemann 406.

[77] See Moule, *Idiom Book*, 57; cf. Schmidt 264. See esp. Rom 2:27 (τὸν διὰ γράμματος καὶ περιτομῆς παραβάτην νόμου); 4:11; 8:25; 14:20.

[78] Cf. Cranfield 2:812; his instrumental reading of διά compels him to reduce γνωρισθέντος to denote *only* this OT attestation of the gospel, and not the apostolic preaching.

[79] Michel 488 n. 19; Zeller 251; and Penna, *Mysterion*, 43 rightly compare 1 QpHab.

fulfilling revelation of the prophetic mysteries in Christ (cf. Rom 1:2) now renders the OT an attendant witness to the proclamation of the gospel.[80] Without these prophetic Scriptures the mystery could not be properly understood.[81]

Some have suggested that "God's wisdom in a mystery", which Paul in 1 Cor 2:6−10 reserved for the mature, is actually disclosed in Ephesians.[82] Certainly we have found that the texts discussed in this section go further than any others in developing the Pauline theme of Christ and the gospel in relation to God's eternal plan of salvation.

4. Excursus: A "Revelation Schema"?

Taking up a proposal of N. A. Dahl,[83] continental form critics for the last 30 years have followed the convention of grouping together a number of Pauline and Deutero-Pauline texts under the heading of "revelation schema".[84] The popularity of this nomenclature makes a brief discussion advisable.

Although the meaning of the term is really an arbitrary matter of scholarly convention,[85] few writers take the trouble to provide a clear definition. It would seem that the basic constituents of this schema are two aspects of God's saving counsel: the fact that it was "once hidden" and secretly foreordained; and that in Christ it has "now been revealed" or made manifest.[86]

Various authors have nevertheless asserted that the "schema" is not specifically Christological in content.[87] Yet while it is true that the focus is never narrowly or exclusively on the person of Christ, it will be apparent from our earlier treatment that Christology in one way or another is crucial to all the texts

For a more general view on the use of the Scriptures in the apostolic enterprise cf. e.g. 2 Tim 3:14 ff.; 4:13.

[80] Cf. Benedict Justinianus (1613), quoted in del Páramo, "Misterio", 258: "Idem vero mysterium ait esse revelatum per scripturas prophetarum secundum praeceptum aeterni Dei, quo voluit per Apostolos prophetarum oracula explicari, atque adeo mysterium in illis occultum in lucem evocari in eum finem, ut omnes gentes fide Christi percepta, legi evangelicae obtemperent."

[81] Thus Penna, *Mysterion*, 43, citing Baulès.

[82] Schlier 21 f., 156; Bruce 245 f., 321.

[83] Dahl, "Beobachtungen", 4 f.

[84] Also sometimes known as "mystery formula": e.g. Gloege, "Offenbarung", 224; cf. Aune, *Prophecy*, 333; Schulte, *Offenbarung*, 23 and n. 1. The various authors give differing lists of the texts in view, including 1 Cor 2:6−10; Col 1:26 f.; Eph 3:4−7, 8−11; Rom 16:25 f.; and sometimes 2 Tim 1:9−11; Tit 1:2 f.; 1 Pet 1:18−21; 1 John 1:1−3; Ign-Magn 6:1; HermSim 9:12.

[85] Thus rightly Wolter, "Weisheit", 298.

[86] Cf. recently also Wolter, "Weisheit", 298.

[87] E.g. Dahl, "Beobachtungen", 5; Lührmann, *Offenbarungsverständnis*, 131 and passim.

in question.[88] It is generally acknowledged that Jewish eschatology with its doctrine of two eons is basic to an understanding of the "schema", although the actual derivation is a matter of dispute.[89] At the same time, Wolter goes so far as to suggest that the specific Jewish background of the schema gives it an anti-Torah bias in the Pauline context: its intention here is to stress that the wisdom of God's age-old redemptive design was not disclosed in the law and in Israel's election, but only in the gospel and its proclamation among the Gentiles.[90]

The problem with the "revelation schema" ultimately arises from its imprecise definition. In 1 Cor 2 the theme is, as Conzelmann recognized, only *in statu nascendi*.[91] Several components integral to the form of later texts are still missing or not yet fully integrated, such as the strong missionary element[92] or the emphasis on a decisive recent disclosure (see above). The absence of these ingredients would seem to exclude this text from the definitive group of examples of the "schema", and to cast doubt on the idea of the latter as a distinct liturgical formula.[93]

Lührmann[94] defines the formula more precisely (albeit rather arbitrarily) by the presence of νῦν and μυστήριον — thereby reducing the number of relevant texts to three: Col 1:26 f.; Eph 3:4 f., 9 f.; Rom 16:25 f. This appears at first sight to remove some of the difficulties and possibly to strengthen his case that the schema is not Pauline. But he fails to recognize that a *Gattung* of only three texts is not a particularly meaningful proposition; moreover, he ignores differences[95] between the three texts chosen.

The question can be pressed further still. If structural elements fail to give accurate definition to this "schema", one might consider the general *theme* of a once hidden mystery being revealed in Christ or the gospel to be a sufficient description. This would also allow for a continuity of development between Paul and the "Deutero-Pauline" writings. However, a closer look makes it apparent

---

[88] Luz, *Geschichtsverständnis*, 287 f. and n. 94 offers a similar critique of Lührmann. Wolter's view ("Weisheit", 305), that 1 Cor 2:6—10 differs from all the other ("Deutero-Pauline") texts in linking the mystery with the cross, would seem to be untrue at least for Col 1:26 f. (see 1:22, 24).

[89] Though Lührmannn, *Offenbarungsverständnis*, 114, 126—129, 133 f. also sees a gnostic background.

[90] Wolter, "Weisheit", 317.

[91] Conzelmann, *Korinther*, 75; "Weisheit", 239.

[92] Cf. Lührmann, *Offenbarungsverständnis*, 131 f. and passim; also recognized by Penna, *Mysterion*, 34—39; Wolter, "Weisheit", 314, 317.

[93] *Pace* Dahl, "Beobachtungen", 4 f.; Lührmann, *Offenbarungsverständnis*, 133; cf. Kamlah, "Untersuchungen", 101, 121.

[94] *Offenbarungsverständnis*, 124—133.

[95] E.g. content (Rom 16:25 f. the gospel of Jesus Christ; Col 1:26 f. word of God/Christ among you; Eph 3:5 f. the Gentiles are fellow heirs) and recipients (Rom 16:25 f. unspecified; Col 1:26 f. "His saints"; Eph 3:5 apostles and prophets).

that in this case the whole idea of a distinct "schema" collapses under the weight of numerous conceptual parallels both within and without the bounds of the NT.[96] What is more, the theme of a saving divine counsel once hidden but now revealed occurs also in contemporary Judaism, e.g. at Qumran (1QpHab 7:2 ff.) or among the Rabbis.[97]

Thus, more helpful than the forced definition of a distinct form-critical unit will be the recognition that Paul views the Christ event and its revelation to the apostles as the decisive historical[98] implementation of God's hidden, age-old plan of salvation. Other early Christian writers thought similarly. This theme was developed in a number of ways, though obviously the use of motifs like "mystery", fulfilment, revelation, and the turn of the ages would be likely. We are dealing, therefore, not with a clearly defined liturgical "schema", but with recurring traditional terms and phrases used to express the patterns of realized eschatology: revelation, redemption, and fulfilment.

5. The Pastoral Epistles

The writer's use of apocalyptic motifs such as the revelation of heavenly mysteries is on the whole rather muted by his own distinctive interests. [Perhaps he is taking his own advice to avoid Ἰουδαϊκοὶ μύθοι, Tit 1:14?].

1 Tim 3:9 speaks of the need for deacons to hold uprightly to the "mystery of faith" (μυστήριον τῆς πίστεως). This reference in the middle of a passage on church order comes without warning, as it were, i.e. without any of the customary contextual markers indicating a connection with hiddenness, revelation, soteriology, eschatology, or the like. Thus it could be considered doubtful whether this text in fact belongs to our discussion or not.

There are no clear parallels to this use of μυστήριον in the accepted Pauline corpus. Assuming that the genitive is epexegetical and that the same correlation of "faith" and "conscience" is in view in 1:19, the reference may be to the mo-

---

[96] Examples might include Gal 3:23−25; 4:3 f.; 2 Tim 1:9 f.; Tit 1:2 f.; 1 Pet 1:10−12, 20; Heb 9:8, 11, 26; Rev 10:7; Matt 11:25−27; 13:16 f. par.; John 1:1−18; IgnMagn 6:1; EpDiogn 8:9−11; HermSim 9.12.1, etc.

[97] E.g. the idea that the Torah was hidden with God since 974 generations before creation, until its revelation at Sinai (b.Zeb 116a; b.Shab 88b − a view deriving from Psa 105:8 and the 26 generations from Adam to Moses); cf. also AssMos 1:12−14; *Memar Marqah* 6:7 and see Wolter, "Weisheit", 317. Schweizer, *Kolosser*, 87 n. 253 explicitly refers to this idea in relation to the "schema".

[98] *Contra* Lührmann's existential interpretation (*Offenbarungsverständnis*, 125): "Dem Schema geht es also nicht so sehr um die geschichtliche Einordnung der Offenbarung als um die Frage . . .: 'Wie bekomme ich teil am Heilsgut?'" A historical intention of the schema is recognized e.g. by Gloege, "Offenbarung", 224.

ral, spiritual and doctrinal *content* of Christian faith (i.e. *fides quae creditur*).[99] A formal appeal to Jewish background material remains somewhat inconclusive;[100] here at any rate one should consider (with Harvey) the common Hellenistic analogy of a discipline of initiation into the mystery cults.[101] *Prima facie* the only real problem with this latter derivation is that the Hellenistic image occurs almost invariably in the plural, whereas 1 Tim 3:9 employs the singular.

But the nature of the μυστήριον in 1 Tim 3:9 is perhaps not to be resolved in isolation. The closely related v. 16 may shed light: "Undeniably great is the mystery of godliness".[102] Here the content of the mystery is clearer: "He who was manifested in the flesh, was justified in the Spirit; he appeared to angels, was preached among the nations, believed in the world, taken up in glory." Obviously this is not the place for an exegesis and interpretation of this disputed text. However, it is clear that this εὐσεβείας μυστήριον carries a distinctly *christological* definition[103] – and one which, despite its interpretive uncertainties, is expressed in unmistakably Jewish, indeed apocalyptic terms. Although the form and style of 3:16 are unfamiliar in Paul, the conscious connection of the mystery with ὅς[104] ἐφανερώθη κτλ. implies that the writer knew this mystery to be God's saving purpose in the incarnation, exaltation, and proclamation of Christ. In this case the differences with the Pauline *homologoumena* certainly do not vanish,[105] but we are given additional indications that the au-

---

[99] Thus many commentators.

[100] Brown, *Mystery*, 68 refers to 1 En 58:5; we might add for comparison the Rabbinic notion that Israel are "keepers of secrets"; as well as the various features of halakhah which are described as "mysteries of Israel" (Sabbath, Mishnah, circumcision, etc.).

[101] Harvey, "Mystery Language", 332. That such metaphors were widespread and possibly employed even without any conscious connection to the pagan cults, can be seen e.g. from Ps-Phoc 229 (his ethical treatise as δικαιοσύνης μυστήρια); and e.g. Ep-Diogn 4:6; but cf. Josephus *Ap* 2:189.

[102] N. B. Huther 152, 162; Holtz 90; Spicq; 107; Wohlenberg 139; Dibelius/Conzelmann 61; Kelly 89; Hanson 84; W. Metzger, *Christushymnus*, 67 et al. declare the mysteries of these two verses to be synonymous. Towner, "Structure", 167 f. wishes to differentiate: 3:9 refers to the content of faith, whereas 3:16 includes in addition "the manner of life that is tied to it." This observation is shrewd, but it would seem not to detract from the likelihood of a substantial overlap between the two mysteries.

[103] For this point cf. e.g. Huther 162; Spicq 106 f.; Kelly 90; Schlatter 113; Lock 44; W. Metzger, *Christushymnus*, 63 f. Note also the θεοσεβείας μυστήριον in EpDiogn 4:6, which, being taken up in 5:3, 7:1 ff. (cf. Meecham, *Diognetus*, 107), is explained in similar terms: God sent His son.

[104] For the superiority of this reading cf. Metzger, *Textual Commentary*, 641. ὅς has no grammatical antecedent, and so is best understood as an integral part of the quoted liturgical fragment.

[105] E.g. Christ personally is manifested rather than the mystery (cf. 1 John 3:5, 8); no clear reference to the eternal design of God (but cf. 1 Tim 2:6; 4:1?); vindication (N.B. ἐδικαιώθη) in the spirit and ascension in glory (but cf. Rom 1:3 f.; Phil 2:9?).

Most curious is Christ's appearance to "angels" (but cf. Col 2:15; Eph 3:10?), for

thor understood μυστήριον in a sense *akin* to that of Paul.[106] For Paul too could speak of the content and substance of faith, i.e. the gospel, as a mystery (1 Cor 2–1; Col 4:3; cf. Eph 3:4; 6:19).[107] And although we are not told explicitly of the mystery's hiddenness (and subsequent revelation), its content here suggests that this dimension must also be present in the writer's mind.[108] [And if to boot the "mystery of godliness" and the "mystery of faith" are in fact substantially the same, a potential parallel with Paul's view in Gal might arise. For there, too, Paul can use πίστις not only of the subjective exercise but also of the objective form and content of faith, 1:23[109] (cf. perhaps 3:23–25, where πίστις, much like a mystery, is first hidden and then revealed).] By calling the mystery "great" or "profound" (μέγα: cf. Eph 5:32) and linking it with the Christian confession (ὁμολογουμένως),[110] the writer elevates the content of the mystery in this hymn to near credal status.[111]

2 Tim 1:9–11 offers the familiar sounding theme of the divine saving counsel of grace having been foreordained (here indeed even *given*, δοθεῖσαν) before the ages, but now manifested by the Christ event and entrusted to the apostle's

---

which perhaps the closest parallels are AscIsa 10:7–15; IgnTrall 9:1; also cf. the delightful quotation in Poole, *Synopsis*, 4:1052: "Christus nunciantibus Angelis conceptus est, natus cantantibus, tentatus ministrantibus, passus consolantibus, suscitatus apparentibus, assumptus comitantibus & tentantibus." But on purely structural grounds the arguments of Micou ("ὤφθη", 201–205) in favour of ἄγγελοι as *human* messengers cannot simply be dismissed. Of particular significance is the apparent disruption of the chronological order by the reading "angels", and the fact that this interpretation leaves us with the unlikely scenario of a christological hymn lacking any reference to the resurrection (the angels at the empty tomb are an implausible explanation; cf. W. Metzger, *Christushymnus*, 97). And since 1 Tim 3:16 is a hymnic quotation, word statistical arguments against ἄγγελοι as "messengers" are rather precarious; cf. at any rate Matt 11:10 par Mark 1:2/Luke 7:27; Luke 7:24; 9:52; [Acts 12:15?; Gal 4:14?]; Jas 2:25; and often in LXX (e.g. Gen 32:3, 6; Josh 7:22; Judg 7:24; Hag 1:13; Mal 1:1; etc.). Recent work in agreement with Micou includes W. Metzger, *Christushymnus*, 91–101 (esp. 96 f.); Murphy-O'Connor, "Redactional Angels", 178–187; earlier Wohlenberg 142; Seeberg, *Katechismus*, 119 f. and others cited there.

[106] Cf. Brown, *Mystery*, 68 (though he perhaps somewhat overstates the case): "Thus the mystery of religion ... sums up admirably all the aspects of the Pauline *mystérion* already seen in the other epistles."

[107] Cf. Spicq 99.

[108] Cf. Dibelius/Conzelmann 61; Kelly 89; Sjöberg, *Der verborgene Menschensohn*, 28. Spicq 99; Jeremias 22 predicate the same for 3:9.

[109] Cf. Bammel, "Galater 1,23", 108 and n. 1, 111 (though he does not think this signifies content, *fides quae creditur*: 108 and n. 3).

[110] *Hapax legomenon* in NT. The reading ὁμολογοῦμεν ὡς (D* 1175 syr.lect.; cf. Wohlenberg 138 f.; Spicq 107; Lewis, "1 Timothy iii.16", 80 f.) could theoretically underlie all uncial MSS. (The only reason why the separation is *obvious* in D* is that, as Tischendorf, *NTG* 1:849 writes, "haec enim sticho seiuncta sunt".) Hanson, "Phrase", 123 n. 1 calls this reading "obviously inferior", but I fail to see why this need be so.

[111] Cf. Spicq 107 f.; Dibelius/Conzelmann 61.

dissemination. Here too a number of phrases and ideas are not paralleled in the *Hauptbriefe* (ἐπιφάνεια; the incarnate Christ as σωτήρ; v. 10b Christ's work as "bringing to light life and immortality through the gospel", etc.). Other aspects of the customary "revealed μυστήριον" idea may be missing or not clearly stated (e.g. its previous hiddenness, the role of the cross). But overall the outline of the Pauline view of the revealed saving design of God is still visible.[112]

Another passage on the revelation of God's ancient salvific design is found in Tit 1:2 f. The phraseology and structure of these verses are in some ways closer to Pauline diction than other relevant passages in the Pastoral Epistles:

> in the hope of eternal life, which God, who cannot deceive, promised before eternal ages (πρὸ χρόνων αἰωνίων) and manifested at the proper time (ἐφανέρωσεν δὲ καιροῖς ἰδίοις),[113] [viz.] His word expressed in proclamation, with which I was entrusted on the order of God our Saviour.

The identification of the *object* hidden and revealed (hope of eternal life, word of God) is unusual but not without parallel (see esp. Col 1:27 – λόγος τοῦ θεοῦ, ἔλπις; cf. Eph 1:18).[114] The decisive revelation of God's purpose is here, as often in Paul, expressly linked with the apostolic office of proclamation; indeed the apposition τὸν λόγον αὐτοῦ ἐν κηρύγματι would appear to *include* Paul's appointed task of preaching the gospel in the very manifestation of the foreordained "hope of eternal life". This rather daring claim is, nevertheless, sufficiently underwritten in Paul's own views on revelation.[115]

Other references to our theme in the Pastorals are only marginally relevant. Thus 2 Tim 4:8 speaks of Paul's crown of righteousness stored up in heaven – a motif familiar from apocalyptic thought (cf. also Rev 22:12 with Isa 40:10; 62:11).[116] Another example might be the statement in Tit 2:11–13; 3:4 on the past "epiphany" of the saving grace of God for all people, and on the future "epiphany" in glory of "the great God and our Saviour Christ Jesus."

---

[112] Of course one might legitimately ask in what sense this is any more "Pauline" than, say, 1 Pet 1:20. See also above on the transferability and unspecificity of the "revelation schema".

[113] A comma should be inserted after ἰδίοις, τὸν λόγον being epexegetical. Cf. Lock 126.

[114] Contrast Col 1:5, where hope is stored up but has not yet been manifested; also Rom 8:24 f.

[115] See above. The various similarities lead Kamlah, "Untersuchungen", 128–130 to consider 2 Tim 1:9 f.; 4:17 f. and Tit 1:1–3 to be *dependent* on Rom 16:25 f., and possibly by the same author.

[116] Hanson 156, citing Dibelius/Conzelmann and Brox, asserts the blatantly un-Pauline character of this idea. But Paul himself clearly speaks in prize/reward language in 1 Cor 9:25; Phil 3:12–14. Cf. further Isa 28:5; Ezek 28:12 LXX; Wisd 5:16; 1 Pet 5:4; Jas 1:12; Rev 2:10; 3:11; TBenj 4:1; AscIsa 7:22; 9:24–26; OdSol 9:8–11; 1 QH 4:7; 9:25; b.Ber 17a [Rab T6]. Regarding "all who love his appearing" see on 1 Cor 2:9 above.

On the whole, then, while the stylistic and conceptual character of the Pastoral Epistles tends to differ from the accepted letters of Paul, various aspects of the apostle's treatment of the "revealed mystery" theme survive intact. Chief among these is the notion that in Christ God's saving purpose has been manifested, and that Paul's divinely appointed ministry is instrumental in its proclamation.

6. The Second Century

The field here is vast; and in light of the topic's importance in early Judaism and Paul it most certainly merits a full-scale treatment in its own right.[117] Here I can offer no more than a superficial "spot check" of some of the writings whose date and/or content might be considered to follow most closely upon the period of the New Testament. My selection is based largely on the criteria of both an early date and an explicit development of the theme at hand; the texts discussed are (in this order) the Didache, Ignatius of Antioch, Justin Martyr, and the Epistle to Diognetus.

6.1. The Didache

Suggested dates for this early Syrian church order range from the middle of the first to the middle of the second century. Only one passage here is potentially of interest to us, viz. Did 11:11. Pending some significant new discoveries, however, the interpretation of the notoriously obscure phrase μυστήριον κοσμικὸν ἐκκλησίας is bound to remain pure guesswork. Suggestions have ranged from references to celibacy or spiritual cohabitation between an ascetic and a virgin (syzygy speculation)[118] to a dubious prophetic practice or teaching.[119]

The context (11:7–12) concerns the distinction between true and false prophets. The one who teaches [διδάσκειν] truth but does not practise [ποιεῖν] it

---

[117] Items of interest include the Apocalypse of Paul, *Epistula Apostolorum; Passio Perpetuae;* the teaching of Elchasai (cf. most recently Luttikhuizen, *The Revelation of Elchasai;* N.B. "Elchasai" = חיל כסי [p. 181 f.]); the Nag Hammadi Library [cf. only the numerous entries in Siegert, *Register* under *OYôNH* (pp. 123–126); *HôP* (p. 166 f.); *QôLP* (p. 192); *mystérion* (p. 273); *sigé* (p. 300); also *apokalypsis* etc. (p. 216); *apokryphon* (p. 217); *phaneroun* etc. (p. 318)]; the Hermetic Writings; Mandaean texts; also Tertullian and Clement of Alexandria; etc.

[118] So Harnack, *Lehre,* 121 f.; also cf. Kraft 171; Aune, *Prophecy,* 413 n. 214, 429 n. 96; and see others cited in Draper, "Commentary", 247. For this idea, an appeal is sometimes made to Eph 5:22–32.

[119] Thus Lake in *Apostolic Fathers,* 1:327 n. 2; Broek-Utne, "Did. 11/11", 577–81 (with a criticism of Harnack); Draper, "Commentary", 248.

accordingly is rejected. But the judgement of a *genuine* prophet who enacts [ποιεῖν εἰς] "the mystery", but does not teach [διδάσκειν] others to practise [ποιεῖν] it, is to be left up to God — "for thus also did the prophets of old". Thus it would seem that the "mystery" must be something which this Christian prophet shares with the OT prophets (despite Hosea this connection would seem to rule out the idea of spiritual cohabitation),[120] but which is not freely accessible to the church at large. The participial clause μὴ διδάσκων δὲ ποιεῖν could be understood in either a modal (concessive: "without teaching") or a conditional sense ("if he does not teach").[121]

Given our ignorance of the historical setting, we may not be able to say more than that the text has in view the privileged esoteric action of a prophet which must not be impugned.[122]

6.2. Ignatius of Antioch

Ignatius, Bishop of Antioch (d. c.110), stands in many ways close to Paul in his understanding of the Gospel.[123] He also claims to have special knowledge of the heavenly world. Writing to the Trallians (5:1 f.), he affirms his own insight and knowledge of celestial mysteries, fearing all the while that his readers are not mature enough to digest such matters:

---

[120] Broek-Utne, "Did. 11/11", 577 f. observes, moreover, that this practice (or celibacy, for that matter) would not likely have been the special prerogative of prophets.

[121] The apparent contrast between ποιῶν κτλ. and διδάσκων κτλ. would seem to commend the concessive reading; but this need not affect the significance of the "mystery".

[122] The reference might be an action (perhaps mystical?) which demonstrates that prophet has access to the counsel and the mysteries of God, as did the prophets of old; cf. Amos 3:7 (N.B. סוד: Aquila ἀπόρρητον); 1 QpHab 7:5; also Num 12:8 [LXX], etc. [If, moreover, a Hebrew רז של העולם or Aramaic/Syriac רזא דעלמא were to stand behind μυστήριον κοσμικόν, the passage might well refer to a mystery of the world to come.] That the specific privilege of the prophets in this context might consist in the knowledge of eschatological mysteries was already suggested by Broek-Utne, "Did 11/11", 579 f. The particular *action* of the prophet could be, as Broek-Utne suggests, unusual decisions such as a sudden journey (Acts 11:27 f.; 21:10 f.) or request for money (Acts 1:27 f.; cf. Did 11:12), which cannot be suggested to others; or it could be a specific secret mystical practice, such as those known from the Rabbis or *Hekhalot* literature.

A parallel (to my knowledge hitherto unnoted) to the use of ποιέω with μυστήριον is in Sir 8:18 (Hebrew): "Do not do before a stranger what is to be kept secret (אל תעש רז לפני זר), for you do not know how it will turn out (מה ילד ספו)." An admittedly more far-fetched (and enigmatic) parallel might be the later Rabbinic idea of "working in the mystery of the world" (עוסק ברזו של עולם = ποιῶν ἐν μυστηρίῳ κοσμικῷ?). In its context (b. Sanh 42a etc.) this expression is a possible reference to judging. Prophets as judges in the eschatological age are mentioned e.g. in SibOr 1:782.

[123] Carr, *Angels*, 136, 142; cf. Bultmann, "Ignatius", 37–51.

Surely I am not unable to write you of heavenly things? But I am afraid lest I harm you who are infants. Pardon me, lest you be choked by what you cannot bear. For I myself, although I am bound and can understand the heavenly things and the angelic places and the archontic formations, not for this I am already a disciple.

Not unlike Paul in 1 Cor 2:6; 3:1 f. (or for that matter the Rabbis),[124] Ignatius believes that a disclosure of heavenly knowledge to his readership at large might be detrimental, since they are not mature enough to cope with it.[125] In his opinion, true Christian discipleship does not at any rate depend on the initiation into esoteric knowledge, but rather on an exemplary lifestyle of meekness, faith, and love (IgnTrall 8:1 f.).[126] But at the same time Ignatius knows himself to be a prophet with knowledge of heavenly mysteries.[127]

Perhaps the best known "mystery" passage in Ignatius is IgnEph 19:1 (another confirmation of his self-estimation as a charismatic):[128] "The virginity of Mary, and her giving birth, as well as the death of the Lord, eluded the Ruler of this world: three mysteries of a cry, which were accomplished in the stillness of God." The term μυστήριον is here used of three individual aspects of God's eternal design in Christ (cf. 19:2; 18:2)[129] — but interestingly the stress lies less on their revelation than on their concealment.[130] The fact that these items are linked with the idea of "mystery"[131] is *eo ipso* less surprising: we know from 1 Cor 2:8 that the cross as an important element of "God's wisdom in a mystery" eluded the rulers of this world;[132] and in AscIsa 11:16 the virgin birth is

---

[124] Schoedel 144 n. 7 thinks the imagery is Hellenistic, and cites references to this effect. But the metaphor of not giving a child adult's food would seem rather to be a commonplace of any culture. Given Ignatius's largely Biblical and Pauline treatment of the mystery motif (so also Nock, "Hellenistic Mysteries", 813), citation of Paul is certainly in order. Carr, *Angels*, 138 affirms that the passage is "consciously modelled upon Paul."

[125] The exception seems to be Polycarp, who is actually enouraged (IgnPol 2:2) to "pray that the invisible things may be revealed to you [τὰ δὲ ἀόρατα αἰτεῖ ἵνα σοι φανερώθη], that you may lack nothing and abound in every gift."

[126] The situation which Ignatius envisions (N.B. 8:1) at Tralles differs somewhat from that at Corinth, in that the Trallians are clearly threatened by docetic opponents who neglect the incarnate Christ in favour of esoteric pursuits (cf. chs. 6—10).

[127] Cf. also IgnEph 20:1 f.; IgnPhld 7:1 f.; IgnSmyr 5:1 f.; cf. further Aune, *Prophecy*, 291—296; and esp. Schlier, *Untersuchungen*, 140—152.

[128] Indeed Cerfaux, *Christian*, 53 considers that the reference to mysteries and the whole style of the passage "indicate heavenly vision which has become doctrine".

[129] Cf. Bauer/Paulsen 44 (the μυστήρια consist of the christological *Heilsdaten*).

[130] Note, however, the significance of κραυγή in this regard (cf. Bauer/Paulsen 44).

[131] But note the absence in this passage of a central notion of "the mystery" (of faith or the like). The virgin birth as μυστήριον occurs also in Justin, *Dial* 43.

[132] Lightfoot 2:78 thinks that the clear reference to 1 Cor 1:20 in 18:1 implies here a specific allusion to 1 Cor 2:8; cf. also Bauer/Paulsen 44.

spoken of in similar terms. But the paradox is that the three self-interpreting[133] "mysteries of a cry" were wrought as God kept silent, ἐν ἡσυχίᾳ θεοῦ.[134]

If these "mysteries" were implemented in the stillness of God, how then was Christ *publicly* manifested to the world (and the powers)? IgnEph 19:2 provides Ignatius's answer: by his heavenly appearance. The αἰῶνες here may[135] or may not[136] be the astral/demonic powers allied with the Ruler of this world; but the revelation of Christ is given to them by the manifestation in heaven of his unspeakable light.[137] The historical incarnation of Christ (cf. 19:3 θεοῦ ἀνθρωπίνως φανερουμένου), then, eluded the evil powers and was only revealed to them by the glory of its manifestation in heaven.[138] The decisive cosmic revelation is here not an earthly but a heavenly event.

At the same time, the incarnation or "going forth" (προέρχομαι)[139] of Jesus

---

[133] They are seemingly unaccompanied by a *word* of revelation. Lightfoot 2:76 renders the genitive κραυγῆς "though destined to be proclaimed aloud"; cf. p. 80, "κραυγή is the correlative to ἡσυχία, as revelation is to mystery". Similarly Schoedel 91 ("The unheralded events of salvation cry out their meaning to those who are able to grasp their significance"). *Pace* Daube ("τρία μυστήρια", 128 f.; similarly Grant 50), who somewhat implausibly tries to link each item with a cry uttered by Elizabeth, Mary's midwife, and Jesus, respectively. Note the explicit *absence* of a midwife in AscIsa 11:14; OdSol 19:9; etc., in the context of the early tradition of the miraculous birth of Jesus; cf. Danilou, *Jewish Christianity*, 214–216.

[134] Ignatius's notion of God's stillness or silence (Bauer/Paulsen 43: a "characteristic of the divine sphere") gives an interesting hue to his idea of revelation. Thus he writes (IgnMagn 8:2), "There is one God, who manifested himself [ἐφανέρωσεν ἑαυτόν] through Jesus Christ his son, who is his word proceeding from silence [αὐτοῦ λόγος ἀπὸ σιγῆς προελθών]." Schoedel 120 f.; Grant 62 et al. deny the need to appeal to Gnostic categories: the parallel with Wisd 18:14–16 can just as easily support a Jewish derivation. We might further point out the popular Biblical and Jewish idea of a cosmic silence preceding a theophany: see e.g. Hab 2:20; Zeph 1:7; Zech 2:13; Rev 8:1; also ExodR 29:9. Ignatius speaks also of the stillness of the earthly Jesus, IgnEph 15:1 f.; cf. the Messianic secret in the Synoptics and in John (e.g. Matt 26:63par Mark 14:61; 27:12, 14; John 19:9); also 1 Pet 2:23; Isa 42:2; 53:7. Bartsch's denial (*Gnostisches Gut*, 54 [ff.]) of any concrete Jesus tradition behind Ignatius's statement lacks persuasiveness.

[135] E.g. Lightfoot 2:80; Schlier, *Untersuchungen*, 28; Schoedel 91 and n. 24; Daniélou, *Jewish Christianity*, 221–224.

[136] E.g. Grant 50.

[137] Lightfoot 2:80 f.; Bartsch, *Gnostisches Gut*, 151, 153 f.; Grant 51; and Schoedel 92 see the "star" of 19:2 as alluding specifically to the star of Bethlehem. Be that as it may – a higher, symbolic meaning of this star must clearly also be intended: this is not simply the star of Matt 2 (though Matt doubtless also allegorizes the astrological meaning, 2:9b; cf. Num 24:17?). Cf. Lightfoot 2:82: "the symbol and the thing symbolized might be blended together".

[138] N.B. a glorious manifestation in heaven which, unlike Phil 2:9; 1 Tim 3:16; [Eph 3:10]; AscIsa 11:23–32; TBenj 9:5; Justin *Dial* 36:5 f., is linked with the nativity/epiphany rather than with the resurrection/ascension of Christ. See also the previous note.

[139] IgnMagn 7:2; 8:2. For a similar idea see already John 8:42; 13:3; 16:27 f.; 17:8, but with ἐξέρχομαι; cf. Schlier, *Untersuchungen*, 35.

is crucial also for the revelation of God's mysteries; He was from eternity with
the Father and was manifested (IgnMagn 6:1). Not only is Christ the λόγος and
self-manifestation of God proceeding out of silence, but He is also the only one
to whom the secrets of God have been entrusted (ὃς μόνος πεπίστευται τὰ
κρυπτὰ τοῦ θεοῦ, Phld. 9:1).[140]

6.3. Justin Martyr

With this early Christian apologist (d. c.160) we encounter an author whose
knowledge and use of the motif of "mysteries" would again merit an independent study — if only for the frequency with which the term μυστήριον occurs
(more than 50 ×). The following remarks can be no more than prolegomena to
such a study.

Justin essentially follows and develops the use of "mystery" found in Philo.
Its broad definition is that of a symbol or (exegetical) allegory; indeed it has
been pointed out that μυστήριον functions synonymously with words such as
παραβολή, σύμβολον, or τύπος.[141] In the plural it can regularly designate
pagan mystery rites.[142] But in the singular its most significant reference is either
to Old Testament typologies (often with reference to a particular text, as in
Philo's allegoresis), or to the saving events and realities of Christianity (the an-
titypes, as it were). Examples of the former are the flood (cf. already 1 Pet
3:20 f.); the sawing asunder of Isaiah with a wooden saw;[143] the linking of God's
blessings for Jacob with the horns [*sic*] of a unicorn (Deut 33:17LXX, as a type
of the cross); or similarly of the outstretched arms of Moses in Exod 17; etc.[144]
The latter use applies e.g. to the sonship of the crucified Christ; to the symbol
of Christ as a lamb; to the idea of regeneration; or generally to the "mystery of
salvation".[145]

In a sense, therefore, the non-cultic uses of μυστήριον in Justin could be summarized as referring broadly to the allegorical (i.e. Christian) meaning of various Old Testament motifs. In a particularly clear passage (*Dial* 44) Justin
spells this out. Trypho is told that the blessings of the Old Testament will not

---

[140] Cf. EpDiogn 8:9. This combination of ideas (Christ, silence, revelation of mysteries) occurs also in Rom 16:26 and later in Gnostic writings, esp. *Trimorphic Protennoia*,
XIII 37:4—30 (*NHL*, p. 463); and cf. Schlier, *Untersuchungen*, 41 f.

[141] Hamilton, "Church", 484; earlier Bornkamm, "μυστήριον", 832; von Soden,
"ΜΥΣΤΗΡΙΟΝ", 202.

[142] E.g. *Apol* 1:25, 27, 54, 66; *Apol* 2:12.

[143] For this popular legend see Heb 11:37 and esp. AscIsa 5:1, 13; 11:41; VitProph 1:1;
b. Yeb 49b; y. Sanh 10, 28c.43 ff.

[144] See e.g. *Dial* 40, 91, 111, 120, 138, 139, etc.

[145] *Apol* 1:13; *Dial* 40, 74, 85, etc.

be inherited by the Jews simply by virtue of being the descendants of Abraham; they are rather dependent on a *faith* akin to that of Abraham, i.e. one which akknowledges Scripture's mysteries (typological meanings). Indeed all those commandments not specifically laid down for righteous living were in fact spoken ἢ εἰς μυστήριον τοῦ Χριστοῦ ἢ διὰ τὸ σκληροκάρδιον τοῦ λάου ὑμῶν, "either in relation to the mystery of Christ or on account of your people's hardness of heart." Elsewhere he affirms that the gift (χάρις) of the interpretation of Scripture has now been transferred to the Christians (*Dial* 82), to whom God has revealed (ἀπεκάλυψεν)[146] its true meaning (*Dial* 100).

Though Justin does not appear to employ the familiar Jewish and Pauline notions of the revelation of heavenly mysteries, he nevertheless represents an interesting development in the Christian use of mystery language. For here we find Philo's idea of charismatic, allegorical interpretation of Scripture fused with a specifically Christian notion of the typological fulfilment hinging on the person and work of Christ. This hermeneutical approach has its roots above all in Paul (e.g. 1 Cor 10:4; Gal 4:21−31), in 1 Peter (e.g. 1:10−12; 3:20 f.), and Hebrews (e.g. 7; 9; 10:1; 12:18−24); but in Justin it comes to flourish fully and richly.

6.4. The Epistle to Diognetus

Date and authorship of this document are disputed and uncertain to a considerable degree, although the relatively pristine state of doctrinal development[147] may be tentatively taken to indicate a date around the middle of the second century.[148]

The theological centre of the Epistle is in Chapters 7− 9.[149] Although neither the Old Testament nor the earthly life of Jesus receives more than a passing reference,[150] the writer's christology is explained with reference to the mysteries of heaven (7:2). The mystery of the Christian religion has been assigned as a stewardship (οἰκονομία 7:1; cf. 1 Cor 4:1, 9:17) not of human but of divine origin (4:6; 5:3); God's sending of His Son (7:4f.) was the establishment of

---

[146] Justin can occasionally use this word in an apparently less theological sense of "to divulge": *Dial* 90, 94 − once of the words of the prophets and once of Justin (with μυστήριον as object).

[147] E.g. christology; but note also the concern to distinguish Christianity from *Judaism* rather than from Gnosticism or pagan cults.

[148] Thus Meecham. Although esp. German scholarship has often opted for a considerably later date, Baumeister, "Datierung", 105−111 has recently presented arguments for a date just before A.D. 200.

[149] Meecham 19.

[150] Meecham 20 explains this in terms of the Gentile orientation.

heavenly truth on earth in form of the Logos, the very Creator of the world (7:2).[151] God's design of salvation had at first been communicated to this Son alone,[152] but then He disclosed it publicly through His Son's manifestation (8:9−11) − the identification of the incarnation with the revelation of the saving mystery of God is not far from the mind of Paul. Those who love God and become His imitators among men are given to speak His mysteries (10:7); this suggests a rather "democratic" understanding of the propagation of God's mystery, viz. by anyone who cares to obtain full knowledge (ἐπίγνωσις) of it (contrast 1 Cor 2:6−10).[153] The probably secondary appendix (Chapters 11−12)[154] speaks of the Christian truth as conveying a knowledge of the mysteries of the Father (11:2), revealed by the Son (11:4, 8; 12:9).

In the Epistle to Diognetus, then, the trend to a generalization of the Pauline "revealed mystery" motif has been further generalized. Here too, however, it refers first and foremost to the gospel of the saving purposes of God as revealed in Jesus Christ.

---

[151] Note the cosmological dimension of christology here in relation to the Christian mystery. This emphasis is more tentative in Paul, e.g. Col 2:3.

[152] Meecham 125 traces this notion to Gen 1:26 LXX ποιήσωμεν ἄνθρωπον, κτλ.

[153] But see 11:8, with its more familiar notion of a disclosure of the things revealed to the author; cf. Meecham 139.

[154] Cf. Meecham 64−68: possibly by Melito or Hippolytus.

Conclusion

In these concluding remarks I will begin by summing up and assessing the fruits of earlier research from the perspective of the present study, before proceeding to a summary and specific conclusions.

1. Evaluation of Previous Research

A proper history of research, albeit a *desideratum*, would unfortunately exceed the present limitations of space. The following remarks are simply to show in brief how my results relate to a few of the more important studies on revelation and on mysteries.

1.1. Revelation

1.1.1. Judaism

Comprehensive examinations of Jewish views of revelation in their own right have been rare indeed. J. B. Frey's lengthy article was a noble attempt in its time, but was not widely followed up. Certainly his ultimately negative conclusions about revelation in post-Biblical Judaism were, and all too often continue to be, characteristic of NT scholars: the Jews searched the Torah, but their approach was mistaken.[1] Oepke's "word/concept" study in *TWNT* devotes less than two pages to the question as here in view;[2] and like the work of numerous other scholars, it is rather dominated by his reading of passages like 1Macc 4:46 on the one hand, and the dismissal of apocalyptic on the other.

However, since the discovery of the Qumran material, a number of major specialized studies have appeared, from which my work has drawn considerable benefit. Rylaarsdam on Jewish Wisdom literature was perhaps somewhat insubstantial, but O. Betz on Qumran, Blenkinsopp on Josephus, Chester on

---

[1] Frey, "Révélation", 509 f.
[2] *TWNT* 3:580 f.

the Targums, and the works of Scholem, Goldberg and others on Rabbinic literature have certainly been some of the milestones along the now more travelled road of historical and literary investigations into Jewish apocalyptic, exegesis, and views of Scripture.

1.1.2. Paul

Much more work has of course been done on the Pauline and NT view of revelation, although some of the major studies have suffered from serious ideological and methodological weaknesses. E. F. Scott's book is rather popular in character and shows no interaction with the Jewish background. Bultmann's seminal essay on revelation takes a distinctly anthropological and existential approach, and is thus perhaps of limited value — although it clearly influenced a number of his students. Oepke works in more appropriately theological terms, but emphasizes *Heilsgeschichte* and eschatological drama at the expense of revelation as divine communication. H. Schulte's book is essentially a collection of word studies, with a neglect of Jewish and a penchant for Gnostic parallels, and with the explicit refusal (p. 85) to provide a conclusion. Wilckens (1961) offers a more useful overview of the NT *concept* of revelation, although he is perhaps unduly constrained by the programmatic orientation ("revelation as history") of the collection in which his essay appears. Downing's 1964 *tour de force* on revelation (or the absence of it) in the NT proves really only the relative unimportance of divine *self*-revelation,[3] but not of revelation as such.

By far the most valuable and substantial contribution to date has been the published dissertation of Lührmann. This contains much that is useful: exegetical interaction with the Pauline texts and with major secondary literature, theological evaluation, and at least a basic awareness of Jewish (and Gnostic) background material. He does not, however, devote a separate section to the study of Jewish sources (but see pp. 84 ff., 98 ff.), and his reference index shows relatively meagre gleanings from the Old Testament, Josephus, the Rabbis, and the Targumim (absent).[4] Although his stated method of evaluating the Pauline data is, expressly like Schulte's (p. 11), somewhat statistical (viz., based on the occurrence of particular Greek verbs), fortunately in practice he rises above this to an examination of whole contexts (e.g. Chapter Four on 2 Cor). My main disagreement with his conclusions is over his basic Bultmannian orientation (p. 155 and passim), which leads him to deny the historical and christological aspects of Paul's view of revelation, and to focus instead on the existential and kerygmatic.[5]

---

[3] Note e.g. "Revelation", 185.

[4] In part this may be due to his declared presupposition (p. 14 n. 4) that the background to Paul's view of revelation is to be sought in "Jewish wisdom including Philo".

[5] This is a criticism also mounted by earlier readers, e.g. Merklein, *Amt*, 194; Luz, *Ge-*

1.2. "Mystery"

In both major and minor contributions, the notion of "mystery" has long received rather more sustained attention. While the so-called History of Religions School had for the most part favoured a flowery array of popular Hellenistic religious motifs, the groundwork for an approach through the OT and Jewish texts was laid by G. Bornkamm and a little earlier by D. Deden in a relatively neglected article (*Gallica sunt, non leguntur?*). The latter's conclusion, twelve years *before* the decisive discovery of the Dead Sea Scrolls, is substantially the same as that of R. E. Brown:

> Nous possédons dans les présupposés juifs tout ce qui est nécessaire pour expliquer le vocabulaire et la formation des idées chrétiennes. . . . En pratique, nous excluons du même coup toute influence réelle de l'hellénisme et de la phraséologie religieuse du paganisme sur la langue de l'Apôtre.[6]

A clear death-knell of the theory of pagan derivation was rung by K. Prümm, who in 1960 concluded a series of articles with a learned but lumbering contribution on "mysteries", in which after detailed study of the Hellenistic evidence he arrives *inter alia* at the conclusion that the Pauline μυστήριον is to be understood on the basis of Qumran and the LXX (i.e. Daniel).[7]

The two most valuable and substantial works are by Brown and Penna. Brown has perhaps done the most to sway scholarly opinion to a Jewish reading of the Pauline notion of mystery. His background work in the Jewish sources is careful and thorough (though he omits specific treatment of the Targums and Rabbinic literature), and this bears good fruit in his reading of the Pauline texts. My discussion above records agreement with him on most exegetical points. However, he pursues what is essentially a word study, largely ignoring thematic/theological connections (e.g. with the OT) as well as words in paradigmatic correlation to μυστήριον (e.g. ἀπόρρητον, ἀπόκρυφον, -κρυπτ-, etc.).

Penna takes for granted Brown's conclusions, without offering much independent work in the Jewish sources (Qumran being a partial exception). But his thematically organized presentation on the whole betrays a good understanding of the texts; unlike Brown he goes on to evaluate some of the attendant theological themes. He also offers (as promised, p. 9) a rather fuller biblio-

---

schichtsverständnis, 287 n. 94. Cf. my Ch. 8, § 1.1 passim. The dissertation of K. L. Burres, "Semantics", is primarily an exercise in structuralist methodology; that of R. E. Sturm, "*Apokalyptô*", I have been unable to obtain. A. Schweitzer's famous *Mysticism of Paul the Apostle*, despite the title, is not of direct relevance to the subject here in view.

[6] Deden, "Mystère", 434; cf. Brown, *Mystery*, 69. Deden's critique of the prevailing History of Religions position (e.g. A. Loisy) focuses on the absence of important pagan terminology from the New Testament (p. 426).

[7] Prümm, "Mystères", 180. See already "Mysterion", 135.

graphy than his predecessors. My main hesitation about this work is that its wholly synthetic and thematic layout has enticed its author into confident generalizations[8] which, though often true, sometimes do less than justice to the texts. Thus e.g. his conclusions about the ecclesiological (67 ff.), anthropological (79 ff.) and non-cosmological (87) nature of the Pauline mystery are based on a good deal of extrapolation.[9]

Two other works deserve a brief mention here. Caragounis's book on μυστήριον in Ephesians is a welcome attempt to remain sensitive to the flavour of the word μυστήριον in Hellenistic religion; but overall the book is unfortunately a disappointment. Chapter 5 on the Jewish background lacks depth and perspective. He employs a diachronic word study of μυστήριον as something "incomprehensible, hard to understand" and then goes on — oblivious to J. Barr's strictures — to impose this on "all subsequent times to the present day".[10] This leads to an emphasis on form rather than content of the mystery: incomprehensibility becomes its *essence*. Apart from this it is difficult to perceive a central thesis, not least because much time is spent on extraneous matters.[11]

Finally, A. E. Harvey, while allowing for the dominance of a Jewish determination of the Biblical and Pauline concept of mystery, has called for greater awareness of "overtones" of Hellenistic mystery metaphors. This of course is a helpful balance to Brown's approach: "Even if all the instances of μυστήριον can be explained' in terms of *raz*, it does not follow that the writer did not intend, and the reader did not pick up, some echo of the Greek mystery-metaphor."[12] However, two points of criticism are in order. First, if the meaning of e.g. the Pauline μυστήριον is predominately Jewish, any intentional *double entendre* in a given context would need to be demonstrated rather than assumed. And secondly, the bridge between "what the writer intended" and "what the reader picked up" is not as secure as Harvey supposes. In any case, "reader re-

---

[8] Beginning with the preface, p. 10: the Pauline μυστήριον "contains *in nuce* all the elaborations of systematic theology." One may (as the present writer) or may not be inclined to agree, but such confidence in the *prolegomena* to an exegetical study is hard to match.

[9] Moreover, e.g. the claim (p. 17) that the Hellenistic mysteries are opposed to the Pauline mystery in every one of their characteristics (including their "absence of moral requirements"), is manifestly incorrect.

[10] *Mysterion*, 32 f.; he calls this "the first and foremost conclusion of this study". It leads to some unlikely interpretations, as of 2 Thess 2:7; Mark 4:11par; Rev 1:20.

[11] Fully half of the text is spent on a general discussion of Eph; little attention is given e.g. to the relationship with Col.

[12] Harvey, "Mystery Language", 331: clearly a critique of Brown's conclusion (*Mystery*, 69).

sponse criticism" in Paul is a risky enterprise at best, and in respect to our topic would merit a separate study.

It remains here to summarize and assess our results.

2. Summary

We set out to inquire into notions of divine revelation and mysteries, and to show that the latter are profitably studied within the framework of the former. It would appear that this endeavour has been successful — not only with regard to Paul, whose notion of God's mysteries is firmly integrated with his understanding of the fundamental revelation in Jesus Christ, but also with regard to early Judaism, where the mysteries of Torah and the mysteries of heaven are consistently associated with special revelation (or lack of it, as the case may be).

2.1. Judaism (cf. the earlier synthetic statement pp. 124—126)

As a corollary to the belief in a fading of the Spirit and of prophecy after the exile, we noted in Judaism a certain reluctance to speak of revelation outside the Torah. But alongside this was a wealth of evidence to suggest that God continued to speak even to the present generation, chiefly through inspired insights (whether exegetical or visionary) granted to privileged interpreters of God's word written. "Mystery" is the name frequently given to the content of such revelation — be it the hidden treasures of Torah or the intricacies of uranography and the heavenly plan of salvation. While the soteriological secrets of heaven serve a purpose of theodicy (thus connecting with OT antecedents of "mystery") and help the writer's community to identify its place within history, halakhic mysteries delineate the distinctive way of life appropriate to that place.

2.2. Paul

In coming to Paul we found, despite a good deal of structural continuity, a fundamental shift in the approach to revelation, in which the Torah has become (not "replaced" by Christ and the gospel, but) the attendant witness to the surpassing end-time revelation of God's righteousness and saving design. Qualified and gifted Christian exegesis unlocks its true message, which was written "altogether for our sake."[13]

---

[13] Next to the "words of the Lord" (including, perhaps, Jesus's approach to halakhah)

2.2.1. In the recent past, God has manifested His righteousness in the historical events of the sacrificial death and resurrection of Jesus; at the same time He has revealed the dispensation of faith in Christ, by which Jews and Gentiles alike are justified.

2.2.2. This revelation of the gospel has been uniquely granted in the past to the apostles (apparently with the resurrection appearances, Gal 1; 1 Cor 15). But it has now been "kerygmatized" in that the present preaching of the gospel continues to reveal the eschatological righteousness and wrath of God, and the apostolic ministry itself constitutes a living demonstration of the truth and knowledge of God. Paul affirms other present-day (esp. prophetic) disclosures as important; indeed they are given as manifestations of the Spirit (1 Cor 12:7, etc.) and in response to prayer (2 Cor 12:8 f.). But these phenomena do not appear to be of permanent, foundational significance to his overall view of revelation.

2.2.3. Against the backdrop of first-century Judaism, the past and present dimensions of revelation suggest the inauguration of the eschaton. Nevertheless the ultimate revelation of Jesus Christ as saviour and judge in glory, and of the believers with Him, is still to come; all that precedes this must be seen in its light.

2.2.4. In Paul as in Judaism, the notion of divine mysteries is intricately linked with revelation.[14] Two levels[15] of publicly taught mysteries have been revealed by the Spirit (1 Cor 2:10 ff.)[16] to the apostles (and prophets), who act as their responsible stewards and dispensers.[17]

(i) "Mystery" or "mysteries" can refer collectively to the saving purposes of God, especially as these are summed up in the message of the gospel of Christ. This usage occurs in 1 Cor and more fully in Col; it is further developed in Eph and later writings.

(ii) A mystery can at the same time denote one particular (sometimes detailed) aspect of God's plan of salvation, especially as this relates to the eschaton. Examples include Rom 11:25 f. and 1 Cor 15:51.

---

the Torah continues to play a supporting ethical role, of a kind not unrelated to certain Jewish Hellenistic ideas.

[14] Cf. Penna's observation (*Mysterion*, 27) that in all 13 (*sic*) Pauline μυστήριον texts a verb of revelation is present: ἀποκαλύπτω, γνωρίζω, γινώσκω, φωτίζω, or λαλέω. Cf. earlier Deden, "Mystère", 419 f.

[15] Similarly Prümm, "Mystères", 219 f.; van Roon, "Wisdom", 216.

[16] This notion is absent from Col; contrast Eph 3:5 etc. Cf. further Part I above; p. 165 n. 37; also p. 144 f. The specific function of the Spirit in Paul's view of revelation would merit further study.

[17] N.B. Illegitimate or evil mysteries do not figure significantly, though 2 Thess 2:7 (μυστήριον τῆς ἀνομίας) appears to present a parallel to Qumran's "counter-mysteries", the evil designs of Belial; cf. e.g. 2 Cor 2:11; 4:4.

2.2.5. The latter category of mysteries of particular doctrine seems to be disclosed with considerable caution, being couched in contexts of traditional language and careful Scriptural proof. Such mysteries are introduced only under certain circumstances, the criteria being the maturity of the audience and its edification on an issue of particular concern.

2.2.6. The mystical revelation of heavenly mysteries and the participation in angelic worship was part of the religious experience both of Paul and of the Corinthian (and perhaps Colossian?) charismatics. However, the apostle considers such matters best reserved for private contemplation; charismatic ἀποκάλυψις at any rate is incomplete where it cannot be rationally formulated and intelligibly communicated to the church for its edification.

2.2.7. In keeping with this principle, Paul himself never bases his authority for the disclosure of a particular μυστήριον on a vision. Rather, each item of new revelation is placed squarely against the background of Scripture and of familiar tradition.[18]

2.2.8. In the doubtfully Pauline and post-apostolic material examined in Chapter 11, we observed a number of significant changes in terminology and orientation. In particular, we found a further continuation of the increasingly collective and general use of "mystery" to denote the gospel of Christ as a whole, or the totality of God's saving purposes for mankind as revealed in him (and pertaining especially to the church). Ignatius and the Epistle to Diognetus stress that the theme of hiddenness and revelation turns decisively on the incarnation of Christ, while Justin Martyr could be said to apply Philo's allegorical interpretation (and mystery terminology) to Paul's christological hermeneutic of the Old Testament.

3. Evaluation of Results

3.1. Revelation

One implication of this view of the Pauline pattern of revelation is its logical symmetry, *mutatis mutandis*, with the corresponding pattern of Judaism. For a similar three-dimensional perspective applies there as well: (i) past salvation event (Exodus) and constitutive revelation (the Torah given to Moses); (ii) present revealed elaboration (through tradition and interpretation) of the past revelation; and (iii) future crowning revelation of the Messiah and/or the King-

---

[18] For a context of congregational worship his envisioned procedure may in fact be similar, since prophecy is subject to testing (1 Cor 14:29), presumably by (*inter alia*) the same criteria of Scripture and tradition. See further Dunn, "Testing", 189f., 192.

dom of God. For Paul the future dimension has already broken into the past and the present; similarly some Jewish writers (notably those of Qumran) share the conjunction of future and present eschatology,[19] as well as the sense of a fundamental revelation in the recent past.[20]

We cannot therefore properly speak of a "bursting" or "abandonment" of the apocalyptic pattern of revelation as disclosure in this age and implementation in the age to come.[21] Paul retains the apocalyptic schema, although he subjects it to considerable modification in light of the actual incursion, in Christ and the Gospel, of God's eschatological righteousness into the present.[22] Three temporal dimensions remain in place, but are subject to a christocentric redefinition and consolidation.

3.2. Revelation of Mysteries

As mere esoterica, mysteries of heaven are of relatively little interest to Paul; in this he is at one with the Mishnah and early Rabbinic Judaism. While he consistently distinguishes between the stewards and the addressees of revelation, his differentiation in 1 Corinthians between two levels of teaching is not explicitly developed in Colossians (and the later letters). Instead, Paul seems to condense his teaching about mysteries into a "grander", more universal conception of "the mystery of Christ", in which Christology and soteriology are one. Thus he counters the threat of esoteric aberrations by homing in on the central gospel message in a movement of increasing exotericism and global perspectives. It may be this inclusive view of the christological mystery, together with his reserve about esoteric matters, which also obviates the need to speak about the more cosmological secrets of heaven. This more comprehensive mystery is also the one which later writers in the Pauline tradition take as their starting point.

A curious feature, *prima facie*, is the complete absence of the category of halakhic mysteries of exegesis, so common in contemporary Jewish writings — this despite a considerable amount of concrete ethical instruction, by no means all of which is simply a matter of commonly accepted norms. But, as we saw, Paul's exegesis generally avoids large areas of halakhah. Moreover, it might well be a violation of his own criteria of οἰκοδομή and τοῖς πᾶσιν πάντα, were

---

[19] See esp. Kuhn, *Enderwartung*, 176–181 and passim. Cf. also e.g. JosAsen 15:4f.

[20] Note esp. the function of the Teacher of Righteousness.

[21] *Pace* e.g. Lührmann, *Offenbarungsverständnis*, 79, 108; Kim, *Origin*, 73. Cf. also Stuhlmacher, *Evangelium*, 79; and 81 n. 2 for his criticism of Lührmann. (Kim appears to have misread Stuhlmacher, since he [74 n. 1] acknowledges indebtedness to the former's pp. 76 ff.)

[22] Cf. also Beker, *Paul*, 145 f.; Soards, "Paul", 149.

he to stun his Gentile churches with exegetical wizardry of the kind practised at Qumran or in the Palestinian *bêth ha-midrash*.[23] Nevertheless, where necessary Paul is quite willing to propose an eschatological mystery derived by exegetical revelation (Rom 11:25; 1 Cor 15:51).

Over all it seems to be true for Paul as for Judaism that the written Torah requires an oral Torah (in his case, christological hermeneutics, gospel tradition, kerygma) to become audible as the word of God εἰς ἡμέτεραν διδασκαλίαν, ללמדך. What is more, it would not be conceptually alien to contemporary Judaism to speak of a revealed Messianic "mystery" as the hermeneutical key to the reading of Scripture and of *Heilsgeschichte* (cf. Qumran, etc.). In this way the interconnection of revelation past and present may help one to see from a different perspective how Paul "reasoned his way into" his understanding of the complex interpretation of Torah: it could be that precisely where Paul's views on revelation seem most removed from Judaism, they in fact remain logically compatible with one of the latter's most basic structures of thought.[24]

Finally, we note the relative subsidence of the theodicy question in Paul's discussion of the revelation of mysteries.[25] While such revelation still accentuates God's sovereignty in history and cosmos, no longer does it serve to hold in hopeful abeyance the believer's painful question, "How long, Oh Lord?" Much of this is no doubt to be attributed to Paul's conviction that in Christ God *has* in fact manifested His righteousness (Rom 3:21 ff., etc.) and thus made the question obsolete: "For all the promises of God find their Yes in him" (2 Cor 1:20; cf. Rom 5:1−11; also e.g. Tit 3:4−7). Potential issues of theodicy do arise (suffering, death), but they seem less intractable. The death of believers proves to be reconcilable with an imminent eschaton, and suffering (at any rate apostolic suffering) is as it were taken on board, made into an integral and necessary part of God's unstoppable movement towards victory and new creation.

In a sense Paul's *theologia crucis* can be seen to turn the theodicy problem on its head: what seems God's folly to "the wise, the scribe, the debater of this age", has in fact become the wisdom of God − "Christ crucified". The hidden salvific dimensions of God's wisdom in this mystery are known by revelation only (1 Cor 2:6−10; cf. 2 Cor 4:3−18, etc.).

But perhaps one area in which Paul *does* face an abiding issue of theodicy (apart from his more personal trouble with the σκόλοψ τῇ σαρκί) is the hardheartedness of Israel. Paul struggles seriously with this issue in Rom 9−11, and after much interaction with Scripture it is finally resolved − again, by revela-

---

[23] Note in this regard the observation of Harnack, p. 156 n. 144 above.

[24] In this respect one of the weaknesses of T. Williams's *Form and Vitality* is his failure to recognize that revelation as "meta-revelation", as interpretation of previously received revelation, is foundational to the logic of doctrinal stability and creativity in both Judaism and early Christianity.

[25] Cf. further Bultmann, *Theologie*, 350.

tion of a mystery: a partial hardening has happened to Israel *until*[26] the fulness
of the Gentiles has come in.

Paul's theology of revelation and mystery had a lasting impact on the early
post–apostolic age. The later letters of the Pauline corpus, along with the
Apostolic Fathers, continue the emphasis on the universal (and especially the
ecclesiological) dimensions of the divine mystery revealed in Christ. Thus the
moving passage in the Epistle to Diognetus 8:9–11, in some ways almost an
exposition of Paul, supplies a most fitting conclusion:

> Having formed a great and unspeakable design, [God] communicated it to this Child
> alone. And so long as he kept it in a mystery and guarded His wise counsel, he
> seemed to neglect us and to be careless; but when he revealed it through his beloved
> Child, and manifested the things prepared from the beginning, he gave us all things
> at once, both to share in his benefits and to see and understand – and which of us
> would ever have expected these things?

---

[26] Note Zeller on the ἄχρι οὗ, above, p. 173 f. n. 82. Cf. further Dunn, *Romans,*
2:278 f.

Bibliography

1. Primary Sources

1.1 Texts and Translations

3 Enoch or The Hebrew Book of Enoch. Edited and Translated by H. Odeberg. Cambridge: University Press, 1928. [Reprinted in The Library of Biblical Studies. New York: Ktav, c1973.]

Aboth de Rabbi Nathan. Edited by S. Schechter. Vienna: Lippe; London: Nutt; Frankfurt: Kauffmann, 1887.

Acta Martyrum. Edited by P. T. Ruinart. Regensburg: Manz, 1859.

Altjüdisches Schrifttum außerhalb der Bibel. Translated by Paul Riessler. Augsburg: Filser, 1928.

Ante-Nicene Christian Library: Translations of the Writings of the Fathers down to A.D. 325. Edited by A. Roberts and J. Donaldson. 24 Vols. Edinburgh: T. & T. Clark, 1867–72.

Apocalypsis Henochi Graece. Edited by M. Black. And *Fragmenta Pseudepigraphorum Quae Supersunt Graeca*. Edited by A.-M. Denis. PVTG 3. Leiden: Brill, 1970.

The Apocrypha of the Old Testament: Revised Standard Version. The Oxford Annotated Apocrypha. Edited by B. M. Metzger. New York: Oxford University Press, 1977.

The Apocryphal Old Testament. Edited by H. F. D. Sparks. Oxford: Clarendon, 1984.

The Apostolic Fathers. Translated by K. Lake. LCL. 2 Vols. Cambridge, MA: Harvard University Press; London: Heinemann, c1912–1913.

Aramaic Texts from Qumran. With Translations and Annotations by B. Jongeling, C. J. Labuschagne, and A. S. van der Woude. Vol. 1. Semitic Study Series 4. Leiden: Brill, 1976.

Aristeas to Philocrates (Letter of Aristeas). Edited by Moses Hadas. Dropsie College Edition Jewish Apocryphal Literature. New York: Harper & Row, 1951.

The Asatir: The Samaritan Book of the "Secrets of Moses". Translated by M. Gaster. London: The Royal Asiatic Society, 1927.

Aus Israels Lehrhallen: Kleine Midraschim zur späteren legendarischen Literatur des Alten Testaments. Translated by A. Wünsche. 5 Vols. Leipzig: Pfeiffer: 1907–10.

The Authorised Daily Prayer Book of the United Hebrew Congregations of the British Commonwealth of Nations. Translated by S. Singer. 2nd ed. London: Eyre & Spottiswoode, 1962.

Baillet, M.; Milik, J. T. et al. *Discoveries in the Judaean Desert*. Vols. 1–7. Oxford: Clarendon, 1955–1982.

The Bible in Aramaic: Based on Old Manuscripts and Printed Texts. Edited by A. Sperber. 4
    Vols. Leiden: Brill, 1959—68.
Biblia Hebraica Stuttgartensia. Edited by K. Elliger and W. Rudolph. New ed. Stuttgart:
    Deutsche Bibelgesellschaft, 1977.
Biblia Sacra Iuxta Vulgatam Versionem. Edited by R. Weber. 2 Vols. Stuttgart: Württem-
    bergische Bibelanstalt, 1969.
The Book of Ben Sira: Text, Concordance and an Analysis of the Vocabulary (Hebrew). The
    Historical Dictionary of the Hebrew Language. Jerusalem: Academy of the Hebrew
    Language/Shrine of the Book, 1973.

Cicero: De Senectute, De Amicitia, De Divinatione. Translated by W. A. Falconer. Vol. 8.
    LCL. London: Heinemann; Cambridge, MA: Harvard University Press, 1923.
Corpus Papyrorum Judaicarum. Edited by V. A. Tcherikover and A. Fuks. 3 Vols. Cam-
    bridge, MA: Harvard University Press, 1957— 1964.
The Dead Sea Scrolls in English. Edited and Translated by G. Vermes. 3rd ed. Harmonds-
    worth: Penguin, 1987. [DSSE. Occasional references to the 2nd ed. (1975) are clearly
    marked.]

Eusebius: The Ecclesiastical History. Translated by K. Lake and J. E. L. Oulton. 2 Vols.
    LCL. Cambridge, MA: Harvard University Press; London: Heinemann, 1926—1932.
ΕΥΣΕΒΙΟΣ ΚΑΙΣΑΡΕΙΑΣ. Βιβλιοθήκη Ἑλλήνων Πατέρων καὶ Ἐκκλησιαστικῶν
    Συγγραφέων 19—29. Athens: Ἔκδοσις τῆς Ἀποστολικῆς Διακονίας τῆς Ἐκκλη-
    σίας τῆς Ἑλλάδος, 1959—1962.

The Fathers According to Rabbi Nathan. Translated by Judah Goldin. New Haven: Yale
    University Press, 1955.
Fitzmyer, Joseph A. and Harrington, Daniel J. A Manual of Palestinian Aramaic Texts.
    Bib et Or 34. Rome: Biblical Institute Press, 1978.
Fragments of Philo Judaeus. Edited by J. R. Harris. Cambridge: University Press, 1886.

Hagiographa Chaldaice. Edited by P. de Lagarde. Leipzig: Teubner, 1873.
The Hebrew Text of the Book of Ecclesiasticus. Edited by I. Lévi. Semitic Study Series 3. 3rd
    ed. Leiden: Brill, 1969.
Hebrew-English Edition of the Babylonian Talmud. Edited by I. Epstein. 20 Vols. London:
    Soncino, 1972—1984.
Hennecke, E. New Testament Apocrypha. 2 Vols. Edited by W. Schneemelcher. Transla-
    tion edited by R. McL. Wilson. London: Lutterworth, 1963—1965.
Héraclite: Allégories d'Homère. Edited and translated by F. Buffière. Collection des Uni-
    versités de France. Paris: Belles Lettres, 1962.
Herford, R. Travers. Pirkê Aboth: The Tractate 'Fathers', from the Mishnah, Commonly
    Called 'Sayings of the Fathers'. 2nd ed. New York: Jewish Institute of Religion/Bloch,
    1930.

Inscriptions Reveal: Documents from the Time of the Bible, the Mishna and the Talmud. Edited
    by Efrat Carmon et al. 2nd ed. Jerusalem: Israel Museum, 1973.
Isbell, Charles D. Corpus of the Aramaic Incantation Bowls. SBLDS 17. Missoula: Scholars
    Press, 1975.

Jellinek, Adolph. Bet ha-Midrasch: Sammlung kleiner Midraschim und vermischter Abhand-
    lungen aus der älteren jüdischen Literatur. 6 vols. in 2. 3rd ed. Jerusalem: Wahrmann,
    1967.

Josephus. Translated by H. St. J. Thackeray (Vols. 1–5), Ralph Marcus (Vols. 5–8) with Allen Wikgren (Vol. 8), and Louis H. Feldman (Vols. 9–10). LCL. London: Heinemann; Cambridge, MA: Harvard University Press, 1926–1965.

Juvenal and Persius. With an English Translation by G. G. Ramsay. LCL. Rev. ed. London: Heinemann; Cambridge, MA: Harvard University Press, 1940.

Kennicott, Benjamin. *Vetus Testamentum Hebraicum, cum Variis Lectionibus.* 2 Vols. Oxford: Clarendon, 1776–1780.

Klein, Michael L. *The Fragment-Targums of the Pentateuch: According to their Extant Sources.* AnBib 76. 2 Vols. Rome: Biblical Institute, 1980.

Knibb, Michael A. *The Book of Enoch: A New Edition in Light of the Aramaic Dead Sea Fragments.* 2 Vols. Oxford: Clarendon, 1978.

Kuhn, Karl Georg. *Der tannaitische Midrasch Sifre zu Numeri.* Rabbinische Texte 2:3. Stuttgart: Kohlhammer, 1959.

Le Déaut, Roger. *Targum du Pentateuque: Traduction des Deux Recensions Palestiniennes Complètes avec Introduction, Parallèles, Notes et Index.* 5 Vols. Sources Chrétiennes 245, 256, 261, 271, 282. Paris: Cerf, 1978–1981.

Levine, Étan. *The Aramaic Version of Qohelet.* New York: Sepher-Hermon, 1978.

Levine, Étan. *The Aramaic Version of Lamentations.* New York: Hermon, 1976.

Levine, Étan. *The Aramaic Version of Ruth.* AnBib 58. Rome: Biblical Institute Press, 1973.

Mekilta de-Rabbi Ishmael. Edited by J. Z. Lauterbach. 3 Vols. Philadelphia: Jewish Publication Society of America, 1933–1935.

Memar Marqah: The Teaching of Marqah. Edited and Translated by J. Macdonald. BZAW 84. 2 Vols. Berlin: Töpelmann, 1963.

Midrasch Tanchuma: Ein agadischer Commentar zum Pentateuch von Rabbi Tanchuma ben Rabbi Abba. Edited by S. Buber. Wilna: Romm, 1885.

Midrash Rabbah. 2 Vols. Wilna: Romm, 1887.

Midrash Rabbah. Edited by H. Freedman and M. Simon. 10 Vols. London: Soncino, 1939.

The Midrash on Psalms. Edited by W. G. Braude. 2 Vols. New Haven: Yale University Press, 1959.

Midrasch Tehillim (Schocher Tob). Edited by S. Buber. Wilna: Romm, 1891.

Milik, J. T. *The Books of Enoch: Aramaic Fragments of Qumrân Cave 4.* Oxford: Clarendon, 1976.

The Mishnah. Translated by H. Danby. Oxford: Oxford University Press, 1933.

Mishnayoth. Edited by P. Blackman. 7 Vols. New York: Judaica Press, 1964.

Montefiore, C. G. and Loewe, H. *A Rabbinic Anthology.* London: Macmillan, 1938. [Repr. New York: Schocken, 1974.]

Montgomery, James A. *Aramaic Incantation Texts from Nippur.* University of Pennsylvania, The Museum: Publications of the Babylonian Section 3. Philadelphia: University Museum, 1913.

The Nag Hammadi Library in English. Edited by J. M. Robinson. Leiden: Brill, 1977.

Naveh, Joseph and Shaked, Saul. *Amulets and Magic Bowls: Aramaic Incantations of Late Antiquity.* Jerusalem: Magnes; Leiden: Brill, 1985.

Neophyti 1: Targum Palestinense MS de la Bibliotheca Vaticana. Edited by A. Diez Macho. 6 Vols. Testos y Estudios 7–11, 20. Madrid/Barcelona: Consejo Superior de Investigaciones Científicas, 1968–1979.

Newsom, Carol. *Songs of the Sabbath Sacrifice: A Critical Edition*. HSS 27. Atlanta: Scholars, 1985.

Novum Testamentum Graece. Edited by E. Nestle et al. 26th ed. (revised). Stuttgart: Deutsche Bibelstiftung, 1981.

The Odes of Solomon: The Syriac Texts. Edited and Translated by J. H. Charlesworth. SBLTT 13 (PS 7). Missoula: Scholars Press, 1977.

The Old Testament Pseudepigrapha. Edited by J. H. Charlesworth. 2 Vols. Garden City: Doubleday, 1983—1985.

Die Oracula Sibyllina. Edited by J. Geffcken. Die griechischen Schriftsteller der ersten drei Jahrhunderte. Leipzig: Hinrichs, 1902.

Origenis Hexaplorum Quae Supersunt: Sive Veterum Interpretum Graecorum in Totum Vetus Testamentum Fragmenta. Edited by F. Field. 2 Vols. Oxford: Clarendon, 1875.

The Oxyrhynchus Papyri. Part XXII. Edited by E. Lobel and C. H. Roberts. Graeco-Roman Memoirs 31. London: Egypt Exploration Society, 1954.

Papyri Graecae Magicae: Die griechischen Zauberpapyri. Edited and Translated by K. L. Preisendanz. 2nd ed. edited by A. Henrichs. Sammlung wissenschaftlicher Commentare 1—2. Stuttgart: Teubner, 1973—1974.

The Penguin Book of Hebrew Verse. Edited by T. Carmi. Harmondsworth: Penguin, 1981.

Peshitta: The Old Testament in Syriac according to the Peshitta Version. Edited by the Peshitta Institute. Vol. 4.3: *Apocalypse of Baruch: 4 Esdras*. Leiden: Brill, 1973.

Pesikta Rabbati: Discourses for Feasts, Fasts, and Special Sabbaths. Translated by W. G. Braude. Yale Judaica Series 18. 2 Vols. New Haven/London: Yale University Press, 1968.

Philo Judaeus: Opera Quae Supersunt. Edited by L. Cohn and P. Wendland. 6 Vols. + Vol. 7: *Indices ad Philonis Alexandrini Opera* (by J. Leisegang). Berlin: de Gruyter, 1896—1926.

Philo. Translated by F. H. Colson (Vols. 2, 6—10) with G. H. Whitaker (Vols. 1, 3—5); and by Ralph Marcus (Supplements 1—2). LCL. London: Heinemann; Cambridge, MA: Harvard University Press, 1929—1953.

Philonenko, Marc. *Joseph et Aséneth: Introduction, Texte Critique, Traduction et Notes*. Studia Post-biblica 13. Leiden: Brill, 1968.

Platonis Opera. Edited by J. Burnet. Vols. 2+4. Scriptorum Classicorum Bibliotheca Oxoniensis. Oxford: Clarendon, 1901— 1902.

Plutarch's Moralia. LCL. Vols 5+8. Translated by F. C. Babbitt, P. A. Clement and H. B. Hoffleit. Cambridge, MA: Harvard University Press; London: Heinemann, 1936+1969.

Pritchard, James B. *Ancient Near Eastern Texts Relating to the Old Testament*. 3rd ed. Princeton: Princeton University Press, 1969.

Pseudo-Jonathan (Thargum Jonathan ben Usiël zum Pentateuch). Edited by M. Ginsburger. Berlin: Calvary, 1903.

Pseudo-Philo's Liber Antiquitatum Biblicarum. Edited by Guido Kisch. University of Notre Dame Publications in Medieval Studies 10. Notre Dame: University of Notre Dame, 1949.

Quinti Septimii Florentis Tertulliani Quae Supersunt Opera. Edited by F. Oehler. 3 Vols. Leipzig: Weigel, 1853.

Raschis Pentateuchkommentar. Translated by S. Bamberger. 3rd ed. Frankfurt: Kauffmann, 1935.

Reitzenstein, R. *Poimandres: Studien zur Griechisch-Ägyptischen und Frühchristlichen Literatur*. Leipzig: Teubner, 1904.

Sancti Eusebii Hieronymi Stridonensis Presbyteri Opera Omnia. Edited by J. P. Migne. 11 Vols. Paris: [the Editor], 1845–1846.

Sepher Ha-Razim: A Newly Recovered Book of Magic from the Talmudic Period: Collected from Genizah Fragments and other Sources (Hebr.). Edited by M. Margalioth. Jerusalem: American Academy for Jewish Research/"Yediot Achronot", 1966. .

Sepher Ha-Razim: The Book of the Mysteries. Translated by M. A. Morgan. SBLTT 25 (PS 11). Chico: Scholars Press, 1983.

Septuaginta: Id est Vetus Testamentum graece iuxta LXX interpretes. Edited by A. Rahlfs. 2 Vols. in 1. Stuttgart: Deutsche Bibelgesellschaft, c1935.

Septuaginta: Vetus Testamentum Graecum Auctoritate Academiae Scientiarum Gottingensis editum. 16 Vols. Göttingen: Vandenhoeck & Ruprecht, 1931–.

Siegert, Folker. *Drei hellenistisch-jüdische Predigten: Ps.-Philon, "Über Jona", "Über Simson" und "Über die Gottesbezeichnung 'wohltätig verzehrendes Feuer'"*. WUNT 20. Tübingen: J.C.B. Mohr (Paul Siebeck), 1980.

Sifre on Deuteronomy. Edited by L. Finkelstein. New York: Jewish Theological Seminary of America, 1969 [= 1939].

Sifre: A Tannaitic Commentary on the Book of Deuteronomy. Translated by R. Hammer. New Haven/London: Yale University Press, 1986.

Synopse zur Hekhalot-Literatur. Edited by P. Schäfer. TSAJ 2. Tübingen: J.C.B. Mohr (Paul Siebeck), 1981.

Staab, Karl. *Pauluskommentare aus der griechischen Kirche*. Neutestamentliche Abhandlungen 15. Münster: Aschendorff, 1933.

Suetonius. Translated by J. C. Rolfe. Vol. 2. LCL. London: Heinemann; Cambridge, MA: Harvard University Press, 1913–1914.

Swete, Henry Barclay. *Theodori Episcopi Mopsuesteni in Epistolas B. Pauli Commentarii*. 2 Vols. Cambridge: University Press, 1880–1882.

Tacitus: The Histories. Translated by Clifford H. Moore. Vol. 1. LCL. London: Heinemann; Cambridge, MA: Harvard University Press, 1925.

Talmud Yerushalmi. Krotoshin: 1866. [Reprinted Jerusalem: Shiloh, 1967.]

Targum de Salmos: Edición Príncipe del Ms. Villa-Amil n. 5 de Alfonso de Zamora. Edited by L. Diez Merino. Biblia Poliglota Complutense: Tradición sefardí de la Biblia Aramea 4:1. Bibliotheca Hispana Biblica 6. Madrid: Instituto "Francisco Suárez", 1982.

The Targum of Isaiah. Edited and translated by J. F. Stenning. Oxford: Clarendon, 1949.

The Targums of Onkelos and Jonathan ben Uzziel on the Pentateuch with the Fragments of the Jerusalem Targum: From the Chaldee. Translated by J. W. Etheridge. New York: Ktav, c1968.

The Testaments of the Twelve Patriarchs: A Critical Edition of the Greek Text. Edited by M. de Jonge. PVTG 1:2. Leiden: Brill, 1978.

Testamentum Iobi. Edited by S. P. Brock. And *Apocalypsis Baruchi Graece*. Edited by J.-C. Picard. PVTG 2. Leiden: Brill, 1967.

Die Texte aus Qumran: Hebräisch und Deutsch. Edited by E. Lohse. 3rd ed. Darmstadt: Wissenschaftliche Buchgesellschaft, 1981.

Tischendorf, Constantinus. *Novum Testamentum Graece*. 3 vols. Leipzig: Giesecke & Devrient/Hinrichs, 1869–1894. [NTG]

Torrey, Charles Cutler. *The Lives of the Prophets: Greek Text and Translation*. JBLMS 1. Philadelphia: SBL, 1946.

Tosephta: Based on the Erfurt and Vienna Codices. Edited by M. S. Zuckermandel. 2nd ed. Jerusalem: Bamberger & Wahrmann, 1937.
The Tosefta. Translated by J. Neusner. 6 Vols. New York: Ktav, 1977–83.
Übersetzung der Hekhalot-Literatur. Vol. 2. Edited by P. Schäfer. TSAJ 17. Tübingen: J.C.B. Mohr (Paul Siebeck), 1987.

Valerii Maximi Factorum et Dictorum Memorabilium Libri Novem. Edited by C. Kempf. Leipzig: Teubner, 1888.

Wettstein, Johann Jacob. *Novum Testamentum Graecum.* 2 Vols. Amsterdam: Dommer, 1751–1752.

Yadin, Yigael. *The Temple Scroll.* 3 vols. and supplementary plates. Jerusalem: Israel Exploration Society, 1983.

1.2. Concordances and Lexica

Aland, Kurt, ed. *Computer-Konkordanz zum Novum Testamentum Graece.* Berlin: de Gruyter, 1980.

Bauer, Walter. *Griechisch-Deutsches Wörterbuch zu den Schriften des Neuen Testaments und der übrigen urchristlichen Literatur.* Rev. 5th ed. Berlin/New York: de Gruyter, 1971.
Brown, Francis, Driver, S. R., and Briggs, Charles A. *A Hebrew and English Lexicon of the Old Testament.* Oxford: Clarendon, [1977].

Cowling, Geoffrey. "Concordance to (Genizah) Fragments of the Palestinian Targum." Unpublished Manuscript. University of Aberdeen, 1968.

Dillmann, C. F. August. *Lexicon Linguae Aethiopicae cum Indice Latino.* New York: Ungar, c1955.

Goldschmidt, Lazarus. *Subject Concordance to the Babylonian Talmud.* Edited by R. Edelmann. Royal Library Lazarus Goldschmidt Collection. Copenhagen: Munksgaard, 1959.

Hatch, Edwin and Redpath, Henry A. *A Concordance to the Septuagint and the other Greek Versions of the Old Testament (Including the Apocryphal Books).* 3 Vols. Oxford: Clarendon, 1897–1906.

Jastrow, Marcus. *A Dictionary of the Targumim, the Talmud Babli and Yerushalmi, and the Midrashic Literature.* 2 Vols. New York: Pardes, 1950.

Kassovsky, Ḥaim Joshua. *Concordantiae totius Mischnae: Omnes Voces Sex Librorum Mischnae.* 2 Vols. Frankfurt: Kauffmann, 1927. (2nd ed. Jerusalem 1956–).
Kassovsky, Ḥaim Joshua. *Thesaurus Talmudis: Concordantiae Verborum quae in Talmude Babilonico Reperiuntur.* Edited by Biniamin Kasowski. 41 Vols. Jerusalem: Ministry of Education & Culture, 1954–82.
Kassovsky, Ḥaim Joshua. *Thesaurus Thosephthae: Concordantiae Verborum quae in Sex Thosephthae Ordinibus Reperiuntur.* Vols. Jerusalem: 1932–.

Kassovsky, Ḥaim Joshua. אוצר התרגום קונקורדנצ'א לתרגום אנקלוס. 5 Vols. in one. Jerusalem: Kiriath Moshe, 1933—40.

Koehler, Ludwig and Baumgartner, Walter. *Hebräisches und Aramäisches Lexikon zum Alten Testament.* 3rd ed. Revised by W. Baumgartner. Edited by B. Hartmann et al. Vols. 1—3. Leiden: Brill, 1967—1983.

Kosovsky, Biniamin. *Otzar Leshon Hatanna'im: Concordantiae Verborum quae in Mechilta d'Rabbi Ismael Reperiuntur.* 4 Vols. Jerusalem: Jewish Theological Seminary of America, 1965—1966.

Kosovsky, Biniamin. *Otzar Leshon Hatanna'im: Concordantiae Verborum quae in Sifra aut Torat Kohanim Reperiuntur.* 4 Vols. Jerusalem: Jewish Theological Seminary of America, 1967—1969.

Kosovsky, Biniamin. *Otzar Leshon Hatanna'im: Thesaurus "Sifrei": Concordantiae Verborum quae in 'Sifrei' Numeri et Deuteronomium Reperiuntur.* 5 Vols. Jerusalem: Jewish Theological Seminary of America, 1970—1974.

Kuhn, Karl Georg, ed. *Konkordanz zu den Qumrantexten.* Göttingen: Vandenhoeck & Ruprecht, 1960.

Kuhn, Karl Georg, ed. "Nachträge zur Konkordanz zu den Qumrantexten." *RQ* 4 (1963—64): 163—234.

Lerimann, Tsevi. אוצר אמרי אבות לתלמודים ולמדרשים ולספרי ראשונים. 5 Vols. Jerusalem: Mass, 1959—69.

Liddell, H. G. and Scott, R. *A Greek-English Lexicon.* Edited by H. S. Jones. 2 Vols. + Supplement (edited by E. A. Barber). Oxford: Clarendon, 1925—68.

Lignée, Hubert. "Concordance de '1Q Genesis Apocryphon'." *RQ* 1 (1958—59): 163—186.

Mandelkern, Solomon. *Veteris Testamenti Concordantiae Hebraicae atque Chaldaicae.* Jerusalem/Tel Aviv: Schocken, 1978.

Mayer, Günter. *Index Philoneus.* Berlin/New York: de Gruyter, 1974.

Reider, Joseph and Turner, Nigel. *An Index to Aquila: Greek-Hebrew, Hebrew-Greek, Latin-Hebrew: With the Syriac and Armenian Evidence.* SVT 12. Leiden: Brill, 1966.

Rengstorf, Karl Heinrich (ed.). *A Complete Concordance to Flavius Josephus.* 4 Vols. & Supplement. Leiden: Brill, 1968—1983.

Schäfer, Peter, ed. *Konkordanz zur Hekhalot-Literatur.* 2 vols. TSAJ 12—13. Tübingen: J.C.B. Mohr (Paul Siebeck), 1986—88. [Vol. 2 *non vidi.*]

Siegert, Folker. *Nag-Hammadi-Register: Wörterbuch zur Erfassung der Begriffe in den koptisch-gnostischen Schriften von Nag-Hammadi mit einem deutschen Index.* Introduction by Alexander Böhlig. WUNT 26. Tübingen: J.C.B. Mohr (Paul Siebeck), 1982.

Smend, Rudolf. *Griechisch-Syrisch-Hebräischer Index zur Weisheit des Jesus Sirach.* Berlin: Reimer, 1907.

Van Zijl, J. B. *A Concordance to the Targum of Isaiah.* SBL Aramaic Studies 3. Missoula: Scholars Press, 1979.

Whitelocke, Lester T. *An Analytical Concordance of the Books of the Apocrypha.* 2 vols. Washington: University Press of America, 1978.

2. Secondary Literature

Aageson, James W. "Scripture and Structure in the Development of the Argument in Romans 9–11." *CBQ* 48 (1986): 265–289.

Abbott, T. K. *A Critical and Exegetical Commentary on the Epistles to the Ephesians and Colossians*. ICC. Edinburgh: T. & T. Clark, n.d. [1897].

Aber, Felix. "Memra und Schechinah." In *Festschrift zum 75jährigen Bestehen des jüdisch-theologischen Seminars Fraenckelscher Stiftung*, 2:1–10. Breslau [Wroclaw]: Marcus, 1929.

Aberbach, Moses and Grossfeld, Bernard. *Targum Onqelos on Genesis 49: Translation and Analytical Commentary*. SBL Aramaic Studies 1. Missoula: Scholars Press, 1976.

Albrektson, Bertil. *History and the Gods: An Essay on the Idea of Historical Events as Divine Manifestations in the Ancient Near East and in Israel*. Coniectana Biblica, O.T. Series 1. Lund: Gleerup, 1967.

Allo, E.-B. *Saint Paul: Première Épître aux Corinthiens*. Études Bibliques. 2nd ed. Paris: Lecoffre (Gabalda), 1956.

Allo, E.-B. *Saint Paul: Seconde Épître aux Corinthiens*. Études Bibliques. 2nd ed. Paris: Lecoffre (Gabalda), 1956. [*2 Corinthiens*].

Altenmüller, Hartwig. "Geheimnis." *Lexikon der Ägyptologie* 2/4 (1976): 510–513.

Altmann, Alexander. "שירי־הקדושה בספרות ההיכלות הקדומה." *Melilah* 2 (Manchester, 1946): 1–24.

Amir, Yehoshua. "Philo and the Bible." *Studia Philonica* 2 (1973): 1–8.

Anderson, A. A. "The Use of *Ruah* in IQS, IQH, and IQM." *JSS* 7 (1962): 293–303.

Assmann, Jan. *Re und Amun: Die Krise des polytheistischen Weltbilds im Ägypten der 18.–20. Dynastie*. OBO 51. Freiburg/Switzerland: Universitätsverlag; Göttingen: Vandenhoeck & Ruprecht, 1983.

Attridge, Harold W. *The Interpretation of Biblical History in the Antiquitates Judaicae of Flavius Josephus*. Harvard Dissertations in Religion 7. Missoula: Scholars Press, 1976.

Aune, David E. *The Cultic Setting of Realized Eschatology in Early Christianity*. SNT 28. Leiden: Brill, 1972.

Aune, David E. "Orthodoxy in First Century Judaism? A Response to N. J. McEleney." *JSJ* 7 (1976): 1–10.

Aune, David E. *Prophecy in Early Christianity and the Ancient Mediterranean World*. Grand Rapids: Eerdmans, 1983.

Aune, David E. "The Use of ΠΡΟΦΗΤΗΣ in Josephus." *JBL* 101 (1982): 419–21.

Bacher, Wilhelm. *Die exegetische Terminologie der jüdischen Traditionsliteratur*. 2 Vols. in 1. Darmstadt: Wissenschaftliche Buchgesellschaft, c1965.

Badenas, Robert. *Christ the End of the Law: Romans 10.4 in Pauline Perspective*. JSNTSup 10. Sheffield: JSOT Press, 1985.

Baeck, Leo. "Offenbarung: III. Im Judentum." *RGG*[2] 4 (1927): 660f.

Baeck, Leo. "The Origin of Jewish Mysticism." In idem, *The Pharisees and other Essays*, 93–105. New York: Schocken, 1947.

Baird, William. "Visions, Revelation, and Ministry: Reflections on 2 Cor 12:1–5 and Gal 1:11–17." *JBL* 104 (1985): 651–662.

Balentine, Samuel E. *The Hidden God: The Hiding of the Face of God in the Old Testament*. Oxford: Oxford University Press, 1983.

Bammel, Ernst. "ΑΡΧΙΕΡΕΥΣ ΠΡΟΦΗΤΕΥΩΝ." *TLZ* 79 (1954): 351–356.

Bammel, Ernst. "Νόμος Χριστοῦ." *SE* 3 [=TU 88] (1964): 120–128.

Bammel, Ernst. "Paulus, der Mose des neuen Bundes." *Theologia* 54 (Athens, 1983): 5–14.

Bandstra, Andrew J. "Did the Colossian Errorists Need a Mediator?" In *New Dimensions in New Testament Study*, 329–343. Edited by R. N. Longenecker and M. C. Tenney. Grand Rapids: Zondervan, 1974.

Barnett, P. W. "The Jewish Sign Prophets — A.D. 40–70: Their Intentions and Origin." *NTS* 27 (1981): 679–697.

Barr, James. "The Concepts of History and Revelation." In idem, *Old and New in Interpretation: A Study of the Two Testaments*, 65–102. London: SCM, 1966.

Barr, James. "Revelation in History." *IDB* Supplementary Volume, 746–749. Nashville: Abingdon, 1976.

Barr, James. "Revelation through History in the Old Testament and in Modern Theology." *Interp* 17 (1963): 193–205.

Barrett, C. K. *A Commentary on the Epistle to the Romans*. Black's NT Commentaries. London: Black, 1957.

Barrett, C. K. *A Commentary on the First Epistle to the Corinthians*. Black's New Testament Commentaries. 2nd ed. London: Black, 1971.

Barrett, C. K. *A Commentary on the Second Epistle to the Corinthians*. Black's New Testament Commentaries. 2nd ed. London: Black, 1973. [*2 Corinthians*]

Barrett, C. K. *From First Adam to Last: A Study in Pauline Theology*. London: Black, 1962.

Barrett, C. K. "New Testament Eschatology." *SJT* 6 (1953): 136–155.

Barth, Christoph. *Diesseits und Jenseits im Glauben des späten Israel*. SBS 72. Stuttgart: KBW, 1974.

Barth, Markus. *Ephesians: Introduction, Translation, and Commentary*. AB 34–34A. 2 Vols. Garden City: Doubleday, 1974.

Bartlett, John R. "Revelation and the Old Testament." In *Witness to the Spirit: Essays on Revelation, Spirit, Redemption*, 11–31. Edited by Wilfrid Harrington. Proceedings of the Irish Biblical Association, Vol. 3. Dublin: Irish Biblical Association; Manchester: Koinonia, 1979.

Barton, John. *Oracles of God: Perceptions of Ancient Prophecy in Israel after the Exile*. London: Darton, Longman & Todd, 1986.

Bartsch, Hans-Werner. *Gnostisches Gut und Gemeindetradition bei Ignatius von Antiochien*. BFCT 2:44. Gütersloh: Bertelsmann, 1940.

Bauckham, Richard J. "Colossians 1:24 Again: The Apocalyptic Motif." *EvQ* 47 (1975): 168–170.

Baumann, Rolf. *Mitte und Norm des Christlichen: Eine Auslegung von 1. Korinther 1,1–3,4*. NTAbh 5. Münster: Aschendorffsche Verlagsbuchhandlung, 1968.

Baumeister, Theofried. "Zur Datierung der Schrift an Diognet." *VC* 42 (1988): 105–111.

Baumgarten, Joseph M. "The Unwritten Law in the Pre-Rabbinic Period." In idem, *Studies in Qumran Law*, 13–35. SJLA 24. Leiden: Brill, 1977. [= *JSJ* 3 (1972): 7–29.]

Bavinck, Herman. *The Philosophy of Revelation*. Grand Rapids: Baker, c1979.

Beardslee, William A. "The Casting of Lots at Qumran and in the Book of Acts." *NT* 4 (1960): 245–252.

Beare, Francis Wright. "The Epistle to the Colossians: Introduction and Exegesis." In *The Interpreter's Bible*, Vol. 11, 131–241. Edited by G. A. Buttrick. New York/Nashville: Abingdon, 1955.

Begg, Christopher T. "Access to Heavenly Treasuries: The Traditionsgeschichte of a Motif." *BN* 44 (1988): 15–20.

Beker, J. Christiaan. *Paul the Apostle: The Triumph of God in Life and Thought.* Philadelphia: Fortress, 1980.

Bengel, Johann Albrecht. *Gnomon Novi Testamenti.* Edited by M. E. Bengel and J. Steudel. 3rd ed. London: Nutt, Williams & Norgate; Cambridge: Macmillan, 1855.

Benoit, Pierre. "Colossiens 2:2–3." In *The New Testament Age: Essays in Honor of Bo Reicke.* Vol. 1, 41–51. Edited by W.C. Weinrich. Macon: Mercer University Press, 1984.

Benoit, Pierre. "Ἅγιοι en Colossiens 1.12: Hommes ou Anges?" In *Paul and Paulinism: Essays in Honour of C. K. Barrett,* 83–99. Edited by M. D. Hooker & S. G. Wilson. London: SPCK, 1982.

Benz, Ernst. *Paulus als Visionär: Eine vergleichende Untersuchung der Visionsberichte des Paulus in der Apostelgeschichte und in den paulinischen Briefen.* Akademie der Wissenschaften und der Literatur, Abhandlungen der Geistes- und Sozialwissenschaftlichen Klasse 1952/2. Mainz: Akademie, 1952.

Berchman, Robert M. "Arcana Mundi: Magic and Divination in the *De somniis* of Philo of Alexandria." *SBL 1987 Seminar Papers,* 403–428. Edited by K. H. Richards. SBLSPS 26. Atlanta: Scholars Press, 1987.

Berger, Klaus. "Zur Diskussion über die Herkunft von I Kor. II.9." *NTS* 24 (1978): 270–283.

Berger, Peter L. *The Heretical Imperative: Contemporary Possibilities of Religious Affirmation.* Garden City: Anchor/Doubleday, 1980.

Berger, Peter L. and Luckmann, Thomas. *The Social Construction of Reality: A Treatise in the Sociology of Knowledge.* Garden City: Anchor/Doubleday, 1967.

Bertholet, Alfred. *Biblische Theologie des Alten Testaments.* Vol. 2: *Die jüdische Religion von der Zeit Esras bis zum Zeitalter Christi.* Grundriss der Theologischen Wissenschaften II 2:2. 2nd ed. Tübingen: J.C.B. Mohr (Paul Siebeck), 1911.

Bertram, G. "Praeparatio evangelica in der Septuaginta." *VT* 7 (1957): 225–249.

Bertram, G. "Vom Wesen der Septuaginta-Frömmigkeit: Zur Prägung der biblischen Gottesvorstellung in der griechischen Übersetzung des Alten Testaments." *WO* 2 (1954–59): 274–284.

Best, Ernest. *A Commentary on the First and Second Epistles to the Thessalonians.* Black's New Testament Commentaries. London: Black, 1972.

Best, Ernest. "The Revelation to Evangelize the Gentiles." *JTS* N.S. 35 (1984): 1–30.

Best, Ernest. "The Use and Non-Use of Pneuma by Josephus." *NT* 3 (1959): 218–225.

Betz, Hans Dieter. "The Concept of Apocalyptic in the Theology of the Pannenberg Group." *Journal for Theology and the Church* 6 (1969): 192–207.

Betz, Hans Dieter. *Galatians: A Commentary on Paul's Letter to the Churches in Galatia.* Hermeneia. Philadelphia: Fortress, 1979.

Betz, Otto. *Offenbarung und Schriftforschung in der Qumransekte.* WUNT 6. Tübingen: J.C.B. Mohr (Paul Siebeck), 1960.

Betz, Otto. "Das Problem des Wunders bei Flavius Josephus im Vergleich zum Wunderproblem bei den Rabbinern und im Johannesevangelium." In *Josephus- Studien: Untersuchungen zu Josephus, dem antiken Judentum und dem Neuen Testament: Otto Michel zum 70. Geburtstag gewidmet,* 23–44. Edited by O. Betz et al. Göttingen: Vandenhoeck & Ruprecht, 1974.

Betz, Otto. "Vision and Recognition in Jewish Apocalypticism." In *Proceedings of the Eighth World Congress of Jewish Studies.* Division A: *The Period of the Bible,* 111–117. Edited by D. Krone. Jerusalem: World Union of Jewish Studies, 1982.

Bieder, W. "Das Geheimnis des Christus nach dem Epheserbrief." *TZ* 11 (1955): 329–343.

Bietenhard, Hans. *Die himmlische Welt im Urchristentum und Spätjudentum.* WUNT 2. Tübingen: J.C.B. Mohr (Paul Siebeck), 1951.

Bikerman, Élie. "La Chaîne de la Tradition Pharisienne." *RB* 59 (1952): 44–54.

Birnbaum, Solomon Asher. "Alphabet, Hebrew: Square Script." *EncJud* 1 (1972): 705–710.

Bittner, Wolfgang. "Gott – Menschensohn – Davidssohn: Eine Untersuchung zur Traditionsgeschichte von Daniel 7,13 f." *Freiburger Zeitschrift für Philosophie* 32 (1985): 343–372.

Black, Matthew. *The Book of Enoch or 1 Enoch: A New English Edition.* SVTP 7. Leiden: Brill, 1985.

Black, Matthew. *Romans.* NCB. London: Oliphants, 1973.

Blank, Josef. "Erwägungen zum Schriftverständnis des Paulus." In *Rechtfertigung: Festschrift für Ernst Käsemann zum 70. Geburtstag.* Edited by J. Friedrich et al. Tübingen: J.C.B. Mohr (Paul Siebeck); Göttingen: Vandenhoeck & Ruprecht, 1976.

Blass, F. and Debrunner, A. *A Greek Grammar of the New Testament and other Early Christian Literature.* Translated & Revised by R. W. Funk. Chicago/London: University of Chicago Press, 1961.

Blenkinsopp, Joseph. *A History of Prophecy in Israel: From the Settlement in the Land to the Hellenistic Period.* London: SPCK, 1984.

Blenkinsopp, Joseph. "Prophecy and Priesthood in Josephus." *JJS* 25 (1974): 239–262.

Blenkinsopp, Joseph. *Prophecy and Canon: A Contribution to the Study of Jewish Origins.* University of Notre Dame Center for the Study of Judaism and Christianity in Antiquity, No. 3. Notre Dame/London: University of Notre Dame Press, 1977.

Blenkinsopp, Joseph. *Wisdom and Law in the Old Testament: The Ordering of Life in Israel and early Judaism.* Oxford Bible Series. Oxford/New York: Oxford University Press, 1983.

Bockmuehl, Markus. "A Note on the Text of Colossians 4:3." *JTS* N.S. 39 (1988): 484–489.

Bockmuehl, Markus. "Das Verb φανερόω im Neuen Testament: Versuch einer Neuauswertung." *BZ* 32 (1988): 87–99.

Bogaert, Pierre. *Apocalypse de Baruch: Introduction, Traduction du Syriaque et Commentaire.* SC 145. 2 Vols. Paris: Cerf, 1969.

Böhl, Felix. "Die Legende vom Verbergen der Lade." *FJB* 4 (1976): 63–80.

Böhlig, Alexander. *Mysterion und Wahrheit: Gesammelte Beiträge zur spätantiken Religionsgeschichte.* Arbeiten zur Geschichte des späteren Judentums und des Urchristentums 6. Leiden: Brill, 1968.

Bonsirven, Joseph. *Exégèse Rabbinique et Exégèse Paulinienne.* Bibliothèque de Théologie Historique. Paris: Beauchesne, 1939.

Borger, R. "Geheimwissen." *Reallexikon der Assyriologie und Vorderasiatischen Archäologie* 3 (1957–71): 188–191.

Bornkamm, Günter. "Die Hoffnung im Kolosserbrief: Zugleich ein Beitrag zur Frage der Echtheit des Briefes." In idem, *Geschichte und Glaube,* Part 2 (=*Gesammelte Aufsätze,* Vol. 4), 206–213. BEvT 53. Munich: Kaiser, 1971.

Bornkamm, Günter. "Μυστήριον κτλ." *TWNT* 4 (1942): 809–834.

Bornkamm, Günter. "Die Offenbarung des Zornes Gottes: Röm 1–3." In idem, *Das Ende des Gesetzes: Paulusstudien,* 9–33. BEvT 16. Munich: Kaiser, 1952.

Botterweck, G. Johannes and Bergman, L. "ידע." *TWAT* 3 (1977–82): 479–512.

Bousset, Wilhelm. *Die Religion des Judentums im späthellenistischen Zeitalter.* Edited by H. Gressmann. HNT 21. 3rd ed. Tübingen: J.C.B. Mohr (Paul Siebeck), 1926.

Bowers, W. Paul. "A Note on Colossians 1:27a." In *Current Issues in Biblical and Patristic Interpretation: Studies in Honor of Merrill C. Tenney Presented by His former Students*, 110–114. Edited by G. F. Hawthorne. Grand Rapids: Eerdmans, 1975.

Bowker, John W. "Merkabah Visions and the Visions of Paul." *JSS* 16 (1971): 157–173.

Bowker, John W. "Mystery and Parable: Mark iv. 1–20." *JTS* N.S. 25 (1974): 301–317.

Bowker, John W. *The Targums and Rabbinic Literature: An Introduction to Jewish Interpretations of Scripture*. Cambridge: University Press, 1969.

Braun, Herbert. "Das himmlische Vaterland bei Philo und im Hebräerbrief." In *Verborum Veritas: Festschrift für Gustav Stählin zum 70. Geburtstag*, 319–27. Edited by Otto Böcher and Klaus Haacker. Wuppertal: Brockhaus, 1970.

Bréhier, Emile. *Les Idées Philosophiques et Religieuses de Philon d'Alexandrie*. Études de Philosophie Médiévale 8. 2nd ed. Paris: Librairie Philosophique J. Vrin, 1925.

Brock, Sebastian. Review of M. D. Koster, *The Peshitta of Exodus*, Studia Semitica Neerlandica 19 (Assen/Amsterdam: van Gorcum, 1977). *JTS* N.S. 29 (1978): 549–51.

Brockington, L. H. "Septuagint and Targum." *ZAW* 66 (1954): 80–86.

Broek-Utne, Albert. "Eine schwierige Stelle in einer alten Gemeindeordnung (Did. 11/11)." *ZKG* 54 (1935): 576–81.

Brooke, George J. "Qumran Pesher: Towards the Redefinition of a Genre." *RQ* 10 (1981): 483–503.

Brooke, George J. *Exegesis at Qumran: 4QFlorilegium in its Jewish Context*. JSOTSup 29. Sheffield: JSOT, 1985.

Brown, Raymond E. *The Semitic Background of the Term "Mystery" in the New Testament*. Facet Books, Biblical Series 21. Philadelphia: Fortress, 1968.

Brownlee, William H. *The Midrash Pesher of Habakkuk*. SBLMS 24. Missoula: Scholars Press, 1979.

Bruce, F. F. *1&2 Thessalonians*. WBC 45. Waco: Word, 1982.

Bruce, F. F. "Biblical Exposition at Qumran." In *Gospel Perspectives*, Vol.3 : *Studies in Midrash and Historiography*, 77–98. Edited by R. T. France and D. Wenham. Sheffield: JSOT, 1983.

Bruce, F. F. "The Colossian Heresy." *BibSac* 141 (1984): 195–208.

Bruce, F. F. *The Epistle of Paul to the Romans: An Introduction and Commentary*. Tyndale NT Commentaries. London: Tyndale, 1963.

Bruce, F. F. *The Epistle to the Galatians: A Commentary on the Greek Text*. NIGTC. Grand Rapids: Eerdmans, 1982.

Bruce, F. F. *The Epistles to the Colossians, to Philemon, and to the Ephesians*. NICNT. Grand Rapids: Eerdmans, 1984.

Bruce, F. F. "Holy Spirit in the Qumran Texts." *ALUOS* 6 (1966–68): 49–55.

Bruce, F. F. "Jews and Christians in the Lycus Valley." *BibSac* 141 (1984): 3–15.

Bruce, F. F. "Josephus and Daniel." *ASTI* 4 (1965): 148–162.

Bruce, F. F. *Paul: Apostle of the Heart Set Free*. Grand Rapids: Eerdmans, 1977.

Buchanan, George Wesley. *Revelation and Redemption: Jewish Documents of Deliverance from the Fall of Jerusalem to the Death of Naḥmanides*. Dillsboro: Western North Carolina Press, 1978.

Buchanan, George Wesley. "The Word of God and the Apocalyptic Vision." In *Society of Biblical Literature 1978 Seminar Papers*, 2:183–192. Edited by Paul J. Achtemeier. Missoula: Scholars Press, 1978.

Büchler, Adolph. *Types of Jewish-Palestinian Piety from 70 B.C.E. to 70 C.E.: The Ancient Pious Men*. New York: Ktav, 1968 [= 1922].

Büchsel, Friedrich. *Der Geist Gottes im Neuen Testament*. Gütersloh: Bertelsmann, 1926.

Buffière, Félix. *Les Mythes d'Homère et la Pensée Grecque.* Paris: Belles Lettres, 1956.
Bujard, Walter. *Stilanalytische Untersuchungen zum Kolosserbrief als Beitrag zur Methodik von Sprachvergleichen.* SUNT 11. Göttingen: Vandenhoeck & Ruprecht, 1973.
Bultmann, Rudolf. "Der Begriff der Offenbarung im Neuen Testament." In idem, *Glauben und Verstehen: Gesammelte Aufsätze,* 3:1–34. 3rd ed. Tübingen: J.C.B. Mohr (Paul Siebeck), 1965.
Bultmann, Rudolf. "Exegetische Probleme des zweiten Korintherbriefes." *Symbolae Biblicae Upsalienses* 9 (1947): 3–31 [= idem, *Exegetica: Aufsätze zur Erforschung des Neuen Testaments,* 298– 322. Edited by E. Dinkler. Tübingen: J.C.B. Mohr (Paul Siebeck), 1967.]
Bultmann, Rudolf. "Γινώσκω κτλ." *TWNT* 1 (1933): 688–719.
Bultmann, Rudolf. "Ignatius und Paulus." In *Studia Paulina: In Honorem Johannis de Zwaan Septuagenarii,* 37–51. [Edited by J. N. Sevenster and W. C. van Unnik.] Haarlem: Bohn, 1953.
Bultmann, Rudolf. *Theologie des Neuen Testaments.* Edited by O. Merk. Uni-Taschenbücher 630. 9th ed. Tübingen: J.C.B. Mohr (Paul Siebeck), 1984.
Bultmann, Rudolf. *Der zweite Brief an die Korinther.* Edited by E. Dinkler. KEKNT Sonderband. Göttingen: Vandenhoeck & Ruprecht, 1976. [*2 Korinther*]
Bultmann, Rudolf and Lührmann, Dieter. "Φαίνω κτλ." *TWNT* 9 (1973): 1–11.
Burchard, Christoph. "The Importance of Joseph and Aseneth for the Study of the New Testament: A General Survey and a Fresh Look at the Lord's Supper." *NTS* 33 (1987): 102–134.
Burkhardt, Helmut. *Die Inspiration heiliger Schriften bei Philo von Alexandrien.* Giessen/Basle: Brunnen, 1988.
Burres, Kenneth Lee. "Structural Semantics in the Study of the Pauline Understanding of Revelation." Ph. D. Dissertation, Evanston, IL (Northwestern University): 1970.

Caird, G. B. Review of Mauro Pesce, *Paulo e gli arconti a Corinto.* In *JTS* N.S. 29 (1978): 543–44.
Callan, Terrance. "Prophecy and Ecstacy in Greco-Roman Religion and in 1 Corinthians." *NT* 27 (1985): 125–140.
Cambier, J. "Le grand mystère concernant le Christ et son Église: Ephésiens 5,22–33." *Bib* 47 (1966): 43–90, 223–242.
Caragounis, Chrys C. *The Ephesian* Μυστήριον: *Meaning and Content.* ConBNT 8. Lund: Gleerup, 1977.
Carmignac, Jean. "Conjecture sur la première ligne de la Règle de la Communauté." *RQ* 2 (1959): 85–87.
Carmignac, Jean. "Description du péhnomène de l'Apocalyptique dans l'Ancien Testament." In *Apocalypticism in the Mediterranean World and the Near East: Proceedings of the International Colloquium on Apocalypticism, Uppsala, August 12–17, 1979,* 163–170. Edited by David Hellholm. Tübingen: J.C.B. Mohr (Paul Siebeck), 1983.
Carr, Wesley. *Angels and Principalities: The Background, Meaning and Development of the Pauline Phrase hai archai kai hai exousiai.* SNTSMS 42. Cambridge: Cambridge University Press, 1981.
Carr, Wesley. "The Rulers of this Age: 1 Corinthians ii. 6–8." *NTS* 23 (1977): 20–35.
Casciaro Ramirez, Jose Maria. "Los Himnos de Qumrân y el 'Misterio' Paulino." *Scripta Theologica* 8 (1976): 9–56.
Casciaro Ramirez, Jose Maria. "El 'Misterio' Divino en los Escritos Posteriores de Qumrân." *Scripta Theologica* 8 (1976): 445–479.

Casciaro Ramirez, Jose Maria. "El Tema del 'Misterio' Divino en la Regla de la Comunidad de Qumrân." *Scripta Theologica* 7 (1975): 481–497. ["Regla"]

Cerfaux, Lucien. *The Christian in the Theology of St Paul*. Translated by Lilian Soiron. London etc.: Chapman, 1967.

Cerfaux, Lucien. "Influence des Mystères sur le Judaïsme Alexandrin avant Philon." *Muson* 37 (1924): 29–88. [= Idem, *Recueil Lucien Cerfaux: Études d'Exégèse et d'Histoire Religieuse de Monseigneur Cerfaux à l'Occasion de son Soixante-Dixième Anniversaire*, 1:65–112. BETL 6–7. Gembloux: Duculot, 1954.]

Cerfaux, Lucien. "Les 'saints' de Jérusalem." *ETL* 2 (1925): 510–529.

Chadwick, Henry. "All Things to All Men." *NTS* 1 (1955): 261–275.

Chadwick, Henry. "Philo and the Beginnings of Christian Thought." In *The Cambridge History of Later Greek and Early Medieval Philosophy*, 133–192. Edited by A. H. Armstrong. Cambridge: Cambridge University Press, 1967.

Charles, R. H. *The Book of Enoch or 1 Enoch: Translated from the Editor's Ethiopic Text*. 2nd ed. Oxford: Clarendon, 1912.

Charles, R. H. *A Critical History of the Doctrine of a Future Life in Israel, in Judaism, and in Christianity*. Jowett Lectures 1898–99. 2nd ed. London: Black, 1913.

Charles, R. H. *Religious Development between the Old and New Testaments*. Home University Library of Modern Knowledge. London: Williams & Norgate; New York: Holt, 1914.

Charlesworth, James H. *The Old Testament Pseudepigrapha and the New Testament: Prolegomena for the Study of Christian Origins*. SNTSMS 54. Cambridge, etc.: Cambridge University Press, 1985.

Chernus, Ira. *Mysticism in Rabbinic Judaism: Studies in the History of Midrash*. Studia Judaica 11. Berlin/New York: de Gruyter, 1982.

Chester, Andrew. *Divine Revelation and Divine Titles in the Pentateuchal Targumim*. TSAJ 14. Tübingen: J.C.B. Mohr (Paul Siebeck), 1986.

Chilton, Bruce D. *A Galilean Rabbi and his Bible: Jesus' Own Interpretation of Isaiah*. London: SPCK, 1984.

Chilton, Bruce D. *The Glory of Israel: The Theology and Provenience of the Isaiah Targum*. JSOTSup 23. Sheffield: JSOT Press, 1983.

Christiansen, Irmgard. *Die Technik der allegorischen Auslegungswissenschaft bei Philon von Alexandrien*. BGBH 7. Tübingen: J.C.B. Mohr (Paul Siebeck), 1969.

Clements, Ronald Ernest. *Prophecy and Covenant*. SBT 43. London: SCM, 1965.

Cohen, A. *Everyman's Talmud*. London: Dent; New York: Dutton, c1949.

Cohen, Norman J. "Shekhinta ba-Galuta: A Midrashic Response to Destruction and Persecution." *JSJ* 13 (1982): 147–159.

Collange, Jean-François. *Énigmes de la Deuxième Épître de Paul aux Corinthiens: Étude Exégétique de 2 Cor. 2,14–7,4*. SNTSMS 18. Cambridge: University Press, 1972.

Collins, John J. *Between Athens and Jerusalem: Jewish Identity in the Hellenistic Diaspora*. New York: Crossroads, 1983.

Collins, John J. "Introduction [to Apocalypse]: Towards the Morphology of a Genre." *Semeia* 14 (1979): 1–20. ["Morphology"]

Collins, John J. "Jewish Apocalyptic against its Hellenistic Near Eastern Environment." *BASOR* 220 (1975): 27–36.

Collins, Marilyn F. "The Hidden Vessels in Samaritan Traditions." *JSJ* 3 (1972): 97–116.

Conzelmann, Hans. *Der erste Brief an die Korinther*. KEKNT 5. [11th ed.] Göttingen: Vandenhoeck & Ruprecht, 1969.

Conzelmann, Hans. *Grundriß der Theologie des Neuen Testaments*. 4th ed. rev. by A. Lindemann. Tübingen: J.C.B. Mohr (Paul Siebeck), 1987.

Conzelmann, Hans. "Paulus und die Weisheit." *NTS* 12 (1966): 231–244.

Copleston, Frederick. *A History of Philosophy*. Vol. 1: *Greece and Rome* (Parts 1+2). Image Books. Garden City: Doubleday, 1962.

Coppens, Joseph. "Le 'Mystère' dans la Théologie Paulinienne et ses Parallèles Qumrâniens." In *Littérature et Théologie Pauliniennes, 142–165*. Recherches Bibliques 5. Bruges: Desclée de Brouwer, 1960.

Couturier, Guy. "La vision du conseil divin: étude d'une forme commune au prophétisme et à l'apocalyptique." *Science et Esprit* 35 (1984): 5–43.

Cranfield, C. E. B. *A Critical and Exegetical Commentary on the Epistle to the Romans*. ICC. 2 Vols. Edinburgh: T. & T. Clark, 1975–1979.

Cranfield, C. E. B. "St. Paul and the Law." *SJT* 17 (1964): 43–68.

Crenshaw, James L. *Prophetic Conflict: Its Effect Upon Israelite Religion*. BZAW 124. Berlin/New York: de Gruyter, 1971.

Cullmann, Oscar. *Christ and Time: The Primitive Christian Conception of Time and History*. Translated by F. V. Filson. Rev. ed. London: SCM, 1962.

Daniélou, Jean. *The Theology of Jewish Christianity*. The Development of Christian Doctrine before the Council of Nicaea, Vol. 1. Translated and edited by J. A. Baker. London: Darton, Longman & Todd, 1964.

Daube, David. "τρία μυστήρια κραυγῆς." *JTS* 16 (1965): 128–129.

Daube, David. "Typology in Josephus." *JJS* 31 (1980): 18–36.

Dautzenberg, Gerhard. "Botschaft und Bedeutung der urchristlichen Prophetie nach dem ersten Korintherbrief (2:6–16; 12–14)." In *Prophetic Vocation in the New Testament and Today*, 131–161. Edited by J. Panagopoulos. NTSup 45. Leiden: Brill, 1977.

Dautzenberg, Gerhard. "Glossolalie." *RAC* 11 (1981): 225–246.

Dautzenberg, Gerhard. *Urchristliche Prophetie: Ihre Erforschung, ihre Voraussetzungen im Judentum und ihre Struktur im ersten Korintherbrief*. BWANT 6:4 (104). Stuttgart, etc.: Kohlhammer, 1975.

Davis, James A. "Wisdom and Spirit: An Investigation of 1 Corinthians 1:18–3:20 against the Background of Jewish Sapiential Traditions in the Greco-Roman Period." Ph. D. Dissertation, Nottingham: 1982.

Davies, W. D. *Paul and Rabbinic Judaism: Some Rabbinic Elements in Paul's Theology*. 4th ed. Philadelphia: Fortress, 1980. [*PRJ*]

Davies, W. D. "Paul and the Law: Reflections on Pitfalls in Interpretation." In idem, *Jewish and Pauline Studies*, 91–122. London: SPCK, 1984. ["Law"]

Davies, W. D. "Reflections on Tradition: The 'Abot Revisited." In *Jewish and Pauline Studies*, 27–48. London: SPCK, 1984. ["Tradition"]

Davies, W. D. *Torah in the Messianic Age and/or the Age to Come*. JBLMS 7. Philadelphia: SBL, 1952.

De Lestapis, S. *L'Énigme des Pastorales de Saint Paul*. Paris: Lecoffre (Gabalda), 1976.

De Pury, Albert. "Sagesse et Révélation dans l'Ancien Testament." *RTP* 27 (1977): 1–50.

De Strycker, Émile. *La Forme la Plus Ancienne du Protévangile de Jacques: Recherches sur le Papyrus Bodmer 5 avec une Édition Critique du Texte Grec et une Traduction Annotée*. Subsidia Hagiographica 33. Brussels: Société des Bollandistes, 1961.

De Villiers, P. G. R. "Revealing the Secrets: Wisdom and the World in the Similitudes of Enoch." *Neotestamentica* 17 (1983): 50–68.

De Wette, W. M. L. *Kurze Erklärung der Briefe an die Colosser, an Philemon, an die Ephesier und Philipper.* Kurzgefasstes exegetisches Handbuch zum Neuen Testament 2:4. Leipzig: Weidmann, 1843.

De Wette, W. M. L. *Kurze Erklärung des Briefes an die Römer.* Kurzgefasstes exegetisches Handbuch zum Neuen Testament 2:1. 4th ed. Leipzig: Weidmann, 1847.

Dean-Otting, Mary. *Heavenly Journeys: A Study of the Motif in Hellenistic Jewish Literature.* Judentum und Umwelt 8. Frankfurt etc.: Lang, 1984.

Deane, William J. *The Book of Wisdom: The Greek Text, the Latin Vulgate and the Authorised English Version: With an Introduction, Critical Apparatus and a Commentary.* Oxford: Clarendon, 1881.

Dechent, H. "Der 'Gerechte' — eine Bezeichnung für den Messias." *TSK* 100 (1927/28): 439–443.

Deden, D. "Le 'Mystère' Paulinien." *ETL* 13 (1936): 405–442.

Dehandschutter, B. "Le Rêve dans l'Apocryphe de la Genèse." In *La Littérature Juive entre Torah et Mischna: Quelques problèmes*, 48–55. Recherches Bibliques 9. Leiden: Brill, 1974.

Deissmann, Adolf. *Paul: A Study in Social and Religious History.* Translated by W. E. Wilson. 2nd ed. London: Hodder & Stoughton, 1926.

Deissner, Kurt. *Paulus und die Mystik seiner Zeit.* 2nd ed. Leipzig/Erlangen: Deichert, 1921.

Del Páramo, Severiano. "El 'misterio' paulino y el sentido literal pleno." *Semana Biblica Española* 15 (1955): 247–266.

Delling, Gerhard. "Die biblische Prophetie bei Josephus." In *Josephus- Studien: Untersuchungen zu Josephus, dem antiken Judentum und dem Neuen Testament: Otto Michel zum 70. Geburtstag gewidmet*, 109–121. Edited by O. Betz et al. Göttingen: Vandenhoeck & Ruprecht, 1974.

Delling, Gerhard. "Josephus und das Wunderbare." In idem, *Studien zum Neuen Testament und zum hellenistischen Zeitalter: Gesammelte Aufsätze 1950–1968*, 130–145. Edited by F. Hahn et al. Göttingen: Vandenhoeck & Ruprecht, 1970.

Delling, Gerhard. "Τέλος κτλ." *TWNT* 8 (1969): 50–88.

Delling, Gerhard. "Wunder — Allegorie — Mythus bei Philon von Alexandreia." In idem, *Studien zum Neuen Testament und zum hellenistischen Zeitalter: Gesammelte Aufsätze 1950–1968*, 72–129. Edited by F. Hahn et al. Göttingen: Vandenhoeck & Ruprecht, 1970.

Dewailly, P. "Mystère et silence dans Rom. xvi.25." *NTS* 14 (1967–68): 111–117.

Dexinger, Ferdinand. *Henochs Zehnwochenapokalypse und offene Probleme der Apokalyptikforschung.* Studia Post-Biblica 29. Leiden: Brill, 1977.

Dexinger, Ferdinand. "Limits of Tolerance in Judaism: The Samaritan Example." In *Jewish and Christian Self-Definition*, Vol. 2: *Aspects of Judaism in the Graeco-Roman Period*, 88–114. Edited by E. P. Sanders et al. London: SCM, 1981.

Dibelius, Martin. *An die Kolosser Epheser: An Philemon.* HNT 12. 2nd ed. Tübingen: Mohr (Siebeck), 1927.

Dibelius, Martin and Conzelmann, Hans. *The Pastoral Epistles: A Commentary on the Pastoral Epistles.* Translated by P. Buttolph & A. Yarbro. Edited by H. Koester. Hermeneia. Philadelphia: Fortress, 1972.

Dienstfertig, Meyer. *Die Prophetologie in der Religionsphilosophie des ersten nachchristlichen Jahrhunderts, unter besonderer Beachtung der Verschiedenheit in den Auffassungen des Philon von Alexandrien und des Flavius Josephus.* [Ph. D. Dissertation, Erlangen] Breslau: Schatzky, 1892. Dommershausen, W. "גּוֹרָל." In *TWAT* 1 (1973): 991–998.

Dotan, Aharon. "The 'Secret' in the Synagogue Inscription of 'Én-Gedi" (Hebrew). *Leshonenu* 35 (1970–71): 211–217.

Downing, F. G. *Has Christianity a Revelation?* Library of Philosophy and Theology. London: SCM, 1964.

Downing, F. G. "Revelation in the New Testament and among its Expounders." *SE* 3 [= TU 88] (1964): 183–186.

Draper, Jonathan Alfred. "A Commentary on the Didache in the Light of the Dead Sea Scrolls and Related Documents." Ph.D. Dissertation, Cambridge: 1983.

Driver, G. R. *The Judaean Scrolls: The Problem and a Solution*. Oxford: Blackwell, 1965.

Drummond, James. *Philo Judaeus; or The Jewish-Alexandrian Philosophy in its Development and Completion*. 2 Vols. London/ Edinburgh: Williams and Norgate, 1888.

Duganzic, Ivan. *Das "Ja" Gottes in Christus: Eine Studie zur Bedeutung des Alten Testaments für das Christusverständnis des Paulus*. Forschung zur Bibel. Würzburg: Echter, 1977.

Dulles, Avery. *Models of Revelation*. Garden City: Doubleday, 1983.

Dunn, James D. G. "Prophetic 'I'-Sayings and the Jesus Tradition: The Importance of Testing Prophetic Utterances within Early Christianity." *NTS* 24 (1978): 175–198.

Dunn, James D. G. *Romans*. WBC 38A–B. Dallas: Word, 1988.

Dunn, James D. G. *Unity and Diversity in the New Testament: An Inquiry into the Character of Earliest Christianity*. London: SCM, 1977.

Dupont, Jacques. *Gnosis: La connaissance religieuse dans les Épîtres de Saint Paul*. Universitatis Catholicae Lovaniensis Dissertationes ad gradum magistri in Facultate Theologica 2:40. 2nd ed. Paris: Gabalda, 1960.

Eaton, John H. "Some Misunderstood Hebrew Words for God's Self-Revelation." *Bible Translator* 25 (1974): 331–338.

Eaton, John H. *Vision in Worship: The Relation of Prophecy and Liturgy in the Old Testament*. London: SPCK, 1981.

Eckstein, Hans Joachim. "'Denn Gottes Zorn wird vom Himmel her offenbar werden': Exegetische Erwägungen zu Röm 1,18." *ZNW* 78 (1987): 74–89.

Eckstein, Hans Joachim. "'Nahe ist dir das Wort': Exegetische Erwägungen zu Röm 10,8." *ZNW* 79 (1988) 205–220.

Ehrlich, Ernst Ludwig. "Tora im Judentum." *EvT* 37 (1977): 536–548.

Ehrlich, Ernst Ludwig. *Der Traum im Alten Testament*. BZAW 73. Berlin: Töpelmann, 1953.

Eichrodt, Walther. "Offenbarung: II Im AT." *RGG*³ 4 (1960): 1599–1601. ["Offenbarung"]

Eising, H. "Die theologische Geschichtsbetrachtung im Weisheitsbuche." In *Vom Wort des Lebens: Festschrift für M. Meinertz zur Vollendung des 70. Lebensjahres 19. Dezember 1950*, 28–40. Edited by N. Adler. NTAbh Supplement 1. Münster: Aschendorffsche Verlagsbuchhandlung, 1951.

Elliger, Karl. *Studien zum Habakuk-Kommentar vom Toten Meer*. BHT 15. Tübingen: J.C.B. Mohr (Paul Siebeck), 1953.

Ellis, E. Earle. "Dating the New Testament." *NTS* 26 (1980): 487–502.

Ellis, E. Earle. *Paul's Use of the Old Testament*. Edinburgh/ London: Oliver & Boyd, 1957.

Ellis, E. Earle. "'Spiritual' Gifts in the Pauline Community." *NTS* 20 (1974): 128–144.

Ellis, E. Earle. "'Wisdom' and 'Knowledge' in 1 Corinthians." *TynBul* 25 (1974): 82–98.

Evans, Craig A. "The Colossian Mystics." *Bib* 63 (1982): 188–205.

Fabry, Heinz-Josef. "סוד: Der himmlische Thronrat als ekklesiologisches Modell." In idem (ed.), *Bausteine biblischer Theologie: Festgabe für G. Johannes Botterweck zum 60. Geburtstag dargebracht von seinen Schülern*, 99–126. BBB 50. Cologne/Bonn: Hanstein, 1977.

Falk, Ze'ev W. "The Temple Scroll and the Codification of Jewish Law." *Jewish Law Annual* 2 (1979): 33–44.

Fascher, Erich. "Deus Invisibilis: Eine Studie zur biblischen Gottesvorstellung." In *Rudolf Otto Festgruß: Aufsätze eines Kollegenkreises zu Rudolf Ottos 60. Geburtstag*, 41–77. Edited by H. Frick. Marburger Theologische Studien 1. Gotha: Klotz, 1931.

Fascher, Erich. *ΠΡΟΦΗΤΗΣ: Eine sprach- und religionsgeschichtliche Untersuchung*. Giessen: Töpelmann, 1927.

Fee, Gordon D. *1 and 2 Timothy, Titus*. A Good News Commentary. San Francisco: Harper & Row, 1984.

Fee, Gordon D. *The First Epistle to the Corinthians*. NICNT. Grand Rapids: Eerdmans, 1987.

Festugière, A.-J. *La Révélation d'Hermès Trismégiste*. Vol. 1: *L'Astrologie et les Sciences Occultes*. Études Bibliques. Paris: Lecoffre (Gabalda), 1944.

Feuillet, André. "L'énigme de I Cor. II,9: Contribution à l'étude des sources de la christologie paulinienne." *RB* 70 (1963): 52–74.

Fichtner, Johannes. *Die altorientalische Weisheit in ihrer israelitisch-jüdischen Ausprägung: Eine Studie zur Nationalisierung der Weisheit in Israel*. BZAW 62. Giessen: Töpelmann, 1933. [*Altorientalische Weisheit*]

Fichtner, Johannes. "Ὀργή: B. III. Der Zorn Gottes im AT." *TWNT* 5 (1954): 395–410.

Fichtner, Johannes. "Die Stellung der Sapientia Salomonis in der Literatur- und Geistesgeschichte ihrer Zeit." *ZNW* 36 (1937): 113–132.

Fichtner, Johannes. *Weisheit Salomos*. HAT 2:6. Tübingen: J.C.B. Mohr (Paul Siebeck), 1938. [*Weisheit*]

Fiddes, P. S. "The Hiddenness of Wisdom in the Old Testament and Later Judaism." D. Phil. Dissertation, Oxford: 1976.

Findlay, G. G. *The Epistles of Paul the Apostle to the Thessalonians*. Cambridge Greek Testament for Schools and Colleges. Cambridge: University Press, 1904.

Finkel, Asher. "The Pesher of Dreams and Scriptures." *RQ* 4 (1963–64): 357–70.

Fishbane, Michael. *Biblical Interpretation in Ancient Israel*. Oxford: Clarendon, 1985.

Fishbane, Michael. "Inner Biblical Exegesis: Types and Strategies of Interpretation in Ancient Israel." In *Midrash and Literature*, 19–37. Edited by G. H. Hartman and S. Budick. New Haven/London: Yale University Press, 1986. ["Exegesis"]

Fishbane, Michael. "Jewish Biblical Exegesis: Presupposition and Principles." In *Scripture in the Jewish and Christian Traditions: Authority, Interpretation, Relevance*, 92–110. Edited by F. R. Greenspahn. University of Denver Center for Judaic Studies. Nashville: Abingdon, 1982. ["Jewish Exegesis"]

Fishbane, Michael. "The Qumran Pesher and Traits of Ancient Hermeneutics." In *Proceedings of the Sixth World Congress of Jewish Studies*, 1:97–114. Edited by Avigdor Shinan. Jerusalem: World Union of Jewish Studies/Jerusalem Academic Press, 1977.

Fishbane, Michael. "Revelation and Tradition: Aspects of Inner-Biblical Exegesis." *JBL* 99 (1980): 343–61.

Fitzmyer, Joseph A. "The Aramaic 'Elect of God' Text from Qumran Cave IV," *CBQ* 27 (1965): 348–72.

Flemington, W. F. "On the interpretation of Colossians 1:24." In *Suffering and Martyrdom in the New Testament: Studies Presented to G. M. Styler by the Cambridge New Testament Seminar*, 84—90. Edited by W. Horbury and B. McNeil. Cambridge, etc.: Cambridge University Press, 1981.

Foerster, Werner. "Der Heilige Geist im Spätjudentum." *NTS* 8 (1962): 117—34.

Fohrer, Georg. *Theologische Grundstrukturen des Alten Testaments*. Theologische Bibliothek Töpelmann 24. Berlin: de Gruyter, 1972.

Fohrer, Georg. "Twofold Aspects of Hebrew Words." In *Words and Meanings: Essays Presented to David Winton Thomas on his Retirement from the Regius Professorship of Hebrew in the University of Cambridge, 1968*, 95—103. Edited by P. Ackroyd and B. Lindars. Cambridge: University Press, 1968.

Fohrer, Georg and Foerster, Werner. "Σῴζω κτλ." *TWNT* 7 (1964): 966—1024.

Forster, A. Haire. "The Meaning of Δόξα in the Greek Bible." *ATR* 12 (1929—30): 311—316.

Francis, Fred O. "The Christological Argument of Colossians." In *God's Christ and His People: Studies in Honour of Nils Alstrup Dahl*, 192—208. Edited by J. Jervell and W. A. Meeks. Oslo etc.: Universitetsforlaget, 1977.

Francis, Fred O. "Humility and Angelic Worship in Col 2:18." In *Conflict at Colossae: A Problem in the Interpretation of Early Christianity Illustrated by Selected Modern Studies*, 163—195. Edited and translated by Fred O. Francis & Wayne A. Meeks. SBLSBS 4. Missoula: Society of Biblical Literature, 1973.

Frankel, Z. *Ueber den Einfluss der palästinischen Exegese auf die alexandrinische Hermeneutik*. Leipzig: Barth, 1851.

Franxman, Thomas W. *Genesis and the "Jewish Antiquities" of Flavius Josephus*. BibOr 35. Rome: Biblical Institute Press, 1979.

Frey, J.-B. "La Révélation d'après les Conceptions Juives au Temps de Jésus-Christ." *RB* 13 (1916): 472—510.

Friedrich, Gerhard. "Εὐαγγελίζομαι κτλ." *TWNT* 2 (1935): 705—735.

Fritsch, Charles T. *The Anti-Anthropomorphisms of the Greek Pentateuch*. Princeton: Princeton University Press, 1943.

Fritsch, Charles T. "A Study of the Greek Translation of the Hebrew Verbs 'To See', with Deity as Subject or Object." In *Eretz-Israel: Archaeological, Historical and Geographical Studies*. Vol. 16: *Harry M. Orlinsky Volume*, 51—56. Edited by B. A. Levine and A. Malamat. Jerusalem: Israel Exploration Society, 1982.

Früchtel, Ursula. *Die kosmologischen Vorstellungen bei Philo von Alexandrien: Ein Beitrag zur Geschichte der Genesisexegese*. ALGHJ 2. Leiden: Brill, 1968.

Fryer, Nico S. L. "The Meaning and Translation of *Hilastérion* in Romans 3:25." *EQ* 59 (1987): 99—116.

Furfey, Paul Hanley. "The Mystery of Lawlessness." *CBQ* 8 (1946): 179—191.

Furnish, Victor Paul. *II Corinthians*. AB 32A. Garden City: Doubleday, 1984.

Gabrion, Hervé. "L'interprétation de l'Écriture dans la littérature de Qumrân." In *Aufstieg und Niedergang der römischen Welt*. Part II: *Principat*. Vol 19:1, pp. 779—848. Berlin/New York: de Gruyter, 1979.

Gadd, C. J. "Some Babylonian Divinatory Methods and their Inter- Relations." In *La Divination en Mésopotamie ancienne et dans les régions voisins: XIVᵉ Rencontre Assyriologique Internationale*, 21—34. Paris: Presses Universitaires de France, 1966.

García Martínez, Florentino. "Las Tablas Celestes en el Libro de los Jubileos." In *Palabra y Vida: Homenaje a José Alonso Díaz en su 70 cumpleaños*, 333—349. Edited by A. Vargas-Machuca and G. Ruiz. Publicaciones de la Universidad Pontifica Comillas Madrid, Serie 1, Estudios 28, Teología 1:15. Madrid: UPCM, 1984.

Gärtner, Bertil. *The Areopagus Speech and Natural Revelation*. ASNU 21. Uppsala: Almqvist & Wiksells; Lund: Gleerup; Copenhagen: Munksgaard, 1955.

Gaster, Theodore H. "A Qumran Reading of Deuteronomy XXXIII 10." *VT* 8 (1958): 217—219.

Gaston, Lloyd. *Paul and the Torah*. Vancouver: University of British Columbia Press, 1987.

Gehman, Henry S. "Adventures in Septuagint Lexicography." *Textus* 5 (1966): 125—132.

Georgi, Dieter. *Unterweisung in lehrhafter Form: Weisheit Salomos*. Jüdische Schriften aus hellenistisch-römischer Zeit 3:4. Gütersloh: Mohn, 1980.

Gerleman, Gillis. *Studies in the Septuagint: I. The Book of Job*. Lunds Universitets Årsskrift N. S. 1.43.2. Lund: Gleerup, 1946.

Gese, Hartmut. "Anfang und Ende der Apokalyptik, dargestellt am Sacharjabuch." *ZTK* 70 (1973): 20—49.

Gilbert, Maurice. "Les raisons de la modération divine (Sagesse 11,21—12,2)." In *Mélanges bibliques et orientaux en l'honneur de M. Henri Cazelles*, 149—162. Edited by A. Caquot and M. Delcor. AOAT 212. Kevelaer: Butzon & Bercker; Neukirchen-Vluyn: Neukirchener, 1981.

Ginzberg, Louis. *The Legends of the Jews*. 7 Vols. Philadelphia: Jewish Publication Society of America, 1909—1938.

Ginzberg, Louis. "Some Observations on the Attitude of the Synagogue towards the Apocalyptic-Eschatological Writings." *JBL* 41 (1922): 115—136.

Glombitza, Otto. "Apostolische Sorge: Welche Sorge treibt den Apostel Paulus zu den Sätzen Röm. xi 25ff.?" *NT* 7 (1965): 312—318.

Gnilka, Joachim. *Der Epheserbrief*. HTKNT 10:2. Freiburg etc.: Herder, 1971.

Gnilka, Joachim. *Der Kolosserbrief*. HTKNT 10:1. Freiburg, etc.: Herder, 1980.

Gnuse, Robert K. *The Dream Theophany of Samuel: Its Structure in Relation to Ancient Near Eastern Dreams and its Theological Significance*. Lanham, MD: University Press of America, 1984.

Goldberg, Arnold M. "Rabban Yoḥanans Traum: Der Sinai in der frühen Merkavamystik." *FJB* 3 (1975): 1—27.

Goldberg, Arnold M. "Rede und Offenbarung in der Schriftauslegung Rabbi Aqibas." *FJB* 8 (1980): 61—79.

Goldberg, Arnold M. "Torah aus der Unterwelt? Eine Bemerkung zu Röm 10,6—7." *BZ* 14 (1970): 127—131.

Goldberg, Arnold M. "Die spezifische Verwendung des Terminus Schekhinah im Targum Onkelos als Kriterium einer relativen Datierung." *Judaica* 19 (1963): 43—61.

Goldberg, Arnold M. *Untersuchungen über die Vorstellung von der Schekhina in der frühen rabbinischen Literatur — Talmud und Midrasch*. Studia Judaica 5. Berlin: de Gruyter, 1969.

Goldenberg, David. "The Halakha in Josephus and in Tannaitic Literature: A Comparative Study." *JQR* 67 (1977): 30—43.

Goodenough, Erwin R. *By Light, Light: The Mystic Gospel of Hellenistic Judaism*. Amsterdam: Philo Press, 1969 [=1935].

Goodenough, Erwin R. *Jewish Symbols in the Greco-Roman Period*. Bollingen Series 37. 13 Vols. New York: Pantheon, 1953—1968.

Goodspeed, Edgar J. *Index Apologeticus sive Clavis Iustini Martyris Operum Aliorumque Apologetarum Pristinorum*. Leipzig: Hinrichs, 1912.

Goppelt, Leonhard. *Theologie des Neuen Testaments*. Edited by J. Roloff. 2 Vols. in 1. Uni-Taschenbücher 850. 3rd ed. Göttingen: Vandenhoeck & Ruprecht, 1981.

Gordon, Robert P. "A Study of Targum Jonathan to the Minor Prophets from Nahum to Malachi: Introduction, Translation and Commentary." Ph. D. Dissertation, Cambridge: 1976.

Grabbe, Lester L. "Orthodoxy in First Century Judaism: What are the Issues?" *JSJ* 8 (1977): 149–153.

Grant, Robert M. *The Apostolic Fathers: A New Translation and Commentary*. Vol. 4: *Ignatius of Antioch*. London, etc.: Nelson, 1966.

Grant, R. M. *The Letter and the Spirit*. London: SPCK, 1957.

Grässer, Erich. "Kol 3,1–4 als Beispiel einer Interpretation secundum homines recipientes." *ZTK* 64 (1967): 139–68.

Gray, John. *I & II Kings: A Commentary*. OTL. London: SCM, 1964.

Grelot, Pierre. "L'eschatologie de la Sagesse et les Apocalypses Juives." In *A La Rencontre de Dieu: Mémorial Albert Gelin*, 165–178. Edited by A. Barucq et al. Bibliothèque de la Faculté Catholique de Théologie de Lyon 8. Le Puy: Mappus, 1961.

Grintz, Yehoshua M. "Balaam: In the Aggadah". *EncJud* 4 (1972): 123–124.

Grözinger, Karl Erich. *Musik und Gesang in der Theologie der frühen jüdischen Literatur: Talmud Midrasch Mystik*. TSAJ 3. Tübingen: Mohr (Siebeck), 1982.

Grözinger, Karl Erich. "Singen und ekstatische Sprache in der frühen jüdischen Mystik." *JSJ* 11 (1980): 66–77.

Grudem, Wayne A. *The Gift of Prophecy in 1 Corinthians*. Washington: University Press of America, 1982.

Gruenwald, Ithamar. *Apocalyptic and Merkavah Mysticicsm*. AGAJU 14. Leiden/Cologne: Brill, 1980.

Guillet, J. "Révélation: II. Nouveau Testament." *DBSup* 56 (1982): 600–618.

Gyllenberg, Rafael. "Kultus und Offenbarung." In *Interpretationes ad Vetus Testamentum pertinentes Sigmundo Mowinckel Septuagenario Missae*, 72–84. Oslo: Land og Kirke, 1955.

Haag, Herbert. "Révélation: I Ancien Testament." *DBSup* 56 (1982): 586–600.

Hafemann, Scott J. *Suffering and the Spirit: An Exegetical Study of II Cor. 2:14–3:3 within the Context of the Corinthian Correspondence*. WUNT 2:19. Tübingen: J.C.B. Mohr (Paul Siebeck), 1986.

Hagner, Donald A. "The Vision of God in Philo and John: A Comparative Study." *JETS* 14 (1971): 81–93.

Hall, Winfield Scott II. "Paul as a Christian Prophet in his Interpretation of the Old Testament in Romans 9–11." Th. D. Dissertation, Chicago (Lutheran School of Theology): 1982.

Halperin, David J. *The Merkabah in Rabbinic Literature*. New Haven: Yale University Press, 1980.

Hamerton-Kelly, R. G. *Pre-Existence, Wisdom and the Son of Man*. SNTSMS 21. Cambridge: Cambridge University Press, 1973.

Hamerton-Kelly, R. G. "The Temple and the Origin of Apocalyptic." *VT* 20 (1970): 1–15.

Hanson, Anthony Tyrrell. "A Quasi-Gnostic Pauline Midrash: 1 Corinthians 2.6–16." In idem, *The New Testament Interpretation of Scripture*, 21–96. London: SPCK, 1980.

Hanson, Paul D. "Apocalypticism." *IDB* Supplement (1976): 28–34.

Hanson, Paul D. *The Dawn of Apocalyptic*. Philadelphia: Fortress, 1975.

Harnack, Adolf (von). "Das Alte Testament in den Paulinischen Briefen und in den Paulinischen Gemeinden." *Sitzungsberichte der Preußischen Akademie der Wissenschaften,* Philosophisch-historische Klasse (1929): 124–141. [= *Kleine Schriften zur Alten Kirche,* Vol. 2 (*Berliner Akademieschriften* 1908–1930), 823–840. Opuscula 9:2. Leipzig: Zentralantiquariat der DDR, 1980.]

Harnack, Adolf (von). *Die Lehre von den zwölf Aposteln: Nebst Untersuchungen zur ältesten Geschichte der Kirchenverfassung und des Kirchenrechts.* Leipzig: Hinrichs, 1884.

Harnack, Adolf (von). "Das Problem des zweiten Thessalonicherbriefs." *Sitzungsberichte der Preußischen Akademie der Wissenschaften,* Philosophisch- historische Klasse (1910): 560–578. [= *Kleine Schriften zur Alten Kirche,* Vol. 2 (Berliner Akademieschriften 1908–1930), 101–119. Opuscula 9:2. Leipzig: Zentralantiquariat der DDR, 1980.]

Harrington, Daniel J. "The Wisdom of the Scribe According to Ben Sira." In *Ideal Figures in Ancient Judaism: Profiles and Paradigms,* 181–188. Edited by G. W. E. Nickelsburg and J. J. Collins. SBLSCS 12. Chico: Scholars Press, 1980.

Harris, Murray J. *Raised Immortal: Resurrection and Immortality in the New Testament.* Marshalls Theological Library. London: Marshall, Morgan & Scott, 1983.

Hartman, Lars. *Prophecy Interpreted: The Formation of Some Jewish Apocalyptic Texts and of the Eschatological Discourse Mark 13 Par.* ConBNT 1. Lund: Gleerup, 1966.

Harvey, A. E. "The Use of Mystery Language in the Bible." *JTS* N.S. 31 (1980): 320–336.

Hayward, C. T. Robert. *Divine Name and Presence: The Memra.* Oxford Centre for Postgraduate Hebrew Studies. Totowa, NJ: Allanheld, Osmun & Co., 1981.

Hayward, C. T. Robert. "The Memra of YHWH and the Development of its Use in Targum Neofiti I." *JJS* 25 (1974): 412–418.

Hayward, C. T. Robert. Review of Domingo Muñoz León, *Gloria de la Shekinah en los Targumim del Pentateuco* (1977). *JJS* 30 (1979): 99–102.

Hayward, C. T. Robert. Review of Domingo Muñoz León, *Dios-Palabra: Memra en los Targumim del Pentateuco* (1974). *JJS* 27 (1976): 94–96.

Hayward, C. T. Robert. "Some Notes on Scribes and Priests in the Targum of the Prophets." *JJS* 36 (1985): 210–221.

Hecht, Richard D. "Scripture and Commentary in Philo." In *Society of Biblical Literature 1981 Seminar Papers,* 129–164. Edited by K. H. Richards. Society of Biblical Literature Seminar Papers Series 20. Chico: Scholars Press, 1981.

Hegermann, Harald. "Philon von Alexandria." In *Literatur und Religion des Frühjudentums: Eine Einführung,* 353–369. Edited by J. Maier and J. Schreiner. Würzburg: Echter; Gütersloh: Mohn, 1973.

Heinemann, Isaak. "Die Kontroverse über das Wunder im Judentum der hellenistischen Zeit." In *Jubilee Volume in Honour of Prof. Bernhard Heller on the Occasion of his Seventieth Birthday.* Edited by A. Scheiber. Budapest: Kertész Jószef Könyvnyomdájában, 1941.

Heinemann, Joseph. *Prayer in the Talmud: Forms and Patterns.* Studia Judaica 9. Berlin/New York: de Gruyter, 1977.

Heinemann, Joseph and Petuchowski, Jakob J. *Literature of the Synagogue.* Library of Jewish Studies. New York: Behrman House, 1975.

Heinisch, Paul. *Das Buch der Weisheit.* EHAT 24. Münster: Aschendorffsche Verlagsbuchhandlung, 1912.

Heinrici, Georg. *Kritisch Exegetisches Handbuch über den ersten Brief an die Korinther.* KEKNT 5. 7th ed. Göttingen: Vandenhoeck & Ruprecht, 1888.

Hemer, Colin J. *The Letters to the Seven Churches of Asia in their Local Setting.* JSNTSup 11. Sheffield: JSOT Press, 1986.

Hengel, Martin. "Anonymität, Pseudepigraphie und 'Literarische Fälschung' in der jüdisch-hellenistischen Literatur." In *Pseudepigrapha I: Pseudopythagorica — Lettres de Platon; Littérature pseudépigraphique juive*, 231—308. Edited by K. von Fritz. Fondation Hardt pour l'Étude de l'Antiquité Classique, Entretiens 18. Geneva: Vandoeuvres, 1972.

Hengel, Martin. *Judentum und Hellenismus: Studien zu ihrer Begegnung unter besonderer Berücksichtigung Palästinas bis zur Mitte des 2. Jh. v. Chr..* WUNT 10. 2nd ed. Tübingen: J.C.B. Mohr (Paul Siebeck), 1973.

Herold, Gerhart. *Zorn und Gerechtigkeit Gottes bei Paulus: Eine Untersuchung zu Röm. 1,16—18.* European University Papers 23:14. Bern: H. Lang; Frankfurt: P. Lang, 1973.

Hill, David. *New Testament Prophecy.* Marshall's Theological Library. London: Marshall, Morgan & Scott, 1979.

Himmelfarb, Martha. "Apocalyptic Ascent and the Heavenly Temple." In *SBL 1987 Seminar Papers*, 210—217. Edited by K. H. Richards. SBLSPS 26. Atlanta: Scholars Press, 1987.

Himmelfarb, Martha. "A Report on Enoch in Rabbinic Literature." In *SBL 1978 Seminar Papers*, 1:259—269. Edited by P. J. Achtemeier. SBLSPS 13. Missoula: Scholars Press, 1978.

Hofius, Otfried. "1 Kor 2,9 und das koptische Testament des Jakob." *ZNW* 66 (1975): 140—142.

Hofius, Otfried. "Das Evangelium und Israel: Erwägungen zu Römer 9—11." *ZTK* 83 (1986): 297—324.

Holl, Karl. "Der Kirchenbegriff des Paulus in seinem Verhältnis zu dem der Urgemeinde." In idem, *Gesammelte Aufsätze zur Kirchengeschichte II: Der Osten*, 44—67. Tübingen: J.C.B. Mohr (Paul Siebeck), 1928. [= *Das Paulusbild in der neueren deutschen Forschung*, 144—178. Edited by K. H. Rengstorf. Wege der Forschung 24. Darmstadt: Wissenschaftliche Buchgesellschaft, 1964.]

Hollander, H. W. and De Jonge, M. *The Testaments of the Twelve Patriarchs: A Commentary.* Studia in Veteris Testamenti Pseudepigrapha 8. Leiden: Brill, 1985.

Holm-Nielsen, Svend. *Hodayot: Psalms from Qumran.* Aarhus: Universitetsforlaget, 1960.

Holtz, Gottfried. *Die Pastoralbriefe.* THKNT 13. Berlin: Evangelische Verlagsanstalt, 1965.

Holtz, Traugott. "Zur Frage der inhaltlichen Weisungen bei Paulus." *TLZ* 106 (1981): 386—400.

Hooker, M. D. "Adam in Romans 1." *NTS* 6 (1960): 297—306.

Hooker, M. D. "Beyond the Things that are Written? St Paul's Use of Scripture." *NTS* 27 (1981): 295—309.

Hooker, M. D. "Were there False Teachers in Colossae?" In *Christ and Spirit in the New Testament: In Honour of Charles Francis Digby Moule*, 315—331. Edited by B. Lindars and S. S. Smalley. Cambridge: University Press, 1973.

Horbury, William. "1 Thessalonians ii.3 as Rebutting the Charge of False Prophecy." *JTS* N.S. 33 (1982): 492—507. ["False Prophecy"]

Horbury, William. "The Benediction of the *Minim* and Early Jewish-Christian Controversy." *JTS* N.S. 33 (1982): 19—61.

Horbury, William. "Extirpation and Excommunication." *VT* 35 (1985): 13—38.

Horbury, William. "Ezekiel Tragicus 106: δωρήματα." *VT* 36 (1986): 37—51.

Horbury, William. "The Messianic Associations of 'the Son of Man'." *JTS* N.S. 36 (1985): 34–55.

Horgan, Maurya P. *Pesharim: Qumran Interpretations of Biblical Books.* CBQMS 8. Washington: Catholic Biblical Association, 1979.

Hornung, Erik. *Der Eine und die Vielen: Ägyptische Göttervorstellungen.* 2nd ed. Darmstadt: Wissenschaftliche Buchgesellschaft, 1973.

Horovitz, Isaiah. ספר שני לוחות הברית. Amsterdam: 1689.

Hruby, Kurt. "Le Concept de Révélation dans la Théologie Rabbinique." *L'Orient Syrien* 11 (1966): 17–50, 169–198.

Hruby, Kurt. "L'influence des apocalypses sur l'eschatologie dans la théologie rabbinique." *L'Orient Syrien* 11 (1966): 291–320.

Hübner, Hans. *Gottes Ich und Israel: Zum Schriftgebrauch des Paulus in Römer 9–11.* FRLANT 136. Göttingen: Vandenhoeck & Ruprecht, 1984.

Hübner, Hans. *Law in Paul's Thought.* Translated by J. C. G. Greig. Edited by J. Riches. Edinburgh: Clark, 1984.

Hurtado, Larry W. "The Doxology at the End of Romans." In *New Testament Textual Criticism: Its Significance for Exegesis: Essays in Honour of Bruce M. Metzger,* 185–199. Edited by E. J. Epp and G. D. Fee. Oxford: Clarendon, 1981.

Huther, Johann Eduard. *Kritisch Exegetisches Handbuch über die Briefe an Timotheus und Titus.* KEKNT 11. 4th ed. Göttingen: Vandenhoeck & Ruprecht, 1876.

Jacob, Edmond. "Wisdom and Religion in Sirach." In *Israelite Wisdom: Theological and Literary Essays in Honor of Samuel Terrien,* 247–260. Edited by J. G. Gammie et al. Missoula: Scholars Press, 1978.

Jeremias, Joachim. *Die Briefe an Timotheus und Titus.* NTD 9. Göttingen: Vandenhoeck & Ruprecht, 1963.

Jeremias, Joachim. *Jerusalem zur Zeit Jesu: Eine kulturgeschichtliche Untersuchung zur neutestamentlichen Zeitgeschichte.* 3rd ed. Göttingen: Vandenhoeck & Ruprecht, 1962.

Jeremias, Jörg. *Theophanie: Die Geschichte einer alttestamentlichen Gattung.* WMANT 10. Neukirchen-Vluyn: Neukirchener Verlag, 1965.

Jervell, Jacob. "Die offenbarte und die verborgene Tora: Zur Vorstellung über die neue Tora im Rabbinismus." *Studia Theologica* 25 (1971): 90–108.

Jewett, Robert. *The Thessalonian Correspondence: Pauline Rhetoric and Millenarian Piety.* Foundations and Facets. Philadelphia: Fortress, 1986.

Johnson, Gary Lance. "Josephus: Heir Apparent to the Prophetic Tradition?" In *Society of Biblical Literature 1983 Seminar Papers,* 337–346. Edited by K. H. Richards. Society of Biblical Literature Seminar Papers Series 22. Chico: Scholars Press, 1983.

Johnson, Luke Timothy. *The Writings of the New Testament: An Interpretation.* Philadelphia: Fortress, 1986.

Kadushin, Max. *The Rabbinic Mind.* New York: Blaisdell, 1965.

Kamlah, Ernst. "Traditionsgeschichtliche Untersuchungen zur Schlußdoxologie des Römerbriefs." Ph. D. Dissertation, Tübingen, 1955.

Käsemann, Ernst. *An die Römer.* HNT 8a. 2nd ed. Tübingen: J.C.B. Mohr (Paul Siebeck), 1974.

Käsemann, Ernst. *Perspectives on Paul.* Translated by M. Kohl. New Testament Library. London: SCM, 1971.

Kaufman, Stephen A. "On Methodology in the Study of the Targums and their Chronology." *JSNT* 23 (1985): 117–124.

Kee, Howard Clark. "The Socio-Cultural Setting of Joseph and Aseneth." *NTS* 29 (1983): 394–413.

Kelly, J. N. D. *A Commentary on the Pastoral Epistles: I Timothy – II Timothy – Titus.* Black's NT Commentaries. London: Black, 1963.

Kertelge, Karl. "Apokalypsis Jesou Christou (Gal 1,12)." In *Neues Testament und Kirche: Für Rudolf Schnackenburg*, 266–281. Edited by J. Gnilka. Freiburg etc.: Herder, 1974.

Kiley, Mark. *Colossians as Pseudepigraphy.* The Biblical Seminar 4. Sheffield: JSOT, 1986.

Kim, Seyoon. *The Origin of Paul's Gospel.* WUNT 2:4. Tübingen: J.C.B. Mohr (Paul Siebeck), 1981.

Kim, Seyoon. *"The 'Son of Man'" as the Son of God.* WUNT 30. Tübingen: J.C.B. Mohr (Paul Siebeck), 1983.

Kittel, Gerhard. "Ἀρχέω κτλ." *TWNT* 1 (1933): 464–467.

Kittel, Gerhard and von Rad, Gerhard. "Δόξα κτλ." *TWNT* 2 (1935): 235–258.

Kloppenborg, J. S. "Isis and Sophia in the Book of Wisdom." *HTR* 75 (1982): 57–84.

Klöpper, A. "Die Offenbarung des verborgenen Mysteriums Gottes (1. Kor. 2,7)." *Zeitschrift für Wissenschaftliche Theologie* 47 (1904): 525–545.

Knierim, Rolf. "Offenbarung im Alten Testament." In *Probleme biblischer Theologie: Gerhard von Rad zum 70. Geburtstag*, 206–235. Edited by Hans Walter Wolff. Munich: Kaiser, 1971.

Knox, Wilfred L. "The Divine Wisdom." *JTS* 38 (1937): 230–237.

Knox, Wilfred L. "A Note on Philo's Use of the Old Testament." *JTS* 41 (1940): 30–34.

Knox, Wilfred L. *St Paul and the Church of the Gentiles.* Cambridge: University Press, 1939. [*Gentiles*].

Kobelski, Paul J. *Melchizedek and Melchireša'.* CBQMS 10. Washington: Catholic Biblical Association, 1981.

Koch, Dietrich-Alex. *Die Schrift als Zeuge des Evangeliums: Untersuchungen zur Verwendung und zum Verständnis der Schrift bei Paulus.* BHT 69. Tübingen: J.C.B. Mohr (Paul Siebeck), 1986.

Koch, Klaus. "Offenbaren wird sich das Reich Gottes." *NTS* 25 (1979): 158–65.

Koch, Klaus. *The Rediscovery of Apocalyptic.* Translated by Margaret Kohl. London: SCM, 1972.

Kohler, Kaufmann. "The Halakik [*sic*] Portions in Josephus' Antiquities." In idem, *Studies, Addresses and Personal Papers*, 69–85. New York: The Alumni Association of the Hebrew Union College (Bloch), 1931.

Kohler, Kaufmann. "Revelation." *JE* 10: (1905): 396–398.

König, F. Eduard. *Der Offenbarungsbegriff des Alten Testaments.* 2 Vols. Leipzig: Hinrichs, 1882.

Kosmala, Hans. *Hebräer – Essener – Christen: Studien zur Vorgeschichte der frühchristlichen Verkündigung.* Studia Post-Biblica 1. Leiden: Brill, 1959.

Kraft, Robert A. *The Apostolic Fathers: A New Translation and Commentary.* Vol. 3: *Barnabas and Didache.* New York etc.: Nelson, 1965.

Krämer, H. "Zur Wortbedeutung 'Mysteria'." *Wort und Dienst* N.S. 6 (1959): 121–125.

Kraus, Hans Joachim. *Psalmen.* BKAT 15:1+2. 5th ed. Neukirchen-Vluyn: Neukirchener, 1978.

Kraus, Hans Joachim. *Theologie der Psalmen.* BKAT 15:3. Neukirchen-Vluyn: Neukirchener, 1979.

Kremer, Jacob. *Was an den Leiden Christi noch mangelt: Eine interpretationsgeschichtliche und exegetische Untersuchung zu Kol. 1,24b.* BBB 12. Bonn: Hanstein, 1956.

Krüger, Paul. "Würdigung der Propheten im Spätjudentum." In *Neutestamentliche Studien: Georg Heinrici zu seinem 70. Geburtstag (14. März 1914)*, 1–12. Edited by A. Deissmann & H. Windisch. Untersuchungen zum Neuen Testament 6. Leipzig: J.C. Hinrichs'sche Buchhandlung, 1914.

Küchler, Max. *Frühjüdische Weisheitstraditionen: Zum Fortgang weisheitlichen Denkens im Bereich des frühjüdischen Jahweglaubens.* OBO 26. Fribourg: Universitätsverlag; Göttingen: Vandenhoeck & Ruprecht, 1979.

Kuhn, Peter. *Gottes Selbsterniedrigung in der Theologie der Rabbinen.* SANT 17. Munich: Kösel, 1968.

Kuhn, Peter. *Offenbarungsstimmen im Antiken Judentum: Untersuchungen zur bat qôl und verwandten Phänomenen.* TSJA 20. Tübingen: J.C.B. Mohr (Paul Siebeck), 1989. [*Non vidi.*].

Kuhn, Heinz-Wolfgang. *Enderwartung und eschatologisches Heil: Untersuchungen zu den Gemeindeliedern von Qumran.* SUNT 4. Göttingen: Vandenhoeck & Ruprecht, 1966.

Kuntz, J. Kenneth. *The Self-Revelation of God.* Philadelphia: Westminster, 1967.

Labat, René, et al., eds. *Les religions du Proche-Orient asiatique: Textes babyloniens, ougaritiques, hittites.* Trésor spirituel de l'humanité. Paris: Fayard/Denoël, 1970.

Lacocque, André. *Daniel et son Temps: Recherches sur le Mouvement Apocalyptique Juif au IIe siècle avant Jésus-Christ.* Le Monde de la Bible. Geneva: Labor et Fides, 1983.

Ladd, George Eldon. "Revelation and Tradition in Paul." In *Apostolic History and the Gospel: Biblical and Historical Essays Presented to F. F. Bruce on his 60th Birthday*, 223–230. Edited by W. W. Gasque and R. P. Martin. Exeter: Paternoster, 1970.

Ladd, George Eldon. *A Theology of the New Testament.* Grand Rapids: Eerdmans, 1984.

Lagrange, M.-J. *Le Judaïsme avant Jésus-Christ.* Études Bibliques. Paris: Librairie Lecoffre, 1931.

Lagrange, M.-J. "Mystères." *RB* 34 (1925): 150–152.

Lampe, G. W. H. *God as Spirit: The Bampton Lectures, 1976.* Oxford: Clarendon, 1977.

Lampe, G. W. H. "'Grievous Wolves' (Acts 20:29)." In *Christ and Spirit in the New Testament: In Honour of Charles Francis Digby Moule*, 253–268. Edited by B. Lindars and S. S. Smalley. Cambridge: University Press, 1973.

Lapide, Pinchas and Stuhlmacher, Peter. *Paul: Rabbi and Apostle.* Translated by L. W. Denef. Minneapolis: Augsburg, 1984.

Larcher, C. *Études sur le Livre de la Sagesse.* Études Bibliques. Paris: Lecoffre, 1969. [*Études*]

Larcher, C. *Le Livre de la Sagesse ou La Sagesse de Salomon.* Études Bibliques N.S. 1, 3. Vols. 1–2. Paris: Lecoffre (Gabalda), 1983–1984. [*Sagesse*]

Latourelle, René. *Theology of Revelation.* New York: Alba House, 1966.

Le Déaut, Roger. *La nuit pascale: Essai sur la signification de la Pâque juive à partir du Targum d'Exode XII 42.* AnBib 22. Rome: Institut Biblique Pontifical, 1963.

Leaney, A. R. C. *The Rule of Qumran and Its Meaning: Introduction, Translation and Commentary.* London: SCM, 1966.

Lebram, Jürgen. "ΜΥΣΤΗΡΙΟΝ ΒΑΣΙΛΕΩΣ." In *Abraham unser Vater: Juden und Christen im Gespräch über die Bibel: Festschrift für Otto Michel zum 60. Geburtstag*, 320–324. Edited by O. Betz et al. AGSU 5. Leiden: Brill, 1963.

Lebram, Jürgen C. H. "Nachbiblische Weisheitstraditionen." *VT* 15 (1965): 167–237.

Lebram, Jürgen C. H. "The Piety of the Jewish Apocalyptists." In *Apocalypticism in the Mediterranean World and the Near East: Proceedings of the International Colloquium on Apocalypticism, Uppsala, August 12–17, 1979*, 171–210. Edited by David Hellholm. Tübingen: J.C.B. Mohr (Paul Siebeck), 1983.

Lebram, Jürgen C. H. "Apokalyptik und Hellenismus im Buche Daniel: Bemerkungen und Gedanken zu Martin Hengels Buch über 'Judentum und Hellenismus'." *VT* 20 (1970): 503—24.

Leenhardt, Franz J. *The Epistle to the Romans: A Commentary.* Translated by H. Knight. London: Lutterworth, 1961.

Leisegang, Johannes. "Griechische Philosophie als Mysterion." *Philologische Wochenschrift* 52 (1932): 1189—96.

Leivestad, Ragnar. "Das Dogma von der prophetenlosen Zeit." *NTS* 19 (1973): 288—299.

Levenson, Jon D. "The Sources of Torah: Psalm 119 and the Modes of Revelation in Second Temple Judaism." In *Ancient Israelite Religion: Essays in Honor of Frank Moore Cross,* 559—574. Edited by Patrick D. Miller et al. Philadelphia: Fortress, 1987.

Lévêque, Pierre. *Aurea Catena Homeri: Une Étude sur l'Allegorie Grecque.* Annales Littéraires de l'université de Besançon. Paris: Belles Lettres, 1959.

Levine, Baruch A. "On the Presence of God in Biblical Religion." In *Religions in Antiquity: Essays in Memory of Erwin Ramsdell Goodenough.* Edited by J. Neusner. SHR 14. Leiden: Brill, 1968.

Lewis, Agnes Smith. "1 Timothy iii.16." *JTS* 19 (1918): 80—81.

Lewy, Hans. *Sobria Ebrietas: Untersuchungen zur Geschichte der antiken Mystik.* BZNW 9. Giessen: Töpelmann, 1929.

Licht, Jacob. *The Thanksgiving Scroll: A Scroll from the Wilderness of Judaea: Text, Introduction, Commentary and Glossary* [Hebrew]. Jerusalem: Bialik Institute, 1957.

Lieberman, Saul. *Hellenism in Jewish Palestine: Studies in the Literary Transmission Beliefs and Manners of Palestine in the I Century B.C.E. — IV Century C.E.* Texts and Studies of the Jewish Theological Seminary of America 18. New York: Jewish Theological Seminary of America, 1950.

Lightfoot, J. B. *The Apostolic Fathers.* [Edited by J. R. Harmer]. 6 vols. London/New York: 1869—91.

Lightfoot, J. B. *Saint Paul's Epistles to the Colossians and to Philemon: A Revised Text with Introductions, Notes, and Dissertations.* 3rd ed. London/New York: Macmillan, 1879.

Lim, Timothy H. "'Not in persuasive words of wisdom, but in the demonstration of the Spirit and power' (I Cor. 2.4)." *NT* 29 (1987): 137—149.

Lincoln, Anthony T. *Paradise Now and Not Yet: Studies in the Role of the Heavenly Dimension in Paul's Thought with Special Reference to his Eschatology.* SNTSMS 43. Cambridge: Cambridge University Press, 1981.

Lincoln, Anthony T. "'Paul the Visionary': The Setting and Significance of the Rapture to Paradise in II Corinthians xii.1—10." *NTS* 25 (1979): 204—20.

Lindars, Barnabas. *Jesus Son of Man.* London: SPCK, 1983.

Lindblom, Johannes. "Die Vorstellung des Sprechens Jahwes zu den Menschen im Alten Testament." *ZAW* 75 (1963): 263—288.

Lindblom, Johannes. *Gesichte und Offenbarungen: Vorstellungen von göttlichen Weisungen und übernatürlichen Erscheinungen im ältesten Christentum.* SHVL 65. Lund: Gleerup, 1968.

Lindner, Helgo. *Die Geschichtsauffassung des Flavius Josephus in Bellum Judaicum: Gleichzeitig ein Beitrag zur Quellenfrage.* AGAJU 12. Leiden: Brill, 1972.

Lohmeyer, Ernst. *Die Briefe an die Kolosser und an Philemon.* KEKNT 9:2. 12th (=5th) ed. Göttingen: Vandenhoeck & Ruprecht, 1961.

Lohmeyer, Ernst. *Vom göttlichen Wohlgeruch.* Sitzungsberichte der Heidelberger Akademie der Wissenschaften, Philosophisch-historische Klasse 1919/9. Heidelberg: Winters Universitätsbuchhandlung, 1919.

Lohse, Eduard. *Die Briefe an die Kolosser und an Philemon.* KEKNT 9:2. 14th (= 1st) ed. Göttingen: Vandenhoeck & Ruprecht, 1968.

Lombard, H. A. "The Character, Epoch (Period), Origins (Motives) and Methods of Jewish Apocalyptic." *Neotestamentica* 12 (1981): 20—40.

Lona, Horacio E. *Die Eschatologie im Kolosser- und Epheserbrief.* Forschung zur Bibel 48. Würzburg: Echter, 1984.

Lock, Walter. *A Critical and Exegetical Commentary on the Pastoral Epistles (I & II Timothy and Titus).* ICC. Edingburgh: T. & T. Clark, 1924.

Lowy, S. *The Principles of Samaritan Bible Exegesis.* Studia Post-Biblica 28. Leiden: Brill, 1977.

Lübking, Hans-Martin. *Paulus und Israel im Römerbrief.* European University Papers 23:260. Frankfurt etc.: Lang, 1986.

Luck, Ulrich. "Die Bekehrung des Paulus und das paulinische Evangelium: Zur Frage der Evidenz in Botschaft und Theologie des Apostels." *ZNW* 76 (1985): 187—208.

Lueken, Wilhelm. *Michael: Eine Darstellung und Vergleichung der jüdischen und der morgenländisch-christlichen Tradition vom Erzengel Michael.* Göttingen: Vandenhoeck & Ruprecht, 1898.

Lührmann, Dieter. *Das Offenbarungsverständnis bei Paulus und in paulinischen Gemeinden.* WMANT 16. Neukirchen-Vluyn: Neukirchener, 1965.

Lust, Johan. "Messianism and Septuagint." In *Congress Volume: Salamanca 1983,* 174—191. Edited by J.A. Emerton. VTSup 36. Leiden: Brill, 1985.

Luttikhuizen, G. P. *The Revelation of Elchasai: Investigations into the Evidence for a Mesopotamian Jewish Apocalypse of the Second Century and Its Reception by Judeo-Christian Propagandists.* TSAJ 8. Tübingen: Mohr (Siebeck), 1985.

Lutzmann, H. "דבר: I. Umwelt: 2. Mesopotamien." In *TWAT* 2 (1977): 98—101.

Luz, Ulrich. "Der alte und der neue Bund bei Paulus und im Hebräerbrief." *EvT* 27 (1967): 318—336.

Luz, Ulrich. *Das Geschichtsverständnis des Paulus.* BEvT 49. Munich: Kaiser, 1968.

MacDonald, John. *The Theology of the Samaritans.* NTL. London: SCM, 1964.

Mack, Burton Lee. *Logos und Sophia: Untersuchungen zur Weisheitstheologie im hellenistischen Judentum.* SUNT 10. Göttingen: Vandenhoeck & Ruprecht, 1973.

Macleod, C. W. Review of A. Maddalena, *Filone Alessandrino* (Milan: Mursia, 1970). *JTS* N.S. 22 (1971): 219 f.

MacMullen, Ramsay. *Paganism in the Roman Empire.* New Haven/ London: Yale University Press, 1981.

Maier, Gerhard. *Mensch und freier Wille: Nach den jüdischen Religionsparteien zwischen Ben Sira und Paulus.* WUNT 12. Tübingen: Mohr (Siebeck), 1971.

Maier, Johann. *The Temple Scroll: An Introduction, Translation & Commentary.* JSOTSup 34. Sheffield: JSOT Press, 1985.

Maneschg, H. "Gott, Erzieher, Retter und Heiland seines Volkes: Zur Reinterpretation von Num 21,4—9 in Weish 16,5—14." *BZ* 28 (1984): 214-229.

Manson, T. W. "ΙΛΑΣΤΗΡΙΟΝ." *JTS* 46 (1945): 1—10.

Manson, T. W. "Some Reflections on Apocalyptic." In *Aux Sources de la Tradition Chrétienne: Mélanges offerts à M. Maurice Goguel à l'occasion de son soixante-dixième anniversaire,* 139—145. Edited by Oscar Cullmann and Pierre Benoit. Bibliothèque Théologique. Neuchatel/Paris: Delachaux & Niestlé, 1950.

Marböck, Johannes. "Gesetz und Weisheit: Zum Verständnis des Gesetzes bei Jesus ben Sira." *BZ* 20 (1976): 1—21.

Marböck, Johannes. "Sir., 38,24–39,11: Der schriftgelehrte Weise: Ein Beitrag zu Gestalt und Werk Ben Siras." In *La Sagesse de l'Ancien Testament*, 293–316. Edited by M. Gilbert. BETL 51. Gembloux: Duculot; Leuven: Leuven University Press, 1979.

Marböck, Johannes. *Weisheit im Wandel: Untersuchungen zur Weisheitstheologie bei Ben Sira.* BBB 37. Bonn: Hanstein, 1971.

Mariotti, Scevola. "L[ivius] L. Andronicus." *KlP* 3:692–695.

Marshall, I. Howard. *1 and 2 Thessalonians*. NCB. Grand Rapids: Eerdmans; London: Marshall, Morgan & Scott, 1983.

Martin, Ralph P. *2 Corinthians*. WBC 40. Waco: Word, 1986.

Martin, Ralph P. *Colossians and Philemon*. NCB. London: Oliphants, 1974.

Marxsen, Willi. *Der zweite Thessalonicherbrief.* Zürcher Bibelkommentare NT 11.2. Zurich: Theologischer Verlag, 1982.

Masson, Charles. *Les Deux Épîtres de Saint Paul aux Thessaloniciens*. CNT 11a. Neuchatel/ Paris: Delachaux & Niestlé, 1957.

Mayer, Reinhold. "Geschichtserfahrung und Schriftauslegung: Zur Hermeneutik des frühen Judentums." In *Die hermeneutische Frage in der Theologie*, 290–355. Edited by O. Loretz and W. Strolz. Freiburg etc.: Herder, 1968.

McEleney, Neil J. "Orthodoxy in Judaism of the First Christian Century." *JSJ* 4 (1973): 19–42.

McEleney, Neil J. "Orthodoxy in Judaism of the First Christian Century: Replies to David E. Aune and Lester L. Grabbe." *JSJ* 9 (1977): 83–88.

McKenzie, John L. *Second Isaiah: Introduction, Translation, and Notes.* AB 20. Garden City: Doubleday, 1968.

McNamara, Martin. *The New Testament and the Palestinian Targum to the Pentateuch.* AnBib 27. Rome: Pontifical Biblical Institute, 1966.

McNamara, Martin. *Targum and Testament: Aramaic Paraphrases of the Hebrew Bible: A Light on the New Testament.* Shannon: Irish University Press, 1972.

Meecham, Henry G. *The Epistle to Diognetus: The Greek Text with Introduction Translation and Notes.* Manchester: Manchester University Press, 1949.

Meeks, Wayne A. "Social Functions of Apocalyptic Language in Pauline Christianity." In *Apocalypticism in the Mediterranean World and the Near East: Proceedings of the International Colloquium on Apocalypticism, Uppsala, August 12–17, 1979*, 687–705. Edited by David Hellholm. Tübingen: J.C.B. Mohr (Paul Siebeck), 1983.

Merkelbach, Reinhold. *Roman und Mysterium in der Antike.* Munich/Berlin: Beck, 1962.

Merklein, Helmut. *Das kirchliche Amt nach dem Epheserbrief.* SANT 33. Munich: Kösel, 1973.

Mertens, Alfred. *Das Buch Daniels im Lichte der Texte vom Toten Meer.* SBM 12. Würzburg: Echter; Stuttgart: KBW, 1971. [*Daniel*]

Metzger, Bruce M. *The Text of the New Testament: Its Transmission, Corruption, and Restoration.* 2nd ed. New York/Oxford: Oxford University Press, 1968.

Metzger, Bruce M. *A Textual Commentary on the Greek New Testament.* 2nd ed. London/ New York: United Bible Societies, 1975.

Metzger, Wolfgang. *Der Christushymnus 1. Timotheus 3,16: Fragment einer Homologie der paulinischen Gemeinden.* Arbeiten zur Theologie 62. Stuttgart: Calwer Verlag, 1979.

Meuzelaar, J. J. *Der Leib des Messias: Eine exegetische Studie über den Gedanken vom Leib Christi in den Paulusbriefen.* Kampen: Kok, 1979.

Meyer, Ben F. "The Pre-Pauline Formula in Rom. 3.25–26a." *NTS* 29 (1983): 198–208.

Meyer, Rudolf. "Προφήτης κτλ.: C. Prophetentum und Propheten im Judentum der hellenistisch-römischen Zeit." *TWNT* 6 (1959): 813–828.

Meyers, Eric M. "The Use of *tôrâ* in Haggai 2:11 ánd the Role of the Prophet in the Restoration Community." In *The Word of the Lord Shall Go Forth: Essays in Honor of David Noel Freedman in Celebration of His Sixtieth Birthday*, 69–76. Edited by C. L. Meyers and M. O'Connor. Winona Lake: Eisenbrauns, 1983.

Michel, Otto. *Der Brief an die Römer*. KEKNT 4. 14th (= 5th) ed. Göttingen: Vandenhoeck & Ruprecht, 1978.

Michel, Otto. "Das Licht des Messias." In *Das Institutum Judaicum der Universität Tübingen in den Jahren 1971–1972*, 155–160. Edited by O. Betz. Tübingen: n. d.

Michel, Otto. *Paulus und seine Bibel*. BFCT 2:18. Gütersloh: Bertelsmann, 1929.

Michel, Otto. "Spätjüdisches Prophetentum." In *Neutestamentliche Studien für Rudolf Bultmann*, 60–66. Edited by W. Eltester. BZNW 21. 2nd ed. Berlin: Töpelmann, 1957.

Michel, Otto. "Studien zu Josephus: Apokalyptische Heilsansagen im Bericht des Josephus (*BJ* 6,290 f. 293–95); ihre Umdeutung bei Josephus." In *Neotestamentica et Semitica: Studies in Honour of Matthew Black*, 240–244. Edited by E. E. Ellis & M. Wilcox. Edinburgh: T. & T. Clark, 1969.

Micou, R. W. "On ὤφθη ἀγγέλοις, 1 Tim iii.16." *JBL* 11 (1892): 201–205.

Milik, J. T. "*Milkî-ṣedeq* et *Milkî-reša'* dans les anciens écrits juifs et chrétiens." *JJS* 23 (1972): 95–144.

Miranda, Juan Peter. *Der Vater, der mich gesandt hat: Religionsgeschichtliche Untersuchungen zu den johanneischen Sendungsformeln: Zugleich ein Beitrag zur johanneischen Christologie und Ekklesiologie*. European University Papers 23:7. Bern: H. Lang; Frankfurt: P. Lang, 1972.

Mitton, C. Leslie. *Ephesians*. NCB. London: Oliphants, 1976.

Mitton, C. Leslie. *The Epistle to the Ephesians: Its Authorship, Origin and Purpose*. Oxford: Clarendon, 1951.

Molitor, Franz Josef. *Philosophie der Geschichte oder über die Tradition in dem alten Bunde und ihre Beziehung zur Kirche des neuen Bundes: Mit vorzüglicher Rücksicht auf die Kabbalah*. Vol. 1. 2nd ed. Münster: Theissing, 1857.

Montefiore, C. G. and Loewe, H. *A Rabbinic Anthology*. London: Macmillan, 1938. [Reprinted New York: Schocken, c1974.]

Moo, Douglas. Review of Heikki Räisänen, *Paul and the Law* and E. P. Sanders, *Paul, the Law and the Jewish People*. *Trinity Journal* N.S. 5 (1984): 92–99.

Moore, George Foot. "Intermediaries in Jewish Theology: Memra, Shekinah, Metatron." *HTR* 15 (1922): 41–85.

Moore, George Foot. *Judaism in the First Centuries of the Christian Era: The Age of the Tannaim*. 3 Vols. Cambridge, MA: Harvard University Press, 1927–1930.

Morris, Leon. *The First and Second Epistles to the Thessalonians: The English Text with Introduction, Exposition and Notes*. The New London Commentary on the New Testament. London/Edinburgh: Marshall, Morgan & Scott, 1959.

Moule, C. F. D. *The Birth of the New Testament*. 3rd. ed. London/San Francisco: Harper, 1981.

Moule, C. F. D. *The Epistles of Paul the Apostle to the Colossians and to Philemon*. Cambridge Greek Testament Commentary. Cambridge etc.: Cambridge University Press, 1957.

Moule, C. F. D. *An Idiom Book of New Testament Greek*. 2nd ed. Cambridge, etc.: Cambridge University Press, 1959.

Moule, C. F. D. "The Influence of Circumstances on the Use of Eschatological Terms." *JTS* N.S. 15 (1964): 1–15.

Moule, C. F. D. "The Problem of the Pastoral Epistles: A Reappraisal." In idem, *Essays in New Testament Interpretation*, 113–132. Cambridge etc.: Cambridge University Press, 1982.

Mühlenberg, Ekkehard. "Das Problem der Offenbarung in Philo von Alexandrien." *ZNW* 64 (1973): 1–18.

Müller, Hans-Peter. "Mantische Weisheit und Apokalyptik." In *Congress Volume: Uppsala 1971*, 268–93. VTSup 22. Leiden: Brill, 1972.

Müller, Karlheinz. "'Die Propheten sind schlafen gegangen' (syrBar 85,3): Nachbemerkungen zur überlieferungsgeschichtlichen Reputation der Pseudepigraphie im Schrifttum der frühjüdischen Apokalyptik: Für Josef Schreiner zum 60. Geburtstag." *BZ* 26 (1982): 179–207.

Müller, Paul-Gerd. "Φανερόω." *EWNT* 3 (1983): 988–991.

Müller, Ulrich B. *Prophetie und Predigt im Neuen Testament: Formgeschichtliche Untersuchungen zur urchristlichen Prophetie.* SNT 10. Gütersloh: Mohn, 1975.

Muñoz León, Domingo. *Dios-Palabra: Memra en los Targumim del Pentateuco.* Institución San Jerónimo 4. Granada: Santa Rita-Monachil, 1974.

Murdock, William R. "History and Revelation in Jewish Apocalyptic." *Interp* 21 (1967): 165–187.

Murphy, Frederick James. *The Structure and Meaning of Second Baruch.* SBLDS 78. Atlanta: Scholars Press, 1985.

Murphy-O'Connor, Jerome. "Redactional Angels in 1 Tim 3:16." *RB* 91 (1984): 178–187.

Muschalek, Georg and Gamper, Arnold. "Offenbarung in Geschichte." *ZKT* 86 (1964): 180–196.

Mussner, Franz. "Contributions Made by Qumran to the Understanding of the Epistle to the Ephesians." In *Paul and Qumran: Studies in New Testament Exegesis*, 159–178. Edited by Jerome Murphy-O'Connor. London etc.: Chapman, 1968.

Myers, Jacob M. *I and II Esdras: Introduction, Translation and Commentary.* AB 42. Garden City: Doubleday, 1974.

Myers, Jacob M. and Freed, Edwin D. "Is Paul Also Among the Prophets?" *Interp* 20 (1966): 40–53.

Neusner, Jacob. *Midrash in Context: Exegesis in Formative Judaism.* Philadelphia: Fortress, 1983.

Neusner, Jacob. *The Rabbinic Traditions about the Pharisees before 70.* 3 vols. Leiden: Brill, 1971.

Neusner, Jacob. "The Rabbinic Traditions about the Pharisees before 70 A.D.: The Problem of Oral Tradition." *Kairos* 14 (1972): 57–70.

Neusner, Jacob. "Scripture and Mishnah: Authority and Selectivity." In *Scripture in the Jewish and Christian Traditions: Authority, Interpretation, Relevance*, 64–85. Edited by F. R. Greenspahn. University of Denver Center for Judaic Studies. Nashville: Abingdon, 1982. ["Authority"]

Newsom, Carol A. "Merkabah Exegesis in the Qumran Sabbath Shirot." *JJS* 38 (1987): 11–30.

Nickelsburg, George W. E. "The Apocalyptic Message of *1 Enoch* 92–105." *CBQ* 39 (1977): 309–328.

Nickelsburg, George W. E. *Jewish Literature between the Bible and the Mishnah: A Historical and Literary Introduction.* London: SCM, 1981.

Nikiprowetzky, V. *Le Commentaire de l'Écriture chez Philon d'Alexandrie: Son Caractère et sa Portée: Observations philologiques.* ALGHJ 11. Leiden: Brill, 1977.

Nissen, Andreas. "Tora und Geschichte im Spätjudentum: Zu Thesen Dietrich Rösslers." *NT* 9 (1967): 241–277.

Noack, Bent. *Spätjudentum und Heilsgeschichte.* Franz Delitzsch Vorlesungen 1968. Stuttgart: Kohlhammer, 1971.

Nock, Arthur Darby. "Hellenistic Mysteries and Christian Sacraments." In *Essays on Religion and the Ancient World,* 2:791– 820. Edited by Z. Stewart. Oxford: Clarendon, 1972. [= *Mnemosyne* 4.5 (1952): 177–213.]

Nock, Arthur Darby. "The Question of Jewish Mysteries." In *Essays on Religion and the Ancient World,* 1:459–468. Edited by Z. Stewart. Oxford: Clarendon, 1972. [=*Gnomon* 13 (1937): 156–165.]

Noth, Martin. "Das Geschichtsverständnis der alttestamentlichen Apokalyptik." In *Gesammelte Studien zum Alten Testament,* 248–273. Theologische Bücherei 6. 3rd ed. Munich: Kaiser, 1966.

Nötscher, Friedrich. *Zur theologischen Terminologie der Qumran-Texte.* BBB 10. Bonn: Hanstein, 1956.

Novak, David. "The Origin of the Noahide Laws." In *Perspectives on Jews and Judaism: Essays in Honor of Wolfe Kelman,* 301–310. Edited by A. A. Chiel. New York: The Rabbinical Assembly, 1978.

Nygren, Anders. *Commentary on Romans.* Translated by C. C. Rasmussen. Philadelphia: Muhlenberg, 1949.

O'Brien, Peter T. *Colossians, Philemon.* WBC 44. Waco: Word, 1982.

O'Neill, J. C. *Paul's Letter to the Romans.* Harmondsworth: Penguin, 1975.

O'Neill, J. C. "The Source of the Christology in Colossians." *NTS* 26 (1980): 87–100.

Oepke, Albrecht. *Der Brief des Paulus an die Galater.* THKNT 9. Edited by J. Rohde. 5th ed. Berlin: Evangelische Verlagsanstalt, 1984.

Oepke, Albrecht. "Καλύπτω κτλ." *TWNT* 3 (1938): 558–597.

Olford, David Lindsay. "An Exegetical Study of Major Texts in Romans which Employ Cultic Language in a Non-Literal Way." Ph.D. Dissertation, Sheffield: 1985.

Oppenheim, A. Leo. *The Interpretation of Dreams in the Ancient Near East.* Transactions of the American Philosophical Society, N.S. 46:3. Philadelphia: American Philosophical Society, 1956).

Otte, Klaus. *Das Sprachverständnis bei Philo von Alexandrien: Sprache als Mittel der Hermeneutik.* BGBE 7. Tübingen: J.C.B. Mohr (Paul Siebeck), 1968.

Otzen, Benedikt. "Heavenly Visions in Early Judaism: Origin and Function." In *In the Shelter of Elyon: Essays on Ancient Palestinian Life and Literature in Honour of G. W. Ahlström,* 199–215. Edited by W. B. Barrick and J. R. Spencer. JSOTSup 31. Sheffield: JSOT, 1984.

Pallis, Alexander. *To the Romans: A Commentary.* Liverpool: Liverpool Booksellers' Co., 1920.

Pascher, Joseph. Η ΒΑΣΙΛΙΚΗ ΟΔΟΣ: Der Königsweg zu Wiedergeburt und Vergottung bei Philon von Alexandrien. Studien zur Geschichte der Kultur des Altertums 17:3/4. Paderborn: Schöningh, 1931.

Patte, Daniel. *Early Jewish Hermeneutic in Palestine.* SBLDS 22. Missoula: Scholars Press, 1975.

Paul, André. "Le concept de la prophétie biblique: Flavius Josèphe et Daniel." *RSR* 63 (1975): 367–384.

Paulsen, Henning. *Die Briefe des Ignatius von Antiochia und der Brief des Polykarp von Smyrna.* 2nd ed. of the commentary by W. Bauer. HNT 18. Tübingen: J.C.B. Mohr (Paul Siebeck), 1985.

Penna, Romano. *Il "Mysterion" Paolino.* Supplementi alla Rivesta Biblica 10. Brescia: Paideia, 1978.

Pépin, Jean. *Mythe et Allgorie: Les origines grecques et les contestations judéo-chrétiennes.* 2nd ed. Paris: Études Augustiniennes, 1976.

Percy, Ernst. *Die Probleme der Kolosser- und Epheserbriefe.* SHVL 39. Lund: Gleerup, 1946.

Perdue, Leo G. *Wisdom and Cult: A Critical Analysis of the Views of Cult in the Wisdom Literatures of Israel and the Ancient Near East.* SBLDS 30. Missoula: Scholars Press, 1977.

Pérez Fernández, Miguel. *Tradiciones Mesianicas en el Targum Palestinense: Estudios Exegéticos.* Institución San Jerónimo 12. Valencia/Jerusalem: Soler, 1981.

Perlitt, Lothar. "Die Verborgenheit Gottes." In *Probleme biblischer Theologie: Gerhard von Rad zum 70. Geburtstag,* 367–382. Munich: Kaiser, 1971.

Pesce, Mauro. *Paolo e gli arconti a Corinto: Storia della ricerca (1888–1975) ed esegesi di 1 Cor. 2,6.8.* Testi e ricerche di Scienze religiose 13. Brescia: Paideia, 1977.

Peters, Norbert. *Das Buch Jesus Sirach oder Ecclesiasticus.* EHAT 25. Münster: Aschendorffsche Verlagsbuchhandlung, 1913.

Petuchowski, Jakob J. "Bibel und Tradition im rabbinischen Judentum." *Tübinger Theologische Quartalsschrift* 161 (1981): 106–44.

Petuchowski, Jakob J. "Judaism as 'Mystery' – The Hidden Agenda?" *HUCA* 52 (1981): 141–52.

Petuchowski, Jakob J. "The Liturgy of the Synagogue: History, Structure, and Contents." In *Approaches to Ancient Judaism,* Vol. 4: *Studies in Liturgy, Exegesis, and Talmudic Narrative,* 1–64. Edited by W. S. Green. Chico: Scholars Press, 1983.

Petuchowski, Jakob J. "Zur rabbinischen Interpretation des Offenbarungsglaubens." In *Offenbarung im jüdischen und christlichen Glaubensverständnis,* 72–86. edited by J. J. Petuchowski & W. Strolz. QD 92. Freiburg, etc.: Herder, 1981.

Philonenko, Marc. "L'apocalyptique qoumrânienne." In *Apocalypticism in the Mediterranean World and the Near East: Proceedings of the International Colloquium on Apocalypticism, Uppsala, August 12–17, 1979,* 211–218. Edited by David Hellholm. Tübingen: J.C.B. Mohr (Paul Siebeck), 1983.

Philonenko, Marc. "Quod oculus non vidit." *TZ* 15 (1959): 51–52.

Piñero-Sáenz, Antonio. "Concepciones de la Inspiración en Filón de Alejandría." In *Salvación en la Palabra: Targum – Derash – Berith: En memoria del profesor Alejandro Diez Macho,* 223–233. Edited by Domingo Muñoz León. Madrid: Ediciones Cristiandad, 1986.

Plöger, Otto. "Prophetisches Erbe in den Sekten des frühen Judentums." *TLZ* 79 (1954): 291–296.

Plöger, Otto. *Theocracy and Eschatology.* Translated by S. Rudman. Oxford: Blackwell, 1968.

Plummer, Alfred. *A Critical and Exegetical Commentary on the Second Epistle of St Paul to the Corinthians.* ICC. Edinburgh: T. & T. Clark, 1915. [*2 Corinthians*]

Ponsot, Hervé. "D'Isaïe, LXIV, 3 à I Corinthiens, II, 9." *RB* 90 (1983): 229–242.

Poole, Matthew. *Synopsis Criticorum Aliorumque S. Scripturae Interpretum.* Vol. 4. London: Flesher/Smith, 1676.

Potin, Jean. *La fête juive de la Pentecôte: Étude des textes liturgiques.* 2 Vols. Lectio Divina 65a–b. Paris: Cerf, 1971.

Poznanski, Adolf. "Über die religionsphilosophischen Anschauungen des Flavius Josephus." Ph.D. Dissertation, Halle-Wittenberg: 1887.

Prato, Gian Luigi. "La lumière interprète de la sagesse dans la tradition textuelle de Ben Sira." In *La Sagesse de l'Ancien Testament*, 293–316. Edited by M. Gilbert. BETL 51. Gembloux: Duculot; Leuven: Leuven University Press, 1979.

Prigent, P. "Ce que l'oeil n'a pas vu." *TZ* 14 (1958): 416–429.

Prümm, Karl. "Mystères." *DBSup* 6 (1960): 1–225.

Prümm, Karl. "'Mysterion' von Paulus bis Origenes: Ein Bericht und ein Beitrag." *ZKT* 61 (1937): 391–425.

Prümm, Karl. "Zur Phänomenologie des paulinischen Mysterion und dessen seelischer Aufnahme: Eine Übersicht." *Bib* 37 (1956): 135–161.

Räisänen, Heikki. *Paul and the Law*. WUNT 29. Tübingen: Mohr (Siebeck), 1983.

Rajak, Tessa. *Josephus: The Historian and His Society*. London: Duckworth, 1983.

Ramsay, Sir William M. *Cities and Bishoprics of Phrygia*. 2 vols. Oxford: Clarendon, 1895.

Raurell, Frederic. "The Religious Meaning of 'Doxa' in the Book of Wisdom." In *La Sagesse de l'Ancien Testament*, 370–383. Edited by M. Gilbert. BETL 51. Gembloux: Duculot; Leuven: University Press, 1979.

Reese, James M. *Hellenistic Influence in the Book of Wisdom and its Consequences*. AnBib 41. Rome: Biblical Institute, 1970.

Refoulé, François. *. . . Et ainsi tout Israël sera sauvé: Romains 11,25–32*. Lectio Divina 117. Paris: Cerf, 1984.

Reicke, Bo. "Chronologie der Pastoralbriefe." *TLZ* 101 (1976): 81–94.

Reinmuth, Eckart. *Geist und Gesetz: Studien zu Voraussetzungen und Inhalt der paulinischen Paränese*. Theologische Arbeiten 44. Berlin: Evangelische Verlagsanstalt, 1985.

Reitzenstein, Richard. *Die hellenistischen Mysterienreligionen nach ihren Grundgedanken und Wirkungen*. 3rd ed. Leipzig/Berlin: Teubner, 1927.

Reitzenstein, R. *Poimandres: Studien zur Griechisch-Ägyptischen und Frühchristlichen Literatur*. Leipzig: Teubner, 1904.

Rendtorff, Rolf. "Geschichte und Wort im Alten Testament." *EvT* 22 (1962): 621–649.

Rendtorff, Rolf. "Offenbarung im Alten Testament." *TLZ* 85 (1960): 833–838.

Rendtorff, Rolf. "Offenbarung und Geschichte." In *Offenbarung im jüdischen und christlichen Glaubensverständnis*, 37–49. Edited by J. J. Petuchowski and W. Strolz. Quaestiones Disputatae 92. Freiburg, etc.: Herder, 1981.

Rendtorff, Rolf. "Die Offenbarungsvorstellungen im Alten Testament." In *Offenbarung als Geschichte*, 21–41. Edited by Wolfhart Pannenberg. KD Beiheft 1. 2nd ed. Göttingen: Vandenhoeck & Ruprecht, 1963.

Rengstorf, Karl Heinrich. "Διδάσκω κτλ." *TWNT* 2 (1935): 138–168.

Reumann, John. "'Stewards of God' – Pre-Christian Religious Application of *Oikonomos* in Greek." *JBL* 77 (1958): 339–349.

Reumann, John. "OIKONOMIA-Terms in Paul in Comparison with Lucan *Heilsgeschichte*." *NTS* 13 (1967): 147–167.

Riches, John. *Jesus and the Transformation of Judaism*. London: Darton, Longman & Todd, 1980.

Ricoeur, Paul. "Herméneutique de l'idée de Révélation." In idem et al., *La Révélation*, 15–54. Publications des Facultés Universitaires Saint-Louis 7. Brussels: Facultés Universitaires Saint-Louis, 1977.

Ridderbos, Herman N. *The Epistle of Paul to the Churches of Galatia*. Translated by H. Zylstra. NICNT. Grand Rapids: Eerdmans, 1953.

Ridderbos, Herman. *De Pastorale Brieven*. Commentaar op het Nieuwe Testament. Kampen: Kok, 1967.

Ridderbos, Herman N. *Paul: An Outline of his Theology*. Translated by J. R. de Witt. Grand Rapids: Eerdmans, 1975.

Riedweg, Christoph. *Mysterienterminologie bei Platon, Philon und Klemens von Alexandrien*. Untersuchungen zur antiken Literatur und Geschichte 26. Berlin/New York: de Gruyter, 1987.

Riesner, Rainer. "Der Christus-Offenbarung nach-denken: Anmerkungen zur paulinischen Hermeneutik in 1 Kor 1,18—2,16." In *Evangelische Schriftauslegung: Ein Quellen- und Arbeitsbuch für Studium und Gemeinde*, 416—423. Edited by J. Cochlovius and P. Zimmerling. Krelingen/Wuppertal: Brockhaus, 1987.

Rigaux, Béda. "Révélation des Mystères et Perfection à Qumran et dans le Nouveau Testament." *NTS* 4 (1958): 237—262.

Rigaux, Béda. *Saint Paul: Les Épîtres aux Thessaloniciens*. Études Bibliques. Paris: Lecoffre (Gabalda); Gembloux: Duculot, 1956.

Ringgren, Helmer. *The Faith of Qumran: Theology of the Dead Sea Scrolls*. Translated by E. T. Sander. Philadelphia: Fortress, 1963.

Ringgren, Helmer. *Religions of the Ancient Near East*. Translated by John Sturdy. London: SPCK, 1973.

Robertson, A. T. *A Grammar of the Greek New Testament in the Light of Historical Research*. 4th ed. Nashville: Broadman, 1934.

Robertson, Archibald and Plummer, Alfred. *A Critical and Exegetical Commentary on the First Epistle of St Paul to the Corinthians*. ICC. 2nd ed. Edinburgh: T. & T. Clark, 1914.

Robinson, D. W. B. "Who Were the Saints?" *RTR* 22 (1963): 45—53.

Robinson, H. Wheeler. *Inspiration and Revelation in the Old Testament*. Oxford: Clarendon, 1946.

Robinson, J. Armitage. *St Paul's Epistle to the Ephesians: A Revised Text and Translation with Exposition and Notes*. 2nd ed. London: Macmillan, 1909.

Robinson, John A. T. *Redating the New Testament*. London: SCM, 1976.

Rochais, Gérard. "Qu'est-ce que l'Apocalyptique?" *Science et Esprit* 36 (1984): 273—286.

Rogerson, John. *The Supernatural in the Old Testament*. Guildford: Lutterworth, 1976.

Rokeah, David. "A New Onomasticon Fragment from Oxyrhynchus and Philo's Etymologies." *JTS* N.S. 19 (1968): 70—82.

Rössler, Dietrich. *Gesetz und Geschichte: Untersuchungen zur Theologie der jüdischen Apokalyptik und der pharisäischen Orthodoxie*. WMANT 3. Neukirchen- Vluyn: Neukirchener, 1960.

Rowland, Christopher. "Apocalyptic Literature." In *It is Written: Scripture Citing Scripture: Essays in Honour of Barnabas Lindars, SSF*, 170—189. Edited by D. A. Carson & H. G. M. Williamson. Cambridge etc.: Cambridge University Press, 1988. ["Literature"]

Rowland, Christopher. "Apocalyptic Visions and the Exaltation of Christ in the Letter to the Colossians." *JSNT* 19 (1983): 73—83. ["Exaltation"]

Rowland, Christopher. *Christian Origins*. London: SPCK, 1985.

Rowland, Christopher. *The Open Heaven: A Study of Apocalyptic in Judaism and Early Christianity*. London: SPCK, 1982.

Rowland, Christopher. "The Visions of God in Apocalyptic Literature." *JSJ* 10 (1979): 137—154. ["Visions"]

Rowley, H. H. *The Faith of Israel: Aspects of Old Testament Thought*. London: SCM, 1956.

Ruppert, Lothar. *Jesus als der leidende Gerechte? Der Weg Jesu im Lichte eines alt- und zwischentestamentlichen Motivs.* SBS 59. Stuttgart: KBW, 1972.

Russell, D. S. *The Method and Message of Jewish Apocalyptic: 200 BC — AD 100.* London: SCM, 1964.

Rylaarsdam, J. Coert. *Revelation in Jewish Wisdom Literature.* Chicago: University of Chicago Press, 1946.

Sabourin, Leopold. "The MEMRA of God in the Targums." *BTB* 6 (1976): 79—85.

Sæbø, M. "סוד." *THAT* 2 (1976): 144—148.

Saldarini, Anthony J. "Apocalypses and 'Apocalyptic' in Rabbinic Literature and Mysticicsm." *Semeia* 14 (1979): 187—205.

Sanday, William and Headlam, Arthur C. *A Critical and Exegetical Commentary on the Epistle to the Romans.* ICC. Edinburgh: T. & T. Clark, 1895.

Sanders, James A. "Torah and Christ." *Int* 29 (1975): 372—390.

Sanders, James A. "Torah and Paul." In *God's Christ and His People: Studies in Honour of Nils Alstrup Dahl,* 132—140. Edited by J. Jervell and W. A. Meeks. Oslo etc.: Universitetsforlaget, 1977.

Sanders, E. P. *Jesus and Judaism.* London: SCM, 1985.

Sanders, E. P. *Paul and Palestinian Judaism: A Comparison of Patterns of Religion.* London: SCM, 1977. [*PPJ*]

Sanders, E. P. *Paul, the Law and the Jewish People.* Philadelphia: Fortress, 1983. [*PLJP*]

Sandmel, Samuel. "Apocalypse and Philo." In *Essays on the Occasion of the Seventieth Anniversary of the Dropsie University,* 383—87. Edited by A. I. Katsh and L. Nemoy. Philadelphia: Dropsie, 1979.

Sandmel, Samuel. *The Genius of Paul: A Study in History.* Philadelphia: Fortress, c1979.

Sandmel, Samuel. *Judaism and Christian Beginnings.* New York: Oxford University Press, 1978.

Sandmel, Samuel. "Philo Judaeus: An Introduction to the Man, his Writings, and his Significance." *ANRW* II 21:1 (1984): 3—46.

Sandmel, Samuel. *Philo of Alexandria: An Introduction.* New York/Oxford: Oxford University Press, 1979.

Sänger, Dieter. *Antikes Judentum und die Mysterien: Religionsgeschichtliche Untersuchungen zu Joseph und Aseneth.* WUNT 2:5. Tübingen: J.C.B. Mohr (Paul Siebeck), 1980.

Sänger, Dieter. "Rettung der Heiden und Erwählung Israels: Einige vorläufige Erwägungen zu Römer 11,25—27." *KD* 32 (1986): 99—119.

Sauer, G. "יעד." In *THAT* 2 (1976): 742—746.

Sayler, Gwendolyn B. *Have the Promises Failed? A Literary Analysis of 2 Baruch.* SBLDS 72. Chico: Scholars Press, 1984.

Schäfer, Peter. "Das 'Dogma' von der mündlichen Torah im rabbinischen Judentum." In idem, *Studien zur Geschichte und Theologie des Rabbinischen Judentums,* 153—197. AGJU 15. Leiden: Brill, 1978.

Schäfer, Peter. "Geist: II. Judentum." *TRE* 12 (1984): 173—178.

Schäfer, Peter. "New Testament and Hekhalot Literature: The Journey into Heaven in Paul and in Merkavah Mysticism." *JJS* 35 (1984): 19—35. ["Journey"]

Schäfer, Peter. "Prolegomena zu einer kritischen Edition und Analyse der Merkava Rabba." *FJB* 5 (1977) 65—93.

Schäfer, Peter. *Rivalität zwischen Engeln und Menschen: Untersuchungen zur rabbinischen Engelvorstellung.* Studia Judaica 8. Berlin/New York: de Gruyter, 1975.

Schäfer, Peter. "Die Termini 'Heiliger Geist' und 'Geist der Prophetie' in den Targumim und das Verhältnis der Targumim zueinander." *VT* 20 (1970): 304—314.

Schäfer, Peter. "Die Torah der messianischen Zeit." *ZNW* 65 (1974): 27–42. [= idem, *Studien zur Geschichte und Theologie des Rabbinischen Judentums*, 198–213. AGJU 15. Leiden: Brill, 1978.]

Schäfer, Peter. *Die Vorstellung vom Heiligen Geist in der Rabbinischen Literatur.* SANT 28. Munich: Kösel, 1972.

Schenk, Wolfgang. "Christus, das Geheimnis der Welt, als dogmatisches und ethisches Grundprinzip des Kolosserbriefes." *EvT* 43 (1983): 138–155.

Schiffman, Lawrence H. "At the Crossroads: Tannaitic Perspectives on the Jewish-Christian Schism." In *Jewish and Christian Self-Definition*, Vol. 2: *Aspects of Judaism in the Graeco-Roman Period*, 115–156. Edited by E. P. Sanders et al. London: SCM, 1981.

Schiffman, Lawrence H. *The Halakhah at Qumran.* SJLA 16. Leiden: Brill, 1975.

Schiffman, Lawrence H. Review of Y. Yadin, *The Temple Scroll. BA* 48 (1985): 122–126.

Schiffman, Lawrence H. *Who Was a Jew? Rabbinic and Halakhic Perspectives on the Jewish-Christian Schism.* Hoboken, NJ: Ktav, 1985.

Schimanowski, Gottfried. *Weisheit und Messias: Die jüdischen Voraussetzungen der urchristlichen Präexistenzchristologie.* WUNT 2:17. Tübingen: J.C.B. Mohr (Paul Siebeck), 1985.

Schlatter, Adolf. *Gottes Gerechtigkeit: Ein Kommentar zumn Römerbrief.* 5th ed. Stuttgart: Calwer Verlag, 1975.

Schlatter, Adolf. *Die Kirche der Griechen im Urteil des Paulus: Eine Auslegung seiner Briefe an Timotheus und Titus.* 2nd ed. Stuttgart: Calwer Verlag, 1958.

Schlatter, Adolf. *Paulus der Bote Jesu: Eine Deutung seiner Briefe an die Korinther.* 2nd ed. Stuttgart: Calwer Verlag, 1956.

Schlatter, Adolf. *Die Theologie der Apostel.* 3rd ed. Stuttgart: Calwer Verlag, 1977.

Schlatter, Adolf. *Die Theologie des Judentums nach dem Bericht des Josefus* [sic]. Beiträge zur Förderung Christlicher Theologie 2:26. Gütersloh: Bertelsmann, 1932.

Schlatter, Adolf. *Wie sprach Josephus von Gott?* BFCT 14:1. Gütersloh: Bertelsmann, 1910.

Schlier, Heinrich. *Der Brief an die Epheser: Ein Kommentar.* 7th ed. Düsseldorf: Patmos-Verlag, 1971.

Schlier, Heinrich. *Der Brief an die Galater.* KEKNT 7. 12th ed. Göttingen: Vandenhoeck & Ruprecht, 1962.

Schlier, Heinrich. "Die Kirche als Geheimnis Christi nach dem Epheserbrief." In *Die Zeit der Kirche: Exegetische Aufsätze und Vorträge*, 299–307. Freiburg: Herder, 1956.

Schlier, Heinrich. "La Notion Paulinienne de la Parole de Dieu." In *Littérature et Théologie Paulinienne*, 127–141. Edited by A. Descamps. Recherches Bibliques 5. Louvain: de Brouwer, 1960.

Schlier, Heinrich. *Religionsgeschichtliche Untersuchungen zu den Ignatiusbriefen.* BZNW 8. Giessen: Töpelmann, 1929.

Schmidt, Hans Wilhelm. *Der Brief des Paulus an die Römer.* THKNT 6. Berlin: Evangelische Verlagsanstalt, 1963.

Schmithals, Walter. *Die Gnosis in Korinth; Eine Untersuchung zu den Korintherbriefen.* FRLANT 66. 2nd ed. Göttingen: Vandenhoeck & Ruprecht, 1965.

Schmitt, Wolfgang O. "Tzetzes, Iohannes." *KlP* 5: 1031–1034.

Schnabel, Eckhard J. *Law and Wisdom from Ben Sira to Paul: A Tradition Historical Enquiry into the Relation of Law, Wisdom, and Ethics.* WUNT 2:16. Tübingen: J.C.B. Mohr (Paul Siebeck), 1985.

Schnackenburg, Rudolf. *Der Brief an die Epheser*. EKKNT 10. Zurich etc.: Benziger; Neukirchen-Vluyn: Neukirchener, 1982.

Schneider, Johannes. "'Mysterion' im Neuen Testament." *TSK* 104 (1932): 255—78.

Schneider, Johannes. *Die Passionsmystik des Apostels Paulus: Ihr Wesen, ihr Hintergrund und ihre Nachwirkungen*. UNT 15. Leipzig: Hinrichs, 1929.

Schoedel, William R. *Ignatius of Antioch: A Commentary on the Letters of Ignatius of Antioch*. Hermeneia. Edited by H. Koester. Philadelphia: Fortress, 1985.

Schoemaker, William Ross. "The Use of רוח in the Old Testament and of πνεῦμα in the New Testament: A Lexicographical Study." *JBL* 23 (1904): 13—67.

Schoeps, H. J. *Paul: The Theology of the Apostle in the Light of Jewish Religious History*. Translated by Harold Knight. London: Lutterworth, 1961.

Scholem, Gershom G. *Jewish Gnosticism, Merkabah Mysticism, and Talmudic Tradition*. 2nd ed. New York: Jewish Theological Seminary of America, 1965.

Scholem, Gershom G. *Major Trends in Jewish Mysticism*. 3rd ed. New York: Schocken, 1954.

Scholem, Gershom G. "Revelation and Tradition as Religious Categories in Judaism." In *The Messianic Idea in Judaism and other Essays on Jewish Spirituality*, 282—303. New York: Schocken, 1971.

Scholem, Gershom G. *Ursprung und Anfänge der Kabbala*. Studia Judaica 3. Berlin: de Gruyter, 1962.

Schreiner, Josef. "Geistbegabung in der Gemeinde von Qumran." *BZ* 9 (1965): 161—180.

Schreiner, Josef. "Hermeneutische Leitlinien in der Septuaginta." In *Die hermeneutische Frage in der Theologie*, 356—394. Edited by O. Loretz and W. Strolz. Schriften zum Gespräch 3. Freiburg etc.: Herder, 1968.

Schulte, Hannelis. *Der Begriff der Offenbarung im Neuen Testament*. BEvT 13. Munich: Kaiser, 1949.

Schürer, Emil. *The History of the Jewish People in the Age of Jesus Christ (175 B.C.—A.D. 135)*. A New English Version Revised and Edited by G. Vermes et al. 3 Vols. Edinburgh: T. & T. Clark, 1973—1987. [Schürer/Vermes, *HJPAJC*]

Schweizer, Eduard. *Der Brief an die Kolosser*. EKKNT 12. Einsiedeln/Cologne: Benziger; Neukirchen-Vluyn: Neukirchener, 1976.

Scott, Ernest Findlay. *The New Testament Idea of Revelation*. London: Ivor Nicholson & Watson, 1935.

Seaford, Richard. "1 Corinthians xiii.12." *JTS* N.S. 35 (1984): 117—120.

Seckler, Max. "Dei verbum religiose audiens: Wandlungen im christlichen Offenbarungsverständnis." In *Offenbarung im jüdischen und christlichen Glaubensverständnis*, 214—236. Edited by J. J. Petuchowski & W. Strolz. Quaestiones Disputatae 92. Freiburg: Herder, 1981.

Seeligmann, I. L. *The Septuagint Version of Isaiah: A Discussion of its Problems*. Mededelingen en Verhandelingen 9, Vooraziatisch-Egyptisch Genootschap "Ex Oriente Lux". Leiden: Brill, 1948.

Segal, Alan F. *Two Powers in Heaven: Early Rabbinic Reports about Christianity and Gnosticism*. SJLA 25. Leiden: Brill, 1977.

Sellin, Gerhard. "Das 'Geheimnis' der Weisheit und das Rätsel der 'Christuspartei': (Zu 1 Kor 1—4)." *ZNW* 73 (1982): 69—96.

Senft, Christophe. *La première Épître de Saint-Paul aux Corinthiens*. CNT 2:7. Neuchatel: Delachaux & Niestlé, 1979.

Sheppard, Gerald T. *Wisdom as a Hermeneutical Construct: A Study in the Sapientializing of the Old Testament*. BZAW 151. Berlin/New York: de Gruyter, 1980.

Siegert, Folker. *Argumentation bei Paulus: gezeigt an Röm 9—11*. WUNT 34. Tübingen: J.C.B. Mohr (Paul Siebeck), 1985.

Siegfried, Carl. *Philo von Alexandria als Ausleger des Alten Testaments an sich selbst und nach seinem geschichtlichen Einfluss betrachtet: Nebst Untersuchungen über die Graecität Philos*. Jena: Dufft, 1875.

Silberman, Lou H. "Unriddling the Riddle: A Study in the Structure and Language of the Habakkuk Pesher (1QpHab)." *RQ* 3 (1961—62): 323—364.

Sjöberg, Erik. *Der Menschensohn im äthiopischen Henochbuch*. SHVL 41. Lund: Gleerup, 1946. [*Menschensohn*]

Sjöberg, Erik. *Der verborgene Menschensohn in den Evangelien*. SHVL 53. Lund: Gleerup, 1955.

Sjöberg, Erik; Stählin, Gustav; and Procksch, Otto. "Ὀργή: D. Das Spätjudentum." *TWNT* 5 (1954): 413—419.

Skehan, Patrick W. and Di Lella, Alexander A. *The Wisdom of Ben Sira*. AB 39. New York: Doubleday, 1987.

Smend, Rudolf. *Die Weisheit des Jesus Sirach*. Berlin: Reimer, 1906.

Smith, D. Moody. "The Pauline Literature." In *It is Written: Scripture Citing Scripture. Essays in Honour of Barnabas Lindars, SSF*, 265—291. Edited by D. A. Carson & H. G. M. Williamson. Cambridge etc.: Cambridge University Press, 1988.

Smith, Jonathan Z. "Wisdom and Apocalyptic." In *Religious Syncretism in Antiquity: Essays in Conversation with Geo Widengren*, 131—156. Edited by B. A. Pearson. Missoula: Scholars Press, 1975.

Smith, Morton. "Goodenough's *Jewish Symbols* in Retrospect." *JBL* 86 (1967): 53—68.

Smith, Morton. "The Occult in Josephus." In *Josephus, Judaism, and Christianity*, 236—256. Edited by Louis H. Feldman & Gohei Hata. Leiden: Brill; Tokyo: Yamamoto Shoten; Detroit: Wayne State University Press, 1987.

Smith, Morton. "On the History of ΑΠΟΚΑΛΥΠΤΩ and ΑΠΟΚΑΛΥΨΙΣ." In *Apocalypticism in the Mediterranean World and the Near East: Proceedings of the International Colloquium on Apocalypticism, Uppsala, August 12—17, 1979*, 9—20. Edited by D. Hellholm. Tübingen: J.C.B. Mohr (Paul Siebeck), 1983.

Smith, Morton. "The Reason for the Persecution of Paul and the Obscurity of Acts." In *Studies in Mysticism and Religion: Presented to Gershom G. Scholem on his Seventieth Birthday by Pupils Colleagues and Friends*, 261—268. Edited by E. E. Urbach et al. Jerusalem: Magnes Press, 1967.

Smolar, Leivy and Aberbach, Moses. *Studies in Targum Jonathan to the Prophets*. Including Pinkhos Churgin, *Targum Jonathan to the Prophets*. Library of Biblical Studies. New York: Ktav; Baltimore: Baltimore Hebrew College, 1983.

Snaith, John G. "Ben Sira's Supposed Love of Liturgy." *VT* 25 (1975): 167—174.

Snaith, John G. "The Importance of Ecclesiasticus." *ExpTim* 75 (1963—64): 66—69.

Soards, Marion L. "Paul: Apostle and Apocalyptic Visionary." *BTB* 16 (1986): 148—150.

Sparks, H. F. D. "1 Kor 2,9: A Quotation from the Coptic Testament of Jacob?" *ZNW* 67 (1976): 269—276.

Spicq, C. *Les Épîtres Pastorales*. Paris: Gabalda (Lecoffre), 1947.

Stadelmann, Helge. *Ben Sira als Schriftgelehrter: Eine Untersuchung zum Berufsbild des vormakkabäischen Sôfêr unter Berücksichtigung seines Verhältnisses zu Priester-, Propheten- und Weisheitslehrertum*. WUNT 2:6. Tübingen: J.C.B. Mohr (Paul Siebeck), 1980.

Stählin, W. "Zum Verständnis von 1. Kor. 2,6—8." In *Verbum Dei Manet in Aeternum: Eine Festschrift für Prof. D. Otto Schmitz zu seinem siebzigsten Geburtstag am 11. Juni 1953*, 94—102. Edited by W. Foerster. Witten: Luther-Verlag, 1953.

Starobinski-Safran, Esther. "La Prophétie de Moïse et sa Portée d'après Philon." In *La Figure de Moïse: Écriture et relectures,* 67–80. Edited by Robert Martin-Achard et al. Publications de la Faculté de Théologie de l'Université de Genève 1. Geneva: Labor et Fides, 1978.

Steinmetz, Franz Josef. *Protologische Heils-Zuversicht: Die Strukturen des soteriologischen und christologischen Denkens im Kolosser- und Epheserbrief.* Frankfurter Theologische Studien 2. Frankfurt: Knecht, 1969.

Stemberger, Günter. "Esoterik: II. Im Judentum." *TRE* 10 (1982): 368–374.

Stemberger, Günter. *Der Leib der Auferstehung: Studien zur Anthropologie und Eschatologie des palästinischen Judentums im neutestamentlichen Zeitalter (ca. 170 v.Cr. [sic] – 100 n.Chr.).* AnBib 56. Rome: Biblical Institute Press, 1972.

Stone, Michael Edward. "Lists of Revealed Things in Apocalyptic Literature." In *Magnalia Dei: The Mighty Acts of God: Essays on the Bible and Archaeology in Memory of G. Ernest Wright,* 414–452. New York: Doubleday, 1976.

Stone, Michael Edward. *Scriptures, Sects and Visions: A Profile of Judaism from Ezra to the Jewish Revolts.* Philadelphia: Fortress, 1980.

[Strack, Hermann L.] and Billerbeck, Paul. *Kommentar zum Neuen Testament aus Talmud und Midrasch.* 7 Vols. Munich: Beck, 1922–1961.

Strack, Hermann L. and Stemberger, Günter. *Einleitung in Talmud und Midrasch. 7th ed. Munich: Beck, 1982.*

Strobel, A. "Schreiben des Lukas? Zum sprachlichen Problem der Pastoralbriefe." *NTS* 15 (1969): 191–210.

Strobel, A. *Untersuchungen zum eschatologischen Verzögerungsproblem auf Grund der spätjüdisch-urchristlichen Geschichte von Habakuk 2,2 ff.* NTSup 2. Leiden: Brill, 1961.

Stuhlmacher, Peter. "'Das Ende des Gesetzes': Über Ursprung und Ansatz der paulinischen Theologie." *ZTK* 67 (1970): 14–39.

Stuhlmacher, Peter. "Erwägungen zum Problem von Gegenwart und Zukunft in der paulinischen Eschatologie." *ZTK* 64 (1967): 423–450.

Stuhlmacher, Peter. *Gerechtigkeit Gottes bei Paulus.* FRLANT 87. 2nd ed. Göttingen: Vandenhoeck & Ruprecht, 1966.

Stuhlmacher, Peter. "Jesustradition im Römerbrief? Eine Skizze." *Theologische Beiträge* 14 (1983): 240–250.

Stuhlmacher, Peter. "Das paulinische Evangelium." In idem (ed.), *Das Evangelium und die Evangelien: Vorträge vom Tübinger Symposium 1982,* 157–182. WUNT 28. Tübingen: J.C.B. Mohr (Paul Siebeck), 1983.

Stuhlmacher, Peter. *Das paulinische Evangelium: I. Vorgeschichte.* FRLANT 95. Göttingen: Vandenhoeck & Ruprecht, 1968.

Stuhlmacher, Peter. "Zur neueren Exegese von Röm 3,24–26." In *Versöhnung, Gesetz und Gerechtigkeit: Aufsätze zur biblischen Theologie,* 117–135. Göttingen: Vandenhoeck & Ruprecht, 1981.

Sturm, Richard Earl. "An Exegetical Study of Paul's Use of the Words *Apokalyptô/Apokalypsis.*" Ph. D. Dissertation, New York (Union Theological Seminary): 1983. [*Non vidi.*]

Styler, G. M. "The Basis of Obligation in Paul's Christology and Ethics." In *Christ and the Spirit in the New Testament: In Honour of Charles Francis Digby Moule,* 175–187. Edited by B. Lindars and S. S. Smalley. Cambridge: University Press, 1973.

Suggs, M. Jack. "'The Word is Near You': Romans 6–10 within the Purpose of the Letter." In *Christian History and Interpretation: Studies Presented to John Knox,* 289–312. Edited by W. R. Farmer et al. Cambridge: University Press, 1967.

Suter, David Winston. "Apocalyptic Patterns in the Similitudes of Enoch." In *Society of Biblical Literature 1978 Seminar Papers*, 1:1—13. SBLSPS 13. Edited by Paul J. Achtemeier. Missoula: Scholars Press, 1978.

Suter, David Winston. *Tradition and Composition in the Parables of Enoch*. SBLDS 47. Missoula: Scholars Press, 1979.

Sweet, John P. M. "The Theory of Miracles in the Wisdom of Solomon." In *Miracles: Cambridge Studies in their Philosophy and History*, 113—126. Edited by C. F. D. Moule. London: Mowbray, 1965.

Swete, Henry Barclay. *An Introduction to the Old Testament in Greek*. 2nd ed. Cambridge: University Press, 1902.

Tabor, James D. *Things Unutterable: Paul's Ascent to Paradise in its Greco- Roman, Judaic, and Early Christian Contexts*. Studies in Judaism. Lanham/London: University Press of America, 1986.

Tasker, R. V. G. *The Second Epistle of Paul to the Corinthians: An Introduction and Commentary*. Tyndale NT Commentaries. London: Tyndale, 1958.

Thackeray, H. St. J. *The Septuagint and Jewish Worship*. The Schweich Lectures 1920. London: British Academy/Oxford University Press, 1921.

Thiselton, Anthony C. "The 'Interpretation' of Tongues: A New Suggestion in the Light of Greek Usage in Philo and Josephus." *JTS* N.S. 30 (1979): 15—36.

Thomson, James G. S. S. *The Old Testament View of Revelation*. Grand Rapids: Eerdmans, 1960.

Tillich, Paul. "Die Idee der Offenbarung." *ZTK* N.S. 8 (1927): 403—412.

Towner, Philip H. "The Structure of the Theology and Ethics in the Pastoral Epistles." Ph.D. Dissertation, Aberdeen: 1984.

Trilling, Wolfgang. *Der zweite Brief an die Thessalonicher*. EKK 14. Zurich etc.: Benziger; Neukirchen-Vluyn: Neukirchener Verlag, 1980.

Urbach, Ephraim E. *The Sages: Their Concepts and Beliefs*. Translated by Israel Abrahams. Publications of the Perry Foundation in the Hebrew University of Jerusalem. 2 Vols. Jerusalem: Magnes Press, 1979.

Urbach, Ephraim E. "Self-Isolation or Self-Affirmation in Judaism in the First Three Centuries: Theory and Practice." In *Jewish and Christian Self- Definition*, Vol. 2: *Aspects of Judaism in the Graeco-Roman Period*, 269—298. Edited by E. P. Sanders et al. London: SCM, 1981.

Urbach, Ephraim E. "The Traditions about Merkabah Mysticism in the Tannaitic Period." In *Studies in Mysticism and Religion: Presented to Gershom G. Scholem on his Seventieth Birthday by Pupils Colleagues and Friends*, 1—28 (Hebrew Section). Jerusalem: Magnes Press, 1967.

Van Bruggen, Jan. *Die geschichtliche Einordnung der Pastoralbriefe*. Theologische Verlagsgemeinschaft. Wuppertal: Brockhaus, 1981.

Van Imschoot, P. "Sagesse et esprit dans l'Ancien Testament." *RB* 47 (1938): 23—49.

Van Roon, A. *The Authenticity of Ephesians*. NTSup 39. Leiden: Brill, 1974.

Van Roon, A. "The Relation between Christ and the Wisdom of God According to Paul." *NT* 16 (1974): 207—239.

Van Unnik, Willem Cornelius. "Flavius Josephus and the Mysteries." In *Studies in Hellenistic Religions*, 244—279. Edited by M. J. Vermaseren. Études Préliminaires aux Religions Orientales dans l'Empire Romain. Leiden: Brill, 1979.

Van Unnik, Willem Cornelius. "Die Prophetie bei Josephus." In idem, *Flavius Josephus als historischer Schriftsteller*, 41–54. Franz Delitzsch Vorlesungen, New Series. Heidelberg: Schneider, 1978.

Vanderkam, James C. *Enoch and the Growth of an Apocalyptic Tradition*. Washington: Catholic Biblical Association of America, 1984.

Vanderkam, James C. "The Prophetic-Sapiential Origins of Apocalyptic Thought." In *A Word in Season: Essays in Honour of William McKane*, 163–176. Edited by J. D. Martin and P. R. Davies. JSOTSup 42. Sheffield: JSOT Press, 1986.

Vanderlinden, E. "Les divers modes de connaissance de Dieu selon Philon d'Alexandrie." *MScRel* 4 (1947): 285–304.

Vermes, Geza. *The Dead Sea Scrolls: Qumran in Perspective*. London: Collins, 1977. [*Scrolls*]

Vermes, Geza. "The Decalogue and the Minim." In idem, *Post-Biblical Jewish Studies*, 37–49. SJLA 8. Leiden: Brill, 1975.

Vermes, Geza. "Haggadah in the Onkelos Targum." *JSS* 8 (1963): 159–169.

Vermes, Geza. *Jesus and the World of Judaism*. London: SCM, 1983. [*World*]

Vermes, Geza. *Jesus the Jew: A Historian's Reading of the Gospels*. London: Collins, 1973.

Vermes, Geza. "The Qumran Interpretation of Scripture in its Historical Setting." *ALUOS* 6 (1966–68): 84–97.

Vermes, Geza. "A Summary of the Law by Flavius Josephus." *NT* 24 (1982): 289–303.

Vermes, Geza. "'The Torah is a Light'." *VT* 8 (1958): 436–438.

Vermes, Geza. *Scripture and Tradition in Judaism: Haggadic Studies*. Studia Post-Biblica 4. Leiden: Brill, 1961.

Vielhauer, Philipp. "Paulus und das Alte Testament." In idem, *Oikodome: Aufsätze zum Neuen Testament*, 2:196–228. Edited by G. Klein. Theologische Bücherei 65. Munich: Kaiser, 1979.

Vogt, E. "'Mysteria' in textibus Qumrân." *Bib* 37 (1956): 247–257.

Volz, Paul. *Die Eschatologie der jüdischen Gemeinde im neutestamentlichen Zeitalter*. 2nd ed. Hildesheim: Olms, 1966 [= 1934].

Volz, Paul. *Der Geist Gottes und die verwandten Erscheinungen im Alten Testament und im anschließenden Judentum*. Tübingen: Mohr (Siebeck), 1910.

Von der Osten-Sacken, P. *Apokalyptik in ihrem Verhältnis zu Prophetie und Weisheit*. Theologische Existenz Heute 157. Munich: Kaiser, 1969.

Von Dobschütz, Ernst. *Die Thessalonicher-Briefe*. KEKNT 10. 7th (= 1st) ed. Göttingen: Vandenhoeck & Ruprecht, 1909.

Von Nordheim, Eckhard. "Das Zitat des Paulus in 1 Kor 2,9 und seine Beziehung zum koptischen Testament Jakobs." *ZNW* 65 (1974): 112–120.

Von Rad, Gerhard. *Theologie des Alten Testaments*. 2 Vols. 4th ed. Göttingen: Vandenhoeck & Ruprecht, 1965.

Von Soden, H. *Die Briefe an die Kolosser, Epheser, Philemon; die Pastoralbriefe*. Hand-Commentar zum NT 3:1. 2nd ed. Freiburg/ Leipzig: 1893.

Von Soden, H. "ΜΥΣΤΗΡΙΟΝ und Sacramentum in den ersten zwei Jahrhunderten der Kirche." *ZNW* 12 (1911): 188–227.

Wacholder, Ben Zion. *The Dawn of Qumran: The Sectarian Torah and the Teacher of Righteousness*. Monographs of the Hebrew Union College 8. Cincinnati: Hebrew Union College Press, 1983.

Ward, Ronald A. *Commentary on 1 & 2 Timothy, Titus*. Waco: Word, 1974.

Watson, Francis. *Paul, Judaism and the Gentiles: A Sociological Approach*. SNTSMS 56. Cambridge, etc.: Cambridge University Press, 1986.

Weber, Ferdinand. *Jüdische Theologie auf Grund des Talmud und verwandter Schriften.* Edited by F. Delitzsch & G. Schnedermann. 2nd ed. Leipzig: Dörffling & Francke, 1897.

Wedderburn, A. J. M. *Baptism and Resurrection: Studies in Pauline Theology against Its Graeco-Roman Background.* WUNT 44. Tübingen: J.C.B. Mohr (Paul Siebeck), 1987.

Weinfeld, Moshe. "The Heavenly Praise in Unison." In *Meqor Hajjim: Festschrift für Georg Molin zu seinem 75. Geburtstag,* 427–437. Edited by I. Seybold. Graz: Akademische Druck- u. Verlagsanstalt, 1983.

Weinfeld, Moshe. *The Organizational Pattern and the Penal Code of the Qumran Sect: A Comparison with Guilds and Religious Associations of the Hellenistic-Roman Period.* Novum Testamentum et Orbis Antiquus 2. Fribourg: Éditions Universitaires; Göttingen: Vandenhoeck & Ruprecht, 1986.

Weiser, Artur. "Zur Frage nach den Beziehungen der Psalmen zum Kult: Die Darstellung der Theophanie in den Psalmen und im Festkult." In *Festschrift Alfred Bertholet zum 80. Geburtstag,* 513–531. Edited by Walter Baumgartner et al. Tübingen: J.C.B. Mohr (Paul Siebeck), 1955.

Weiss, Johannes. *Der erste Korintherbrief.* KEKNT 5. 2nd (=9th) ed. Göttingen: Vandenhoeck & Ruprecht, 1910.

Wellhausen, Julius. "Zur apokalyptischen Literatur." In *Apokalyptik,* 58–66. Edited by Klaus Koch and Johann Michael Schmidt. Wege der Forschung 365. Darmstadt: Wissenschaftliche Buchgesellschaft, 1982. [= Idem, *Skizzen und Vorarbeiten,* 6:225–234. Berlin: Reimer, 1899.]

Wenham, David. *The Rediscovery of Jesus' Eschatological Discourse.* Gospel Perspectives 4. Sheffield: JSOT, 1984.

Werner, Jürgen. "Allegorische Dichtererklärung." *KlP* 1:274.

Westcott, Brooke Foss. *Saint Paul's Epistle to the Ephesians: The Greek Text with Notes and Addenda.* London: Macmillan, 1906.

Westerholm, Stephen. "On Fulfilling the Whole Law (Gal. 5:14)." *SEÅ* 51–52 (1986–87): 229–237.

Westermann, Claus. *Das Buch Jesaja: Kapitel 40–66.* ATD 19. Göttingen: Vandenhoeck & Ruprecht, 1966.

Westermann, Claus. *Lob und Klage in den Psalmen.* 5th ed. Göttingen: Vandenhoeck & Ruprecht, 1977.

Westermann, Claus and Albertz, Rainer. "גלה." In *THAT* 1 (1971): 418–426.

Wewers, Gerd A. *Geheimnis und Geheimhaltung im rabbinischen Judentum.* Religionsgeschichtliche Versuche und Vorarbeiten 35. Berlin: de Gruyter, 1975.

White, John L. "Introductory Formulae in the Body of the Pauline Letter." *JBL* 90 (1971): 91–97.

White, John L. "Saint Paul and the Apostolic Letter Tradition." *CBQ* 45 (1983): 433–444.

Whybray, R. N. *Isaiah 40–66.* NCB. London: Oliphants, 1975.

Widmann, Martin. "1 Kor 2,6–16: Ein Einspruch gegen Paulus." *ZNW* 70 (1979): 44–53.

Wieder, Naphtali. *The Judean Scrolls and Karaism.* London: East & West, 1962.

Wieder, Naphtali. "The Term קץ in the Dead Sea Scrolls and in Hebrew Liturgical Poetry." *JJS* 5 (1954): 22–31.

Wilckens, Ulrich. "Die Bekehrung des Paulus als religionsgeschichtliches Problem." *ZTK* 56 (1959): 273–293.

Wilckens, Ulrich. *Der Brief an die Römer.* 3 Vols. EKK 6:1–3. Zurich, etc.: Benziger; Neukirchen-Vluyn: Neukirchener, 1978–82.

Wilckens, Ulrich. "Das Kreuz Christi als die Tiefe der Weisheit Gottes: Zu 1. Kor 2,1—16." In *Paolo a una Chiesa Divisa: (1 Cor 1—4)*, 68—81. Edited by L. de Lorenzi. Serie Monografica di "Benedictina": Sezione biblico-ecumenica 5. Rome: Abbazia di S. Paolo fuori le mura, 1980.

Wilckens, Ulrich. "Das Offenbarungsverständnis in der Geschichte des Urchristentums." In *Offenbarung als Geschichte*, 42—90. Edited by W. Pannenberg. KD Supplement 1. Göttingen: Vandenhoeck & Ruprecht, 1961.

Wilckens, Ulrich. *Weisheit und Torheit: Eine exegetisch- religionsgeschichtliche Untersuchung zu 1. Kor. 1 und 2*. BHT 26. Tübingen: J.C.B. Mohr (Paul Siebeck), 1959.

Wilckens, Ulrich. "Zu 1Kor 2,1—16." In *Theologia Crucis — Signum Crucis: Festschrift für E. Dinkler zum 70. Geburtstag*, 501—537. Edited by A. Andresen and G. Klein. Tübingen: J.C.B. Mohr (Paul Siebeck), 1979.

Willet, Andrew. *Hexapla: That Is, A Six-Fold Commentarie upon the most Divine Epistle of the holy Apostle S. Paul to the Romanes*. Cambridge: Legge (University), 1611.

Willi-Plein, Ina. "Das Geheimnis der Apokalyptik." *VT* 27 (1977): 62—81.

Williams, A. Lukyn. "The Cult of the Angels at Colossae." *JTS* 10 (1909): 413—438.

Williams, Trevor. *Form and Vitality in the World and in God: A Christian Perspective*. Oxford: Clarendon, 1985.

Wilson, Andrew M. and Wills, Lawrence. "Literary Sources of the *Temple Scroll*." *HTR* 75 (1982): 275—288.

Wilson, Stephen G. *Luke and the Pastoral Epistles*. London: SPCK, 1979.

Winston, David. "Was Philo a Mystic?" In *Studies in Jewish Mysticism: Proceedings of Regional Conferences Held at the University of California, Los Angeles and McGill University in April, 1978*, 15—39. Edited by J. Dan and F. Talmage. Cambridge, MA: Association for Jewish Studies, 1982.

Winston, David. *The Wisdom of Solomon: A New Translation with Introduction and Commentary*. AB 43. Garden City: Doubleday, 1979.

Winter, Martin. *Pneumatiker und Psychiker in Korinth: Zum religionsgeschichtlichen Hintergrund von 1. Kor. 2,6—3,4*. Marburger Theologische Studien 12. Marburg: Elwert, 1975.

Wohlenberg, G. *Die Pastoralbriefe (der erste Timotheus-, der Titus- und der zweite Timotheusbrief)*. Kommentar zum NT 13. Leipzig: Deichert, 1906.

Wolfson, Harry Austryn. *Philo: Foundations of Religious Philosophy in Judaism, Christianity, and Islam*. Structure and Growth of Philosophic Systems from Plato to Spinoza 2. 2 Vols. Cambridge, MA: Harvard University Press, 1947.

Wolter, Michael. "Verborgene Weisheit und Heil für die Heiden: Zur Traditionsgeschichte und Intention des 'Revelationsschemas'." *ZTK* 84 (1987) 297—319.

Worrell, John Edward. "Concepts of Wisdom in the Dead Sea Scrolls." Ph.D. Dissertation, Claremont, CA (Claremont Graduate School), 1968.

Wright, N. T. *The Epistles of Paul to the Colossians and to Philemon: An Introduction and Commentary*. Tyndale NT Commentaries. Leicester: Inter-Varsity; Grand Rapids: Eerdmans, 1986.

Wyschogrod, Michael. "The Law: Jews and Gentiles." In *Speaking of God Today: Jews and Lutherans in Conversation*, 3—14. Edited by P. D. Opsahl and M. H. Tanenbaum. Philadelphia: Fortress, 1974.

Wyschogrod, Michael. "A New Stage in Jewish–Christian Dialogue." *Judaism* 31 (1982): 355—65.

Yadin, Yigael. *The Message of the Scrolls*. New York: Simon & Schuster, 1957.

Yates, Roy. "A Note on Colossians 1:24." *EvQ* 42 (1970): 88—92.

Yates, Roy. "'The Worship of Angels' (Col 2:18)." *ExpTim* 97 (1985—86): 12—15.

Zeilinger, Franz. *Der Erstgeborene der Schöpfung: Untersuchungen zur Formalstruktur und Theologie des Kolosserbriefes.* Vienna: Herder, 1974.

Zeitlin, Solomon. "Dreams and their Interpretation." *JQR* 66 (1975–76): 1–18.

Zeller, Dieter. *Der Brief an die Römer.* Regensburger Neues Testament. Regensburg: Pustet, 1984.

Zeller, Dieter. *Juden und Heiden in der Mission des Paulus: Studien zum Römerbrief.* Forschung zur Bibel 1. Stuttgart: Katholisches Bibelwerk, 1973.

Ziegert, Paul. "Über die Ansätze zu einer Mysterienlehre aufgebaut auf den antiken Mysterien bei Philo Judäus." *TSK* 76 (1894): 706–732.

Zimmerli, Walther. "'Offenbarung' im Alten Testament: Ein Gespräch mit R. Rendtorff." *EvT* 22 (1962): 15–31.

Zobel, Hans-Jürgen. "גלה." *TWAT* 1 (1973): 1018–1031.

Zunz, [Leopold]. *Die gottesdienstlichen Vorträge der Juden, historisch entwickelt: Ein Beitrag zur Alterthumskunde und biblischen Kritik, zur Literatur- und Religionsgeschichte.* Edited by N. Brüll. 2nd ed. Frankfurt: Kauffmann, 1892.

Additions to the Bibliography

Dahl, Nils Alstrup. "Formgeschichtliche Betrachtungen zur Christusverkündigung." In *Neutestamentliche Studien für Rudolf Bultmann,* 3–9. Edited by Walter Eltester. BZNW 21. Belin: Töpelmann, 1954.

Gloege, Gerhard. "Offenbarung und Überlieferung." *TLZ* 79 (1954): 213–236.

Guthrie, Donald. *New Testament Introduction.* 3rd ed. Downers Grove: Inter-Varsity, 1970.

Guthrie, Donald. *The Pastoral Epistles.* Tyndale New Testament Commentaries. Grand Rapids: Eerdmans, 1957.

Hamilton, J. D. B. "The Church and the Language of Mystery: The First Four Centuries." *ETL* 53 (1977): 479–494.

Hatch, Edwin. *Essays in Biblical Greek.* Oxford: Clarendon, 1889.

Hill, R. "Synoptic 'Basileia' and Pauline 'Mysterion'." *EstBib* 45 (1987): 309–324. [Non Vidi.]

Kennedy, H. A. A. *St. Paul and the Mystery Religions.* London: Hodder & Stoughton, 1913.

Lock, Walter. *A Critical and Exegetical Commentary on the Pastoral Epistles.* ICC. Edinburgh: T. & T. Clark, 1978 [= 1924].

Index of Passages

Old Testament

New Testament

Old Testament Apocrypha and Pseudepigrapha

Dead Sea Scrolls

14:14	14, 53, 55
15:1	8, 52
15:2	197
16:11	53
16:16	53
17:7	8, 52
17:9	53

1QpHab

2:2f	47
2:6-9	47
2:8	61
7	49
7:1-8	47
7:1ff.	50
7:1	96
7:2	47, 135, 210
7:4	96
7:5-13	54
7:5	53, 167, 214
7:7	96
7:8	53
7:12	96
7:14	53, 199
7:15	161
12:7	153

1QS

1:3	47, 49
1:8	159
1:9	44
2:2	159
3:3	159
3:9	159
3:13	49
3:17-4:26	50
3:20-24	197
3:23	53, 96
4:1	55
4:17	53
4:18	53, 161
4:2-6	50
4:6	53
4:6	53
4:6	53
4:6	67
4:22	48, 53, 159
5:3	52
5:9	44
5:11	43, 53
5:11f	42
5:24	159
6:3	45
6:6	45
6:7	45
6:16	52

6:16f	159
6:16ff	52
6:18	52
6:19	54
6:19f	159
6:22	52
8:1-12	159
8:1f	159
8:1	43, 49
8:10-12	159
8:11f	43, 45
8:14f	153
8:15-18	159
8:15f	43, 47
8:15	44
8:16	52, 165
8:20f	159
8:9f	159
9:5f	159
9:7	52
9:8f	159
9:10	52
9:13	44
9:18	53, 54, 201
9:19	44, 48, 159
9:2	159
9:22	50
10:1	43
11:19	
11:3	52, 53, 54
11:5-8	54
11:5	53
11:6	52, 54, 165
11:7	8, 52
11:7ff	54
11:19	52, 53

1QSa

1:1f	45
1:6-8	51
1:9	8, 52
1:17	159
1:20	8, 52

1QSb

4:22-26	169
5:22	159

2Q24	52
4Q159	45
4Q160	49, 52

4Q176

16:2	52, 53, 54

4Q180

1:3	37

| 4Q186 | 52 |

4Q280

2:6	56

4Q286

10.ii.2-12	56

4Q401

14.ii:24	53
14.ii	55
17:4-6	55
17:6	53

4Q402

4:11	55
4:14	55

4Q403

1.i:18-20	55
1.ii:27	53, 55

4Q405

3.ii:9	53

4Q502

1:5	55

4Q503

51.v:13	56

4Q508

2:4	44

4Q511

2 II 6	53
44-47 I 6	53
48-51 II 7	53

| 4QAmram | 53 |

4QAmramᵇ

1:10ff	52

4QCatenaᵃ

1-4:13f.	51

4QEnᶜ

5.ii:26	161
5.ii:26f	48

Philo

Josephus

Rabbinic Literature

(Tractates are listed in alphabetical order)

Targums

Peshitta

Jewish Magical Texts

Samaritan Literature

Patristic Literature (in alphabetical order)

Gnostic Texts

Other Ancient Sources

Index of Modern Authors

Index of Subjects